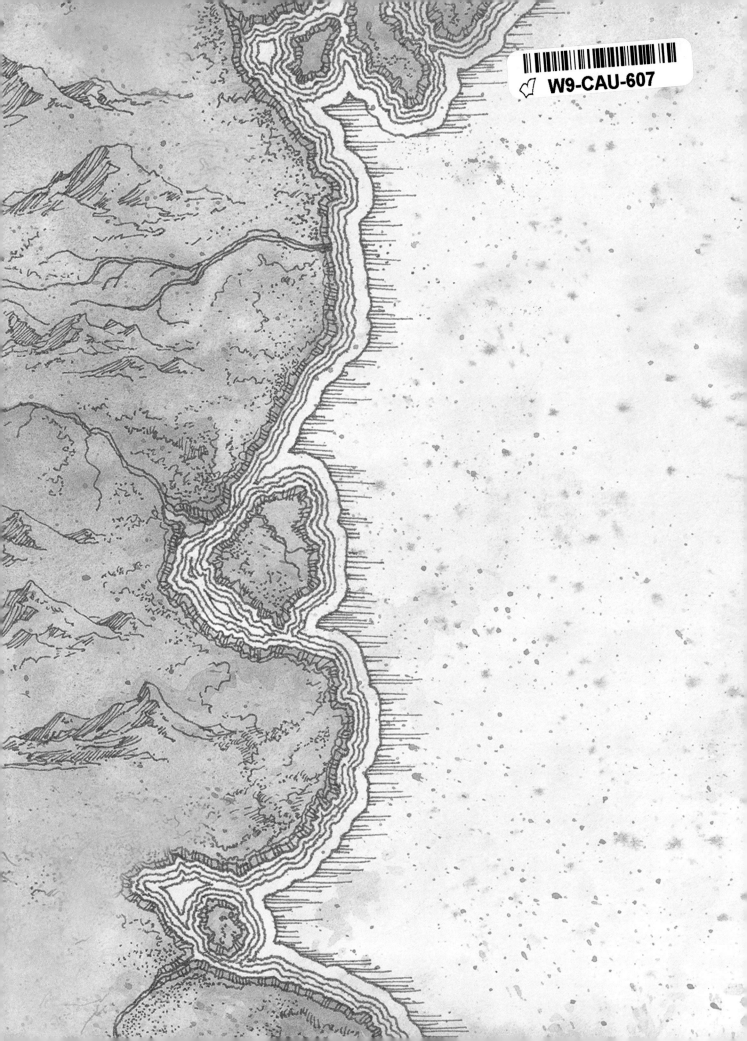

STATES AND REGIONS

Series Authors

Dr. Richard G. Boehm

Claudia Hoone

Dr. Thomas M. McGowan

Dr. Mabel C. McKinney-Browning

Dr. Ofelia B. Miramontes

Series Consultants

Dr. Alma Flor Ada

Dr. Phillip Bacon

Dr. W. Dorsey Hammond

Dr. Asa Grant Hilliard, III

HARCOURT BRACE & COMPANY

Orlando Atlanta Austin Boston San Francisco Chicago Dallas
New York Toronto London

SERIES AUTHORS

Dr. Richard G. Boehm
Professor
Department of Geography
  and Planning
Southwest Texas State University
San Marcos, Texas

Claudia Hoone
Teacher
Ralph Waldo Emerson School #58
Indianapolis, Indiana

Dr. Thomas M. McGowan
Associate Professor
Division of Curriculum
  and Instruction
Arizona State University
Tempe, Arizona

Dr. Mabel C. McKinney-Browning
Director
Division for Public Education
American Bar Association
Chicago, Illinois

Dr. Ofelia B. Miramontes
Associate Professor
School of Education
University of Colorado
Boulder, Colorado

SERIES CONSULTANTS

Dr. Alma Flor Ada
Professor
School of Education
University of San Francisco
San Francisco, California

Dr. Phillip Bacon
Professor Emeritus of Geography
  and Anthropology
University of Houston
Houston, Texas

Dr. W. Dorsey Hammond
Professor of Education
Oakland University
Rochester, Michigan

Dr. Asa Grant Hilliard, III
Fuller E. Callaway Professor
  of Urban Education
Georgia State University
Atlanta, Georgia

MEDIA AND LITERATURE SPECIALISTS

Dr. Joseph A. Braun, Jr.
Professor of Elementary
  Social Studies
Department of Curriculum
  and Instruction
Illinois State University
Normal, Illinois

Meredith McGowan
Youth Librarian
Tempe Public Library
Tempe, Arizona

GRADE-LEVEL CONSULTANTS AND REVIEWERS

John M. Fischer
Teacher
5th Avenue Alternative School
Columbus, Ohio

Carol A. Flanagan
Teacher
St. Brendan School
Hilliard, Ohio

Donna M. Hard
Teacher
W. E. Cundiff Elementary School
Vinton, Virginia

David J. Kush
Teacher
Conemaugh Valley Elementary
  School
Johnstown, Pennsylvania

Mel Miller
Social Studies Consultant
Macomb Intermediate
  School District
Clinton Township, Michigan

Dr. Paul E. Phillips
Professor of Geography
Geosciences Department
Fort Hays State University
Hays, Kansas

Printed in the United States of America

ISBN: 0-15-302040-7

2 3 4 5 6 7 8 9 10   032   99 98 97

CONTENTS

UNIT 1

CHAPTER 1

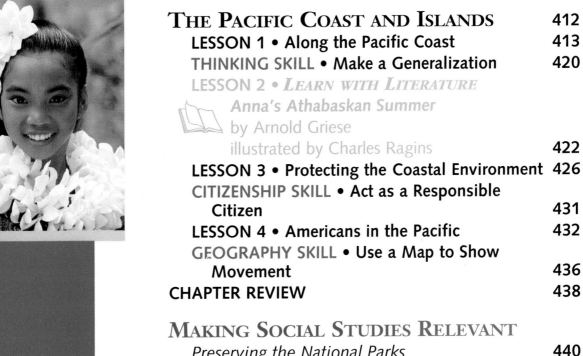
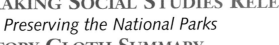

F.Y.I.

BUILDING CITIZENSHIP

FEATURES

MAPS

CHARTS, GRAPHS, DIAGRAMS, TABLES, AND TIME LINES

ATLAS

CONTENTS

ATLAS

THE WORLD: POLITICAL

ARCTIC OCEAN

Greenland
(DENMARK)

ALASKA
(U.S.)

CANADA

NORTH
AMERICA

Azores
(PORTUGAL)

UNITED STATES

Bermuda
(U.K.)

ATLANTIC
OCEAN

Area of inset

Midway
Islands
(U.S.)

Tropic of Cancer

MEXICO

CAPE VERDE

HAWAII
(U.S.)

PACIFIC
OCEAN

VENEZUELA

GUYANA
SURINAME

COLOMBIA

FRENCH GUIANA
(FRANCE)

Equator

ECUADOR

Galápagos
Islands
(ECUADOR)

BRAZIL

Tokelau
(N.Z.)

KIRIBATI

SOUTH
AMERICA

PERU

WESTERN
SAMOA

American
Samoa
(U.S.)

Cook
Islands
(N.Z.)

French
Polynesia
(FRANCE)

BOLIVIA

TONGA

PARAGUAY

CHILE

Tropic of Capricorn

Niue
(N.Z.)

Pitcairn
(U.K.)

Easter Island
(CHILE)

URUGUAY

ARGENTINA

PACIFIC
OCEAN

Falkland
Islands
(U.K.)

South
Georgia
(U.K.)

Antarctic Circle

CENTRAL AMERICA AND THE CARIBBEAN

UNITED STATES

Gulf of Mexico

ATLANTIC
OCEAN

BAHAMAS

Tropic of Cancer

MEXICO

CUBA

Turks and
Caicos (U.K.)

Cayman
Islands
(U.K.)

DOMINICAN
REPUBLIC

Puerto
Rico
(U.S.)

HAITI

Anguilla (U.K.)

St. Martin (FRANCE AND NETH.)

ANTIGUA AND BARBUDA

Montserrat (U.K.)

Guadeloupe (FRANCE)

Virgin Islands
(U.S. AND U.K.)

ST. KITTS
AND NEVIS

DOMINICA

BELIZE

JAMAICA

Caribbean Sea

Martinique (FRANCE)

ST. LUCIA

GUATEMALA

HONDURAS

BARBADOS

EL SALVADOR

NICARAGUA

Aruba
(NETH.)

Netherlands
Antilles
(NETH.)

ST. VINCENT AND
THE GRENADINES

GRENADA

PACIFIC OCEAN

Panama
Canal

TRINIDAD AND
TOBAGO

A2

0   200   400 Miles

0   200   400 Kilometers

Azimuthal Equal-Area Projection

COSTA
RICA

PANAMA

VENEZUELA

GUYANA

COLOMBIA

ARCTIC OCEAN

Arctic Circle

ICELAND

Area of inset

EUROPE

RUSSIA

ASIA

KAZAKHSTAN

MONGOLIA

GEORGIA
ARMENIA
TURKEY
AZERBAIJAN
TURKMENISTAN
KYRGYZSTAN
TAJIKISTAN

NORTH
KOREA

JAPAN

PACIFIC
OCEAN

CYPRUS
LEBANON
ISRAEL
SYRIA

CHINA

SOUTH
KOREA

Canary Is.
(SPAIN)

MOROCCO

TUNISIA

IRAQ

IRAN

AFGHANISTAN

JORDAN

KUWAIT

PAKISTAN

NEPAL

BHUTAN

STERN
HARA
ROCCO)

ALGERIA

LIBYA

EGYPT

BAHRAIN
QATAR
SAUDI
ARABIA

U.A.E.

OMAN

INDIA

BANGLADESH

BURMA
(MYANMAR)

LAOS

TAIWAN

AURITANIA

MALI

NIGER

CHAD

SUDAN

ERITREA

YEMEN

THAILAND

VIETNAM

PHILIPPINES

Northern
Mariana Islands
(U.S.)

MARSHALL
ISLANDS

NEGAL

BURKINA
FASO

AFRICA

DJIBOUTI

CAMBODIA

Guam (U.S.)

GUINEA

BENIN
NIGERIA

CENTRAL
AFRICAN REPUBLIC

ETHIOPIA

BRUNEI

PALAU

FEDERATED
STATES OF
MICRONESIA

SIERRA
LEONE
LIBERIA

CÔTE
D'IVOIRE

EQU.
GUINEA

CAMEROON

UGANDA

SOMALIA

MALDIVES

SRI
LANKA

GUINEA–
BISSAU

GHANA
TOGO

CONGO

RWANDA

KENYA

MALAYSIA

HE
GAMBIA

SÃO TOMÉ
AND PRÍNCIPE

GABON

ZAIRE

BURUNDI

SINGAPORE

INDONESIA

NAURU

KIRIBATI

PAPUA
NEW GUINEA

TUVALU

CABINDA
(ANGOLA)

TANZANIA

SEYCHELLES

INDIAN
OCEAN

SOLOMON
ISLANDS

ANGOLA

ZAMBIA

MALAWI

COMOROS

VANUATU

FIJI

MOZAMBIQUE

MADAGASCAR

New
Caledonia
(FRANCE)

NAMIBIA

ZIMBABWE

BOTSWANA

MAURITIUS

AUSTRALIA

Reunion
(FRANCE)

ATLANTIC
OCEAN

SOUTH
AFRICA

SWAZILAND

LESOTHO

NEW
ZEALAND

N
W   E
S

Kerguelen
Archipelago
(FRANCE)

0   1,000   2,000 Miles

0   1,000   2,000 Kilometers

Scale accurate at equator
Robinson Projection

ANTARCTICA

National border

Abbreviations

EQU. GUINEA	EQUATORIAL GUINEA
NETH.	NETHERLANDS
N.Z.	NEW ZEALAND
U.A.E.	UNITED ARAB EMIRATES
U.K.	UNITED KINGDOM
U.S.	UNITED STATES

EUROPE

FINLAND

NORWAY

SWEDEN

ESTONIA

RUSSIA

LATVIA

North
Sea

LITHUANIA

UNITED
KINGDOM

DENMARK

KALININGRAD
(RUSSIA)

BELARUS

IRELAND

NETHERLANDS

POLAND

GERMANY

UKRAINE

BELGIUM

0   200   400 Miles

0   200   400 Kilometers
Azimuthal Equal-Area Projection

LUXEMBOURG

CZECH
REPUBLIC

SLOVAKIA

MOLDOVA

LIECHTENSTEIN

AUSTRIA   HUNGARY

ROMANIA

SWITZERLAND

SLOVENIA

N
W   E
S

FRANCE

SAN
MARINO

CROATIA

BOSNIA AND
HERZEGOVINA

YUGOSLAVIA

BULGARIA

Black
Sea

ATLANTIC
OCEAN

ANDORRA

MONACO
Corsica
(FRANCE)

ITALY

MACEDONIA

TURKEY

VATICAN
CITY

ALBANIA

PORTUGAL

SPAIN

Sardinia
(ITALY)

GREECE

A3

Balearic Islands
(SPAIN)

GIBRALTAR
(U.K.)

Mediterranean Sea

Sicily
(ITALY)

MALTA

Crete
(GREECE)

ARCTIC OCEAN

180° 160° W 140° W 120° W 100° W 80° W 60° W

80° N

Beaufort Sea

Queen Elizabeth Islands

Greenland

Baffin Island

Mt. McKinley
20,320 ft.
(6,194 m)

Mackenzie

Great Bear Lake

Great Slave Lake

Hudson Bay

Bering Sea

Yukon R.

Mt. Logan
19,524 ft.
(5,951 m)

NORTH AMERICA

Aleutian Islands

Gulf of Alaska

ROCKY MOUNTAINS

Great Lakes

Newfoundland

40° N

Vancouver Island

Columbia R.

GREAT PLAINS

Missouri R.

Ohio R.

APPALACHIAN MTS.

Azores

Mt. Whitney
14,494 ft.
(4,418 m)

Colorado R.

Mississippi R.

Bermuda

ATLANTIC OCEAN

Gulf of Mexico

Bahamas

Hawaiian Islands

Tropic of Cancer

20° N

Citlaltepetl
18,701 ft.
(5,700 m)

Yucatán Peninsula

Cuba

Hispaniola

West Indies

Cape Verde Islands

PACIFIC OCEAN

Caribbean Sea

Galápagos Islands

Orinoco River

Guiana Highlands

Equator

Polynesia

AMAZON

Amazon R.

BASIN

SOUTH AMERICA

20° S

ANDES MOUNTAINS

Atacama Desert

Brazilian Highlands

Gran Chaco

Paraná River

Tropic of Capricorn

Mt. Aconcagua
22,831 ft.
(6,959 m)

Pampa

40° S

Patagonia

Falkland Islands

Strait of Magellan

Tierra del Fuego

Cape Horn

60° S

Antarctic Circle

Antarctic Peninsula

80° S

Ross Sea

180° 160° W 140° W 120° W 100° W 80° W 60° W

NORTHERN POLAR REGION

ASIA

Sea of Okhotsk

120° E

90° E

60° E

30° E

EUROPE

Kamchatka Peninsula

Novaya Zemlya

Severnaya Zemlya

Barents Sea

Baltic Sea

150° E

New Siberian Is.

70° N

0   400   800 Miles

0   400   800 Kilometers
Azimuthal Equidistant Projection

ARCTIC OCEAN

North Pole

Svalbard

Norwegian Sea

North Sea

180°

Wrangel Island

80° N

Bering Sea

Bering Strait

British Isles

BROOKS RANGE

Beaufort Sea

North Magnetic Pole

Queen Elizabeth Islands

Greenland

Iceland

70° N

ATLANTIC OCEAN

150° W

Baffin Bay

60°

Arctic Circle

30° W

50° W

A4

NORTH AMERICA

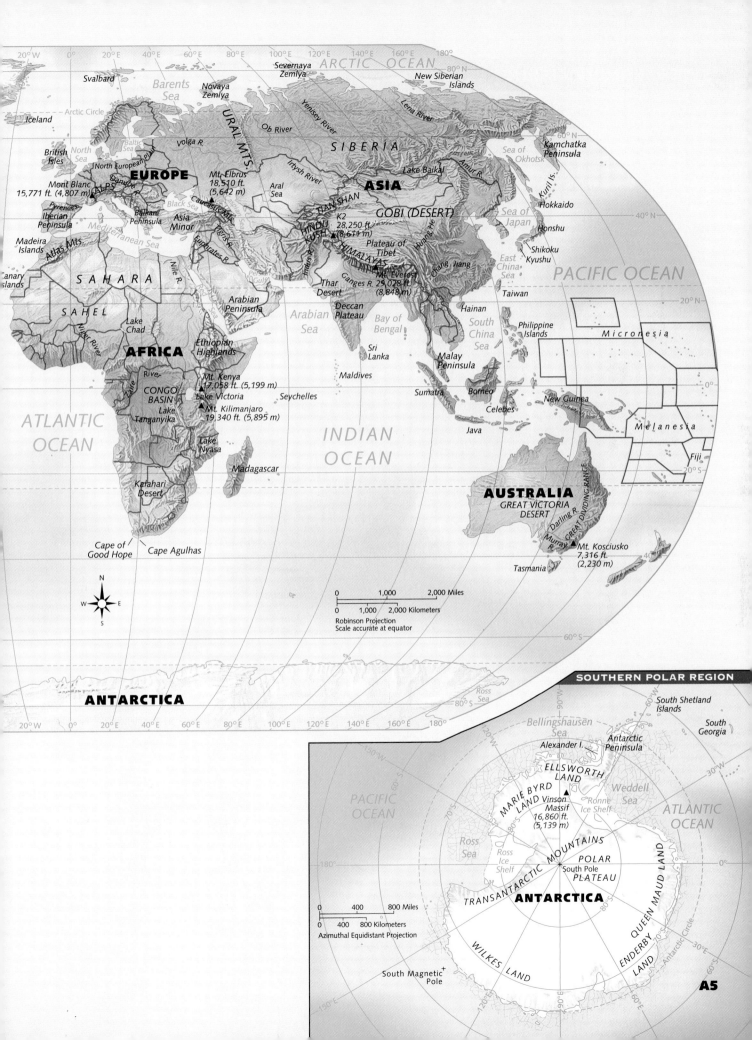

ARCTIC OCEAN

Svalbard
Barents Sea
Severnaya Zemlya
Novaya Zemlya
New Siberian Islands
Iceland
Arctic Circle
British Isles
North Sea
Baltic Sea
URAL MTS.
Ob River
Yenisey River
Lena River
SIBERIA
Kamchatka Peninsula
Sea of Okhotsk
60° N
Volga R.
EUROPE
North European Plain
Danube R.
ALPS
Mont Blanc 15,771 ft. (4,807 m)
Pyrenees
Iberian Peninsula
Black Sea
Caucasus Mts.
Mt. Elbrus 18,510 ft. (5,642 m)
Aral Sea
Irtysh River
TIAN SHAN
Lake Baikal
Amur R.
ASIA
K2 28,250 ft. (8,611 m)
GOBI (DESERT)
Plateau of Tibet
Kuril Is.
Hokkaido
40° N
Kamchatka
Honshu
Madeira Islands
Atlas Mts.
Mediterranean Sea
Balkan Peninsula
Asia Minor
Tigris R.
Euphrates R.
HINDU KUSH
HIMALAYAS
Chang Jiang
Huang He
Shikoku
Kyushu
Sea of Japan
East China Sea
PACIFIC OCEAN
Canary Islands
SAHARA
Nile R.
Red Sea
Persian Gulf
Indus R.
Thar Desert
Ganges R.
Mt. Everest 29,028 ft. (8,848 m)
Taiwan
20° N
SAHEL
Lake Chad
Arabian Peninsula
Arabian Sea
Deccan Plateau
Bay of Bengal
Hainan
South China Sea
Philippine Islands
Micronesia
Niger River
AFRICA
Ethiopian Highlands
Sri Lanka
Maldives
Malay Peninsula
0°
Congo River
CONGO BASIN
Mt. Kenya 17,058 ft. (5,199 m)
Lake Victoria
Mt. Kilimanjaro 19,340 ft. (5,895 m)
Seychelles
Sumatra
Borneo
Celebes
New Guinea
Melanesia
ATLANTIC OCEAN
Zaire River
Lake Tanganyika
Lake Nyasa
INDIAN OCEAN
Java
Fiji
20° S
Kalahari Desert
Madagascar
AUSTRALIA
GREAT VICTORIA DESERT
GREAT DIVIDING RANGE
Darling R.
Cape of Good Hope
Cape Agulhas
Murray R.
Mt. Kosciusko 7,316 ft. (2,230 m)
40° S
Tasmania

0   1,000   2,000 Miles
0   1,000   2,000 Kilometers
Robinson Projection
Scale accurate at equator

N
W   E
S

ANTARCTICA
80° S
Ross Sea
60° S

20° W 0° 20° E 40° E 60° E 80° E 100° E 120° E 140° E 160° E 180°

South Shetland Islands
Bellingshausen Sea
Antarctic Peninsula
South Georgia
60° S
PACIFIC OCEAN
Alexander I.
ELLSWORTH LAND
MARIE BYRD LAND
Vinson Massif 16,860 ft. (5,139 m)
Ronne Ice Shelf
Weddell Sea
ATLANTIC OCEAN
30° W
Ross Sea
Ross Ice Shelf
TRANSANTARCTIC MOUNTAINS
POLAR PLATEAU
South Pole
ANTARCTICA
QUEEN MAUD LAND
180°
WILKES LAND
ENDERBY LAND
Antarctic Circle
30° E
0°

0   400   800 Miles
0   400   800 Kilometers
Azimuthal Equidistant Projection

South Magnetic Pole

A5

ARCTIC OCEAN

Bering Strait

Beaufort Sea

Viscount Melville Sound

Baffin Bay

Greenland
(DENMARK)

ALASKA
(U.S.)

Fairbanks

Anchorage

Whitehorse

Juneau

Gulf of Alaska

Bering Sea

Yukon River

Mackenzie River

Liard River

Great Bear Lake

Yellowknife

Great Slave Lake

CANADA

Foxe Basin

Hudson Strait

Arctic Circle

Davis Strait

Peace River

Athabasca River

Lake Athabasca

Hudson Bay

Labrador Sea

Edmonton

Calgary

Saskatoon

Saskatchewan R.

Regina

Lake Winnipeg

Winnipeg

James Bay

Vancouver

Seattle

Portland

Puget Sound

Columbia

Snake R.

Boise

UNITED STATES

Thunder Bay

St. Lawrence River

Great Lakes

Ottawa

Toronto

Quebec

Montreal

St. John

St. John's

Gulf of St. Lawrence

Salt Lake City

Great Salt Lake

Missouri R.

Chicago

Detroit

Albany

Boston

Cleveland

New York City

Reno

Denver

St. Louis

Indianapolis

Philadelphia

Washington, D.C.

San Francisco

Las Vegas

Colorado R.

Richmond

Norfolk

Los Angeles

Phoenix

Memphis

Atlanta

Raleigh

San Diego

Tucson

El Paso

Dallas

Charleston

Savannah

Hermosillo

Rio Grande

Houston

New Orleans

Jacksonville

Chihuahua

San Antonio

Gulf of Mexico

Tampa

Miami

BAHAMAS

Nassau

Honolulu

HAWAII
(U.S.)

PACIFIC OCEAN

ATLANTIC OCEAN

30° N

Tropic of Cancer

MEXICO

Monterrey

Durango

León

Tampico

Havana

CUBA

HAITI

Port-au-Prince

Santo Domingo

Guadalajara

Mexico City

Veracruz

JAMAICA

Kingston

PUERTO RICO (U.S.)

DOMINICAN REPUBLIC

Acapulco

Puebla

BELIZE

Belmopan

GUATEMALA

Guatemala

HONDURAS

Caribbean Sea

San Salvador

Tegucigalpa

EL SALVADOR

Managua

Maracaibo

Caracas

GUYANA

SURINAME

NICARAGUA

San José

Panama City

Paramaribo

COSTA RICA

PANAMA

VENEZUELA

Georgetown

Cayenne

Medellín

FRENCH GUIANA (FRANCE)

Cali

Bogotá

COLOMBIA

Quito

Belém

Galápagos Islands
(ECUADOR)

Guayaquil

Manaus

Rio Negro

Amazon R.

Equator

ECUADOR

Iquitos

Fortaleza

Trujillo

PERU

Recife

Lima

Cuzco

BRAZIL

Tapajós River

Xingu R.

Tocantins R.

Salvador

FRENCH POLYNESIA
(FRANCE)

Papeete

Lake Titicaca

La Paz

Brasília

São Francisco R.

Arequipa

BOLIVIA

Goiânia

Belo Horizonte

Sucre

Campo Grande

Rio de Janeiro

Antofagasta

PARAGUAY

São Paulo

Tropic of Capricorn

Salta

Asunción

Curitiba

San Miguel de Tucumán

Paraná R.

CHILE

Pôrto Alegre

Córdoba

30° S

Valparaíso

Rosario

URUGUAY

Santiago

Buenos Aires

Montevideo

La Plata

Concepción

Rio de la Plata

Mar del Plata

Valdivia

Bahía Blanca

ARGENTINA

Falkland Islands
(U.K.)

Punta Arenas

South Georgia
(U.K.)

0   1,000   2,000 Miles
0   1,000   2,000 Kilometers
Miller Cylindrical Projection

N
W   E
S

⎯⎯ National border
⊛ National capital
• City

A6

150° W   120° W   90° W   60° W

ARCTIC OCEAN

Ellesmere Island

North Magnetic Pole

Queen Elizabeth Islands

Melville Island

Devon Island

Baffin Bay

Greenland

Beaufort Sea

Banks Island

Viscount Melville Sound

Victoria Island

Baffin Island

Davis Strait

Point Barrow

Brooks Range

Arctic Circle

Mt. McKinley
20,320 ft.
(6,194 m)

Yukon River

Great Bear Lake

Foxe Basin

Cape Farewell

60° N

Yukon Plateau

Mackenzie Mts.

Mackenzie River

Great Slave Lake

Hudson Strait

Labrador Sea

Alaska Range

Mt. Logan
19,524 ft.
(5,951 m)

Coast Mountains

Liard River

River

Hudson Bay

Labrador

Gulf of Alaska

Peace River

Lake Athabasca

James Bay

Kodiak Island

Alaska Peninsula

Athabasca R.

CANADIAN

SHIELD

Newfoundland

Aleutian Islands

Queen Charlotte Islands

Saskatchewan River

Lake Winnipeg

GREAT

Gulf of St. Lawrence

Vancouver Island

Coast Ranges

Puget Sound

Cascade Range

Missouri River

Great Lakes

St. Lawrence R.

Nova Scotia

Bay of Fundy

Black Hills

Mississippi

PLAINS

INTERIOR PLAINS

Ohio R.

APPALACHIAN MTS.

Cape Cod
Long Island

Sierra Nevada

Great Salt Lake

GREAT BASIN

Snake River

Platte R.

Arkansas

Ozark Plateau R.

River

Cape Hatteras

ATLANTIC OCEAN

Mt. Whitney
14,494 ft. (4,418 m)

ROCKY

MOUNTAINS

Colorado R.

Rio

COASTAL PLAIN

30° N

Death Valley
(lowest point in N.A.)
-282 ft. (-86 m)

Sonoran Desert

Grande

Gulf of California

Baja California

Sierra Madre Occidental

Sierra Madre Oriental

Gulf of Mexico

Bahamas

Hawaiian Islands

Tropic of Cancer

Citlaltépetl
18,701 ft.
(5,700 m)

Yucatán Peninsula

Cuba

Greater Antilles

Hispaniola

Puerto Rico

PACIFIC

OCEAN

Lake Nicaragua

Caribbean Sea

Lesser Antilles

Isthmus of Panama

Lake Maracaibo

Orinoco R.

Guiana Highlands

Line

Chimborazo
20,561 ft.
(6,267 m)

Llanos

Rio Negro

Amazon R.

Cape São Roque

Islands

Galápagos Islands

Equator

AMAZON BASIN

ANDES

Marquesas Islands

Huascarán
22,205 ft.
(6,768 m)

Tapajós River

Xingu River

Tocantins R.

São Francisco River

Mato Grosso Plateau

Brazilian Highlands

Cook Islands

Tuamotu Archipelago

Society Islands

Lake Titicaca

MOUNTAINS

Tropic of Capricorn

Paraguay R.

Gran Chaco

Iguazú Falls

Atacama Desert

Paraná

Uruguay R.

Mt. Aconcagua
22,831 ft.
(6,959 m)

30° S

Rio de la Plata

Pampa

0   1,000   2,000 Miles
0   1,000   2,000 Kilometers
Miller Cylindrical Projection

Valdés Peninsula
(lowest point in S.A.)
-131 ft. (-40 m)

Patagonia

N
W   E
S

▲ Mountain peak
▼ Point below sea level
— National border
≈ Waterfall

Falkland Islands

South Georgia

A7

Strait of Magellan

Tierra del Fuego

Cape Horn

60° W

150° W   120° W   90° W   60° W   30° W

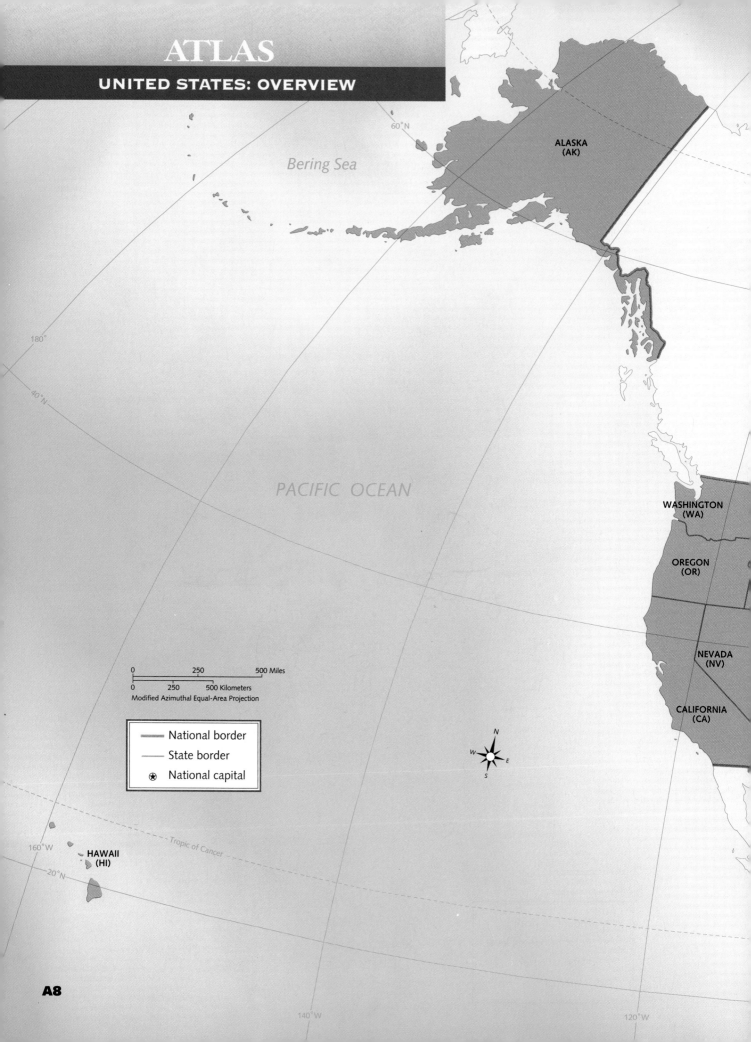

60° N

Bering Sea

ALASKA
(AK)

180°

40° N

PACIFIC OCEAN

WASHINGTON
(WA)

OREGON
(OR)

NEVADA
(NV)

CALIFORNIA
(CA)

0   250   500 Miles

0   250   500 Kilometers

Modified Azimuthal Equal-Area Projection

| National border |
| State border |
| ⊛ National capital |

N
W   E
S

160° W

HAWAII
(HI)

Tropic of Cancer

20° N

140° W

120° W

RUSSIA

ARCTIC OCEAN

170°E

70°N

ALASKA

Arctic Circle

60°N

120°W

CANADA

Yukon River

Fairbanks

Anchorage

Bering Sea

60°N

Juneau

180°

170°W

160°W

150°W

140°W

130°W

PACIFIC OCEAN

50°N

40°N

0   250   500 Miles

0   250   500 Kilometers

CANADA

120°W

110°W

Seattle
Tacoma
Olympia
Spokane
WASHINGTON

Great Falls

Helena   **MONTANA**

Portland   Columbia River

Salem

Billings

Eugene

OREGON   **IDAHO**

Boise

Snake River

WYOMING

Pocatello

Casper

Ogden

Cheyen

Great Salt Lake

NEVADA

Reno
Carson City

Salt Lake City

Provo

Sacramento

San Francisco   Oakland
San Jose

UTAH

Denve

Colorad
Sprin

Fresno

COLORADO   Puebl

CALIFORNIA   Las
Vegas

Flagstaff

Santa Fe

Bakersfield

Albuquerque

PACIFIC OCEAN

Los Angeles   San Bernardino

ARIZONA

NEW MEXICO

San Diego

Phoenix

Roswell

Tucson

El Paso

Rio Grande

▢ Northeast	⊛	National capital
▢ Southeast	★	State capital
▢ Middle West	•	Major city
▢ Southwest	〜	National border
▢ West	—	State border

MEXICO

N
W   E
S

160°W   *PACIFIC OCEAN*   155°W

Honolulu

HAWAII

20°N

Hilo

0   125   250 Miles

0   125   250 Kilometers

0   250   500 Miles

0   250   500 Kilometers

Albers Equal-Area Projection

110°W

120°W

110°W

ATLAS

UNITED STATES: PHYSICAL

RUSSIA

ARCTIC OCEAN

70°N

Brooks Range

ALASKA

Seward Peninsula

Yukon River

St. Lawrence Island

170°E

60°N

Mt. McKinley 20,320 ft. (6,194 m) △

Alaska Range

Bering Sea

180°

0   250   500 Miles
0   250   500 Kilometers

50°N

Aleutian Islands

170°W   160°W   150°W   140°W   130°W

Arctic Circle

120°W

CANADA

Yukon River

60°N

Gulf of Alaska

Kodiak Island

CANADA

120°W   110°W

CANADA

Range

Mt. Rainier 14,410 ft. (4,392 m) ▲   WA

▲ Mt. St. Helens 8,364 ft. (2,549 m)

Columbia River

▲ Mt. Hood 11,235 ft. (3,427 m)

OR

Coast Ranges

Cascade Ranges

Columbia Plateau

ROCKY

Bitterroot Range

Salmon River Mountains

Snake River

ID

Fort Peck Lake

MT

Yellowstone River

Bighorn Mts.

Teton Range

Wind River Range

WY

40°N

Cape Mendocino

Pyramid Lake

Donner Pass Lake Tahoe

NV

GREAT BASIN

Great Salt Lake

Wasatch Range

Uinta Mts.

Great Divide Basin

Mt. Elbert 14,433 ft. (4,399 m)

MOUNTAINS

Front Range

Sierra Nevada

Sacramento River   San Joaquin Valley

Central Valley

Mt. Whitney 14,494 ft. (4,418 m) ▲

UT

Colorado River

Lake Powell

San Juan Mts.

Sangre

CO

PACIFIC OCEAN

Point Conception

Coast Ranges

CA

Death Valley -282 ft. (-86 m) ▼

Mojave Desert

Lake Mead

Grand Canyon

Colorado Plateau

AZ

Salton Sea

Imperial Valley

Sonoran Desert

Baldy Peak 11,403 ft. (3,476 m) ▲

NM

Channel Islands

30°N

130°W

20°N

Legend

Tundra
Evergreen forest
Mixed forest
Grassland
Arid
Mountain
National border
State border
▲ Mountain peak
△ Highest point
▼ Lowest point

MEXICO

Guadalupe Peak 8,749 ft. (2,667 m) ▲

Rio Grande

HAWAII

160°W   155°W

PACIFIC OCEAN

Kauai

Niihau   Oahu   Molokai

Lanai   Maui

Kahoolawe

Hawaii

Mauna Kea 13,796 ft. (4,205 m) ▲

20°N

0   100   200 Miles
0   100   200 Kilometers

N
W   E
S

0   250   500 Miles
0   250   500 Kilometers

Albers Equal-Area Projection

120°W   110°W

A12

CANADA

ME
Mt. Katahdin
5,267 ft.
(1,605 m)

Lake of
the Woods

Upper
Red Lake
Lower
Red Lake

ND

Mesabi
Range

Isle
Royale

Lake
Superior

Keweenaw
Peninsula

Upper Peninsula

Lake Huron

St. Lawrence River

VT
Lake
Champlain

White Mts.

Mt. Washington
6,288 ft.
(1,917 m)

Cape Ann

Leech
Lake

Mille
Lacs
Lake

Wisconsin River

Adirondack
Mountains

NY

Green Mts.

NH

MN

Lake
Oahe

WI

MI

Lower Peninsula

Lake Michigan

Lake
St. Clair

Niagara
Falls

Finger
Lakes

Hudson R.

Connecticut R.

MA

Cape
Cod

SD

Black
Hills

Missouri

River

Mississippi River

Lake
Winnebago

Lake Erie

CT

RI

North Platte R.

Sand Hills

IA

Illinois River

Wabash River

OH

PA

Long
Island

NE

Platte River

INTERIOR

IL

IN

MD

DE

Delaware
Bay

South Platte R.

PLAINS

CENTRAL PLAINS

Ohio River

WV

VA

Potomac R.

Cape
Charles

Chesapeake
Bay

Missouri River

MO

Allegheny Mts.

James R.

Smoky Hills

Lake of
the Ozarks

KY

Roanoke R.

Albemarle
Sound

KS

Harry S. Truman
Reservoir

Cumberland
Gap

Cape
Hatteras

Red Hills

Ozark Plateau

Lake
Barkley

Mt. Mitchell
6,684 ft.
(2,037 m)

NC

Cape Fear River

Arkansas River

Cumberland R.

Canadian

OK

River

Ouachita
Mountains

AR

Tennessee R.

TN

APPALACHIAN MOUNTAINS

PIEDMONT

SC

Cape
Fear

Red River

Stone
Mountain

Savannah River

COASTAL PLAIN

Llano
stacado

Pecos River

Sabine River

MS

Tombigbee R.

Alabama R.

GA

Ocmulgee R.

Oconee R.

Altamaha R.

ATLANTIC
OCEAN

Chattahoochee R.

Edwards
Plateau

TX

Brazos River

Colorado River

Toledo
Bend
Reservoir

Sam
Rayburn
Reservoir

LA

AL

Okefenokee
Swamp

St. Johns River

Cape
Canaveral

Lake
Pontchartrain

Mobile
Bay

Galveston
Bay

Mississippi
Delta

FL

Gulf of Mexico

Tampa
Bay

Lake
Okeechobee

Everglades

BAHAMAS

Cape
Sable

Florida Keys

Straits of Florida

CUBA

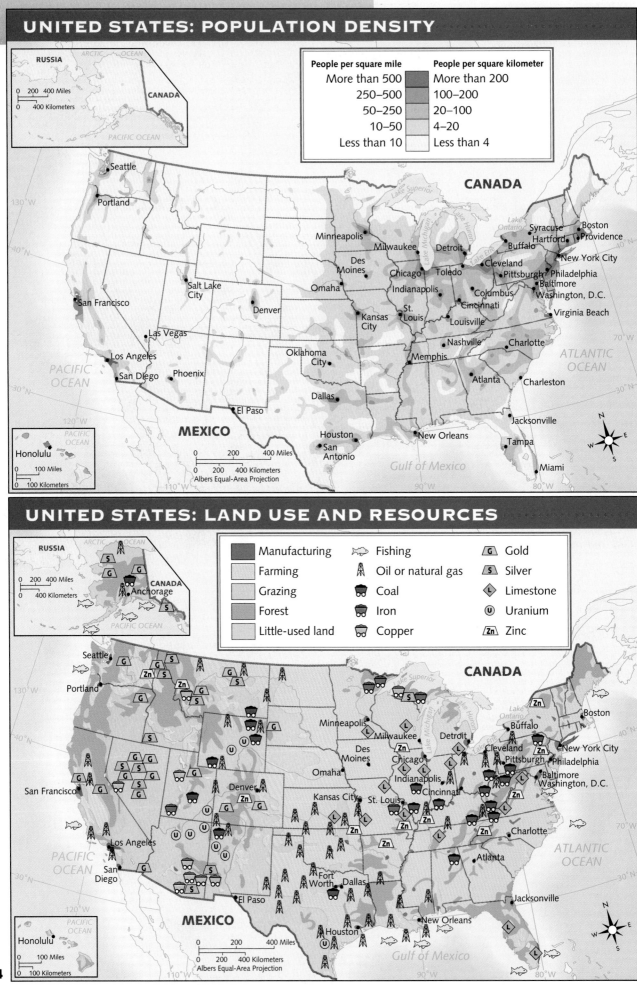

UNITED STATES: POPULATION DENSITY

People per square mile
- More than 500
- 250–500
- 50–250
- 10–50
- Less than 10

People per square kilometer
- More than 200
- 100–200
- 20–100
- 4–20
- Less than 4

RUSSIA
ARCTIC OCEAN
CANADA
PACIFIC OCEAN
0 200 400 Miles
0 400 Kilometers

Seattle
Portland
Minneapolis
Milwaukee
Detroit
CANADA
Lake Superior
Lake Michigan
Lake Huron
Lake Erie
Lake Ontario
Syracuse
Boston
Hartford
Providence
Buffalo
New York City
Des Moines
Chicago
Toledo
Cleveland
Pittsburgh
Philadelphia
Baltimore
Salt Lake City
Omaha
Indianapolis
Columbus
Cincinnati
Washington, D.C.
San Francisco
Denver
Kansas City
St. Louis
Louisville
Virginia Beach
Las Vegas
Nashville
Charlotte
Los Angeles
Oklahoma City
Memphis
ATLANTIC OCEAN
PACIFIC OCEAN
San Diego
Phoenix
Atlanta
Charleston
Dallas
El Paso
MEXICO
Houston
San Antonio
New Orleans
Jacksonville
Tampa
Gulf of Mexico
Miami
Honolulu
PACIFIC OCEAN
0 100 Miles
0 100 Kilometers
0 200 400 Miles
0 200 400 Kilometers
Albers Equal-Area Projection
130°W 120°W 110°W 90°W 80°W 70°W
40°N 30°N

UNITED STATES: LAND USE AND RESOURCES

- Manufacturing
- Farming
- Grazing
- Forest
- Little-used land
- Fishing
- Oil or natural gas
- Coal
- Iron
- Copper
- G Gold
- S Silver
- L Limestone
- U Uranium
- Zn Zinc

RUSSIA
ARCTIC OCEAN
CANADA
S
G
G
Anchorage
S
PACIFIC OCEAN
0 200 400 Miles
0 400 Kilometers

Seattle
Portland
Minneapolis
CANADA
Lake Superior
Lake Michigan
Lake Huron
Lake Ontario
Boston
Buffalo
Zn
Detroit
Cleveland
New York City
Des Moines
Chicago
Pittsburgh
Philadelphia
Omaha
Indianapolis
Cincinnati
Baltimore
Washington, D.C.
San Francisco
Denver
Kansas City
St. Louis
Charlotte
Los Angeles
San Diego
Fort Worth
Dallas
Atlanta
PACIFIC OCEAN
El Paso
Jacksonville
MEXICO
Houston
New Orleans
ATLANTIC OCEAN
Honolulu
Gulf of Mexico
0 100 Miles
0 100 Kilometers
0 200 400 Miles
0 200 400 Kilometers
Albers Equal-Area Projection
130°W 120°W 110°W 90°W 80°W 70°W
40°N 30°N

A14

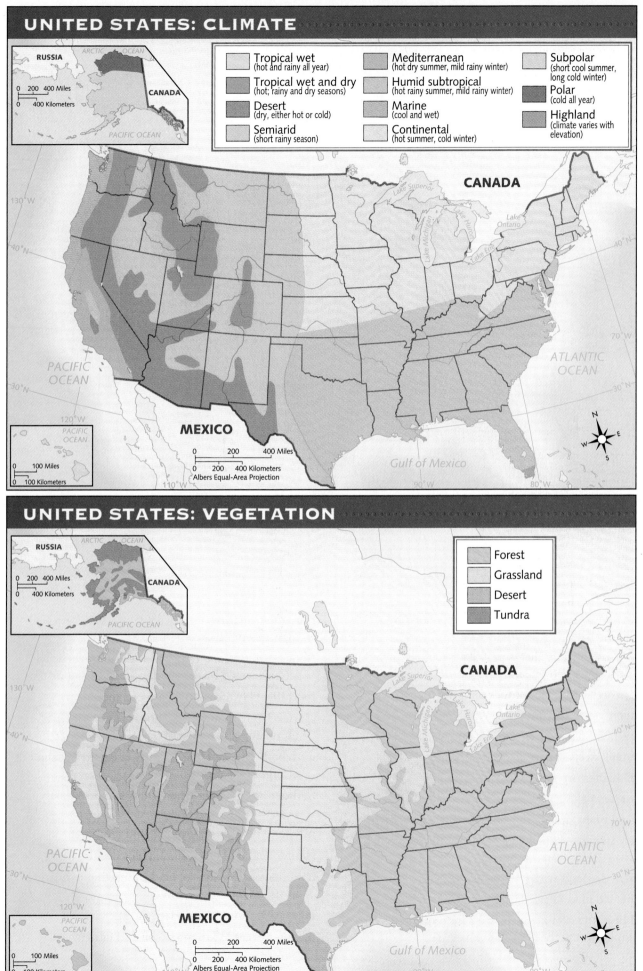

UNITED STATES: CLIMATE

Tropical wet
(hot and rainy all year)

Tropical wet and dry
(hot; rainy and dry seasons)

Desert
(dry, either hot or cold)

Semiarid
(short rainy season)

Mediterranean
(hot dry summer, mild rainy winter)

Humid subtropical
(hot rainy summer, mild rainy winter)

Marine
(cool and wet)

Continental
(hot summer, cold winter)

Subpolar
(short cool summer, long cold winter)

Polar
(cold all year)

Highland
(climate varies with elevation)

RUSSIA
CANADA
0   200   400 Miles
0   400 Kilometers
PACIFIC OCEAN

CANADA

Lake Superior
Lake Michigan
Lake Huron
Lake Ontario
Lake Erie

130°W
40°N
30°N
70°W
80°W
90°W
110°W
120°W

PACIFIC OCEAN

ATLANTIC OCEAN

MEXICO

Gulf of Mexico

PACIFIC OCEAN
0   100 Miles
0   100 Kilometers

0   200   400 Miles
0   200   400 Kilometers
Albers Equal-Area Projection

N
W   E
S

UNITED STATES: VEGETATION

Forest
Grassland
Desert
Tundra

RUSSIA
CANADA
0   200   400 Miles
0   400 Kilometers
ARCTIC OCEAN
PACIFIC OCEAN

CANADA

Lake Superior
Lake Michigan
Lake Huron
Lake Ontario
Lake Erie

130°W
40°N
30°N
70°W
110°W
120°W

PACIFIC OCEAN

ATLANTIC OCEAN

MEXICO

Gulf of Mexico

PACIFIC OCEAN
0   100 Miles
0   100 Kilometers

0   200   400 Miles
0   200   400 Kilometers
Albers Equal-Area Projection

N
W   E
S

A15

ATLAS
GEOGRAPHY TERMS

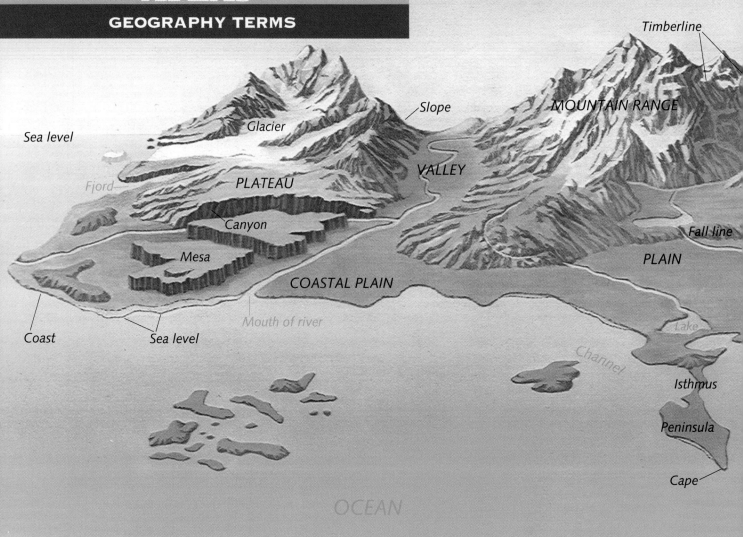

Timberline

Slope

MOUNTAIN RANGE

Glacier

Sea level

Fjord

PLATEAU

VALLEY

Canyon

Fall line

Mesa

PLAIN

COASTAL PLAIN

Coast

Sea level

Mouth of river

Lake

Channel

Isthmus

Peninsula

Cape

OCEAN

basin bowl-shaped area of land surrounded by higher land

bay body of water that is part of a sea or ocean and is partly enclosed by land

bluff high, steep face of rock or earth

canyon deep, narrow valley with steep sides

cape point of land that extends into water

channel deepest part of a body of water

cliff high, steep face of rock or earth

coast land along a sea or ocean

coastal plain area of flat land along a sea or ocean

delta triangle-shaped area of land at the mouth of a river

desert dry land with few plants

dune hill of sand piled up by the wind

fall line area along which rivers form waterfalls or rapids as the rivers drop to lower land

fjord deep, narrow part of a sea or ocean, between high, steep banks

floodplain flat land that is near the edges of a river and is formed by the silt deposited by floods

foothills hilly area at the base of a mountain

glacier large ice mass that moves slowly down a mountain or across land

gulf body of water that is partly enclosed by land but is larger than a bay

harbor area of water where ships can dock safely near land

hill land that rises above the land around it

island land that has water on all sides

isthmus narrow strip of land connecting two larger areas of land

lake body of water with land on all sides

marsh lowland with moist soil and tall grasses

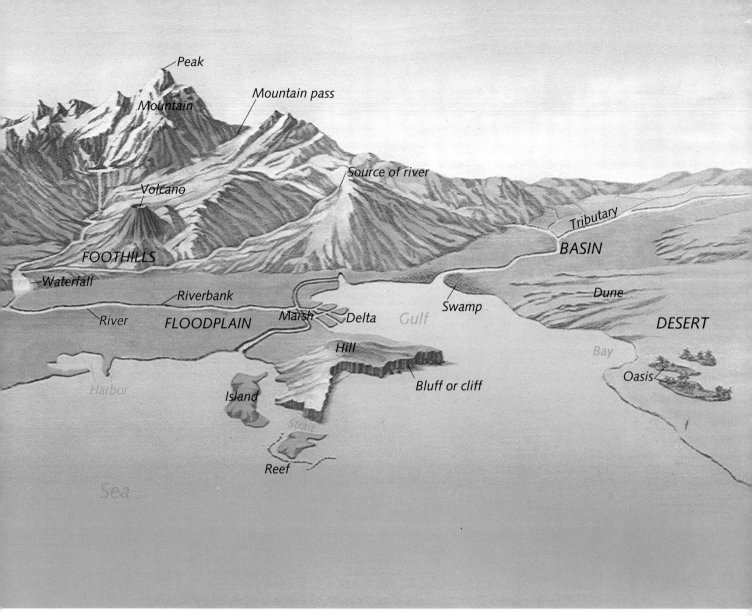

Peak

Mountain

Mountain pass

Volcano

Source of river

Tributary

BASIN

FOOTHILLS

Waterfall

Riverbank

Dune

River

FLOODPLAIN

Marsh

Delta

Swamp

DESERT

Gulf

Hill

Bay

Oasis

Harbor

Bluff or cliff

Island

Strait

Reef

Sea

mesa flat-topped mountain with steep sides

mountain highest kind of land

mountain pass low place between mountains

mountain range row of mountains

mouth of river place where a river empties into another body of water

oasis area of water and fertile land in a desert

ocean body of salt water larger than a sea

peak top of a mountain

peninsula land that is almost completely surrounded by water

plain flat land

plateau area of high, flat land with steep sides

reef ridge of sand, rock, or coral that lies at or near the surface of a sea or ocean

river large stream of water that flows across the land

riverbank land along a river

sea body of salt water smaller than an ocean

sea level the level that is even with the surface of an ocean or sea

slope side of a hill or mountain

source of river place where a river begins

strait narrow channel of water connecting two larger bodies of water

swamp area of low, wet land with trees

timberline line on a mountain above which it is too cold for trees to grow

tributary stream or river that empties into a larger river

valley low land between hills or mountains

volcano opening in the Earth, often raised, through which lava, rock, ashes, and gases are forced out

waterfall steep drop from a high place to a lower place in a stream or river

Why Study SOCIAL STUDIES?

> 66 Every one of you already holds the important office of citizen. Over time you will become more and more involved in your community. You will need to know more about what being a citizen means. Social studies will help you learn about citizenship. That is why social studies is important in your life. 99
>
> The authors of *Stories in Time*

THE POWERFUL IDEAS OF SOCIAL STUDIES

These students are being good citizens. What actions make you a good citizen?

All people are alike in some ways, but each person has different ways of thinking, feeling, and acting.

Think about the many groups you are a part of. You are also a member—or **citizen**—of your town or city, your state, and your country. Citizens work to improve all the groups they belong to and to make the world a better place.

To help you think, feel, and act as a citizen, *Stories in Time* begins every lesson with a question. That question links you to the lesson's story. Each question also connects you with one or more of five powerful ideas that citizens need to understand in order to make decisions.

POWERFUL IDEA NUMBER *1*
COMMONALITY AND DIVERSITY

In some ways people everywhere are alike. We all have basic needs for things like food, clothing, and shelter. We all laugh, get angry, and have our feelings hurt. These are examples of our commonality, or what we all share. At the same time, we need to understand that each person is different from everyone else. We all have different ways of thinking, feeling, and acting. That is our diversity.

Like people, places can also have features in common. For example, many places on Earth have similar landforms. A **landform** is one of the shapes that make up the Earth's surface, such as mountains, hills, or plains. However, every place on Earth is different in some way.

POWERFUL IDEA NUMBER *2*
CONFLICT AND COOPERATION

Because people have different wants and needs, they may have conflicts, or disagreements. But people can often overcome their conflicts by cooperating, or working together. In social studies you will learn about ways people have found to settle their disagreements. You will also learn ways to cooperate and to resolve conflicts in your own life.

POWERFUL IDEA NUMBER *3*
CONTINUITY AND CHANGE

Although some things change over time, other things stay the same. Many things have stayed the same for years and will probably stay the same in the future. This means that they have continuity. Understanding continuity and change can help you see how things in the world have come to be as they are.

POWERFUL IDEA NUMBER *4*
INDIVIDUALISM AND INTERDEPENDENCE

Citizens can act by themselves to make a difference in the world. Their actions as individuals may be helpful or harmful to other citizens. But much of the time, people do not act alone. They depend on others to help them. Such interdependence connects citizens with one another and affects their lives.

People once listened to music on a machine called a phonograph. Today, people listen to music recorded on CDs, or compact discs. What other examples of change can you think of?

POWERFUL IDEA NUMBER *5*
INTERACTION WITHIN DIFFERENT ENVIRONMENTS

People behave in ways that affect other people. People's actions also affect their surroundings, or **environment** . This is true of their home environment, their school environment, or other environments they may be a part of. In turn, people's environments can affect their actions. Understanding such interactions, or how people and places affect one another, is important to understanding why things happened in the past and why things happen today.

The individuals on this soccer team must learn to work together. Members of a team depend on one another.

 What are the five powerful ideas of social studies?

How To

Read Social Studies

Why Is This Skill Important?

Social studies is made up of many different stories about people, places, and events. An event is something that happens. Sometimes you read these stories in library books. Other times you read them in textbooks, like this one. Knowing how to read social studies in a textbook can make it easier to study and to do your homework. It will help you identify main ideas and important people, places, and events.

Understand the Process

You can follow these steps to read any lesson in this book.

1. Preview the whole lesson.
  • Look at the title and headings to find out what the lesson is about.

• Look at the pictures, the captions, and the questions for clues to help you decide what is most important in the lesson.
• Think about the Link to Our World question at the beginning of the lesson to find out the purpose of the lesson.
• Read the statement labeled Focus on the Main Idea. It gives you the key idea that the lesson teaches.
• Look at the Preview Vocabulary list to see what new terms will be introduced.

2. Read the lesson for information on the main idea. As you read, you will come across checkpoint questions. Each has this mark ✓ next to it. Be sure to find the answers to these questions before you continue reading the lesson.

3. When you finish reading the lesson, say in your own words what you have learned.

4. Look back over the lesson. Then answer the review questions—from memory, if possible. The lesson review will help you check your understanding. It will also help you to think critically and to show what you know.

Think and Apply

Use the four steps in Understand the Process each time you are asked to read a lesson in *Stories in Time*.

GEOGRAPHY

Each story you will read in this book has a setting. The setting of a story includes the place where it happens. Knowing about places is an important part of **geography**—the study of the Earth's surface and the way people use it. Studying geography helps you answer the following questions about a place.

- **Where is it? (location)**
- **What is it like there? (place)**
- **How are the lives of people shaped by this place? How is this place shaped by what people do? (human-environment interactions)**
- **How and why do people, ideas, and goods move to and from this place? (movement)**
- **How is this place like other places? How is it different? (regions)**

The answers to these questions tell you what you need to know in order to understand setting. These five topics are so important that many people call them the five themes, or key topics, of geography.

1. LOCATION

Everything on Earth has its own location. A **location** is where something can be found. You can describe location in many ways. You can use numbers and street names to give the location of a place. You can also describe the location of a place by telling what it is near. For example, is your school located near a shopping mall? Is it located across the street from a park?

2. PLACE

Geographers—the people who study geography—look at what makes one place different from another place. As you know, every place on Earth has special features that make it different from all other places. Some of these are its **physical features**, or features that have been formed by nature. The physical features of a place include its landforms, bodies of water, and other natural resources. A **natural resource** is something found in nature that

Street signs, like these in Amarillo, Texas, help people locate places. What other things tell location?

Some of the Earth's physical features, such as this stone arch in Utah's Arches National Park, have unusual shapes.

people can use. **Climate**, or the kind of weather a place has over a long time, is another physical feature of a place.

Many places also have **human features**, or features that have been made by people. Human features include buildings, farms, airports, bridges, and highways. What people do and the number of people who live in an area are human features, too.

3. HUMAN-ENVIRONMENT INTERACTIONS

Geographers also study how humans and the environment interact, or affect each other. Sometimes people change the environment, but the environment can also affect people. For example, the environment can affect the kinds of jobs that people do. It can even affect the kinds of food people eat, the way they dress, and the kinds of homes they live in.

4. MOVEMENT

Each day people in different parts of the United States and the world interact with one another. People and goods move from place to place in cars and trucks and in trains, ships, and airplanes. Ideas move from one place to another in newspapers, on television and radio,

This human feature—a memorial to Chief Crazy Horse—is being carved into a mountainside in South Dakota.

and by telephone. Geography helps you understand how people, goods, and ideas got to where they are.

5. REGIONS

To study a place more closely, geographers sometimes divide the Earth into different regions. A **region** is an area with at least one feature that sets it apart from other areas. A region can be a small area, such as your school's library or cafeteria, that is set aside for some purpose. Or it can be a much larger area, such as a city, a state, or a country. A region can be described by such things as the climate, the landforms, or the plant life that exists there. A region can also be described by a common language or a common way of life.

✓ **What are the five themes of geography?**

To keep warm in northern Alaska's cold climate, this girl wears a heavy coat called a parka. How does the environment affect you?

GLOBES AND MAPS
THE TOOLS OF GEOGRAPHY

What do you usually think of when you hear the word *geography*? Most people think of globes and maps. That is because globes and maps are important tools of geography. They can help you locate the places you read about. They can also help you better understand the Earth and its people.

GLOBES

A globe is a model of the Earth. Because the Earth has the shape of a **sphere**, or ball, a globe is also a sphere. Globes are the best models that we have of the Earth.

Find the North Pole and the South Pole on the drawing of the Earth on this page. Notice the line that circles the Earth halfway between the North Pole and the South Pole. This line is called the **equator**. The equator is the same distance from the North Pole and the South Pole. Although you can see the equator on a globe or map, there is no such line on the Earth.

The equator divides the Earth into a northern half and a southern half. The Earth is a sphere, so half of it is called a **hemisphere**. *Hemi* means "half." The equator divides the Earth into the Northern Hemisphere and the Southern Hemisphere. The Earth can also be divided into the Western Hemisphere and the Eastern Hemisphere.

Globes are good models because they look so much like the Earth. However, globes are not always easy to use. For example, you cannot see the details about a small place on a globe. You cannot see all of a globe at one glance, either. No matter how you turn a globe, you can see only half of it at a time.

MAPS

A map is a drawing of a place. Unlike globes, however, maps are flat. Because they are flat, they cannot show the true shape of the Earth. Even so, maps are very useful.

THE EARTH

North Pole

Northern Hemisphere

Equator

Southern Hemisphere

South Pole

OCEANS AND CONTINENTS

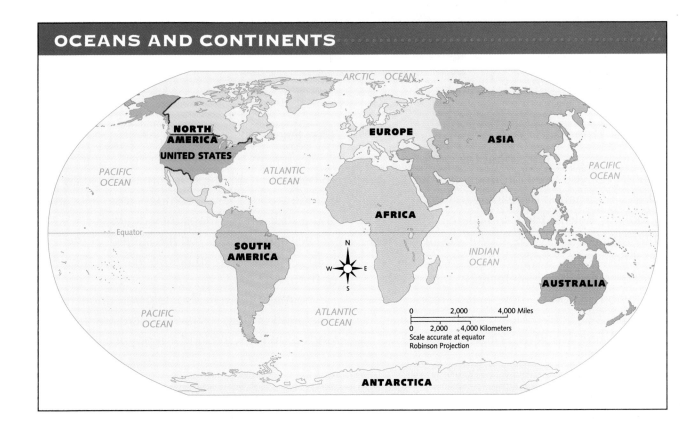

Look at the map on this page. As you can see, most of the Earth is covered by water. In fact, bodies of water cover more than seven-tenths of the Earth's surface. Bodies of water include rivers, lakes, seas, and oceans.

Most of the Earth's water is in the oceans. If you look closely at the map, you will see that all the oceans are connected. Together they make one huge world ocean.

Because the world ocean is so big, it is usually divided into four parts. From largest to smallest, these are the Pacific Ocean, the Atlantic Ocean, the Indian Ocean, and the Arctic Ocean.

On this map you can also see the continents. A **continent** is one of the seven main areas of land on the Earth. The seven continents, from largest to smallest, are Asia, Africa, North America, South America, Antarctica, Europe, and Australia. All of the United States, except for the island state of Hawaii, is in North America.

 **How are globes different from maps?**

Maps
by Dorothy Brown Thompson

High adventure
　And bright dream—
Maps are mightier
　Than they seem:

Ships that follow
　Leaning stars—
Red and gold of
　Strange bazaars—

Ice floes hid
　Beyond all knowing—
Planes that ride where
　Winds are blowing!

Train maps, maps of
　Wind and weather,
Road maps—taken
　Altogether

Maps are really
　Magic wands
For home-staying
　Vagabonds!

How To

Read a Map

Why Is This Skill Important?

To answer questions about the world around you, you need information. You can get this information by reading this book, by looking at its pictures and charts, and by studying its maps. Maps tell you about the five themes of geography—location, place, human-environment interactions, movement, and regions. Knowing how to read maps is an important skill both for learning social studies and for taking action as a citizen.

The Parts of a Map

Most maps have several things in common. To help you read maps, mapmakers usually include a title, a key, a compass rose, a locator, and a scale on the maps they draw.

The map title tells you the subject of the map. Look at the map below. What is the title of this map?

The map title may also help you understand what kind of map is shown. There are many kinds of maps. One kind is a physical map. It

THE UNITED STATES

RUSSIA
ARCTIC OCEAN
ALASKA
CANADA
Juneau
PACIFIC OCEAN
0 200 400 Miles
0 400 Kilometers

⊛ National capital
★ State capital
— National border
— State border

CANADA

0 200 400 Miles
0 200 400 Kilometers
Albers Equal-Area Projection

Olympia
WA
Salem
OR
ID
Boise
Helena
MT
ND
Bismarck
MN
St. Paul
SD
Pierre
WY
Cheyenne
NE
Lincoln
IA
Des Moines
Sacramento
Carson City
NV
Salt Lake City
UT
Denver
CO
KS
Topeka
MO
Jefferson City
WI
Madison
Lake Superior
Lake Michigan
Lake Huron
MI
Lansing
IL
IN
Indianapolis
OH
Columbus
Lake Erie
Lake Ontario
NH
ME
Augusta
Montpelier
VT
Concord
Boston
NY
Albany
MA
Hartford
Providence
RI
CT
PA
Harrisburg
NJ
Trenton
Dover
DE
MD
Annapolis
Washington, D.C.
WV
Charleston
VA
Richmond
Springfield
KY
Frankfort
CA
Santa Fe
AZ
Phoenix
NM
OK
Oklahoma City
AR
Little Rock
TN
Nashville
NC
Raleigh
Columbia
SC
Atlanta
GA
PACIFIC OCEAN
ATLANTIC OCEAN
MS
Jackson
AL
Montgomery
LA
Baton Rouge
TX
Austin
FL
Tallahassee
N
E
W
S

HAWAII
Honolulu
0 100 Miles
0 100 Kilometers
PACIFIC OCEAN

MEXICO
Gulf of Mexico

shows mostly landforms and bodies of water. Another kind of map is a political map. It shows mostly cities and state or national boundaries. **Boundary** is another word for *border,* or the outside edge of a place. What two countries share a national border with the United States?

The **locator** is a small map or globe that shows where the place on the main map is located in a state, in a country, or in the world. The locator on the map of the United States is a globe that shows North America. The United States is shown in red.

⊛	National capital
★	State capital
——	National border
——	State border

The **map key**, which is sometimes called a map legend, explains what the symbols on the map stand for. A **symbol** is something that stands for something else. On a map, a symbol represents a real object in the world. Symbols on maps may be colors, patterns, lines, or other special marks. On the map on page 26, a star is used to show a state capital. What symbol is used to show the national capital?

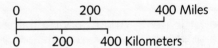

The **map scale** compares a distance on a map with a distance in the real world. A map scale helps you find the real distance between places on a map. Each map in this book has a scale that shows both miles and kilometers.

Find Alaska and Hawaii on the map of the United States. These states are not shown where they really are. Hundreds of miles separate them from the other 48 states. To show the whole area between Alaska, Hawaii, and the other states, the map would have to be much larger, or each part of the map would have to be much smaller. Instead, Alaska and Hawaii are each shown in an **inset map**, or a small map within a larger map. The boxes around Alaska and Hawaii show that they are inset maps.

An inset map often has its own map scale. Look at Alaska on the map of the United States. On the Earth, Alaska is more than twice the size of Texas, but on the map, Alaska is much smaller than Texas. This is because the scales on the inset map and the main map are different.

The **compass rose**, or direction marker on a map, shows the main directions, or cardinal directions. The **cardinal directions** are north, south, east, and west. The compass rose also helps you find the **intermediate directions**, or the directions between the cardinal directions. Intermediate directions are northeast, southeast, southwest, and northwest.

Understand the Process

To help you find places on a map, map-makers sometimes add lines that cross each other to form a pattern called a **grid**. Study the map of Arkansas below. Around the grid are letters and numbers. In this grid the columns, which run up and down, have numbers. The rows, which run left and right, have letters. Each square on the map can be identified by its letter and number.

A map with a grid may have an index such as the one you see beside this map. The index helps you find the names of the places you are looking for. It lists them in alphabetical order. The index also gives the grid letter and number for each place.

1. Find Little Rock, Arkansas's capital, in the map index. What are Little Rock's grid letter and number?

2. Find the letter *B* and the number *2* on the grid. Put a finger of one hand on the letter *B* and a finger of your other hand on the number *2*. Move your fingers toward each other, along row B and column 2. You will find Little Rock in the square where your fingers meet.

3. Now find Fayetteville on the map. In what square is it located? In what square is the city of Fort Smith located?

4. What city is located in square *C-3*? Check your answer with the map index.

Think and Apply

Look at the map of Arkansas again. Identify the parts of the map, and discuss with a partner what the map tells you about Arkansas. Then take turns using the map grid to find different places in the state.

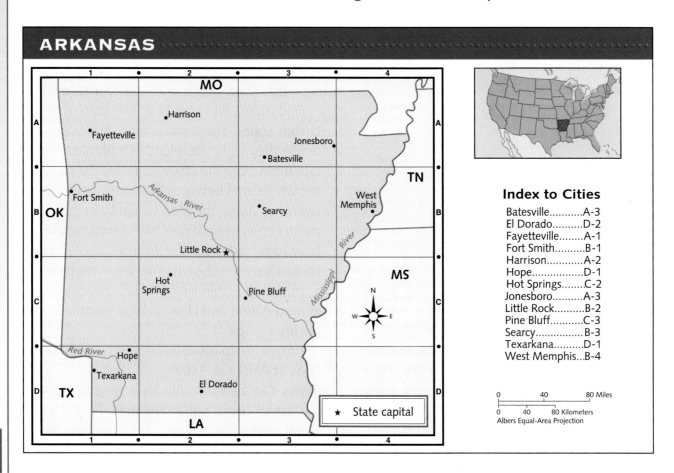

ARKANSAS

Index to Cities

Batesville...........A-3
El Dorado..........D-2
Fayetteville........A-1
Fort Smith..........B-1
Harrison............A-2
Hope................D-1
Hot Springs........C-2
Jonesboro..........A-3
Little Rock..........B-2
Pine Bluff...........C-3
Searcy...............B-3
Texarkana..........D-1
West Memphis...B-4

0   40   80 Miles
0   40   80 Kilometers
Albers Equal-Area Projection

HISTORY

Geography is just one of the subjects you will learn about in social studies. Another is **history**—the study of the past. Studying history helps you see the links between the past and the present. As you read about the past in *Stories in Time*, ask yourself the questions below. They will help you think like a historian, a person who studies the past.

WHAT HAPPENED?

To find out what really happened in the past, you need proof that it happened. You can find proof by studying what people have written or said. Some records of the past are made by people who saw or took part in an event. Other records do not link to an event directly. They were made at a later time by someone who did not take part in the event.

WHEN DID IT HAPPEN?

One way to understand a story of the past is to put events in the order in which they took place. The dates used in a story can help you do this. So can time lines. A time line is a diagram that shows the events that took place during a certain period of time. Time lines can help you understand how one event may have led to another.

WHO TOOK PART IN IT?

To understand the stories of the past, you need to know about the people in the stories and the times in which they lived. A good way to learn about people from their own points of view is to read what they said about something. You will have a chance to do that in this book.

HOW AND WHY DID IT HAPPEN?

Many events in history are linked. To find links between events, you will need to analyze them. **Analyzing** is a way of thinking in which you break something down into its parts and look closely at how those parts are connected. When you analyze an event, you look at things such as who was involved and what the time period was like.

History lets you come face to face with people from the past.

 What questions can you ask yourself when you read about the past?

CIVICS AND GOVERNMENT

Civics and government is the study of citizenship and the ways in which citizens govern themselves. A **government** is a group of people who lead a community, state, or nation. The main job of government is to make and carry out laws. Laws help people live together in order and safety.

Citizens have an important part in making government work. The laws that guide the actions of people are written and carried out by citizens. In *Stories in Time* you will learn about how government works. You will also learn how people and events have shaped our nation's government.

Voters Register Here!

ECONOMICS

An **economy** is a system for providing and using goods and services. The study of how people do these things is called **economics**. In *Stories in Time* you will read about how people make, buy, sell, and trade goods to get what they need or want. You will also learn how the economy of the United States has changed over time.

CULTURE

In *Stories in Time* you will read about people from different parts of the United States and the world. You will explore how they live and their ways of thinking and expressing ideas. You will look at their families and communities and how people make their living. All these things make up a **culture**, or a way of life. Every group has a culture. In *Stories in Time* you will discover many cultures in the story of the United States, past and present.

> ✓ **What kinds of things do you learn when you study civics and government, economics, and culture?**

How To

Work Together in Groups

Why Is This Skill Important?

Learning social studies is sometimes easier when you work with a partner or in a group. Many projects you will work on in your social studies class would be difficult for one person to do. If you work with other students, however, each of you can have a simpler job.

To complete group projects, each group member needs to cooperate with the others. Knowing how to work together is an important skill for students and for all citizens.

Understand the Process

Suppose you are working with other students on a group project, such as putting on a class play, painting a large mural, or cleaning up the school yard or a community park. You and the other group members might find it helpful to follow a set of steps.

1. Organize and plan together.
   - Set your goal as a group.
   - Share your ideas.
   - Cooperate with others to plan your work.
   - Make sure everyone has a job.
2. Act on your plan together.
   - Take responsibility for your jobs.
   - Help one another.
   - If there are conflicts, take time to talk about them and to work them out.
   - Show your group's finished work to the rest of the class.
3. Talk about your work.
   - Discuss what you learned by working together.

Think and Apply

Follow these steps for working together as you take part in the activities in *Stories in Time*.

UNIT 1

LAND, PEOPLE, AND REGIONS

The United States has different climates and landforms.

Workers often use natural resources to earn their living.

People's actions can change the environment.

UNIT 4
The Middle West

UNIT 5
The Southwest

UNIT 6
The West

The United States has different kinds of land, bodies of water, and climates. It has many valuable natural resources, too. The United States also has people who come from many countries around the world. Those people may have different beliefs and ways of doing things, and they live in different places. Yet all Americans are part of one nation.

← Niagara Falls, in New York

People from all over the world have come to live in the United States.

Americans share one national government.

States are just one way people can divide the United States into regions.

WELCOME TO WISCONSIN

Buffalo Co

ALMANAC

Land, People, and Regions

Did You Know?

The United States of America is the fourth-largest country in the world in size and the third-largest country in population. Only Russia, Canada, and China are larger. Only China and India have more people.

LAND	SIZE	CLIMATE	POPULATION*	LEADING PRODUCTS AND RESOURCES

THE UNITED STATES OF AMERICA

Highest Point:
Mt. McKinley, in Alaska
20,320 feet
(6,194 m)

Lowest Point:
Death Valley, in California
282 feet (86 m) below sea level

3,615,292 square miles
(9,363,563 sq km)

Highest Temperature:
134°F (57°C) at Death Valley, in California, on July 10, 1913

Lowest Temperature:
-80°F (-62°C) at Prospect Creek, Alaska, on January 23, 1971

Rainiest Place:
Mount Waialeale, in Hawaii
average yearly rainfall of 460 inches (1,168 cm)

Driest Place:
Death Valley, in California
average yearly rainfall of 2 inches (5 cm)

268,702,000

*The most recent figure available

Farming:
Beef cattle, chickens, corn, cotton, eggs, hogs, milk, soybeans, wheat

Fishing:
Crabs, salmon, shrimp

Manufacturing:
Airplanes, cars and trucks, chemicals, clothing, computers, electronic equipment, gasoline, machinery, medicines, metal products, paper, plastics, printed materials, processed foods

Mining:
Coal, natural gas, oil

Washington, D.C., became the nation's capital in 1800.

The United States uses about 400 billion gallons of water each day.

THE UNITED STATES

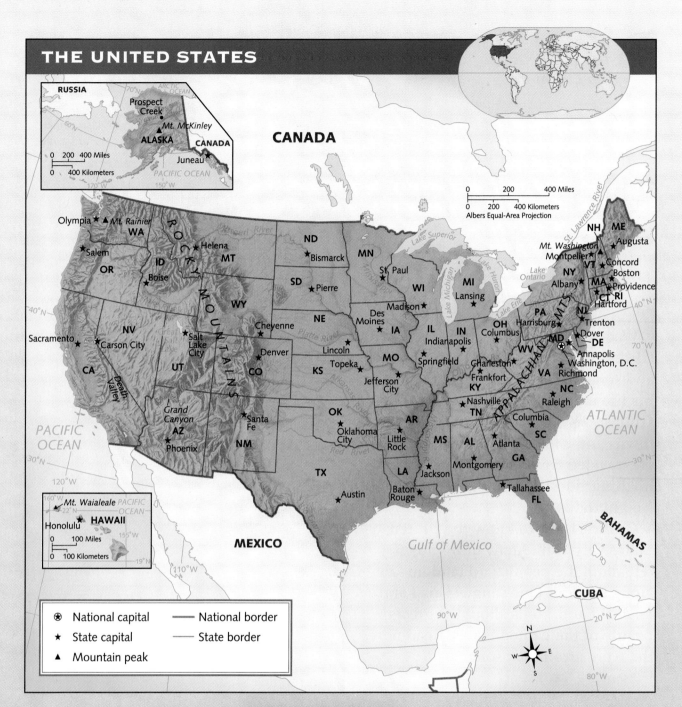

RUSSIA

Prospect Creek
▲ Mt. McKinley
ALASKA
CANADA
Juneau
PACIFIC OCEAN

0 200 400 Miles
0 400 Kilometers

CANADA

0 200 400 Miles
0 200 400 Kilometers
Albers Equal-Area Projection

Olympia ★ ▲ Mt. Rainier
WA
Salem ★
OR
ID
Boise ★
Helena ★
MT
ROCKY MOUNTAINS

ND
Bismarck ★
SD
Pierre ★
WY
Cheyenne ★
NE

MN
St. Paul ★
WI
Madison ★
Des Moines ★
IA
Lincoln ★

Lake Superior
MI
Lansing ★
Lake Michigan
Lake Huron
Lake Erie

NH ME
Mt. Washington ▲ Augusta ★
Montpelier ★ VT Concord ★
NY Boston ★
Albany ★ MA Providence
CT RI
Hartford ★

Sacramento ★
NV
Carson City ★
CA
Death Valley

Salt Lake City ★
UT
Denver ★
CO

Topeka ★
KS
MO
Jefferson City ★

IL
Springfield ★
IN
Indianapolis ★
OH
Columbus ★
PA
Harrisburg ★
WV
Charleston ★
VA
Richmond ★

NJ
Trenton ★
Dover ★ DE
MD
Annapolis ★
Washington, D.C. ☆

PACIFIC OCEAN

Grand Canyon
AZ
Phoenix ★
NM
Santa Fe ★

OK
Oklahoma City ★
TX
Austin ★

AR
Little Rock ★
LA
Baton Rouge ★

KY
Nashville ★
TN
MS
Jackson ★
AL
Montgomery ★
Atlanta ★
GA

NC
Raleigh ★
Columbia ★
SC
APPALACHIAN MTS.

ATLANTIC OCEAN

Mt. Waialeale ▲
HAWAII
Honolulu ★
PACIFIC OCEAN

0 100 Miles
0 100 Kilometers

MEXICO

Gulf of Mexico

Tallahassee ★
FL

BAHAMAS

CUBA

⊛ National capital
★ State capital
▲ Mountain peak

— National border
— State border

N
W E
S

The nation's greatest snowfall in one year—1,122 inches (2,850 cm)—fell on Washington's Mount Rainier between July 1971 and June 1972.

The United States has more than 75,000 elementary schools.

The wind on Mount Washington, in New Hampshire, once blew at 231 miles (372 km) per hour.

This Land Is Your Land

by Woody Guthrie

Woody Guthrie (GUH•three) (1912–1967) was an American singer and songwriter. He spent much of his life moving from place to place. Guthrie visited the back roads and towns and cities of the United States. He traveled from coast to coast, often hitching rides aboard slow-moving freight trains.

Guthrie came to know the United States very well. Many of his songs tell about the people and land he saw along the way. One song, "This Land Is Your Land," tells about the great beauty of the United States. Read now the words from that song.

Redwoods are among the world's tallest living trees. They grow along the Pacific coast of the United States, in California and Oregon.

This land is your land.
This land is my land.
From California to the New York island;
From the redwood forest to the Gulf Stream waters;
This land was made for you and me.

As I was walking that ribbon of highway,
I saw above me that endless skyway.
I saw below me that golden valley,
This land was made for you and me.

I've roamed and rambled and I followed my footsteps
To the sparkling sands of her diamond deserts,
And all around me a voice was sounding,
"This land was made for you and me."

When the sun came shining and I was strolling
And the wheat fields waving and the dust clouds rolling,
As the fog was lifting a voice was chanting,
"This land was made for you and me."

Much of the southwestern United States is desert.

THE AMERICAN LANDSCAPE

66 There is no part of the world where the names are so rich, poetical, humorous, and picturesque as the United States of America. All times, races, and languages have brought their contributions. . . . **99**

Robert Louis Stevenson, 1879

The Statue of Liberty is a symbol of freedom that welcomes newcomers to the United States.

A LAND OF *D*IFFERENT *L*ANDS

*L*ink to Our World

How are places different from one another?

Focus on the Main Idea
As you read this lesson, compare and contrast the major landforms of the United States.

Preview Vocabulary
coastal plain   **canyon**
peninsula   **mountain range**
plateau   **fertile**
basin

Robert Louis Stevenson was one of the best-liked writers of the late 1800s.

The writer Robert Louis Stevenson was very worried. He had just received word that his sweetheart, Fanny, was ill in America. Stevenson knew that he must go to be with Fanny. He did not know, however, that his trip would be a lesson in the geography of the United States.

THE COASTAL PLAIN

On August 7, 1879, Stevenson left his home in Europe and boarded a waiting ship. The ship took ten mostly stormy days to cross the Atlantic Ocean and reach New York City. As the ship neared the east coast of the United States, Stevenson looked out on a broad, tree-filled coastal plain. A **coastal plain** is low land that lies along an ocean.

The land near New York City is part of a much larger region of low land called the Coastal Plain. The Coastal Plain begins along the coast of Massachusetts. At that point it is only a narrow strip of land. The Coastal Plain gets wider as it goes on south toward the Florida peninsula (puh•NIN•suh•luh). A **peninsula** is land almost entirely surrounded by water. From Florida the Coastal Plain stretches west along the Gulf of Mexico into Texas and Mexico.

The coast along the Atlantic Ocean and the Gulf of Mexico often has large bays. Offshore are many low, sandy islands.

✓ **What kind of land lies along the Atlantic and Gulf coasts of the United States?**

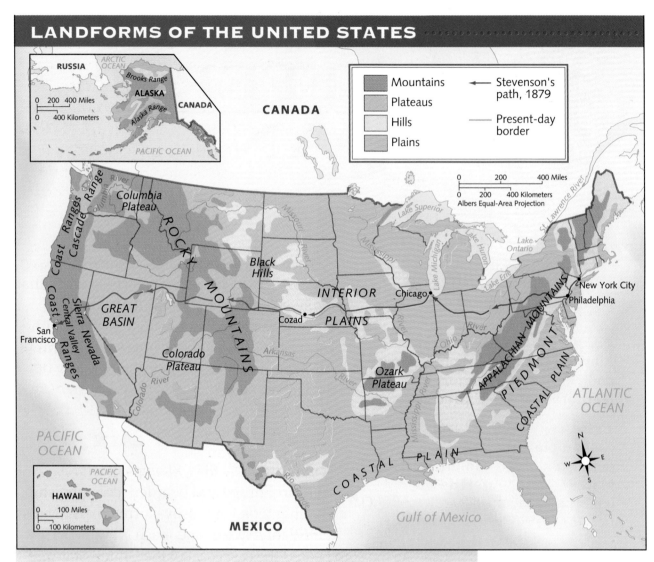

Map legend:
- Mountains
- Plateaus
- Hills
- Plains
- ← Stevenson's path, 1879
- — Present-day border

PLACE The four main landforms in the United States are mountains, plateaus, hills, and plains.

■ What landform covers most of the middle of the country?

THE APPALACHIAN MOUNTAINS

Stevenson did not stay in New York City for long. Fanny lived on the Pacific coast of the United States—in San Francisco, California. To reach San Francisco, Stevenson climbed aboard a train and began the long journey west.

Not long after the train passed through Philadelphia, Pennsylvania, the land began to change. The Coastal Plain gave way to wide valleys and rolling hills. This area of high land on the eastern side of the Appalachian (a•puh•LAY•chee•uhn) Mountains is called the Piedmont (PEED•mahnt). *Piedmont* means "foot of the mountain."

The tree-covered Appalachians rise above the Piedmont. The Appalachians cover much of the eastern part of the United States. They go all the way from northern Alabama to Canada.

 **What mountains cover much of the eastern United States?**

THE INTERIOR PLAINS

To the west of the Appalachian Mountains, the land gets flat again. Here, in the center of the United States, Stevenson saw other plains. They are called the Interior (in•TIR•ee•er) Plains. The word *interior* means "inside." These huge plains stretch across the middle of the United States and north into Canada.

Much of this land is very flat, but there are some hills. In a few places, like the Black Hills of South Dakota and the Ozark Plateau (pla•TOH) in Missouri and Arkansas, the land rises sharply. A **plateau** is high, mostly flat land.

In the northeastern part of the Interior Plains are the five Great Lakes. The Great Lakes are the world's largest group of freshwater lakes. In fact, they could cover the whole United States with about 9 feet (3 m) of water!

During the long journey across the Interior Plains, Stevenson wrote about the land he saw. "The country was flat . . . but far from being dull. All through Ohio, Indiana, Illinois, and Iowa . . . it was rich and various. . . . The tall corn pleased the eye; the trees were graceful. . . ."

By the time the train pulled into the station at Cozad (koh•ZAD), in the middle of Nebraska, the Interior Plains had changed. Now the land had almost no trees and few rivers. The land seemed to look the same for mile after mile. Stevenson wrote that a person "may walk five miles and see nothing; ten, and it is as though he had not moved; twenty, and still he is in the midst of the same great level, and has approached no nearer to the one object in view, the flat horizon."

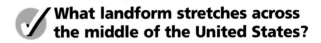

What landform stretches across the middle of the United States?

THE ROCKY MOUNTAINS

As Stevenson's train moved westward, the flat Interior Plains gave way to other mountains. For the first time, Stevenson saw the Rocky Mountains, rising sharply toward the sky. They mark the western edge of the Interior Plains.

The Rocky Mountains cover much of the western United States. They stretch north from New Mexico through Canada and into Alaska. Because the Rockies are so high, many of their peaks are covered with snow all year.

What landform marks the western edge of the Interior Plains?

Farms, like this one in Illinois, cover much of the land on the Interior Plains.

THE LAND BETWEEN THE MOUNTAINS

Stevenson's train took two days to cross the Rocky Mountains. Then the land changed once again. Now Stevenson looked out the window and saw only "desolate and desert scenes, fiery hot and deadly weary."

Between the Rocky Mountains on the east and other mountains farther west is a large area of land that is mostly dry. It is sometimes called the Intermountain Region. Part of this land is the Great Basin, the largest desert in the United States. A **basin** is low, bowl-shaped land with higher ground all around it. Other large deserts lie south of the Great Basin, in Arizona and California.

Not just basins but other physical features mark this area. These include mountains and valleys, plateaus, and canyons. A **canyon** is a deep, narrow valley with steep sides. The two largest plateaus here are the Columbia Plateau to the north and the Colorado Plateau to the southeast.

✔ **What kind of land is found west of the Rocky Mountains?**

California's Death Valley is one of the hottest, driest places in the United States. Only plants that need very little water, like this cactus, can live there.

MORE MOUNTAINS AND VALLEYS

Once Stevenson's train left the desert land behind, more mountain ranges lay ahead. A **mountain range** is a group of connected mountains. Lying just inside California is the Sierra Nevada (see•AIR•ah neh•VAH•dah). *Sierra Nevada* means "snowy mountain range" in Spanish. The land on the eastern side of the Sierra Nevada is very steep. In some places it is so steep that passengers on Stevenson's train were pinned against their seats as the train climbed up the mountains!

Other mountains lie north of the Sierra Nevada, in Washington and Oregon. These are the Cascade Range. West of the Sierra Nevada and the Cascade Range are large valleys with **fertile**, or rich, land. The largest is California's Central Valley.

Next to the Pacific Ocean are the Coast Ranges. These low mountains give much of the Pacific coast a rocky, rugged look. At many places these mountains drop sharply into the Pacific Ocean. Unlike the Atlantic coast, the Pacific coast has very little flat land along it.

Farmers in California's Central Valley grow vegetables, such as lettuce, and fruits for much of the country. What kinds of crops grow where you live?

Twenty-four days after he had left his home in Europe, Stevenson arrived in San Francisco. There he met Fanny, who was well again. The two were married a short time later.

Stevenson had traveled from coast to coast, but he saw only a small part of the United States. Because our country is large, it has many places to see. That is one reason for this book—to help you get to know the United States of America.

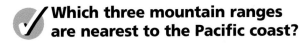 **Which three mountain ranges are nearest to the Pacific coast?**

LESSON 1 REVIEW

Check Understanding

1. **Recall the Facts**   How does land along the Atlantic coast differ from land along the Pacific coast?
2. **Focus on the Main Idea**   What major landforms are found in the United States?

Think Critically

3. **Think More About It**   How might land affect the way of life in an area?
4. **Link to You**   Which of the landforms that Stevenson saw are most like the land where you live?

Show What You Know

 **Map Activity**   Use an outline map of the United States, or draw one yourself. Then use a different color to show where each of the following areas is—the Coastal Plain, the Piedmont, the Appalachian Mountains, the Interior Plains, the Rocky Mountains, the Great Basin, the Sierra Nevada, the Cascade Range, and the Coast Ranges. Label each area, and add a title and a key to your map. Share your map with family members.

RIVERS CHANGE THE LAND

Link to Our World

How do rivers change the land?

Focus on the Main Idea
Read to find out how rivers can both wear down and build up land.

Preview Vocabulary

groundwater	drainage basin
source	erosion
channel	floodplain
mouth	delta
tributary	levee
river system	dam

All living things need water.

In all parts of the United States, rivers cross the land, even in deserts. Some of these rivers are wide and deep. Others are narrow and shallow. Some rivers are always full of water, while others have just a little for much of the year. Yet all rivers change the land.

ACROSS THE LAND

It is a dark day in northern California. Clouds hide the sun and cover the tops of the nearby mountains. Large drops of rain begin to fall on the highway. Drivers start their windshield wipers and turn on their lights. It promises to be a real downpour.

What happens to all the water? Some dries up. Some sinks into the soil to become **groundwater**, or the water beneath the Earth's surface. The rest runs down the land's surface and becomes part of the Sacramento (sa•kruh•MEN•toh) River or some other river.

The place where a river begins is its **source**. Like many rivers, the Sacramento begins high in the mountains. Not all rivers start in mountains, though. Some begin when lakes spill over. Others are formed by water pouring out of springs under the ground.

No matter where or how they begin, all rivers flow from higher to lower ground. Along the way, each river carves a path, or channel, through the land. A **channel** is the deepest part of a river or other body of water. The bottom of a river is called the riverbed. The land along the sides is its banks.

At the end of a river is its mouth. A river's **mouth** is the place where a river empties into some larger body of water. The larger body of water may be another river, a lake, or an ocean.

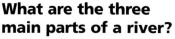 **What are the three main parts of a river?**

DRAINING THE LAND

As a river crosses the land, it may be joined by tributaries (TRIH•byuh•tair•eez). A **tributary** is a stream or river that flows

Two rivers meet in Pittsburgh, Pennsylvania, to form the Ohio River. Pittsburgh has more than 720 bridges—more than any other city in the United States.

SOURCE OF THE OHIO RIVER

OHIO

Ohio River

Allegheny River

•Pittsburgh

PENNSYLVANIA

Monongahela River

Ohio River

0   10   20 Miles
0   10   20 Kilometers
Albers Equal-Area Projection

WEST VIRGINIA

LOCATION The city of Pittsburgh was built at the source of the Ohio River.
■ How do you think Pittsburgh's location has helped the city grow?

into a larger stream or river. Tributaries are also called branches.

Together, a river and its tributaries make up a **river system**. The Ohio River, for example, is part of a huge river system. Two rivers, the Allegheny (a•luh•GAY•nee) and the Monongahela (muh•nahn•guh•HEE•luh), meet in Pittsburgh, Pennsylvania, to form the Ohio River. From there the Ohio River flows almost 1,000 miles (1,600 km) south-west to Cairo, Illinois. Along its path many tributaries join the Ohio. Among them are the Kentucky, Wabash, and Tennessee rivers.

The Ohio River is itself a tributary of an even larger river system—the Mississippi River system. The mighty Mississippi's source is Lake Itasca (eye•TAS•kuh), in Minnesota. From there the river flows 2,348 miles (3,779 km) south to the Gulf of Mexico. Some other major tributaries of the Mississippi are the Missouri, Illinois, Arkansas, and Red rivers.

All river systems drain, or carry water away from, the land around them. The land drained by a river system is its **drainage basin**. When a river is long, its drainage basin can be quite large. The

Mississippi River system drains most of the land between the Rocky and the Appalachian mountains.

Sooner or later, water in most rivers reaches an ocean. This is not true of all rivers, however. In basins, like the Great Basin, rivers flow into low-lying land. As you know, a basin is low, bowl-shaped land. If you pour water into a bowl, it just sits there. In a bowl there is no place for the water to go.

Land in the Great Basin has mountains all around it. The rivers that flow down from those mountains have no place to go. Some of the rivers flow into desert lands and dry up. Others flow into muddy pools that are not very deep or into a lake. The largest of these lakes is the Great Salt Lake in Utah.

 **How are rivers in the Great Basin different from most other rivers?**

WEARING DOWN THE LAND

For millions of years the Colorado River has been carving the walls of the Grand Canyon in northern Arizona. It was not until 1869, however, that anyone would try the 277-mile (446-km) trip through the canyon. In that year John Wesley Powell led a group of scientists down the Colorado River. Powell had decided that following the Colorado River through the Grand Canyon would add "to the great sum of human knowledge."

Powell strapped a chair to the deck of his boat and set off down the churning, swirling river. During the dangerous 3-month trip, he looked up at canyon walls so high that they threatened to

Where?

The Great Salt Lake

The water in rivers dissolves tiny amounts of salt found in the soil. Most rivers carry this salt to the ocean. The rivers that flow into the Great Salt Lake, however, deposit salt there. Over time the water in the lake has become very salty. In fact, the Great Salt Lake is saltier than any ocean. It is so salty that no fish can live in its water.

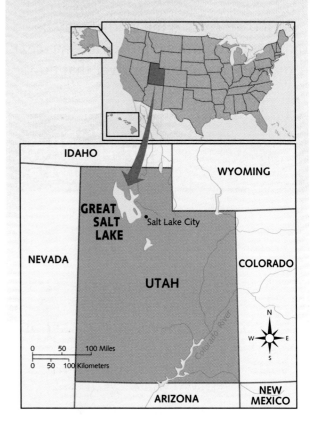

block out the sun. To form the Grand Canyon, the Colorado River has slowly cut its way deeper and deeper through layers of rock. Parts of the canyon are now 1 mile (more than 1 km) deep and 18 miles (29 km) wide!

Rivers have great power to shape the Earth. In fact, the erosion (ih•ROH•zhuhn) caused by flowing water has formed many of the Earth's physical features.

As the Colorado River widened and deepened its course over millions of years, it formed the Grand Canyon. Today, visitors can ride mules to the canyon's bottom.

Erosion is the wearing away of the Earth's surface. As one scientist has noted, "There is no force on this planet more powerful than water flowing over time."

Flowing water acts to erode, or wear down, the Earth's surface. A river's current, or constantly moving water, sweeps rocks and sand down the river. It also carries soil that has been washed into the river by rain or melting snow. As the rocks, sand, and soil are bounced and tumbled by the current, they scrape along the bed of the river and its banks. This causes the river to carve an even deeper and wider path.

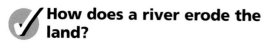 **How does a river erode the land?**

BUILDING UP THE LAND

Where there are mountains, the land is steep. Rivers flow swiftly. When a river reaches flat land, however, its current slows. The river begins to drop the sand and soil it has been carrying. Some may gather into sandbars, or islands in a river. As sandbars grow, they can block a river and make it carve out a new path.

A river also can add new soil to its floodplain. A **floodplain** is the low, flat land along a river. When a river floods, water spreads out over the floodplain. As the floodwaters flow back into the river's channel, they leave silt behind. Silt is fine sand and soil. It builds up from flood after flood, and it is good for farming.

MAJOR RIVERS OF THE UNITED STATES

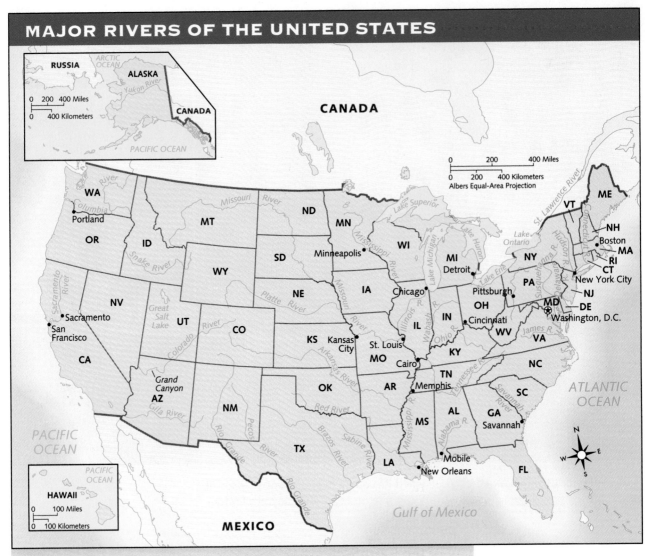

 **PLACE** The Mississippi River is our country's longest and widest river.
■ Which of the Mississippi's tributaries are shown on this map?

A river drops silt at its mouth, too. If there is no strong current to carry the silt away, it begins to build up. Over time the silt can form a delta. A **delta** is the triangle-shaped land at a river's mouth. A delta also has rich soil.

How can rivers build up the land?

FLOODS AND PEOPLE

At one time or another, most rivers flood. When people live and work on floodplains, floods can do much more than just cover the ground with muddy water. They can destroy homes and crops and people's lives.

People who chose to settle along the Mississippi River knew the dangers they faced. Yet people were sure they could overcome the dangers. In 1722 a French engineer decided that New Orleans, Louisiana, could be saved from the waters of the Mississippi by "building a good dike [wall] of earth along the front of the city beside the river." Soon the

Mississippi River had its first levee (LEH•vee). A **levee** is a high wall made of earth. It is built along the banks of a river to control flooding.

Over time more levees were built along the Mississippi River system. Several dams were built, too. A **dam** is a wall built across a river to hold back water. A dam can protect against flooding by not letting too much water flow through a river at one time.

 **What have people done to control flooding on rivers?**

THE FLOOD OF '93

People who live near rivers try to protect themselves and their property, but floods still take place. In the summer of 1993, for week after week, heavy rains fell across much of the Interior Plains. Water levels in the Mississippi River and in many of its tributaries began to rise. Up and down the Mississippi, people asked the same two questions over and over again. Were the levees high enough? Would the levees hold?

People worked day and night, piling bags filled with sand onto the levees. They were afraid that the water would rise higher than the levees or that the levees would break. Their worst fears came true. Many levees did not hold.

The rivers spread out across the land. "It's as if another Great Lake has been added to the United States," said Vice President Al Gore. In all, some 8 million acres of land were flooded. Almost 70,000 people were forced from their homes.

Why did levees fail to protect some areas against flooding?

People in Clarksville, Missouri, used thousands of bags filled with sand to hold back floodwaters from their city during the flood of 1993.

LESSON 2 REVIEW

Check Understanding

1. **Recall the Facts**   Why is a river system's drainage basin sometimes very large?
2. **Focus on the Main Idea**   How can rivers wear down and build up the land?

Think Critically

3. **Think More About It**   Why do you think people sometimes choose to live on floodplains?

Show What You Know

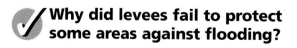 **Observe Your Environment** Running water is always eroding the land. Look around you—at home, at school, and in your neighborhood. What examples of water erosion do you see? Describe each one.

HOW TO

Use an Elevation Map

Why Is This Skill Important?

Did you ever ride up a steep hill on a bike or up a mountain in a car? Then you know that the height of land can change from place to place. Sometimes you travel uphill as you go from one place to another. At other times you travel downhill. But how high is the land at those places? What is the difference in height between them? To answer those questions, you need to use a map that shows elevation (eh•luh•VAY•shuhn). **Elevation** is the height of the land.

Land that is level with the surface of the ocean is said to be at **sea level**. The elevation of all land is measured from sea level, usually in feet or meters. The elevation of land at sea level is zero. Mt. McKinley in Alaska is the highest mountain in the United States. Its elevation is 20,320 feet (6,194 m). In other words, the top of Mt. McKinley is 20,320 feet (6,194 m) higher than sea level.

Understand the Process

The elevation map of the United States on page 51 uses color to show **relief** (rih•LEEF), or differences in elevation. It also uses shading to show relief. Shaded areas on the map help you see where hills and mountains are located, but they do not give you elevations. To find elevations, you must understand what each color stands for. The map key can help you do that.

Find the map key. Notice that the map does not give exact elevations. Instead, each color represents a range of elevations. That is, each color stands for an area's highest and lowest elevations and all of the elevations in between.

1. Find Miami, Florida, on the map. The area around Miami is colored dark green. That tells you that the land near Miami is from

The Coast Ranges rise sharply above the Pacific coast of California.

0 to 655 feet (0 to 200 m) above sea level. What is the elevation of the land east of Denver, Colorado?

2. What range of elevations is shown by the color brown?

3. What color is used to show elevations below sea level? Which state has two large areas with elevations below sea level?

Besides helping you find the elevation of an area, an elevation map can help you discover which way a river flows. Rivers can flow from north to south, from west to east, or in any other direction, but they always flow from higher elevations to lower elevations. The source of a river is always at a higher elevation than its mouth is.

4. Find the source of the Mississippi River. What is the elevation of the land at the source of the Mississippi River?

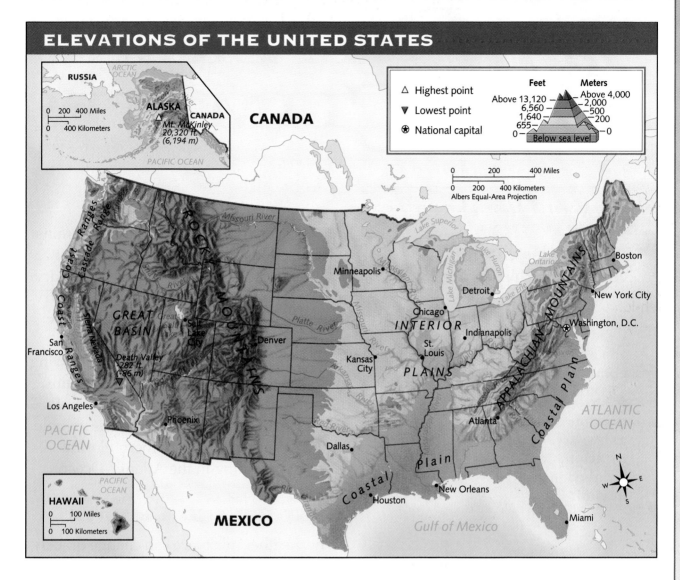

ELEVATIONS OF THE UNITED STATES

RUSSIA

ARCTIC OCEAN

ALASKA

CANADA

0 200 400 Miles
0 400 Kilometers

Mt. McKinley
20,320 ft.
(6,194 m)

PACIFIC OCEAN

△ Highest point
▼ Lowest point
✱ National capital

Feet   Meters
Above 13,120 — Above 4,000
6,560 — 2,000
1,640 — 500
655 — 200
0 — 0
Below sea level

CANADA

0 200 400 Miles
0 200 400 Kilometers
Albers Equal-Area Projection

Missouri River

Lake Superior

Lake Michigan

Lake Huron

Lake Ontario

Lake Erie

Boston

Coast Ranges

Cascade Range

ROCKY MOUNTAINS

Minneapolis

Detroit

New York City

GREAT BASIN

Sierra Nevada

Salt Lake City

Denver

Platte River

Chicago

INTERIOR

Indianapolis

Washington, D.C.

APPALACHIAN MOUNTAINS

Coast Ranges

San Francisco

Death Valley
282 ft.
(-86 m)

Kansas City

St. Louis

PLAINS

Coastal Plain

Los Angeles

Phoenix

Dallas

Atlanta

ATLANTIC OCEAN

PACIFIC OCEAN

Coastal

Plain

New Orleans

Houston

Miami

HAWAII

0 100 Miles
0 100 Kilometers

PACIFIC OCEAN

MEXICO

Gulf of Mexico

N W E S

5. Move your finger south along the Mississippi River to the Gulf of Mexico. Your finger is moving **downstream**, or toward the river's mouth. What is the elevation of the land at the mouth of the Mississippi River?

6. Now trace the river back to its source. Your finger is moving **upstream**, or toward the river's source.

7. Find the source of the Rio Grande. Trace the river downstream to its mouth. In which direction does the Rio Grande mainly flow?

8. Find the Savannah River. In which direction does that river mainly flow?

Think and Apply

Suppose that during your summer vacation, you and your family wanted to take a trip by canoe on the Missouri River. The source of the Missouri River is in the Rocky Mountains. Its mouth is at the Mississippi River, near the city of St. Louis, Missouri. What is the elevation of the land around the Missouri River's source? What is the elevation of the land around the Missouri River's mouth? In which direction does the Missouri River mainly flow? Would it be better to start your trip at the river's source, in the Rocky Mountains, or at its mouth, in Missouri? Explain your answer.

A LAND OF DIFFERENT CLIMATES

LESSON 3

Link to Our World

What causes different climates within a country?

Focus on the Main Idea
Read this lesson to understand some of the things that affect climate in the United States.

Preview Vocabulary
precipitation
axis
rotation
revolution
humidity

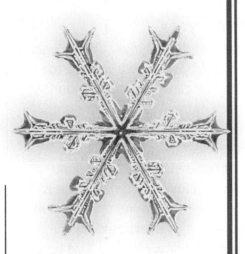

As many as 100 tiny ice crystals may cling together to form a single snowflake.

The summer of 1993 brought heavy rains to places along the Mississippi River, but other lands in the United States were as dry as dust. The United States is a large country with many kinds of land. So weather may be very different in different parts of the country on the same day. It may be snowing in Colorado, high in the Rocky Mountains, or sleet may be falling along the shore of Lake Erie in Ohio. At the same time, people on the Coastal Plain in southern Florida may be swimming in the Atlantic Ocean.

WEATHER AND CLIMATE

The weather in a place can change quickly. It may change from day to day or even from hour to hour—from sunny to stormy or from warm to cold. The weather is made up of many things. Some of these are the daily high and low temperatures, wind direction and speed, and amount of precipitation (prih•sih•puh•TAY•shuhn). **Precipitation** is water, as in rain, sleet, or snow, that falls to the Earth's surface.

While weather is the day-to-day conditions in a place, climate is the kind of weather a place has over time. For example, the weather one day in Los Angeles, California, might be rainy and cool. As scientists study the weather of southern California over time, however, they understand that the climate there is generally dry and warm.

 How is weather different from climate?

THE EARTH'S ROTATION

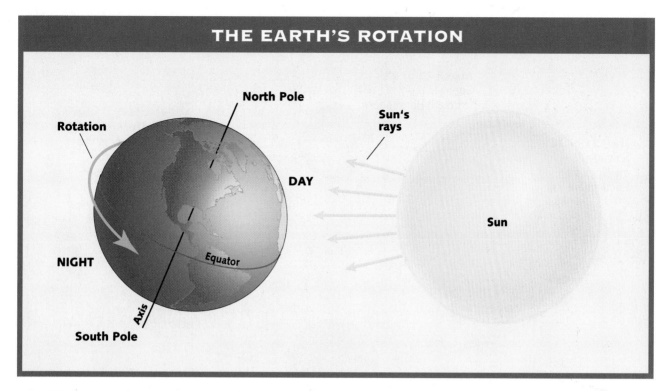

LEARNING FROM DIAGRAMS As the Earth rotates, parts of it are always moving into the sun's light.
■ Why is it nighttime on the side of the Earth facing away from the sun?

MOVEMENTS OF THE EARTH

The Earth gets all its heat from the sun. The Earth, however, is not heated evenly. Some places get more of the sun's warming rays than other places. How much warmth a place gets from the sun's rays and when it gets that warmth are mostly caused by the Earth's movements.

The Earth is always spinning, like a top, around its axis (AK•suhs). The **axis** is a make-believe line that runs through the Earth from the North Pole to the South Pole. It takes one day to make one **rotation** (roh•TAY•shuhn), or complete turn of the Earth. The diagram above shows how this daily rotation from west to east causes day and night.

While the Earth spins on its axis, it follows an orbit, or path, around the sun.

Each **revolution** (rev•uh•LOO•shuhn), or trip around the sun, covers about 595 million miles (958 million km). It takes one year to complete.

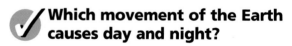
Which movement of the Earth causes day and night?

SEASONS

Because the Earth is tilted on its axis, places on the Earth get different amounts of sunlight and heat at different times of the year. It is the tilt of the axis as the Earth moves around the sun that gives us seasons.

Look at the diagram on page 54. On June 21 or 22 each year, the North Pole is tilted the most toward the sun. Because of this, places in the Northern Hemisphere get more of the sun's direct rays. This

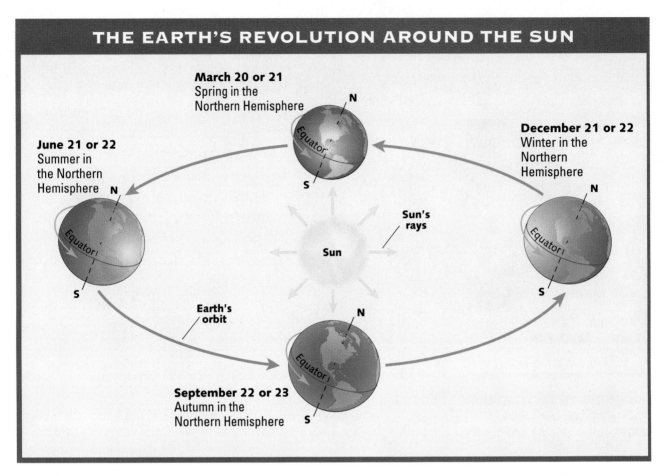

THE EARTH'S REVOLUTION AROUND THE SUN

March 20 or 21
Spring in the
Northern Hemisphere

June 21 or 22
Summer in
the Northern
Hemisphere

December 21 or 22
Winter in the
Northern
Hemisphere

Sun's rays

Sun

Earth's orbit

September 22 or 23
Autumn in the
Northern Hemisphere

LEARNING FROM DIAGRAMS   As the Earth moves around the sun, the seasons change.
■ When does winter begin in the Northern Hemisphere?

causes longer days and warmer temperatures. It is the beginning of summer in the Northern Hemisphere.

At the same time, however, the South Pole tilts away from the sun. Because of this, places in the Southern Hemisphere have shorter days and cooler temperatures. It is winter in the Southern Hemisphere. The seasons are the opposite of those in the Northern Hemisphere.

Find where Earth is on December 21 or 22. Now the South Pole is tilted the most toward the sun. Most of the sun's direct rays fall on places in the Southern Hemisphere. It is the beginning of summer in the Southern Hemisphere. What season is it in the Northern Hemisphere?

At other times of the year, the Earth's axis is not tilted either toward or away from the sun. On March 20 or 21, the sun's rays fall directly on the equator. On that day every place on Earth has equal hours of daylight and darkness. It is the beginning of spring in the Northern Hemisphere. It is the beginning of autumn in the Southern Hemisphere.

On September 22 or 23, the sun's rays again fall directly on the equator. Every place on Earth has equal hours of daylight and darkness. Autumn is beginning in the Northern Hemisphere. What season is beginning in the Southern Hemisphere?

 **What causes seasons?**

DISTANCE FROM THE EQUATOR

Direct rays from the sun give more heat than indirect rays. Because places close to the equator get more of the sun's direct rays, they also get more heat. Places close to the equator, then, usually have the warmest climates.

Places far from the equator—to the north and to the south—get less of the sun's heat. This helps explain why Hawaii, the state closest to the equator, has a much warmer climate than Alaska, the state farthest from the equator.

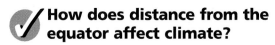 **How does distance from the equator affect climate?**

LAND AND WATER

The uneven heating and cooling of land and water also affect climate. San Francisco, California, is about the same distance north of the equator as Denver, Colorado. San Francisco, however, is usually much cooler than Denver in the summer and much warmer than Denver in the winter.

This happens because land cools off and heats up more quickly than water. Since San Francisco is located near the Pacific Ocean, the ocean helps keep it cooler in the summer and warmer in the winter. The ocean also adds humidity (hyoo•MIH•duh•tee) to the air. **Humidity** is the amount of moisture in the air. Denver is located far away from the ocean. The air there is much drier than in San Francisco.

Oceans can affect climate in another way, too. Juneau (JOO•noh) is located on Alaska's southern coast. Minneapolis (mih•nee•A•puh•luhs), Minnesota, is located much farther south. Juneau, however, is often warmer in the winter. The water that flows in the Pacific Ocean off the coast of Juneau is warm. The winds that blow over that warm water help keep Juneau warmer during the winter.

 **How can large bodies of water affect climate?**

Polar bears have thick, white fur that helps keep them warm in northern Alaska's cold climate.

JANUARY TEMPERATURES IN THE UNITED STATES

°F -20° 0° 20° 40° 60° 80°

°C -29° -18° -7° 4° 16° 27°

PLACE This map shows the average January temperatures in the United States.
■ What is the temperature for St. Louis?

JULY TEMPERATURES IN THE UNITED STATES

°F 40° 60° 70° 80° 90° 100°

°C 4° 16° 21° 27° 32° 38°

PLACE This map shows the average July temperatures in the United States.
■ Which is warmer, Denver or Memphis?

ELEVATION

Climate is affected by elevation, too. Albuquerque (AL•buh•ker•kee), New Mexico, is about the same distance north of the equator as Memphis, Tennessee, is. Albuquerque, however, is much cooler than Memphis in both summer and winter. That is because Albuquerque is located nearly 1 mile (more than 1 km) above sea level, while Memphis is only 331 feet (101 m) above sea level.

Places at higher elevations are usually cooler than places at lower elevations. Temperatures drop about 3°F (almost 2°C) for every 1,000 feet (305 m) in height. Because of that, many tall mountains, such as the Rockies, may be covered with snow all year long.

✓ **How does elevation affect climate?**

LESSON 3 REVIEW

Check Understanding

1. **Recall the Facts** Why do most places at the equator have warm climates?
2. **Focus on the Main Idea** What are some of the things that affect climate?

Think Critically

3. **Link to You** Which things most affect the climate where you live?

Show What You Know

Build a Model Paint plastic foam balls to make models of the Earth and the sun. Use string to hang the models from the ends of coat hangers. Then use them to show how the Earth's movements cause day and night and the seasons.

A RICH LAND

Link to Our World

How do different resources make different kinds of work possible?

Focus on the Main Idea
As you read, look for ways in which resources affect the kinds of jobs people in the United States do.

Preview Vocabulary
product	manufacturing
mineral	service
fuel	economy
human resource	

The United States is a large country with many landforms and climates. It is also rich in natural resources. In fact, few nations in the world have as many different natural resources as the United States. Those resources have helped make the United States strong. They have also given Americans many choices.

USING NATURAL RESOURCES

The land itself is one of our most important natural resources. Early explorers found the soil "fat and lusty." They thought the rich soil could be "adapted to cultivation of every kind . . ." and "whatever is sown there will yield an excellent crop."

Farmland covers about half the area of the United States. Fertile soil, mostly mild climates, and a lot of rainfall help American farmers grow huge amounts of food. In fact, they grow enough food not only to feed Americans but also to sell to other countries. Some important crops grown in the United States are corn, wheat, soybeans, and cotton. Many fruits and vegetables are also raised, along with cattle, chickens, hogs, and sheep.

Trees are another very important natural resource. One early settler wrote that there was "wood of sundry sorts, some very great, and all tall: birch, beech, ash, maple, spruce, cherry tree,

Hogs are raised on many farms in the United States.

Trees supply lumber, paper, and other wood products. How do people use the natural resources found where you live?

American fishers today catch more than 6 million tons of fish a year in waters off the coasts of the United States. Among their catch are oysters, shrimp, lobsters, and other kinds of shellfish.

✓ **Why is fertile soil an important natural resource?**

OTHER RICHES

The United States has many kinds of rocks and minerals (MIN•ruhlz), too. A **mineral** is a natural substance found in rocks. Copper, gold, silver, and other metals come from minerals.

The United States leads the world in the production of minerals. People use rocks and minerals for buildings, machines, and many products. Because the United States has so many kinds of rocks and minerals, Americans have many choices among the products they can make and use.

The United States is also rich in fuels (FYOO•uhlz). A **fuel** is a natural resource used to make heat or energy. Coal, oil, and natural gas are all fuels. People use fuels to cook, to heat buildings, and to make machines work.

The walls of the Washington Monument in Washington, D.C., are covered with white marble that came from Maryland.

yew, oak, very great and good...." Today forests cover nearly one-third of our country's land. Most of them supply lumber, paper, and other wood products. A **product** is something that people make or grow, usually to sell. The United States cuts more lumber and makes more paper than any other country does.

The United States is also a leading producer of fish products. An early sailor whose ship was off the coast of present-day Massachusetts talked about the fishing. There were so many codfish that "we threw numbers of them overboard again.... For the schools of mackerel, herrings, cod and other fish that we saw as we went and came from shore were wonderful...."

Gold is just one of the valuable metals found in the United States. The country's largest gold mine is in South Dakota.

No one nation on Earth has every natural resource that people use. The United States has most of them, though. Along with fertile soil, forests, minerals, and fuels, the United States has a good supply of fresh water. An early settler described a land "with such fresh waters running through the woods as I was almost ravished at the first sight thereof." Today, our many rivers, lakes, and streams provide water both for drinking and for use by farms and factories. Some rivers are used to make electric power.

✓ **How do people use minerals and fuels?**

EARNING A LIVING

The United States is rich in natural resources, like minerals, fuels, and water. The United States is also rich in human resources. **Human resources** are workers and the ideas and skills that they bring to their jobs.

Each day millions of Americans leave their homes and go to work. The kinds of jobs they do sometimes depend on where they live. That is because people often do work that has to do with the resources around them.

Not all resources are distributed, or spread out, equally. Not every place has enough of every resource it needs. For example, many areas of the United States have plenty of fresh water. But as Robert Louis Stevenson saw when he traveled across the country, other places are dry and have few trees. Certain minerals or fuels may be found in one place but not in another place.

Because the United States has many kinds of resources, workers have different kinds of jobs. Some Americans work on farms, plowing and planting the land. Some fish the waters along the coasts or cut down trees in forests. Some mine coal. Other Americans work in manufacturing (man•yuh•FAK•chuh•ring) jobs, usually in factories. **Manufacturing** is the making of goods.

Different jobs need different kinds of skills. This worker uses a computer at her job. What are some other skills that workers might need?

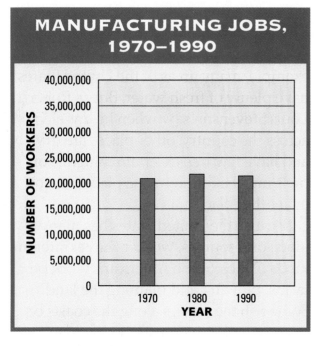

MANUFACTURING JOBS, 1970–1990

NUMBER OF WORKERS

40,000,000
35,000,000
30,000,000
25,000,000
20,000,000
15,000,000
10,000,000
5,000,000
0

1970 1980 1990
YEAR

LEARNING FROM GRAPHS A bar graph makes it easier to compare large numbers. This bar graph shows the number of manufacturing jobs in the United States between 1970 and 1990.

■ What has happened to the number of manufacturing jobs since 1970?

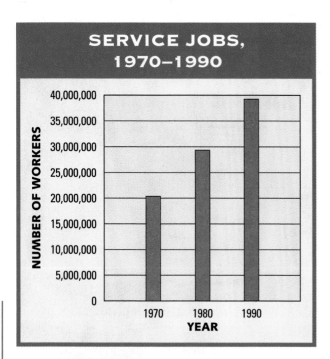

SERVICE JOBS, 1970–1990

NUMBER OF WORKERS

40,000,000
35,000,000
30,000,000
25,000,000
20,000,000
15,000,000
10,000,000
5,000,000
0

1970 1980 1990
YEAR

LEARNING FROM GRAPHS This bar graph shows the number of service jobs in the United States between 1970 and 1990.

■ What has happened to the number of service jobs since 1970?

The United States has the fuel needed to run the machines in factories. It also has many of the natural resources needed to make things. Together, these help make the United States the world's leading manufacturing nation. About one-fifth of all workers in the United States work in manufacturing jobs. Most manufacturing jobs are near large cities.

When factories are built, towns and cities near them often grow. Dothan (DOH•thuhn), Alabama, is one such town. In the 1940s Dothan was what was called a "Saturday town." Saturday was the only day of the week when Dothan was busy. That was the day nearby farmers came to town to sell

This worker in Stamford, Connecticut, has a manufacturing job. She helps make machines that are used in post offices across the country.

This gas-station worker in Dothan, Alabama, provides services for his customers.

their crops and buy things they needed. When factories were built in the town, however, people moved there to take jobs.

As manufacturing in Dothan grew, so did the number of people working in service jobs. A **service** is an activity that people do for others, such as caring for their health, fixing their cars, cleaning their houses, or delivering their mail. Like other jobs, service jobs are done for pay. Teachers, police officers, and lawyers are all service workers. So are secretaries, cooks, and firefighters.

Manufacturing is still an important activity in our country's economy (ih•KAH•nuh•mee), but more people now work in service jobs than in factories. An **economy** is a system for providing and using goods and services. Today more than one-third of all workers in the United States hold service jobs. If other groups of workers, such as people who work for stores, banks, and insurance companies, are included, then more than three-fourths of all workers hold service jobs.

✓ **How are manufacturing jobs different from service jobs?**

*L*SSON 4 REVIEW

Check Understanding

1. **Recall the Facts**   How does having large areas of fertile soil help the United States?
2. **Focus on the Main Idea**   How can resources affect the kinds of jobs people do?

Think Critically

3. **Think More About It**   Why are the skills and talents of each worker important?
4. **Link to You**   What kinds of jobs do most people in your community have? Why do you think that is so?

Show What You Know

Chart Activity   Make a chart listing at least five natural resources. Under each resource, list as many jobs as you can that depend on that resource. For example, under *oil* you might list *gas-station attendant* or *fuel-oil delivery person*. Compare your chart with those of classmates.

Use a Land Use and Resource Map

Why Is This Skill Important?

Do you wonder where some of the products that you use each day come from? Do you know where most goods in the United States are manufactured? Where are most of the natural resources found that are used to make those goods? Do you know where the oil came from that was used to make gasoline for your family's car? What about the trees that were used to make the paper in this book? To find the answers to questions like these, you need a map that shows where some resources are found and how the land is used to produce others.

Understand the Process

The map on page 63 is a land use and resource map. It uses colors to show **land use**, or how most of the land in a place is used. But the map does not show every forest or every farming or manufacturing area in the United

Miners in northern Minnesota use giant machines to dig iron from holes in the ground. These deep holes are known as open-pit mines.

Iron is used to make steel frames for buildings. Here, a worker welds a steel frame together.

States. It shows only the main ones. Look at the map key to see which color stands for each kind of land use.

1. Which color shows areas where manufacturing is the most important land use? Where does most of that manufacturing take place?
2. How is most of the land in Illinois and Iowa used? How is that land use different from the way most land in Wyoming and Utah is used?
3. Find the color for little-used land. Little-used land is land that is not used much because it is too steep, wet, dry, or rocky. Where is most of South Carolina's little-used land?

The map on page 63 uses picture symbols to show some natural resources of the United States. Each symbol is shown at or near the place where the resource is found. The map does not show every resource in the country,

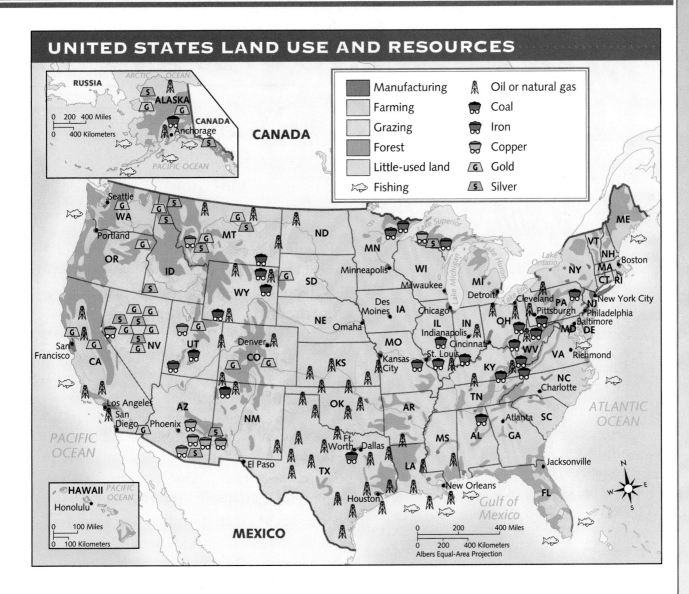

UNITED STATES LAND USE AND RESOURCES

Map Key:
- Manufacturing
- Farming
- Grazing
- Forest
- Little-used land
- Fishing
- Oil or natural gas
- Coal
- Iron
- Copper
- Gold
- Silver

because the United States has too many resources to show on just one map. So the map shows only some of the most important ones. To find out what resource each symbol stands for, look at the map key again.

4. Find the symbol labeled *Oil or natural gas.* Then find Texas on the map. The symbol shows the parts of Texas where much oil and natural gas are found. What important natural resource is found in northern Minnesota and northern Michigan?

5. In which states is copper found?

6. Which resources are found in and under the waters along the coasts of the United States?

Think and Apply

Draw a land use and resource map of your state. Use encyclopedias and library books to find out how people use the land in your state and what natural resources are found there. Use colors to show the different land uses, and make a map key to tell what each color stands for. Choose different symbols to stand for all of the important natural resources. Draw the symbols on the map, and explain what they stand for in the map key. Share your map with other students in your class. Then use it to teach members of your family about land use and resources in your state.

PEOPLE AND THE ENVIRONMENT

L *ink to Our World*

What changes do people cause when they use natural resources?

Focus on the Main Idea
Read to find out how people change the environment when they use natural resources.

Preview Vocabulary
adapt
conservation
scarce
recycle
pollution

People depend on natural resources for almost everything they need. People at work also depend on natural resources to make or grow products. As people at home and at work use those resources, however, they cause changes to their environment.

FARMING THE LAND

As you know, the United States has a lot of land with fertile soil. Before that land can be used for farming, however, it must often be plowed. Plowing land is one way that people **adapt**, or change, their environment to make it more useful to them.

When people first plowed the fertile lands of Iowa, the topsoil was as deep as 16 inches (41 cm). Now in many places, only 6 to 8 inches (15 to 20 cm) of topsoil are left. What happened to all that rich soil? It eroded away.

When people use the land, they often do things that help wind and rain wear down the Earth's surface. People cut down trees, whose roots help hold soil in place. They blast away the sides of mountains. They also plow the land, turning under grasses that cover the soil.

....

Huge clouds of dust and dirt blew across parts of Oklahoma, Kansas, and Texas during the 1930s.

On hilly land, farmers often plow across the side of a hill, rather than up and down. This helps keep the soil from washing away.

> ❝ *IT WAS DARK AS THE MIDDLE OF THE NIGHT, and it stayed that way all day.* ❞
>
> Bessie Zentz of Goodwell, Oklahoma

In the 1930s, in much of Oklahoma, Kansas, and Texas, little rain fell. Some places had no rain at all for months. As the ground dried up, strong winds blew the plowed soil away.

Wind-blown dirt and dust soon covered fences and roads. It was impossible to get away from the blowing dust. "The dust storms scared us to pieces," one woman from Goodwell, Oklahoma, said. "It was dark as the middle of the night, and it stayed that way all day."

Farmers learned that they had to do something to protect soil and other natural resources. Protecting our natural resources and using them wisely is called **conservation** (kahn•ser•VAY•shuhn).

Most farmers all over the country now use different methods of soil conservation. Sometimes they plant rows of trees between their fields to help block the wind. In hilly places, they usually plow their fields in a way that keeps the rain from washing the soil away. Other methods let farmers plant crops without even plowing fields.

✔ **What can happen if farmers do not use soil conservation?**

SAVING TREES

The United States has many forests, but people cut down many trees each year. Some are cut to clear land for new buildings or highways. Most are cut for their wood.

In the past, Americans often cut down trees without planting new ones. Many people believed that natural resources would last forever. People thought there

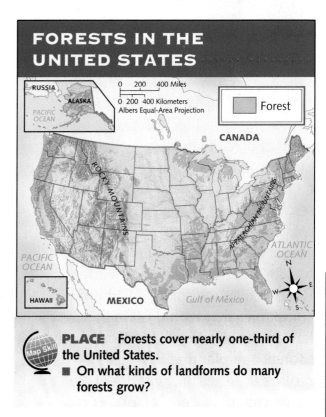

FORESTS IN THE UNITED STATES

RUSSIA
ALASKA
PACIFIC OCEAN
0 200 400 Miles
0 200 400 Kilometers
Albers Equal-Area Projection
Forest
CANADA
ROCKY MOUNTAINS
APPALACHIAN MOUNTAINS
ATLANTIC OCEAN
PACIFIC OCEAN
HAWAII
MEXICO
Gulf of México

🌐 **PLACE** Forests cover nearly one-third of the United States.
■ On what kinds of landforms do many forests grow?

Theodore Roosevelt 1858–1919

Theodore Roosevelt was the twenty-sixth President of the United States. He was sickly as a child, but he exercised often and spent a lot of time outdoors. During his travels to the American West, Roosevelt learned to care deeply about nature. He became the first President to work hard to save forests and wilderness areas.

would always be another forest, another source of clean water, or another acre of land. Over time, however, Americans came to understand that all resources are **scarce**, or limited. All resources need to be used wisely.

Some of the very earliest efforts at conservation were made to save our forests. In 1903 President Theodore Roosevelt spoke out against lumber companies that would "skin the land, and abandon it. . . ." Companies soon began planting new trees to replace the ones they cut down. To save even more trees, many people now **recycle** paper products, or use them again. Recycling can help save many trees.

✓ **Why should trees and other natural resources be used wisely?**

PROTECTING WATER AND AIR

People also change the environment when they use water. People pump water from rivers. They make new lakes and dig wells into the ground. They even lay pipes across the land to take water to dry places.

Most places in the United States have enough fresh water. Yet people must conserve, or save, water if they want it to last. Americans can help conserve water by not using too much water every day.

Just conserving water is not enough, however. People must also think about pollution (puh•LOO•shuhn). **Pollution** is anything that makes a natural resource dirty or unsafe to use.

Arbor Day is a special day for planting trees. These students are planting a pine seedling, or young tree.

The salt used to melt ice and snow on highways can pollute groundwater.

Many of the things people do cause pollution. In states with snowy climates, salt is put on highways to melt ice and snow. The salt in the melted snow can sink into the ground. There it slowly gets into the water supply and pollutes it. Today people are trying to find ways to use less salt on highways and to stop water pollution in other ways.

Like water, air can be polluted by things people do. Most cars, trucks, machines, and factories add some pollution to the air. Air pollution does not stay in one place either. Wind can blow it from place to place.

How can people's actions cause pollution?

USING UP LIMITED RESOURCES

Some resources can be replaced. New trees can grow. Rain can refill rivers and lakes. Other resources, such as minerals and fuels, cannot be replaced. When they are used up, there will be no more.

Americans use a lot of minerals and fuels. To conserve minerals, they can recycle many products, such as glass bottles and tin cans. To conserve fuels, people can put better insulation in their houses so that they need less oil or natural gas for heating. They can drive less and at slower speeds. That will help them use less gasoline.

Another way to slow the use of fuels is to find other sources of energy. Already scientists have found ways to heat homes by using energy from the sun. They have found ways to make electricity out of the power of the wind. They have made engines that can run on fuel made from grains like corn instead of gas.

Why is it important to conserve minerals and fuels?

LESSON 5 REVIEW

Check Understanding

1. **Recall the Facts** What do people do to conserve forests and trees?
2. **Focus on the Main Idea** How do people change the environment when they use natural resources?

Think Critically

3. **Think More About It** What might happen if certain minerals and fuels are used up?

Show What You Know

Art Activity Design a poster or a button showing a way to conserve a natural resource. Use your poster or button to explain how your idea will help conserve that natural resource.

CONNECT MAIN IDEAS

Use this organizer to show that you understand how the chapter's main ideas are connected. First copy the organizer onto a separate sheet of paper. Then complete it by writing three examples for each main idea.

The United States has many landforms.

1. _____
2. _____
3. _____

Landforms

Rivers

The American Landscape

Rivers both wear down and build up the land.

1. _____
2. _____
3. _____

Climate

Resources

People and the Environment

Different things affect climate in the United States.

1. _____
2. _____
3. _____

People change the environment when they use natural resources.

1. _____
2. _____
3. _____

Resources affect the kinds of jobs people in the United States do.

1. _____
2. _____
3. _____

WRITE MORE ABOUT IT

1. **Write a Descriptive Letter**   Imagine that you are writing a letter to someone who lives in another country. You want that person to know what the United States looks like. In your letter, describe each of the major landforms of the United States.

2. **Compare and Contrast**   Suppose that you have been asked to write a story about rivers in the United States for a nature magazine. In your story, explain how rivers can both wear down the land and build it up. Draw pictures to go with your story.

USE VOCABULARY

Write the term that correctly matches each definition.

economy   pollution
erosion   revolution
floodplain   rotation
peninsula   scarce
plateau   service

1. land that is almost entirely surrounded by water

2. high, mostly flat land

3. the wearing away of the Earth's surface

4. low, flat land along a river

5. one complete turn of the Earth

6. one trip around the sun by the Earth

7. an activity that people do for others

8. a system for providing and using goods and services

9. limited

10. anything that makes a natural resource dirty or unsafe to use

CHECK UNDERSTANDING

1. What landform covers much of the western United States?

2. What is a river system? What do all river systems do?

3. Why does the sun not heat the Earth evenly?

4. Why is fertile soil an important resource for the United States?

5. How are human resources important to businesses?

6. What do people use fuel for?

THINK CRITICALLY

1. **Think More About It**   How does having many landforms make the United States a more interesting country in which to live?

2. **Link to You**   What things does your family do to help conserve resources?

APPLY SKILLS

How to Use an Elevation Map
Imagine that you are planning a trip between any two cities shown on the elevation map on page 51. Lay a ruler across the map to connect the two cities. Then write the name and elevation of each city, and tell the elevation of the highest land you will cross on your trip. List the names of any rivers you will cross, and tell in which direction each one flows.

How to Use a Land Use and Resource Map   Use the map on page 63 to answer these questions.

1. Where are the major manufacturing areas in California located?

2. Where is most of the little-used land in Texas?

3. Which fuels are found in West Virginia?

READ MORE ABOUT IT

Up River by Frank Asch. Simon & Schuster. As two boys help clean up Otter Creek, a retired teacher points out wildlife and tells them fascinating secrets about the creek.

U.S.A. by Martha Ellen Zenfell. Silver Burdett. This book gives readers a close look at the land and people of the United States.

CHAPTER 2

WE, THE MANY PEOPLE

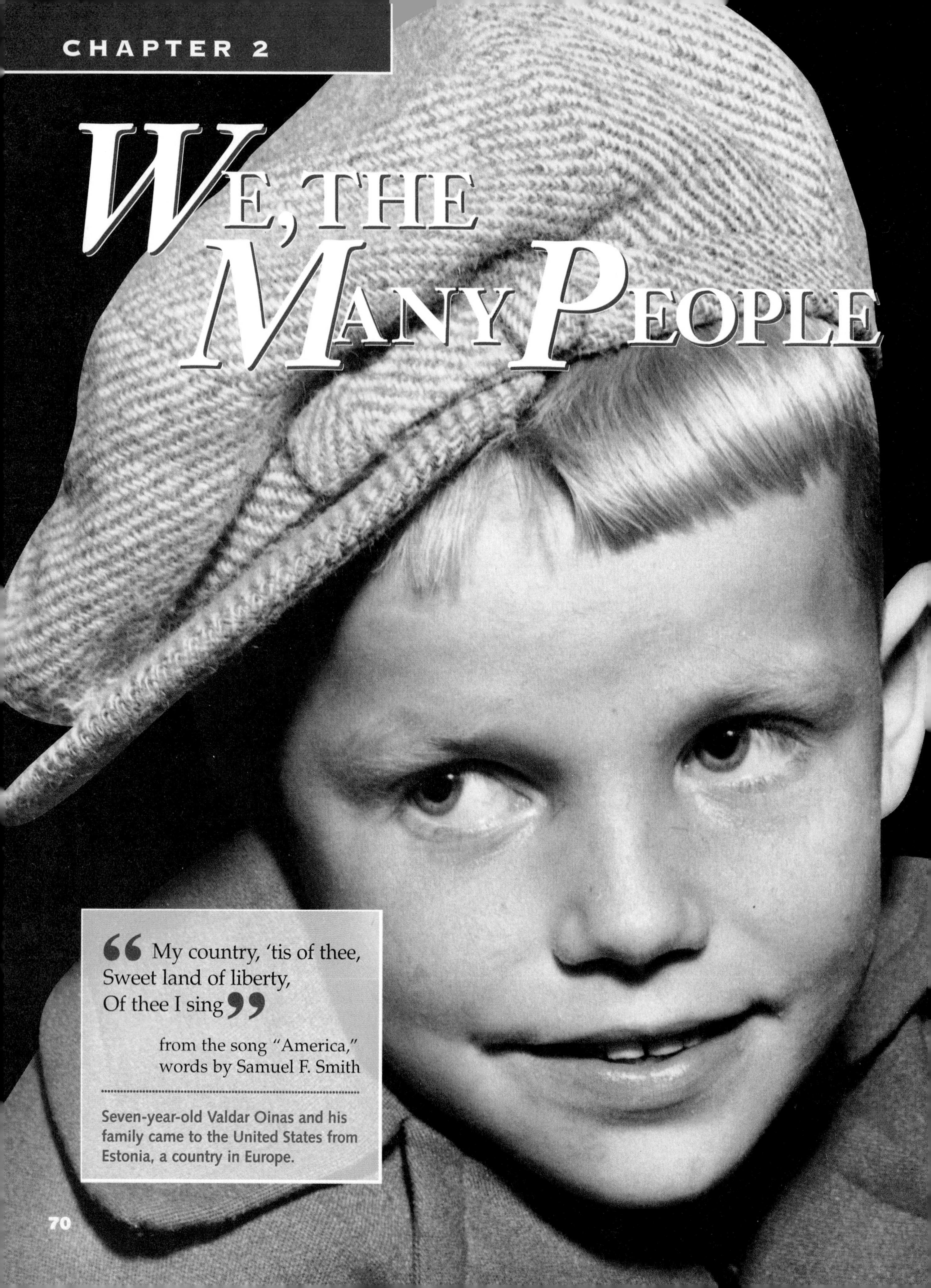

66 My country, 'tis of thee,
Sweet land of liberty,
Of thee I sing 99

from the song "America,"
words by Samuel F. Smith

Seven-year-old Valdar Oinas and his
family came to the United States from
Estonia, a country in Europe.

70

LESSON 1

PEOPLE FROM MANY PLACES

Link to Our World

Why are there different ways of life in one country?

Focus on the Main Idea
As you read, look for reasons why there are different ways of life in the United States.

Preview Vocabulary

custom	religion
immigrant	slavery
ancestor	poverty
isthmus	ethnic group
wealth	culture

These beautiful Easter eggs were made by the Russian jeweler Fabergé (fab•er•ZHAY).

People in the United States can choose all kinds of foods to eat. Do you like tacos, spaghetti, or egg rolls best? Between meals, would you choose an orange or an apple? Each of these foods is different. Yet all of them share something. People first brought them to the United States from other places.

SPECIAL WAYS

When people come to live in a new place, they often bring their customs with them. A **custom** is a usual way of doing things. Shaking hands when you meet someone is a custom. Waving good-bye when you leave is another.

Many American customs came from other places. Do you trick people on April Fools' Day? English settlers brought this custom to America. Do you color eggs at Easter? Immigrants (IH•mih•gruhnts) from Ukraine, Russia, and Poland brought this custom to America. An **immigrant** is a person who comes to live in a country from some other place.

Immigrants also brought holidays with them, such as Saint Patrick's Day and the Chinese New Year. They brought new ways of doing things. They brought different kinds of music and dance, too. Even the languages that most Americans speak are from other countries.

Most Americans speak English, but many of the words they use come from other languages. In fact, many of the things that Americans use each day first

In Brooklyn, New York, immigrants from the West Indies celebrate Carnival Day each spring.

ancestors (AN•ces•terz) who came from other countries. An **ancestor** is an early family member.

The first people to live in what would become the United States were the American Indians, or Native Americans. Thousands of years ago an isthmus (IS•muhs) joined Asia to North America. An **isthmus** is a narrow piece of land that connects two larger land areas. Some people believe that the Indians' ancestors walked across this isthmus from Asia. They were following herds of animals,

came from other places. That includes some of the foods we eat. Immigrants from Mexico first brought tacos to the United States. Italian immigrants gave us spaghetti. Immigrants from China gave us egg rolls. Spanish explorers planted the first oranges in America. The English came carrying bags of apple seeds.

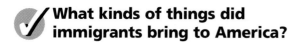 **What kinds of things did immigrants bring to America?**

DIFFERENT PLACES

In the 1850s writer Herman Melville said, "We are not a nation so much as a world." He was saying the United States is made up of people from many other places. People have come here from so many places that this country is called a nation of immigrants. Most people born here have parents, grandparents, or

Where?

The Land Bridge

Today about 50 miles (80 km) of sea separate North America and Asia. Thousands of years ago, however, great sheets of ice covered much of the Earth. In fact, so much water turned into ice that the water level in the oceans dropped. This caused a piece of land, or a land bridge, to appear. It connected North America and Asia.

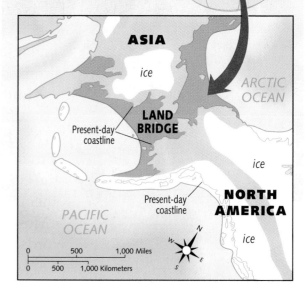

This portrait of Christopher Columbus is thought to show how he really looked. No paintings of Columbus were done while he was alive.

could freely follow their **religion**, or beliefs about God or gods.

Not every group came to America by choice, however. Most Africans who reached America had been taken from their homes and sold into slavery. **Slavery** is making one person the property of another person. Enslaved people were used as workers. Slavery ended in the United States after the Civil War. Abraham Lincoln was President during that war.

✓ **Why is the United States often called a nation of immigrants?**

which they hunted for food. Eventually the Indians settled all over the Americas.

People reached North America from Europe much later. About 1,000 years ago the Vikings came to North America. This group stayed only a few years.

In 1492 Christopher Columbus sailed to America from Spain. He was trying to reach China, where he wanted to trade for gold and other riches. Columbus thought he could reach China by sailing west.

Columbus did not reach China. He did, however, return to Spain with tales of riches. After hearing his stories, other explorers crossed the Atlantic Ocean.

By the early 1700s many Europeans had settled in North America. They came from different parts of Europe, but most of them were looking for the same thing— a better life. Some dreamed of **wealth**, or riches. Some just wanted a chance to own their own land. Others came so they

EUROPEANS IN NORTH AMERICA, 1713

ARCTIC OCEAN

Greenland

0   600   1,200 Miles
0   600   1,200 Kilometers
Azimuthal Equal-Area Projection

PACIFIC OCEAN

NORTH AMERICA

St. Lawrence River

Mississippi River

Rio Grande

ATLANTIC OCEAN

Gulf of Mexico

English
French
Spanish

SOUTH AMERICA

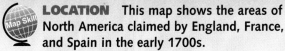

LOCATION This map shows the areas of North America claimed by England, France, and Spain in the early 1700s.
■ Who claimed most of the land in the southwestern part of North America?

DIFFICULT DECISIONS

Over time millions of people from all over the world came to the United States. Some of the towns and cities they moved to were named for the places they came from. That is why we have place names like Germantown in Ohio and Holland in Michigan.

Immigrants had to make a hard decision before coming to America. Should they stay at home, where things were known? Or should they leave for a new life in a new land?

Mary Antin's family faced those questions in the 1880s. They could decide to

This photograph of Mary Antin (left) and her sister was taken several years before her family came to live in the United States.

stay in Plotzk (PLAWTSK), their small village in what was then a part of Russia. If they did, they would be together in their home. But they would go on facing poverty and a hard life with little freedom. **Poverty** means being very poor.

If they left Plotzk, Mary's family would be apart for a very long time. Mary's father would have to go to the United States on his own, find a job, and save money. Only then could he afford to send for the rest of the family. If they left Plotzk, the family would have to leave their friends and favorite things behind. They would have to learn new customs and a new language, too. Still, going to America would mean chances for a better life—and freedom!

Mary wrote in her diary, "Many family councils were held before it was agreed that the plan must be carried out. Then came the parting; for it was impossible for the whole family to go at once. I remember . . . father waving his hat for our special benefit, and saying—the last words we heard him speak as the train moved off—'Good-bye, Plotzk, forever!'" Three years later Mary and the rest of her family joined her father in the United States.

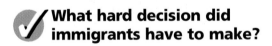 **What hard decision did immigrants have to make?**

A MIX OF PEOPLE

Today people still come to the United States from all over the world. In fact, more than a half million newcomers enter the United States in most years. These people belong to many ethnic (ETH•nik) groups. An **ethnic group** is a group made up of people from the same country,

Each May the people of Holland, Michigan, celebrate their city's Dutch culture at the Tulip Festival. These Klompen dancers wear Dutch costumes. A worker (left) makes wooden shoes, another example of Dutch culture.

people of the same race, or people with a common way of life.

Every ethnic group has its own way of life, or **culture**. The culture of a group is made up of its customs and beliefs. A culture includes language, religion, art, music, clothing, food, games, and holidays. Each ethnic group has brought some of its culture to the United States. Having so many cultures mixed together means that Americans can enjoy a richer life. It also helps explain why people in the United States seem so different from one another in so many ways.

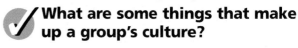 **What are some things that make up a group's culture?**

LESSON 1 REVIEW

Check Understanding

1. **Recall the Facts** Why did early European settlers come to North America?

2. **Focus on the Main Idea** What are some reasons for the different ways of life in the United States?

Think Critically

3. **Think More About It** Suppose the United States had not been settled by people from so many places. How might the United States be different?

Show What You Know

 Writing Activity Describe some cultural differences that you have noticed. They may be in your community or in some place you have visited. Give possible reasons for those differences.

HOW TO

Make a Thoughtful Decision

Why Is This Skill Important?

Think of a time when you made a bad decision. Perhaps you said or did something and later wished you had not. Maybe someone's feelings were hurt.

The decisions you make can have good or bad consequences (KAHN•suh•kwen•suhz). A **consequence** is what happens because of an action. If you decide to go swimming in a safe place, you will get some good exercise and have fun. However, if you swim in an unsafe place, you could be hurt or become ill. To make thoughtful decisions, you need to think about the consequences before you act.

Remember What You Have Read

You have read about Mary Antin, a girl from Russia. Her family's goal was to have freedom and a better life, so they decided to leave their homeland and come to the United States. Think about their decision and its consequences for the family.

1. If Mary's family had stayed in Russia, what might have been the consequences—both good and bad?

2. Explain the good and bad consequences of their coming to the United States.

Understand the Process

Here are some steps you can use to help you make wise decisions.

- Identify a goal.
- Make a list of choices that might help you reach your goal.
- Think about the possible consequences—both good and bad—of each choice.
- Decide which choice you think will have the best consequences.
- Think about your choice. Could it have bad consequences you have not thought of? If so, you may need to make a different choice.
- Make the best choice and follow it.

Think and Apply

Think about a decision that you made recently. What were the consequences of your decision? Do you think your decision was a thoughtful one? Explain.

BUILDING CITIZENSHIP

MARY'S FAMILY MAKES A DECISION

The Goal

Freedom and a better life

Choice 1—Stay in Russia	Choice 2—Go to the United States
Possible consequences: **Good** 1. The family would remain together **Bad** 1. Poverty 2. A hard life	Possible consequences: **Good** 1. A chance for a better life 2. Freedom **Bad** 1. The family would be apart for a long time 2. Have to leave friends and favorite things 3. Have to learn new customs and a new language

LESSON **2**

~~~
LEARN
with
LITERATURE

Focus on Culture
and Change

Nary's Story

from *Who Belongs Here? An American Story*

BY MARGY BURNS KNIGHT • ILLUSTRATED BY ANNE SIBLEY O'BRIEN

Nary was born in Cambodia (kam·BOH·dee·uh), a small country in Southeast Asia. When Nary was very young, a terrible war broke out in Cambodia. Both of his parents were killed by government soldiers. Nary, his grandmother, and his uncle escaped to the nearby country of Thailand (TY·land). They later came to live in the United States.

Nary and his family came to the United States to escape the dangers and hardships in their homeland. Nary has seen many changes in his life since coming to the United States. Some things, however, remain the same. Read to find out how Nary's life has changed and how it has remained the same.

Nary was sad and confused after his parents died. He cried as his grandmother carried him on her back through the jungle to Thailand. He had tried to run, but the blisters on his feet were bleeding. His uncle told him to be quiet because they were running from the soldiers and didn't want to be caught.

In Thailand they lived for several years in a crowded refugee camp where Nary sometimes went to school and his uncle and grandmother helped in the health clinic.

Nary traveled to the U.S. on a plane. Around his neck he wore a tag with his name, picture, and date of arrival in New York City. Nary was very happy to be moving to the States, but he was nervous because he wasn't sure what was going to happen. Nary's family was met at the airport by their sponsor who helped them settle into their new home.

refugee
(reh•fyu•JEE)
a person who travels to another country to escape danger

tuberculosis
(tu•ber•kyuh•LOH•suhs)
a lung disease

When Nary's family arrived in the U.S. his grand-mother was carrying a plastic bag. In it were identity papers, two family photos, and x-rays that showed that her family didn't have active tuberculosis. Nary brought with him his memories of Cambodia and Khmer, the language he learned as a baby. Some days learning English is frustrating for Nary, but his friends and teachers are helping him. On rainy days he laughs as he tells his grandmother it's raining cats and dogs.

Nary had little to eat during the war in Cambodia. He is amazed by the amount of food in his local grocery store.

His grandmother sends money to Cambodia each month so her relatives can buy seeds to plant rice.

Nary eats rice every day. Sometimes he eats it with meat or vegetables. He likes it when pizza and ice cream are served at school for lunch.

Nary admires Dith Pran because he is working for peace in Cambodia. Like Nary, Dith Pran escaped from the killing fields of Cambodia. Now he travels around the U.S. talking about his hopes for his homeland. It is hard for him to repeat his sad stories, but he wants peace in Cambodia and feels it is important to talk about the terrible things that have happened and continue to happen there.

In Nary's new home soldiers don't pound on the door and tell him to get out as they did in Cambodia. Nary likes his new freedom. . . .

Literature Review

1. How did Nary's life change, and how did it stay the same?
2. Explain why not being able to speak English would make life difficult for newcomers like Nary.
3. Imagine that you have just come to live in the United States. Write a short diary entry that tells how your life has changed.

A UNITED COUNTRY

LESSON 3

Link to Our World

What things help unite, or bring together, all the people living in one country?

Focus on the Main Idea
Read to find out what helps unite people living in the United States.

Preview Vocabulary

independence	majority rule
government	right
democracy	responsibility
representative	
democracy	

What is an American? Ask a hundred people, and you will get a hundred different answers. That is because Americans are different from one another in so many ways. Americans have come to the United States from all over the world. They sometimes speak different languages and eat different foods. They often have different customs. Yet in some ways, Americans also have much in common.

AMERICANS SHARE MANY THINGS

Americans share a way of life. We learn about one another from television, newspapers, and magazines. We go to school together. We go to movies. We like certain sports. All these things help bring us together as a people.

Americans are united when they rise together before a baseball game to sing the national anthem. Americans feel pride when they salute the flag as it passes by in a parade. Americans promise to be loyal to the United States when they say the Pledge of Allegiance.

❝I pledge allegiance to the Flag of the United States of America, and to the Republic for which it stands, one Nation under God, indivisible, with liberty and justice for all.❞

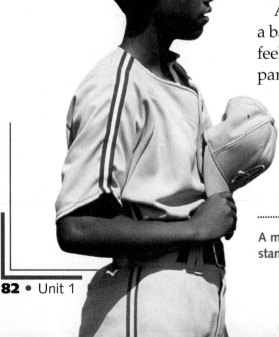

A member of a high school baseball team in Austin, Texas, stands as the national anthem is played.

UNITED STATES GOVERNMENT HOLIDAYS

HOLIDAY	OBSERVED
New Year's Day	January 1
Martin Luther King, Jr., Day	third Monday in January
Washington's Birthday	third Monday in February
Memorial Day	last Monday in May
Independence Day	July 4
Labor Day	first Monday in September
Columbus Day	second Monday in October
Veterans Day	November 11
Thanksgiving Day	fourth Thursday in November
Christmas Day	December 25

On the Fourth of July, fireworks light up the skies over Boston, Massachusetts, and over other cities across the United States. How do people in your community celebrate this holiday?

LEARNING FROM TABLES Most government holidays are observed throughout the country.
■ Which holiday is observed on the last Monday in May?

Americans also share their country's history, or past. One Russian immigrant remembered how reading about the history of the United States made him feel a part of America. He said, "As I read . . . it dawned on me gradually what was meant by *my country*. The people all desiring noble things and striving for them together."

One way that people remember their country's history is by celebrating its holidays. One of the most important holidays in the United States is Independence Day, or the Fourth of July. On that date in 1776, the United States declared its **independence**, or freedom, from English rule. Each July 4, millions of Americans get together to enjoy this holiday.

How do national holidays help unite Americans?

*W*hat?

Independence Day

Even the first leaders of the United States thought that July 4 was an important day. One leader, John Adams, said, "It ought to be solemnized with pomp and parade, with shows, games, . . . bells, bonfires, and illuminations, from one end of this continent to the other. . . ." Although Independence Day was celebrated for many years, it was not made an official holiday until 1941.

This painting by the American artist Norman Rockwell is called *Freedom of Speech*. What do you think Rockwell was trying to say in this painting?

lead a community, state, or country. The main job of government is to make and carry out laws. Because everyone must follow them, laws help unite people. Laws also help settle disagreements.

In the United States our government is a democracy (dih•MAH•kruh•see). A **democracy** is a form of government in which the people rule. In a democracy people are free to make choices about their lives and their government. They often make their choices by voting.

The United States is a democracy, but citizens do not vote on every law. There are more than 260 million people in the United States today. That many people cannot get together in one place to make every law. Instead, citizens elect representatives (reh•prih•ZEN•tuh•tivs), or leaders. Those representatives, in turn, make decisions about the laws for all the people. This system is called a **representative democracy**.

SHARING CERTAIN BELIEFS

Americans share a deep belief in freedom. Americans believe in freedom of religion, freedom to work, freedom to say what they want, freedom to move around, and freedom to meet with other people. Freedom has always drawn people from other places to the United States. "We call no man master here," wrote one English immigrant.

Another immigrant told family members who had stayed in Germany, "If you wish to see our whole family living in a country where freedom of speech obtains, . . . if you wish to be really happy and independent, then come here."

Americans share their government, too. A **government** is a group of people who

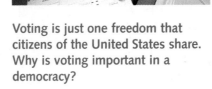

Voting is just one freedom that citizens of the United States share. Why is voting important in a democracy?

What do you usually do when you and your friends cannot decide which of two games to play? Like other Americans, you most likely vote. You and your friends agree to play the game that gets the most votes, or the majority. This way of deciding is called **majority rule**.

Democracy is based on majority rule. In the United States each citizen over eighteen gets one vote. Majority rule is a way to make choices that are fair to most people and that most people agree with.

But *all* people in the United States have certain rights—even those people who do not agree with the majority. A **right** is a freedom that belongs to you. The majority cannot make decisions that take away those rights. For example, all Americans are free to say what they think about government. All Americans are free to worship as they please. All Americans have the right to a fair trial.

 In a representative democracy, who makes decisions about the laws for all the people?

SHARING RESPONSIBILITIES

Americans enjoy many rights, but Americans also have many responsibilities. A **responsibility** is something that a person should do. Some responsibilities, like obeying traffic signs and going to school, are required by law. Other responsibilities are things that good citizens do by choice. These things include voting, learning about the country, working hard, and treating others fairly.

Sharing responsibilities can help bring people together. Americans often help one another in times of need. Americans also work together to solve problems. By working together, Americans can share their different ideas. By sharing their ideas, they can find the best ways to solve problems.

 How does sharing responsibilities help unite Americans?

These people are part of a group called Habitat for Humanity. They work together, without pay, to build homes for needy families.

 LESSON 3 REVIEW

Check Understanding

1. **Recall the Facts**   What makes our government a democracy?
2. **Focus on the Main Idea**   What helps unite people living in the United States?

Think Critically

3. **Personally Speaking**   What qualities do you think an immigrant who leaves his or her homeland has?
4. **Explore Viewpoints**   Do you think majority rule is always fair? Explain.

Show What You Know

 Writing Activity   Draw a picture or cut out photographs from old magazines to show an idea or belief that helps unite Americans. Then write a short paragraph explaining why you think it helps.

Understand National Symbols

Why Is This Skill Important?

Does your school have a symbol? Perhaps it is a powerful panther or a proud eagle. You may even have your school's symbol on a T-shirt or a notebook. Displaying the symbol lets everyone know that you are proud of your school.

The United States also has symbols. These symbols remind us of our nation's heritage. A **heritage** is a way of life, a custom, or a belief that has come from the past and continues today.

Understand the Process

The symbols on these two pages represent parts of our nation's heritage. Each of these symbols has a special meaning for citizens of the United States.

Many people feel proud when they see the United States flag. Look closely at the picture of the flag. Its three colors stand for values that are important to Americans. Red represents courage, white is for goodness, and blue is for care and justice. The 13 stripes on the flag represent the first 13 states. What do the stars stand for?

The Great Seal of the United States is used on all important government papers. It shows that the United States is an independent nation. On the seal is an eagle, a bird known for its strength and freedom. In one claw the eagle holds an olive

The Great Seal of the United States

branch—a symbol that shows the United States wants to live in peace. In the other claw the eagle holds arrows. What do you think the arrows stand for?

The Liberty Bell

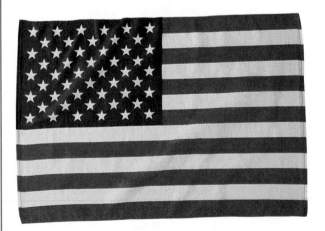

The United States flag

The Liberty Bell hangs in Philadelphia, Pennsylvania. It was rung in 1776 to celebrate the signing of the Declaration of Independence. Today the Liberty Bell represents the freedom that the people of the United States enjoy.

Uncle Sam

The Tomb of the Unknowns

Uncle Sam is a cartoon symbol of the United States. The name probably comes from *U.S.*—the country's initials. But the name was inspired by a real person. During the War of 1812, the letters *U.S.* were printed on the sides of barrels of food sold to the army by a business person named Samuel Wilson. Over time, Wilson became known as Samuel "Uncle Sam" Wilson.

The Statue of Liberty was the first thing that many European immigrants saw as they entered the United States. The huge statue represents the freedom and opportunity the United States offers to newcomers.

The Statue of Liberty

The Tomb of the Unknowns is a monument in Arlington National Cemetery, in Arlington, Virginia. A **monument** is something that is built to remind people of the past. The Tomb of the Unknowns holds the remains of four unidentified soldiers killed in World War I, World War II, the Korean War, and the Vietnam War, but it honors all the men and women who have given their lives in our country's wars.

Think and Apply

Each state also has symbols, reminding people of that state's heritage. Use an encyclopedia and other books in the library to find out about the symbols of your state, such as the state flag, the state seal, or a state monument. Choose one symbol, and draw a picture of it. Then write a paragraph that explains what the symbol represents. Tell why it is an important part of your state's heritage.

BUILDING CITIZENSHIP

PEOPLE AND GOVERNMENT

LESSON 4

L ink to Our World

How does government help unite the people in a country?

Focus on the Main Idea
As you read, look for ways in which the United States government unites the people in the 50 states.

Preview Vocabulary
federal
revolution
Declaration of Independence
Constitution
legislative branch
Congress
executive branch
judicial branch
Supreme Court

Local governments decide where stoplights are needed on city streets.

Americans are different in many ways. Yet there are many things that unite them, such as their belief in freedom and democracy. National symbols like the flag also unite Americans. So does government.

LEVELS OF GOVERNMENT

Every morning, people in the Conway Woods neighborhood hated leaving for work or school. Driving a car from Conway Woods onto the main highway was dangerous. There had already been several accidents. Some people thought they should talk with government leaders about putting up a stoplight. But which government leaders should they talk with?

In the United States there are three levels of government. Each community has its own government, called the local government. Then there are the state governments. Finally, there is a **federal**, or national, government for the whole country.

These three levels of government help people solve problems that they could not solve alone, like putting up a stoplight. Each level of government, however, handles problems of a different size or kind.

Some things that governments do are important only to the people in a community. These things include fixing city streets, picking up garbage, and buying fire trucks. In cases like these, people in the local community can best decide what to do.

One responsibility of state governments is building and repairing highways (above). Not even floodwaters can stop mail delivery (right). Delivering the mail is a responsibility of the federal government.

Other choices affect all the people in one state. For example, state governments take care of problems like building highways and paying for state parks. State governments also make laws about businesses and laws for drivers.

Some things, however, have to do with everyone in the United States. We need an army to protect the whole nation. We must be able to mail letters and travel from state to state. The federal government deals with matters of those kinds.

People get many services from local, state, and federal governments. But all those government services cost money. Police, teachers, and other public workers must be paid.

People pay for government services when they pay taxes. Each level of government collects taxes. People often pay taxes on the money they earn and on the

property they own. When they buy certain things, people may also pay a sales tax. Paying taxes is a responsibility shared by all Americans.

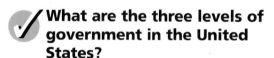 **What are the three levels of government in the United States?**

A WRITTEN PLAN OF UNITY

The United States is a country made up of states, each with its own government. The early leaders of the United States had to figure out a plan for a federal government. The plan had to unite the states as one nation.

Our nation's early leaders believed in self-government. That is, they wanted the people of the United States to govern themselves. After all, the people had

What?

The National Archives

Visitors can see both the Declaration of Independence and the Constitution at the National Archives (AR•kyvz) Building in Washington, D.C. For safety, both are sealed in heavy cases made of bronze and glass. At a moment's notice, the cases can be lowered into a safe.

fought a long war against England to win that right. That war was the American Revolution (rev•uh•LOO•shuhn). A **revolution** is a large, sudden change in government or in people's lives.

The United States declared its independence from England in 1776. Thomas Jefferson, a leader from Virginia, was asked to write a statement explaining why the country thought it should be free. That statement is called the **Declaration of Independence**. In it Jefferson wrote about freedom. He said that all people have a right to "Life, Liberty and the pursuit of Happiness." *Liberty* is another word for *freedom*.

Jefferson explained that "Governments are instituted among Men, deriving their just powers from the consent of the governed. . . ." In other words, Jefferson was saying that a government gets its power from the people. This was the basic idea that would unite all Americans under one federal government.

The plan for the country's federal government is given in a document called the **Constitution**. The Constitution also describes the rights that people in the United States have. Everyone must obey the Constitution. It is the "supreme law of the land."

The Constitution set up three branches, or parts, to the federal government. Each branch of government has a separate job to do. Each branch is just as important as the other two.

✔️ **What document gives the plan for the federal government?**

....

LEARNING FROM TIME LINES This time line shows some key events in the early history of the United States.
■ Was the Constitution written before or after the American Revolution ended?

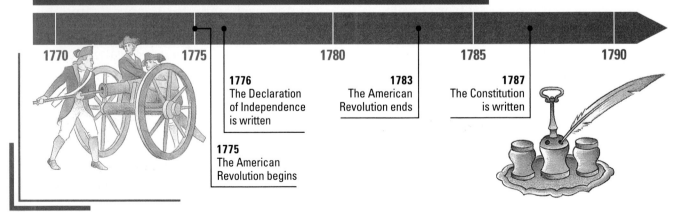

INDEPENDENCE FOR THE UNITED STATES

1770   1775   1780   1785   1790

1776
The Declaration of Independence is written

1775
The American Revolution begins

1783
The American Revolution ends

1787
The Constitution is written

The leader of the House of Representatives is called the Speaker. Here, the Speaker of the House, Newt Gingrich, swears in newly elected members.

THE LAWMAKING BRANCH

One branch of government is the legislative (LEH•juhs•lay•tiv) branch. The main job of the **legislative branch** of government is to make laws. In the federal government this branch is called **Congress**. Congress makes laws for the whole nation.

Congress is made up of two parts. One part is the Senate. The voters of each state elect two senators to represent them in the Senate.

The other part of Congress is the House of Representatives, sometimes called the House for short. Like members of the Senate, members of the House are elected by the voters in each state. But the number of representatives a state elects depends on how many people live there. States with more people, like California and Texas, have more representatives in the House.

Congress meets in the Capitol Building in Washington, D.C. There, members make laws that touch all our lives. A member of Congress once said that the United States is "a government of the people," and that "Congress is the people." He was saying how important the legislative branch is in a representative democracy.

What is the main job of the legislative branch?

CARRYING OUT LAWS

Another branch of the federal government is the executive (ig•ZEH•kyuh•tiv) branch. The main job of the government's **executive branch** is to see that the laws passed by Congress are carried out. The executive branch often suggests laws to Congress as well.

In the federal government the head of the executive branch is the President. The

President Bill Clinton (right) and Vice President Al Gore (left) lead the federal government's executive branch.

President directs the workers who collect taxes and run the government. Voters elect a President and Vice President every four years.

The President has one of the most important and difficult jobs in the world.

The President deals with other countries on behalf of the United States. The President also is the leader of the military.

 What is the main job of the executive branch?

THE COURTS

The judicial (ju•DIH•shuhl) branch is the third branch of the federal government. The main job of the **judicial branch** is to see that laws are carried out fairly. The judicial branch also decides how people who break laws should be punished.

The judicial branch is made up of all the federal courts. The most important court in the country is the **Supreme Court**. It is made up of nine judges, called justices. Decisions made by the justices apply to everyone in the country.

The main job of the Supreme Court is to make sure that the Constitution is followed. The Court must decide if laws passed by Congress or actions taken by

Supreme Court justices are chosen by the President but approved by the Senate. Justices serve on the Supreme Court for life.

LEGISLATIVE BRANCH	EXECUTIVE BRANCH	JUDICIAL BRANCH
	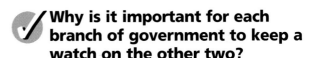	
Congress	President	Federal courts

LEARNING FROM CHARTS This chart shows how the United States government is divided into three branches.

■ Which branch of the federal government is the President part of?

the President agree with the Constitution. The Court also decides if state laws and courts follow the Constitution.

✓ What is the main job of the judicial branch?

WORKING TOGETHER

The three branches of the federal government work together. At the same time, each branch also keeps watch on the other two. That way, no one branch can become too powerful.

The federal government helps unite Americans. It makes laws for everyone to

obey. It also sets up common ways of doing things. The Constitution, for example, gives Congress the right to make bills and coins used for money. That way, Americans can use the same money in every state.

Even the coins that we carry in our pockets help remind us that Americans are united. Each coin carries the national motto, or saying, *E Pluribus Unum* (EE PLUR•uh•bus OO•nuhm). These Latin words mean "out of many, one."

✓ Why is it important for each branch of government to keep a watch on the other two?

LESSON 4 REVIEW

Check Understanding

1. **Recall the Facts** What are the three branches of the federal government?
2. **Focus on the Main Idea** What are some ways the United States government unites all the people living in the 50 states?

Think Critically

3. **Cause and Effect** What problems might it cause if each state made its own money?

Show What You Know

Chart Activity Draw a large triangle on a sheet of paper. Inside the triangle, write *Our Federal Government*. On each point of the triangle, write the name of one branch of government. Beside each name write what the branch does and who or what is the head of that branch. Compare your chart with those of classmates.

CONNECT MAIN IDEAS

Use this organizer to show that you understand how the chapter's main ideas are connected. First copy the organizer onto a separate sheet of paper. Then complete it by writing three examples for each main idea.

There are different ways of life in the United States.

1. _____
2. _____
3. _____

Different things help unite people living in the United States.

1. _____
2. _____
3. _____

We, the Many People

The United States government unites the people in the 50 states.

1. _____
2. _____
3. _____

WRITE MORE ABOUT IT

1. **Explain Differences**   Suppose a visitor asked you to explain why there are so many different customs and ways of life in the United States. Write a paragraph or two to explain those differences.

2. **Write a Letter**   Imagine that you are an immigrant who has recently come to live in the United States. Write a letter to a friend in your native country. Describe the many things Americans share. Be sure to tell about rights and responsibilities.

3. **Write a Report**   In the United States there are three different levels of government—local, state, and federal. Write a short report that explains what each level of government does. Tell how each of the levels affects you, your family, or your community.

USE VOCABULARY

Write a term from this list to complete each of the sentences that follow.

custom   immigrant
democracy   majority rule
ethnic group   right

1. Shaking hands when you meet someone is a _____.

2. An _____ is a person who comes to live in a country from some other place.

3. An _____ is made up of people from the same country, people of the same race, or people with a common way of life.

4. A _____ is a form of government in which the people rule.

5. When decisions are made by voting, people follow _____.

6. A _____ is a freedom a person has.

CHECK UNDERSTANDING

1. Who were the first people to live in what is now the United States?

2. Most groups of people came to America by choice. Which group did not come by choice?

3. What kinds of things make up a group's culture?

4. Why do the citizens of the United States elect representatives?

5. How is majority rule important to a democracy?

6. What is the Constitution?

7. What are the three branches of the federal government? What is the main job of each branch?

THINK CRITICALLY

1. **Cause and Effect** Many ethnic groups have come to live in the United States. How has this affected the country?

2. **Explore Viewpoints** Is majority rule always the best way to decide things? Explain your answer.

3. **Link to You** What responsibilities do you have as a citizen?

APPLY SKILLS

How to Make a Thoughtful Decision
Imagine that you have been asked to play in an important ball game. But the ball game will take place at the same time as a going-away party for a friend. What steps would you follow to make a thoughtful decision about what to do?

How to Understand National Symbols
Think about what the United States means to you. Then create your own national symbol. Explain what the different parts of the symbol stand for.

READ MORE ABOUT IT

The Earliest Americans by Helen Roney Sattler. Clarion. This book explains who the earliest Americans were and describes how they lived.

Klara's New World by Jeanette Winter. Knopf. Klara must leave behind everything she has ever known when her family moves to America.

The National Government by Barbara Silberdick Feinberg. Franklin Watts. This book describes the Constitution and the national government.

CHAPTER 3

LOOKING AT REGIONS

> **"** We look at maps and we see the United States, North America, and Africa as something drawn on a piece of paper. The same landforms. [From space] you don't see the boundaries. Your concepts of neighborhoods expand significantly. **"**
>
> United States astronaut Fred Gregory

UNDERSTANDING REGIONS

L nk to Our World

How does dividing large places into regions make it easier for people to understand their world?

Focus on the Main Idea
As you read, look for different ways in which people divide the United States into regions.

Preview Vocabulary
relative location
county
county seat

Kevin lives in Milford, a small city in Connecticut.

The United States is a country with many differences. The country is just too big to study all at once, so people often divide it into smaller regions. As you know, a region is an area with at least one feature that sets it apart from other areas.

REGIONS AROUND YOU

Like many Americans, Kevin lives in a city. A city is one kind of region. A city and all the people who live there share a place on Earth.

Kevin lives in Milford, Connecticut. If Kevin wanted to describe the location of his city, he might tell you that it is in the state of Connecticut. He might tell you that Milford lies between the cities of Bridgeport and New Haven. That would tell you Milford's **relative location**, or its position in relation to other places on the Earth. However, it would not tell you much about the city itself.

Milford is a small city, but it has different parts. Some parts have old houses built on narrow streets. Some have new houses built close together. Other houses are built in an area along the beach. In Milford's downtown area, there are stores and places to eat. Other parts of the city have office buildings and factories.

Rather than describe the whole city, with all its differences, Kevin might tell you just about his neighborhood. A neighborhood is another kind of region. In Kevin's neighborhood, most of the houses are built of wood. Most have a second floor. Each has a separate

Milford, Connecticut

The city of Milford is on Long Island Sound near the mouth of the Housatonic (hoo•suh•TAH•nik) River. Milford began as a shipbuilding center in 1639. Today businesses in the city make such things as brass goods and electric motors.

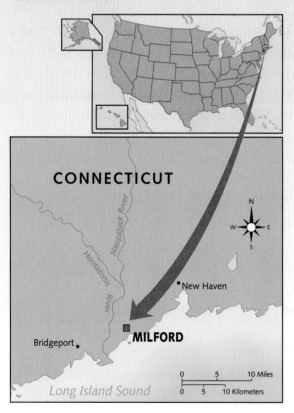

CONNECTICUT

Naugatuck River

Housatonic River

N
W • E
S

• New Haven

Bridgeport •

■ **MILFORD**

| 0 | 5 | 10 Miles |
| 0 | 5 | 10 Kilometers |

Long Island Sound

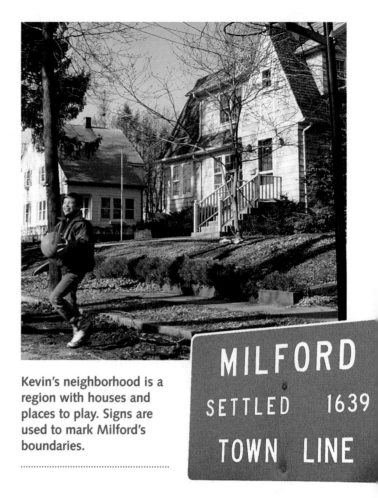

Kevin's neighborhood is a region with houses and places to play. Signs are used to mark Milford's boundaries.

MILFORD
SETTLED 1639
TOWN LINE

garage. Those features make Kevin's neighborhood different from others in Milford.

To better understand Kevin's neighborhood, you can divide it into smaller regions. One street can form a region. The block on which Kevin lives could be a region, too. Even his yard could be studied as a small region.

It would be easy for Kevin to describe his yard or his block. However, it would be very hard for him to describe every house or every building in Milford. By making smaller regions, people can more easily learn and talk about a place.

✓ **Why do people divide places into regions?**

REGIONS WITHIN CITIES

People can define a region by using just about any feature. It may be a region that shares a place, such as Kevin's neighborhood. It may be a region that shares a government. A city is a region that shares a government. All the people who live in a city live by the same laws. They have the same city leaders.

A region that shares a government has exact boundaries. Everyone might not agree about which street marks the end of Kevin's neighborhood, but everyone knows exactly where Milford begins and ends. Its boundaries are set by law. Its city limits are clearly marked with signs.

Cities can be divided into still other kinds of regions. Many cities are divided into a number of voting districts. Voters in each district elect their own leaders to the city's government. Voters who live in one district cannot vote in another district.

Cities are sometimes divided into a number of school districts, too. The families who live in a school district usually send their children to that district's schools. Cities can also be divided into other kinds of districts, such as fire districts and library districts. You live in many different regions all at the same time.

 How is a region that shares a government different from other kinds of regions?

REGIONS WITHIN STATES

Regions are different sizes. Some are small, like Kevin's neighborhood. Some are large, like a state. Like a city, each state has its own government. It also has exact boundaries set by law.

Nearly every state is divided into smaller parts called counties. A **county** is a part of a state that has its own government. Louisiana is divided into smaller regions called parishes. Alaska is divided into boroughs (BUHR•ohz).

The town or city that is the center of government for a county is called the **county seat**. The county government is another kind of local government. It takes care of the county's roads. It runs the county's courts. Many counties also have a sheriff to see that laws are obeyed.

City, county, and state boundaries are important to governments, but people

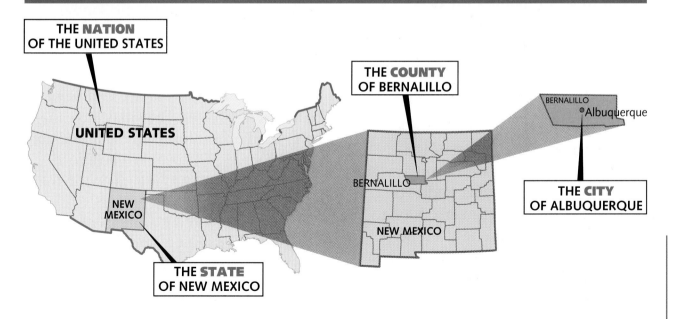

REGIONS WITHIN REGIONS

THE **NATION** OF THE UNITED STATES

THE **COUNTY** OF BERNALILLO

UNITED STATES

BERNALILLO
Albuquerque

BERNALILLO

THE **CITY** OF ALBUQUERQUE

NEW MEXICO

NEW MEXICO

THE **STATE** OF NEW MEXICO

LEARNING FROM DIAGRAMS The United States can be divided into regions of different sizes.
■ Which region covers a larger area, a county or a state?

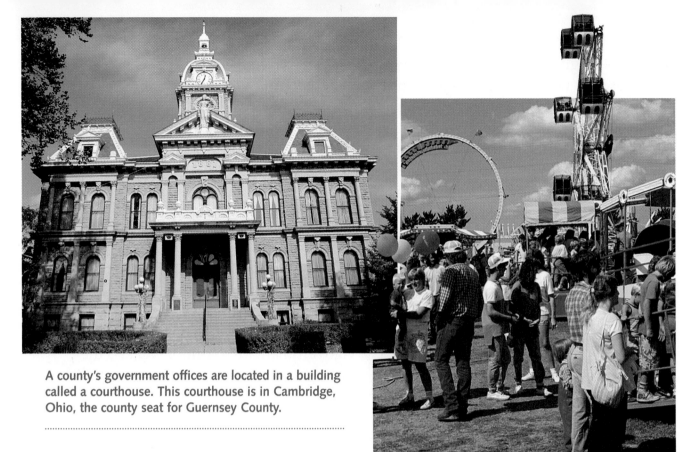

A county's government offices are located in a building called a courthouse. This courthouse is in Cambridge, Ohio, the county seat for Guernsey County.

cross them all the time in their daily lives. People often live in one city or county but work in another one. Some people even live in one state but work or shop in another state.

Many counties across the country hold fairs each year. This fair is in Wexford County, in Michigan.

✓ **Into what smaller parts are most states divided?**

REGIONS WITHIN THE COUNTRY

You know that the United States is made up of 50 states. Each state is a region. It has its own government as well as its own cities, landforms, bodies of water, and resources. It can take a long time to study 50 states, one at a time. So studying the states is not always the best way to study the whole country.

People often group states into larger regions. That makes it easier to compare areas of the United States. In this book the states are grouped into five regions. These regions are the Northeast, the Southeast, the Middle West, the Southwest, and the West.

The states in each region are alike in many ways. They are all in the same part of the United States. They may have the same kind of landforms, climate, and natural resources. The people who live in those states often earn their living in the same ways.

In this book you will read about each of those five regions. You will meet the people who live there. You will learn how the regions are alike and how they are different.

✓ **Why do people sometimes group states into regions?**

REGIONS OF THE UNITED STATES

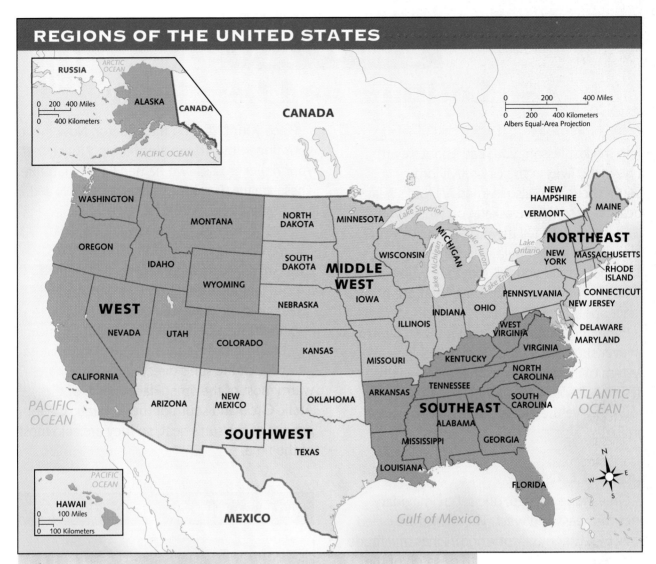

 REGIONS The 50 states are often grouped into five regions. The states in each region are all in the same part of the country.
■ In which region of the United States is your state found?

*L*SSON 1 REVIEW

Check Understanding

1. Recall the Facts Why do people need to divide large places into regions?

2. Focus on the Main Idea How do people divide the United States into regions?

Think Critically

3. Think More About It Why are exact boundaries important for regions that share a government?

4. Link to You What are some of the different regions that you live in?

Show What You Know

 Map Activity Draw a map of your state or community. Divide that area into regions based on different features. Share your map with classmates. Explain to them why you made the regions the way you did.

Use Latitude and Longitude

Why Is This Skill Important?

In the last lesson, you read about Kevin, a boy who lives in the city of Milford, Connecticut. You also learned Milford's relative location. If someone asked you where you lived, you might tell them the name of your town or its location relative to a nearby city. But what would you tell someone who wanted to know your town's **absolute location**, or its exact position on the Earth's surface?

Long ago, mapmakers thought of a way to answer such a question. They developed a system of imaginary lines that could be used to describe absolute location. Using that system, you can give the global address of any place on Earth.

Lines of Latitude

On a globe or map, one set of imaginary lines runs east and west. These lines are called **lines of latitude** (LA•tuh•tood). Lines of latitude are used to tell how far north or south of the equator a place is. Because lines of latitude are always the same distance apart, they are also called **parallels** (PAIR•uh•lehlz). Parallel lines never meet.

Find the equator on Map A. The equator itself is a line of latitude that divides the Earth in half. It is marked 0° (zero degrees). The equator is the starting point for measuring latitude.

Lines of latitude are measured in degrees north and south from the equator. Lines of latitude in the Northern Hemisphere are marked with an *N*. The *N* tells you that the line is north of the equator. The North Pole is marked 90°N. The South Pole is marked 90°S. The *S* tells you that its location is south of the equator. It is in the Southern Hemisphere.

Place your finger on the equator. Now move your finger toward the North Pole. Notice that your finger crosses two named lines of latitude. These are the **Tropic of Cancer** at 23½°N and the **Arctic Circle** at 66½°N.

Place your finger on the equator again. Move your finger toward the South Pole. Once again, your finger crosses two named lines of latitude—the **Tropic of Capricorn** at 23½°S and the **Antarctic Circle** at 66½°S.

Find the area between the Tropic of Cancer and the Tropic of Capricorn. Places in this area get more of the sun's direct rays, so they are warm most of the time. Places north of the Arctic Circle and south of the Antarctic Circle get less of the sun's heat, so they are cold most of the time.

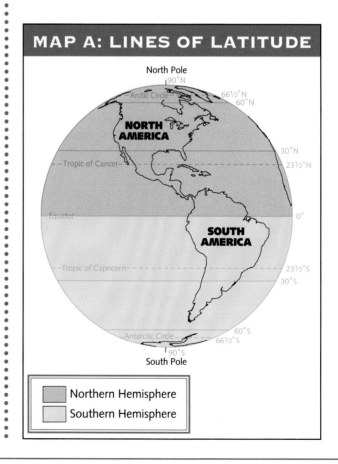

MAP A: LINES OF LATITUDE

North Pole
90°N
Arctic Circle
66½°N
60°N
NORTH AMERICA
30°N
Tropic of Cancer
23½°N
Equator
0°
SOUTH AMERICA
Tropic of Capricorn
23½°S
30°S
60°S
Antarctic Circle
66½°S
90°S
South Pole

- Northern Hemisphere
- Southern Hemisphere

Lines of Longitude

Another set of imaginary lines runs north and south on a globe or map. These lines are called **lines of longitude** (LAHN•juh•tood), or **meridians** (muh•RIH•dee•uhnz). Lines of longitude can be used to tell how far east or west of the prime meridian a place is. The **prime meridian** divides the Earth into the Eastern Hemisphere and the Western Hemisphere. Like the equator, the prime meridian is marked 0° (zero degrees). It is the starting point for measuring longitude.

Find the prime meridian on Map B. As you can see, lines of longitude are numbered east and west from the prime meridian. Lines of longitude in the Eastern Hemisphere are marked with an *E* for east. The lines in the Western Hemisphere are marked with a *W* for west. Lines of longitude meet at the North and South poles. They are farthest apart at the equator.

MAP C: LATITUDE AND LONGITUDE GRID

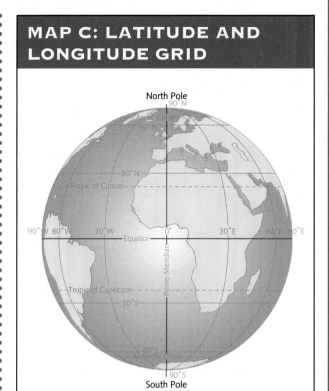

Longitude is measured up to 180° east of the prime meridian and 180° west of the prime meridian. Since 180°E and 180°W are the same meridian, it is just labeled 180°, without an *E* or a *W*.

Together, lines of latitude and longitude form a grid. You can see this grid on Map C.

Understand the Process

The grid formed by lines of latitude and longitude can help you locate any place on the Earth. Look at Map D on page 104. It shows the United States with lines of latitude and longitude and their number labels.

1. Find the parallel that runs through New Orleans, Louisiana. New Orleans is located at 30°N latitude. What line of longitude runs through New Orleans?
2. Write New Orleans' latitude and longitude together, with the latitude first. New Orleans is located at 30°N, 90°W. This is the city's absolute location.

MAP B: LINES OF LONGITUDE

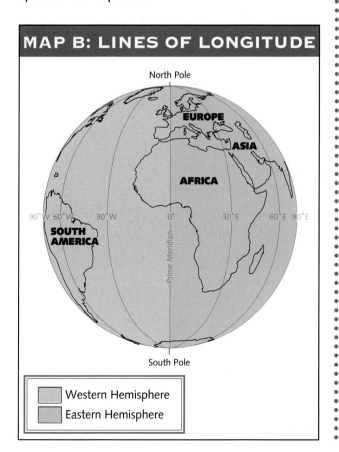

Western Hemisphere
Eastern Hemisphere

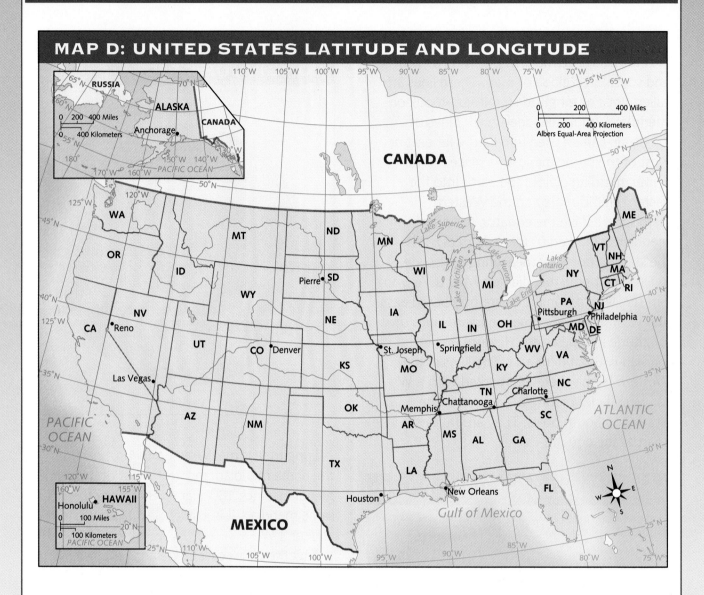

MAP D: UNITED STATES LATITUDE AND LONGITUDE

Sometimes the place you are looking for is not exactly where two lines cross. But lines of latitude and longitude can still help you find the place. You just have to look near where the closest lines of latitude and longitude cross.

3. Suppose you were asked to tell which city is located near 35°N, 80°W. First find the line of latitude labeled 35°N. Then run your finger along that line until it crosses the line of longitude labeled 80°W. What city is located near there?

4. What city is located near 40°N, 90°W?

5. What city is located near 35°N, 85°W?

Think and Apply

Use the map above to tell what city is located near each of these latitudes and longitudes.

45°N, 100°W
40°N, 120°W
40°N, 105°W

Give the closest latitude and longitude for each of these cities.

Memphis, Tennessee
St. Joseph, Missouri
Philadelphia, Pennsylvania
Houston, Texas

LOOKING AT DIFFERENT REGIONS

LESSON 2

Link to Our World

How can different regions be alike?

Focus on the Main Idea
As you read, look for ways regions of the United States can be both alike and different.

Preview Vocabulary

natural vegetation	industry
broadleaf tree	urban
needleleaf tree	suburb
recreation	suburban
agriculture	rural

Regions can be based on the kinds of trees that grow in a place.

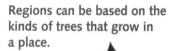

It is easier for people to understand a place if they divide it into smaller regions. There are many ways to do that. When regions are set up using one feature, they still share other features with other regions.

PHYSICAL FEATURES

Look out the window. How would you describe the place where you live? Do you see mountains? Or is the land low and flat? Is the climate warm or cold? Is it wet or dry? What kinds of animals live nearby? What do the trees look like?

The answers to these questions depend on where you live. The United States does not look the same in all places. Students in other parts of the country might describe a very different-looking place from the one you see.

Regions can be based on any feature. Often the feature is chosen because of what people want to know. If they want to know how climate affects the way people live, they might divide the United States into regions with similar climates.

Climate is just one physical feature people use to set up regions. They also use landforms to set up regions—mountain regions and plains regions, to name two kinds.

Regions can be based on wildlife and natural vegetation (veh•juh•TAY•shuhn), too. **Natural vegetation** is the plant life that grows naturally in an area. A forest ranger

ONE STATE, THREE REGIONS

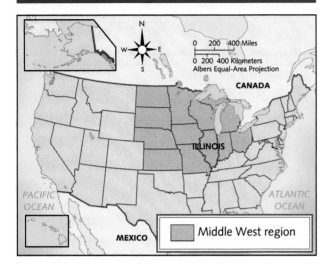

Middle West region

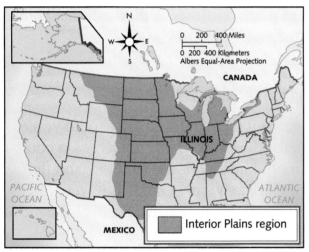

Interior Plains region

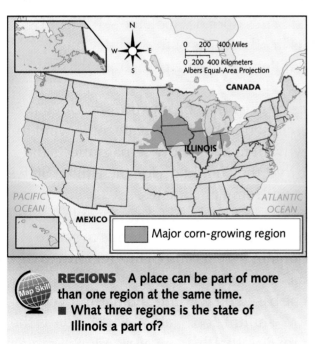

Major corn-growing region

REGIONS A place can be part of more than one region at the same time.
■ What three regions is the state of Illinois a part of?

might divide the United States into regions based on the kinds of trees that grow in different places.

A forest ranger would know the region in the Appalachian Mountains where broadleaf forests grow. A **broadleaf tree** has wide, flat leaves. In autumn its leaves turn colors and fall to the ground. Maple, oak, walnut, cherry, and hickory are all broadleaf trees.

Farther south, on the Coastal Plain, are large needleleaf forests. A **needleleaf tree** has long, sharp leaves that look like needles. Most needleleaf trees, such as pines and firs, stay green all year.

Because of different landforms and resources, people in different regions enjoy different kinds of recreation (reh•kree•AY•shuhn). **Recreation** is what people do to have fun. In mountain regions, people can ski. In coastal regions, they can swim in the ocean.

Unlike regions set up by law, regions based on physical features have no exact boundaries. Two regions often overlap. In places between the broadleaf and needleleaf forests, both kinds of trees grow side by side.

✓ **On what kinds of physical features can regions be based?**

WHAT PEOPLE USE AND MAKE

The United States can be divided into regions based on the kinds of natural resources found in an area. The states of Texas, Oklahoma, and Louisiana all have large deposits of oil. Other states could also be grouped by how much oil they have. This would help people study the country's oil resources.

The Southeast and the Southwest are major cotton-producing regions of the United States.

Other regions can be formed by the way people use natural resources to earn their living. In mining regions many people work at mining rocks, minerals, or fuels. In lumbering regions many people earn their living cutting down trees for wood. In manufacturing regions many people work in factories. In still other regions many people use the land for **agriculture** (A•grih•kuhl•cher), or farming.

Regions can also be based on the products that people make or grow. In the United States most cotton is grown in the Southeast and the Southwest. Most wheat is grown in the Middle West. In other farming regions corn or vegetables may be the main crop.

Some regions are based on what product most of their factories make. Around San Jose, California, the making of computer parts is a major industry. An **industry** is all the businesses that make one kind of product or provide one kind of service.

 What are some kinds of regions that are based on the way people use natural resources?

Where?

Silicon Valley

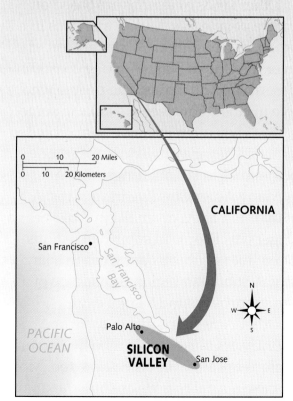

The area near San Jose is sometimes called Silicon Valley. Silicon is a material used to make computer parts. Several factories in Silicon Valley manufacture the tiny chips that allow computers to work.

Many Americans live in suburbs close to large cities. The city in this picture is New Orleans, Louisiana.

WHERE PEOPLE LIVE

Other kinds of regions are based on where people live. Most Americans live in **urban**, or city, regions. Cities are found all over the United States—along coasts, in deserts, and on plains. The people who live in cities, however, are alike in some ways. They often live in or near crowded spaces. They may live close together, sometimes in tall buildings.

Many Americans live in suburbs. A **suburb** is a town or small city built near a larger city. People in suburban regions often live in suburbs but work in a larger city. A **suburban** region is made up of all the suburbs around a large city.

Other Americans live in **rural**, or country, regions. People who live in rural regions are alike in some ways, too. Most homes in rural regions are built far apart.

People in rural regions sometimes have to drive a long way to go to school, go to the doctor, or go shopping.

 How are urban and rural regions different?

CULTURAL REGIONS

Still another kind of region is one based on culture. Dividing a place into cultural regions helps show the customs and beliefs of the people who live there. A cultural region may be based on the main ethnic group that lives in a place. It can also be based on the religion that most of the people there follow, on the kinds of foods most of the people eat, or on the language most of the people speak.

English is spoken in most places in the United States, but many cities have neighborhoods where other languages are spoken. In San Francisco's Chinatown,

San Francisco's Chinatown is a region based on culture. What are some things that make this neighborhood special?

These houses in Orange County, California, are being built on land that was once part of a farming region.

the background of most of the people is Chinese. Many people in Chinatown speak Chinese, so signs are often written in Chinese as well as in English.

What kinds of things might people in a cultural region have in common?

CHANGING REGIONS

The place where you live can be part of several regions all at the same time. You may live in a plains region along the Atlantic coast. You may live in a suburban region in the Northeast. You may also live in a manufacturing region. Each of those tells something different about the place where you live.

Over time, however, a place may change. The features that once made it part of a region may no longer be the same. A city may no longer be part of a manufacturing region if its industries shut down. If a new resource is found, an area may become part of another kind of region.

Americans live in different kinds of regions, yet they share many things. People often shop in the same kinds of stores and eat in the same kinds of restaurants. They often play the same sports— soccer, baseball, football, and basketball—wherever they live.

How can a region change over time?

*L*SSON 2 REVIEW

Check Understanding

1. **Recall the Facts** How are regions based on physical features different from regions set up by law?
2. **Focus on the Main Idea** How can regions of the United States be both alike and different?

Think Critically

3. **Cause and Effect** What might cause the boundaries of a wildlife or natural vegetation region to change?

Show What You Know

Diorama Activity Think about the kinds of regions that could be created where you live. Choose one of those regions. Then make a diorama to show that region's main features. Build your diorama in an empty box turned on its side.

LESSON 3

LINKING REGIONS

Link to Our World

How do the people of one region depend on the people of other regions?

Focus on the Main Idea
As you read, look for things that help link people in different regions.

Preview Vocabulary
**technology
transportation
trade
specialize
interdependence
communication**

The Dewar family reunion is held each summer. Family members from all over the country attend.

People use different features to set up regions. So each region of the United States has something special. However, the people who live in each region must also depend on products and resources from other regions.

FROM REGION TO REGION

A hundred years ago members of the Dewar (DOO•er) family lived close to one another. They all lived in towns or cities in the Northeast. Today the Dewars live in places as far away as Texas and the state of Washington. One cousin lives in England. Yet family members talk to one another and see one another often. As another cousin explains, "Our family lives all over the country, but we like to get together at least once a year at our family reunion."

Like the Dewars, many American families are spread out across the country and around the world. Today's technology (tek•NAH•luh•jee), however, makes it possible for them to stay close. **Technology** is the way people use new ideas to make tools and machines. Such things as telephones and airplanes help connect people in different regions. So do computers and television.

 **Why is technology important to many families today?**

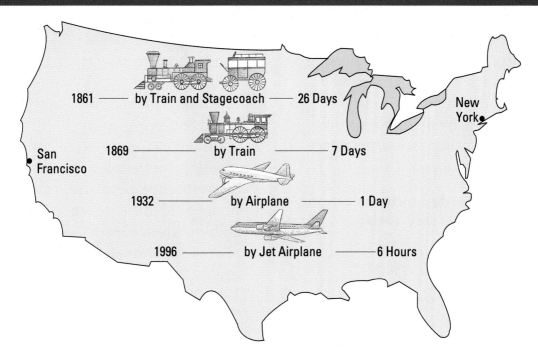

1861 —— by Train and Stagecoach —— 26 Days

1869 —— by Train —— 7 Days

1932 —— by Airplane —— 1 Day

1996 —— by Jet Airplane —— 6 Hours

San Francisco

New York

LEARNING FROM CHARTS   Modern technology has reduced the amount of time needed to travel from coast to coast.
- What methods of transportation did people use to travel from New York to California in 1861? About how long did the trip take?

MOVING PEOPLE AND GOODS

One way technology helps link people in different regions is by making transportation easier. **Transportation** is the way people and goods are moved from place to place.

Airplanes allow people to travel a long way very quickly. Still, Americans travel four times as often in cars as they do in planes. Millions of miles of roads link all the states except Hawaii.

Transportation links people in different regions. It also helps trade. **Trade** is the buying and selling of goods. Without good transportation, trade between regions would not be easy.

 **What is transportation?**

DEPENDING ON OTHER REGIONS

Different regions may have different kinds of natural resources. So workers in different regions often grow or make different products. Along the coast of South Carolina, many workers specialize (SPEH•shuh•lyz) in fishing. To **specialize** is to work at only one kind of job. These men and women can specialize because they do not also have to grow wheat for bread or make gasoline. They can depend on workers in other regions for those products.

Think about all the products you and your family use each day. Your clothes may have been made in a factory in the Southeast with cotton grown in Texas. Your family's car may have been built in

Michigan with parts made in California. The food you eat was grown on farms and ranches all across the United States.

No one region can meet all the needs and wants of its people. People depend on resources and products from every region of the United States. This depending on each other for resources and products is called **interdependence** (in•ter•dih•PEN•duhns).

✓ **Why is interdependence among regions necessary today?**

STAYING IN TOUCH

Interdependence among regions is possible because the United States has good transportation. Before people can trade goods, however, they must know what to send and where to send it. People find out those things through communication (kuh•myoo•nuh•KAY•shuhn). **Communication** is the way people send and receive information.

Communication helps link people in different regions. Each day, mail carriers take millions of letters to and from places all over the United States. People also use the telephone to call family, friends, and businesses in faraway places. In fact, more than a million calls are made in the United States every day.

Cellular (SEL•yuh•ler) telephones make it possible for people to call from anywhere. One man even used a cellular phone to call his wife while he was climbing Mount McKinley, in Alaska!

People now use fax machines to send "instant" letters over telephone lines. They also use computers connected to telephone lines to "talk" to each other.

Television helps link people, too. When television was new, people in different parts of the country saw different shows.

LEARNING FROM GRAPHS The number of households in the United States with television sets has gone up steadily since 1970.
■ About how many households had television sets in 1995?

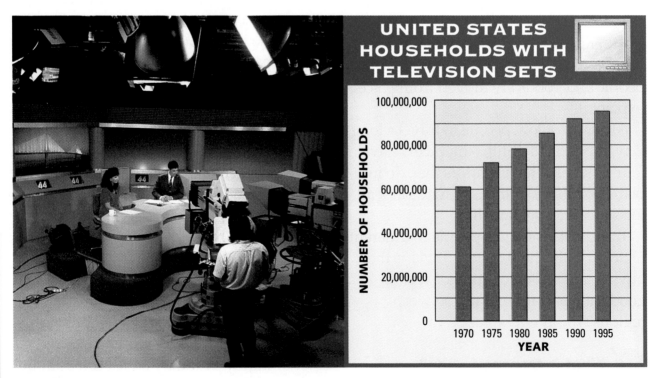

UNITED STATES HOUSEHOLDS WITH TELEVISION SETS

NUMBER OF HOUSEHOLDS

100,000,000

80,000,000

60,000,000

40,000,000

20,000,000

0

1970 1975 1980 1985 1990 1995
YEAR

TRANSPORTATION AND COMMUNICATION

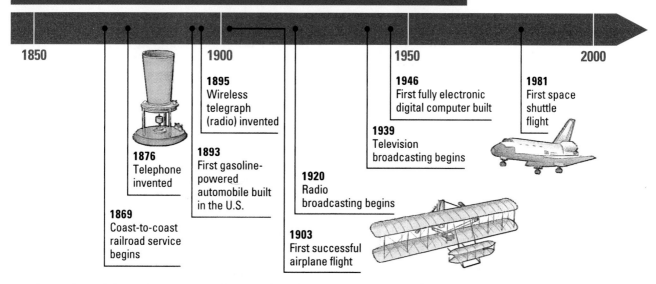

1850   1900   1950   2000

1895
Wireless
telegraph
(radio) invented

1876
Telephone
invented

1893
First gasoline-
powered
automobile built
in the U.S.

1946
First fully electronic
digital computer built

1981
First space
shuttle
flight

1939
Television
broadcasting begins

1920
Radio
broadcasting begins

1869
Coast-to-coast
railroad service
begins

1903
First successful
airplane flight

LEARNING FROM TIME LINES This time line shows some important events in
the history of transportation and communication.
■ When was the telephone invented?

Cellular telephones
use radio waves
instead of wires
to send and
receive
messages.

Today people in all parts of the country
watch many of the same shows. Television
news tells about things that happen in other
parts of the country. Other shows let people
see what life is like in different regions.

 **What is communication?**

LSSON 3 REVIEW

Check Understanding

1. **Recall the Facts** Why do workers in
   different regions often grow or make
   different products?
2. **Focus on the Main Idea** What kinds of
   things help link people in different regions?

Think Critically

3. **Think More About It** Why would
   trade between different regions be more
   difficult without good transportation and
   communication?

Show What You Know

Writing Activity Imagine
the United States without
good transportation and
communication. Write a
paragraph telling three or four
ways your life might be different without
these two links to other people.

CONNECT MAIN IDEAS

Use this organizer to show that you understand how the chapter's main ideas are connected. First copy the organizer onto a separate sheet of paper. Then complete it by writing three examples to support each main idea.

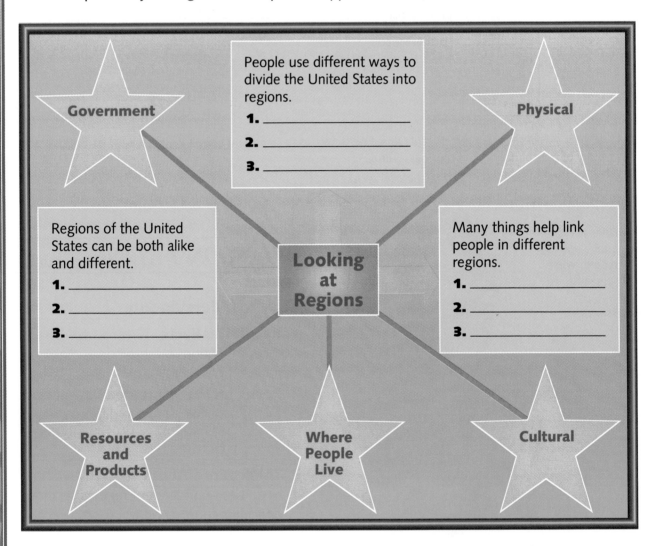

Government

People use different ways to divide the United States into regions.

1. _____
2. _____
3. _____

Physical

Regions of the United States can be both alike and different.

1. _____
2. _____
3. _____

Looking at Regions

Many things help link people in different regions.

1. _____
2. _____
3. _____

Resources and Products

Where People Live

Cultural

WRITE MORE ABOUT IT

1. **Write a Letter** Write a letter to someone who lives in another region of the United States. Tell him or her what it is like to live where you do. Tell some of the things your region has to offer.

2. **Explain How** People use products from every region of the United States. Write a paragraph that explains how technology, transportation, and communication link the place where you live with other places.

USE VOCABULARY

Use each term in a sentence that helps explain its meaning.

1. county
2. agriculture
3. industry
4. urban
5. technology
6. transportation
7. trade
8. specialize
9. interdependence
10. communication

CHECK UNDERSTANDING

1. What is relative location?

2. How is it useful to divide a large area into smaller regions?

3. Which is larger, a county or a state?

4. What is natural vegetation?

5. How can the physical features of a region affect recreation?

6. How do regions based on physical features differ from regions set up by law?

7. Do more Americans live in urban regions or rural regions?

8. What are suburbs?

9. What are some things cultural regions are based on?

10. How does technology help connect people in different regions?

11. How does transportation help trade in the United States?

THINK CRITICALLY

1. **Think More About It**   Why is it important for a region with one government to have exact boundaries?

2. **Link to You**   What kinds of recreation do you and your family enjoy? How might the things you do for recreation be different if you lived in another region?

3. **Explore Viewpoints**   Why do people choose different regions to live in?

4. **Cause and Effect**   How might people change a region?

5. **Personally Speaking**   Television allows people to see what is happening in other places as it happens. Do you think that is always good? Explain your answer.

APPLY SKILLS

 How to Use Latitude and Longitude   Find a world map in an atlas. Use the latitude and longitude grid to answer these questions.

1. Is a place that is located at 40°N, 20°E in the Eastern Hemisphere or the Western Hemisphere?

2. What kind of climate might you expect to find if you visited a city near 0°, 80°W?

3. What country would you be in if you were at 40°N, 100°W?

READ MORE ABOUT IT

Communication by Piero Ventura. Houghton Mifflin. This history of communication gives interesting facts about inventions.

From Sea to Shining Sea. Edited by Amy L. Cohn. Scholastic. The stories and songs in this collection come from different regions of the United States and different times in its past.

The Last Dragon by Susan Miho Nunes. Clarion. Peter Chang spends the summer with a great-aunt in Chinatown.

FIELD TRIPS OF THE FUTURE

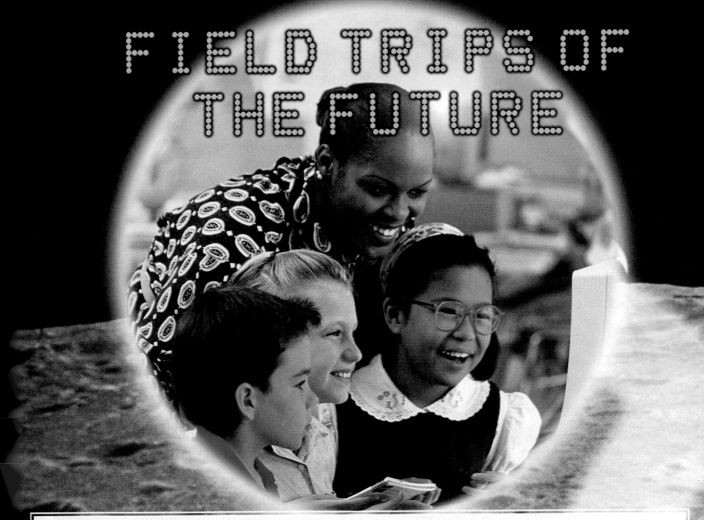

Learning how to use a computer has become an important new part of learning. In some schools students use computers to communicate with students in other regions of the United States and in other regions of the world. Students in Indiana, for example, can learn about North Carolina or Japan from students who live there. In one school in Rhode Island, students use computers to learn the geography of the United States. One student said, "We learned so many things about our country. . . . It was neat to get mail from other classes each day. We're learning so much from each other."

In the future, students will use computer technology for more than sending and receiving electronic mail, or e-mail. By using special goggles and gloves connected to their computers, they will be able to "visit" almost any place they choose— even other planets! They will be able to "move around" a place by simply turning their head or pointing a finger. Because this technology makes the experience seem real, it is called virtual reality.

How do you think using virtual reality might help students? Do you think its use would have problems as well? Hold a classroom debate about the changes computer technology is bringing about today. Discuss whether you think these changes are good or bad.

Some businesses use virtual reality to teach workers how to use machinery. This worker (left) is learning how to operate a front-end loader.

Virtual reality allows a person to experience exciting adventures. This girl (right) is using virtual reality to learn what it is like to ski down a mountainside.

STORY CLOTH

A story cloth uses pictures instead of words to tell a story. Study the pictures shown in this story cloth to help you review what you read about in Unit 1.

Summarize the Main Ideas

1. The United States has different landforms, bodies of water, and climates.

2. People use different resources to earn their living and to meet their needs.

3. People change the environment when they use limited natural resources.

4. Different groups from all over the world have brought their cultures to the United States.

5. Americans share one national government.

6. People often divide the United States into regions.

7. People who live in one region depend on products and resources from other regions. Technology helps link people in different regions.

Write About a Main Idea   Choose one of the main ideas from the list above. Then find pictures in the story cloth that tell something about that main idea. Use those pictures to help you write sentences that give details about the main idea.

COOPERATIVE LEARNING WORKSHOP

Remember

- Share your ideas.
- Cooperate with others to plan your work.
- Take responsibility for your work.
- Show your group's work to the class.
- Discuss what you learned by working together.

Activity 1
Draw a Map

Use encyclopedias and library books to help you list some of the country's important natural resources. Compare your list with the lists of others in your group. Find out where in the country the resources are located. Then work together to draw a resource map of the United States. Create different symbols to mark the places where the resources are located. Add your symbols to a map key.

Activity 2
Make a Collage

Work together to make a collage that shows some of the United States' many ethnic groups and cultures. Cut from newspapers and magazines pictures that show different customs, holidays, and ways of life. Paste your pictures onto a large sheet of paper, and give your collage a title. Display the collage, and talk to your classmates about how people in the United States can enjoy richer lives because of the country's mix of cultures.

Activity 3
Make a Conservation Book

To show people how they can help the environment, make a conservation book. Explain how people change or pollute the environment, and give ideas for ways they can conserve natural resources. To illustrate your book, draw pictures or cut some from magazines and newspapers. Give your book a title, and display it where others in your school can read it.

USE VOCABULARY

Write a term from this list to complete each of the sentences that follow.

coastal plain   drainage basin
culture   trade
custom   tributary

1. A _____ is low land that lies along an ocean.

2. The Ohio River is a _____ of the Mississippi River.

3. The land drained by a river system makes up its _____.

4. A _____ is the usual way of doing things.

5. An ethnic group has its own _____, or way of life.

6. _____ is the buying and selling of goods.

CHECK UNDERSTANDING

1. How is a mountain different from a mountain range?

2. How does erosion change the land?

3. Why is Juneau, Alaska, often warmer in the winter than Minneapolis, Minnesota?

4. How are manufacturing jobs different from service jobs?

5. What is the most important court in the United States?

THINK CRITICALLY

1. **Link to You** What things from other cultures have become part of your life?

2. **Cause and Effect** Plowing the land has caused soil to erode. What are some ways farmers can help conserve the soil?

3. **Explore Viewpoints** Why do you think many immigrants want to keep their native cultures and traditions in their new countries?

4. **Personally Speaking** American workers often specialize. In what kind of job would you like to specialize? Why?

APPLY GEOGRAPHY SKILLS

 How to Use Latitude and Longitude Use the map below to answer the questions.

1. Which line of longitude passes through Zanesville?

2. What city is nearest to 41°N, 84°W?

3. What lines of latitude and longitude meet closest to Ohio's capital, Columbus?

OHIO

0   40   80 Miles
0   40   80 Kilometers
Albers Equal-Area Projection

CANADA

Lake Erie

MI

Toledo

Cleveland

Tiffin

Akron Youngstown

Ottawa

Lima

Mansfield

PA

IN

OHIO

Columbus

Springfield

Zanesville

Dayton

Marietta

Cincinnati

Pomeroy

Ohio River

WV

★ State capital

KY

42°N

41°N

40°N

39°N

85°W   84°W   83°W   82°W   81°W

UNIT 2

THE NORTHEAST

Connecticut   Delaware   Maine   Maryland   Massachusetts   New Hampshire

Mystic Seaport, in Connecticut

A Maine lobster

Plimoth Plantation, in Massachusetts

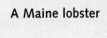

122 Unit 2

The region of the United States known as the Northeast stretches from Maine to Maryland. It is the smallest region of the United States in size. Yet in many places the Northeast is crowded with people.

The Northeast has great cities. It also has tiny villages, tree-covered hills, rocky shores, and sandy beaches. It is rich in history, too. Of the country's first 13 states, 9 are in the Northeast.

← Boston, Massachusetts

New Jersey	New York	Pennsylvania	Rhode Island	Vermont

The United Nations Building, in New York City

Independence Hall, in Philadelphia, Pennsylvania

Gathering maple sap for syrup in Vermont

Unit 2 • **123**

ALMANAC

The Northeast

Did You Know?

There are 11 states in the Northeast. Of those states, 6 are known together as the New England states. The other 5 states are known as the Middle Atlantic states. The nation's capital, Washington, D.C., is also a part of the Northeast.

STATE	CAPITAL	NICKNAME	POPULATION*
THE NEW ENGLAND STATES			
Connecticut (CT)	Hartford	Constitution State	3,268,000
Maine (ME)	Augusta	Pine Tree State	1,236,000
Massachusetts (MA)	Boston	Bay State	5,959,000
New Hampshire (NH)	Concord	Granite State	1,144,000
Rhode Island (RI)	Providence	Ocean State	998,000
Vermont (VT)	Montpelier	Green Mountain State	584,000
THE MIDDLE ATLANTIC STATES			
Delaware (DE)	Dover	First State	736,000
Maryland (MD)	Annapolis	Old Line State	5,180,000
New Jersey (NJ)	Trenton	Garden State	8,015,000
New York (NY)	Albany	Empire State	18,198,000
Pennsylvania (PA)	Harrisburg	Keystone State	12,210,000

*The most recent figures available

TEN LARGEST CITIES

1. New York, New York
2. Philadelphia, Pennsylvania
3. Baltimore, Maryland
4. Washington, D.C.
5. Boston, Massachusetts
6. Pittsburgh, Pennsylvania
7. Buffalo, New York
8. Newark, New Jersey
9. Rochester, New York
10. Jersey City, New Jersey

LEADING PRODUCTS AND RESOURCES

Farming:
Apples, beef cattle, blueberries, cranberries, dairy cows, potatoes, poultry
Fishing:
Clams, crabs, fish, lobsters, scallops
Manufacturing:
Chemicals, clothing, dairy products, electrical equipment, lumber, maple syrup, medicines, paper products, plastics, printed materials, processed foods
Mining:
Coal, gravel, iron, natural gas, oil, sand, stone, zinc

The Verrazano-Narrows Bridge, in New York, has the longest span of any bridge in the United States—4,260 feet (1,298 m).

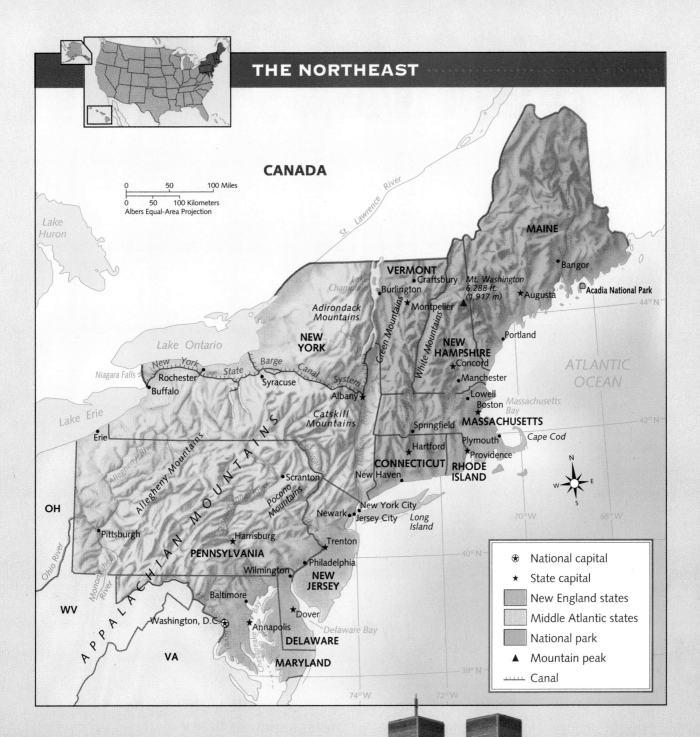

CANADA

0   50   100 Miles

0   50   100 Kilometers

Albers Equal-Area Projection

Lake Huron

St. Lawrence River

MAINE

• Bangor

Lake Champlain

VERMONT

• Craftsbury

Mt. Washington 6,288 ft. (1,917 m) ▲

• Augusta

◻ Acadia National Park

Adirondack Mountains

Burlington ★ Montpelier

44° N

NEW YORK

Green Mountains

White Mountains

NEW HAMPSHIRE

Portland

Lake Ontario

New ★ *York*

★ Concord

State

Barge

Canal

ATLANTIC OCEAN

Niagara Falls

Rochester

Syracuse

System

Manchester

• Lowell

Buffalo

Albany ★

Catskill Mountains

Massachusetts Bay

• Boston

Erie

Allegheny Mountains

Springfield

MASSACHUSETTS

42° N

Cape Cod

Hartford ★

Plymouth

★ Providence

A P P A L A C H I A N   M O U N T A I N S

CONNECTICUT

New Haven

RHODE ISLAND

N

OH

Scranton

Pocono Mountains

Newark

New York City

Jersey City

Long Island

W — E

70° W

68° W

S

Pittsburgh

★ Harrisburg

Susquehanna River

Trenton ★

PENNSYLVANIA

Philadelphia

Delaware River

⊛ National capital

★ State capital

◻ New England states

40° N

Wilmington

NEW JERSEY

◻ Middle Atlantic states

◻ National park

Monongahela River

Ohio River

WV

Baltimore

★ Dover

▲ Mountain peak

Washington, D.C. ⊛

★ Annapolis

DELAWARE

⊦⊦⊦⊦ Canal

Chesapeake Bay

Delaware Bay

VA

MARYLAND

38° N

74° W

72° W

Ice was an important "crop" in the Northeast. In the days before electric refrigerators, ice was used to cool food. It was cut from frozen rivers and lakes and shipped to places all over the United States. In 1890, 3 million tons were cut in the state of Maine alone.

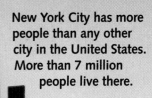

New York City has more people than any other city in the United States. More than 7 million people live there.

A RIVER RAN WILD

by LYNNE CHERRY

American Indians were the first people to live on the land that is today the Northeast region of the United States. One group, the Nashuas (NA·shuh·wuhz), lived along a river in what are now the states of New Hampshire and Massachusetts. There they used the natural resources around them to meet their needs. Read now about the Nashuas and the river named for them.

northern raven

scarlet tanager

wolf

black-capped chickadee

kingfisher

wolverine

bass

passenger pigeon

gray squirrel

muskrat

otter

flying squirrel

wren

Long ago a river ran wild through a land of towering forests. Bears, moose, and herds of deer, hawks and owls all made their homes in the peaceful river valley. Geese paused on their long migration and rested on its banks. Beavers, turtles, and schools of fish swam in its clear waters.

One day a group of native people, searching for a place to settle, came upon the river valley. From atop the highest mountain, known today as Mt. Wachusett, they saw the river nestled in its valley, a silver sliver in the sun.

They came down from the mountain, and at the river's edge they knelt to quench their thirst with its clear water. Pebbles shone up from the bottom.

"Let us settle by this river," said the chief of the native people. He named the river Nash-a-way—River with the Pebbled Bottom.

northern oriole

white-tailed deer

red fox

Canada goose

beaver

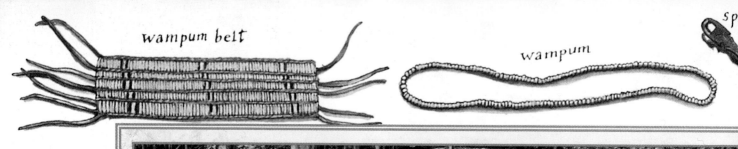
wampum belt

wampum

sp

woven baskets

zucchini

woven baskets

clay pipes

pestle

By the Nash-a-way, Chief Weeawa's people built a village. They gathered cattails from the riverbanks to thatch their dwellings. In the forest they set fires to clear brush from the forest floor. In these clearings they planted corn and squash for eating. They made arrows for hunting and canoes for river travel.

When the Indians hunted in the forest or caught salmon in the river, they killed only what they needed for themselves for food and clothing. They asked all the forest creatures that they killed to please forgive them.

The Nashua people saw a rhythm in their lives and in the seasons. The river, land, and forest provided all they needed.

mortar

arrowheads

quiver and bow

stone ax

shell hoe

stone hoe

arrow

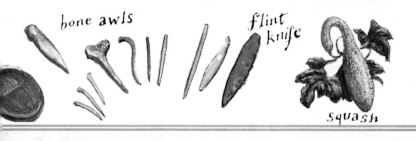

bone awls

flint knife

squash

The Nashua had lived for generations by the clear, clean, flowing river when one day a pale-skinned trader came with a boatload full of treasures. He brought shiny metal knives, colored beads, and cooking kettles, mirrors, tools, and bolts of bright cloth. His wares seemed like magic. The Nashua welcomed him, traded furs, and soon a trading post was built.

In the many years that followed, the settlers' village and others like it grew and the Nash-a-way became the Nashua. The settlers worked together to clear land by cutting down the forests, which they thought were full of danger—wilderness that they would conquer. They hunted wolves and beaver, killing much more than they needed. Extra pelts were sent to England in return for goods and money.

The settlers built sawmills along the river, which the Nashua's current powered. They built dams to make the millponds that were used to store the water. They cut down the towering forest and floated tree trunks down the river. The logs were cut up into lumber, which was used for building houses.

antler flaking tools

wooden bowl

CHAPTER 4

ALONG THE NORTHEAST COAST

> 66 City, oh, city
> of glory and grace,
> of breathtaking towers
> that soar into space,
> of bottomless canyons,
> steel, rivet, and stone;
> City, oh, city,
> how mighty you've grown. 99
>
> from the poem
> "City, Oh, City"
> by Jack Prelutsky

A construction worker in the Northeast

NEWCOMERS BRING CHANGES

LESSON 1

Link to Our World

How can the physical features of a place affect its growth?

Focus on the Main Idea
Read to find out how places along the Northeast region's coast have grown and changed over time.

Preview Vocabulary

cape
harbor
colony
port
raw material

import
export
international trade

Sailing ships were used to explore the coast of North America.

American Indians found many uses for the Northeast's natural resources. Those same resources later attracted settlers from Europe. The Europeans began to build settlements. Over time, many of those settlements grew into large cities.

EXPLORING THE COAST

In 1614 an English explorer named John Smith sailed along the northeast coast of what is now the United States. Smith saw tall, thick forests and many bays and capes. A **cape** is a point of land that reaches out into the ocean. Smith named the land New England. Today New England is made up of the states of Connecticut, Maine, Massachusetts, New Hampshire, Rhode Island, and Vermont.

John Smith told others about the land he had seen. Six years later a small boat sailed along the same coast. In the boat were about a dozen people. They were looking for a good place to build a new settlement.

One of the people in the boat, probably a man named Edward Winslow, wrote about the adventure. "The seas were grown so great that we were much troubled and in great danger. . . . Yet, by God's mercy, recovering ourselves, we had the flood with us, and struck into the harbor." A **harbor** is a place where ships can dock safely.

 What physical features are found along the New England coast?

AT HOME IN A NEW LAND

The harbor that the boat entered was Plymouth Bay, in present-day Massachusetts. After exploring the land nearby, Winslow and the others returned to the larger ship that had carried them across the Atlantic Ocean from England. They quickly gave the good news to the people waiting on board the *Mayflower*. Plymouth Bay was deep enough for ships. Better still, there was fresh water, land for farming, and trees for building homes.

The people who came on the *Mayflower* are now called Pilgrims because they made a long journey for religious reasons. In England the Pilgrims were not allowed to follow their own religion. Over time they decided to start their own colony (KAH•luh•nee) in North America. A **colony** is a settlement started by people who leave their own country to live in another land.

Life in the new colony was hard for the Pilgrims. They had little food. During the first winter, more than half of them died. The rest of the Pilgrims

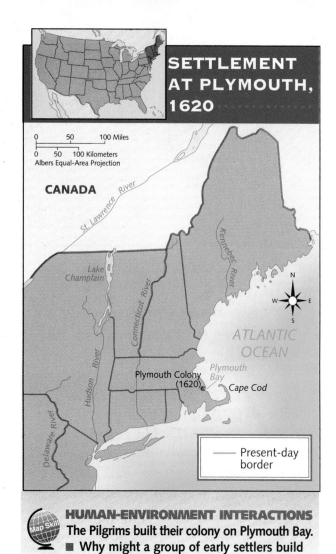

SETTLEMENT AT PLYMOUTH, 1620

0   50   100 Miles
0   50   100 Kilometers
Albers Equal-Area Projection

CANADA

St. Lawrence River

Kennebec River

Lake Champlain

Connecticut River

Hudson River

Delaware River

ATLANTIC OCEAN

Plymouth Colony (1620)

Plymouth Bay

Cape Cod

——— Present-day border

HUMAN-ENVIRONMENT INTERACTIONS
Map Skill
The Pilgrims built their colony on Plymouth Bay.
■ Why might a group of early settlers build their colony on a bay?

might not have lived through the next year if the Indians had not helped them.

Before the Pilgrims came to Plymouth Bay, an Indian named Tisquantum had been taken as a slave to Spain. He later ran away and spent several years in England before returning home. While

This wicker cradle (far left) was used by Peregrine White, a child born on the *Mayflower*. The mirror was also used on the *Mayflower*.

in England, Tisquantum, or Squanto, as the English called him, learned English. Because Squanto had learned English, he was able to teach the Pilgrims how to live in their new land. He showed them how to plant corn, catch fish, and hunt wild animals.

✓ **What resources did the Pilgrims look for when they chose a place for their colony?**

SQUANTO

Squanto helped the Pilgrims survive at Plymouth.

cities. Many cities, like Boston, became important centers of trade. Goods from all across New England were brought to Boston and traded on its docks. From Boston, ships could take goods almost anywhere.

Ships were important to colonists—the people living in colonies. After all, ships were their only link to the rest of the world. Ships brought them tools, clothing, and other manufactured goods from

CENTERS OF TRADE

Soon more people from Europe came to New England and started colonies. Like the Pilgrims, they used the region's many resources. They fished in the bays and the ocean. They trapped animals for fur. They cut down trees to build homes and ships. They built sawmills along the rivers.

As more people came to live along the New England coast, settlements grew into

By the early 1700s Boston had become a busy city. Why was Boston a good place for trade?

Where?

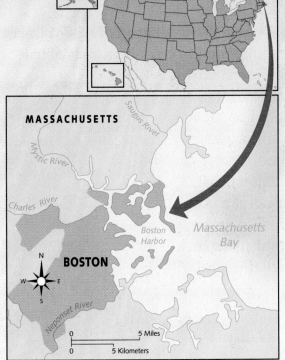

Boston, Massachusetts

Boston is New England's largest city and its leading center of trade. Boston is located on Massachusetts Bay at the mouths of the Charles and Mystic rivers.

MASSACHUSETTS
Saugus River
Mystic River
Charles River
Boston Harbor
Massachusetts Bay
BOSTON
N W E S
Neponset River
0 5 Miles
0 5 Kilometers

Europe. Those goods were then sold or traded for fish, furs, lumber, and other products from New England.

Large and busy port cities grew up all along the Northeast region's coast. A **port** is a trading center where ships are loaded and unloaded. Many ports, like New York City and Baltimore, Maryland, were built on harbors where rivers flow into the Atlantic Ocean. New York City, the busiest port in the Northeast today, was built on a harbor at the mouth of the Hudson River. Baltimore was built where the Patapsco (puh•TAP•skoh) River empties into Chesapeake (CHEH•suh•peek) Bay.

Other ports in the Northeast were built on rivers. Philadelphia, for example, was built on the Delaware River. The Delaware River flows into Delaware Bay.

 Why did many cities in the Northeast become centers of trade?

TRADING NEEDED GOODS

Do you know what a LoLo is? A LoLo is a ship built to carry hundreds of truck-size metal boxes called containers. Each container is filled with products.

After a LoLo docks at a port, workers use a crane to lift each container from

A crane lowers a container onto a waiting truck.

the ship. The containers are loaded onto trucks or trains or are stacked on the ground. When the ship is empty, it is loaded with other containers. This action explains the ship's name—Lift-on, Lift-off, or LoLo for short.

The LoLo moves goods in and out of ports. Many of the ships that sail in and out of ports in the Northeast are taking goods from one part of the United States to another. Some ships carry food. Others carry products made in factories. Still others haul raw materials. A **raw material** is a resource in its natural state, such as a mineral, that can be used to manufacture a product.

LEARNING FROM GRAPHS This graph shows the value of imports coming into different regions of the United States.
■ Which two regions get the most imports?

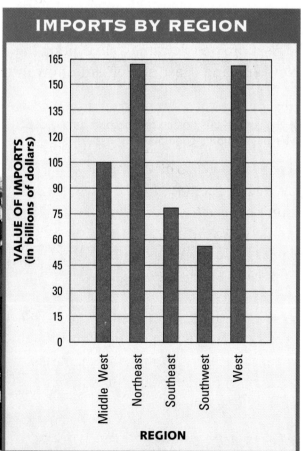

IMPORTS BY REGION

VALUE OF IMPORTS (in billions of dollars)

REGION: Middle West, Northeast, Southeast, Southwest, West

Ships like this one carry hundreds of containers to and from places around the United States and the world.

Ports also link the Northeast and other places in the United States with other countries. Each day, imports from all over the world arrive in the ports of the United States. An **import** is a good brought into one country from another country, most often to be sold.

The United States also uses its ports to send exports to other countries. An **export** is a good shipped from one country to another. Many businesses in the United States make money by selling exports to people in other countries.

Thanks to **international trade**, or trading among nations, people can buy goods their own countries cannot make or grow. Most of those goods are carried from country to country by ship. Ships can carry more goods and are cheaper to use than airplanes.

 How do ports link the United States with other countries?

LESSON 1 REVIEW

Check Understanding

1. **Recall the Facts** Why were ships important to colonists?
2. **Focus on the Main Idea** How have places along the Northeast region's coast grown and changed over time?

Think Critically

3. **Link to You** What physical features have helped your region grow?
4. **Think More About It** How might life in the United States be different without ports?

Show What You Know

Art Activity Make a poster that shows how the Northeast region's coast has changed. Divide a large piece of paper in half. On one side, draw a scene that shows how the coast might have looked when John Smith sailed there. On the other half, show how the coast might look today.

Read a Cutaway Diagram

Why Is This Skill Important?

Most people like to know how things work. To do that, sometimes they need to know what things look like on the inside. However, it is not always possible to take an object apart to see inside it. You would not want to take apart your television to see how it works.

Sometimes you may just wonder what something is like inside. Do you wonder about submarines or space shuttles? What other things have made you wonder, "What is it like inside?"

Cutaway Diagrams

There is a kind of drawing that can help you answer this question. It is called a cutaway diagram. A **cutaway diagram** shows the outside and inside of an object at the same time. The artist "cuts away" part of the drawing to make a kind of window. Looking through that window, you can see inside the object. Cutaway diagrams can let you see inside a television set, a building, or a large cargo ship.

Ships from all over the world load and unload cargo in port cities in the Northeast. Many of those ships are dry bulk cargo ships. These ships carry dry cargo, such as grain, sugar, or coal, in bulk. *Bulk* means that the cargo is carried loose in a big pile instead of in containers.

Understand the Process

The cutaway diagram on page 137 shows some of the ways a dry bulk cargo ship can be loaded and unloaded.

1. Find the cutaway "window" that shows the inside of the ship. What part of the ship is shown? Name one part of the ship that is shown on the rest of the diagram.
2. You can see that the hold, or cargo area, of a dry bulk cargo ship is divided into several parts. Each part of the hold is covered by a hatch. Why do you think the hold on this ship has more than one part?
3. Find the part of the hold labeled *A*. Here grain is being loaded using a large chute.

All cargo ships are important to trade. This dry bulk cargo ship is being loaded with grain.

A DRY BULK CARGO SHIP

Hatches

Vacuum tube

Scoop

Chute

Coal

B.

Sugar

A.

C.

Cabin

Grain

Hold

The cargo slides down the chute and into the ship's hold.

4. Now find the part of the hold labeled *B*. If the cargo is not too heavy, machines may pull it out through a large vacuum tube. The machines are like giant vacuum cleaners. What cargo is being unloaded from the ship this way?

5. Now find the part of the hold labeled *C*. Sometimes the cargo is too heavy to be unloaded using vacuum tubes. So dockworkers use power scoops or large grab buckets. The scoop or bucket reaches down

into the ship's hold, grabs some of the loose cargo, and lifts it out. Then the scoop or bucket drops the cargo into a truck or railroad car. What cargo is being unloaded from the ship by this method?

Think and Apply

Use an encyclopedia or library books to find out how some object works—perhaps a flashlight or a camera. Then draw a cutaway diagram of that object. Add labels to your diagram, and use it to explain to classmates how the object works.

A REGION OF CITIES

LESSON 2

Link to Our World

In what ways are all cities alike?

Focus on the Main Idea
Read to find out how cities in the Northeast are like cities in other parts of the United States.

Preview Vocabulary
population
urban growth
prejudice
central business district
urban sprawl
metropolitan area
megalopolis

Early cities in the Northeast were often built on harbors or along the rivers that flowed into harbors. Today much of the Northeast is crowded with cities. Each one is different, but they all share some features with cities everywhere.

INDUSTRIES AND GROWTH

Over time, cities in the Northeast grew larger both in size and in population. **Population** is the number of people who live in a place. The population of New York City grew from just 60,000 people in 1800 to more than 3 million people in 1900.

New York City's Orchard Street was a busy place when this photograph was taken in 1898. Orchard Street was part of a crowded neighborhood called the Lower East Side.

New industries were the chief reason for this **urban growth**, or the growth of cities. Old industries, such as fishing, shipbuilding, and trade, were joined by new ones. The new industries included factories, printing plants, and machine shops. Many of the new industries started in coastal cities to be near ports.

Many people moved to cities to find jobs. Some of the people came from rural areas of the United States. Others were immigrants. They came mostly from places in Europe.

✓ Why did many people move to coastal cities in the Northeast?

IMMIGRANTS CROWD INTO CITIES

Before airplanes, most immigrants came to the United States just as the Pilgrims had—on ships. Many entered the United States through Ellis Island. Ellis Island was an immigration center in New York Harbor. As they sailed into the harbor, immigrants were greeted by the Statue of Liberty. At the base of the statue is a poem, "The New Colossus," written by Emma Lazarus (LAZ•uh•ruhs). It describes how the Statue of

Liberty welcomes immigrants to America. The poem ends,

> 66Give me your tired, your poor,
> Your huddled masses yearning to breathe free,
> The wretched refuse of your teeming shore.
> Send these, the homeless, tempest-tost to me.
> I lift my lamp beside the golden door!99

Because so many immigrants settled in cities in the Northeast, the cities there grew larger and more crowded. In one neighborhood of New York City, called the Lower East Side, hundreds of thousands of people lived close together. They often had little money, so many

What?

Ellis Island

Between 1892 and 1954, more than 12 million immigrants from at least 50 countries entered the United States through Ellis Island. Today Ellis Island is part of the Statue of Liberty National Monument.

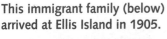

This immigrant family (below) arrived at Ellis Island in 1905.

Immigrants in New York City often lived in crowded tenements (top). Many earned their living by working in factories, like this clothing factory (above).

Pauline Newman (right) was just one of the thousands of immigrants who came to New York City.

immigrants had to live in rundown apartment buildings called tenements (TEH•nuh•muhnts). One newspaper reporter found that "two small rooms in a six-story tenement were made to hold a family of father, mother, twelve children, and six boarders." A boarder is someone who pays to live in another person's home.

Like other groups of immigrants, many Jews had come to the United States to find work. Other Jews had come to try to escape the prejudice (PREH•juh•duhs) they faced in Europe because of their religion. **Prejudice** is an unfair feeling of hatred or dislike for a group because of their background, race, or religion. In the United States, Jews could freely follow their religion.

Pauline Newman was one of the many Jewish immigrants living on the Lower East Side. Most immigrants had to work long hours for little pay. Pauline had a job in a clothing factory. "We started work at 7:30 in the morning and during the busy season we worked until 9 in the evening. . . . The employers had a sign that said: If you don't come in on Sunday, don't come in on Monday. You were expected to work every day if they needed you and the pay was the same whether you worked extra or not."

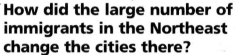

" **YOU WERE EXPECTED TO WORK EVERY DAY** *if they needed you. . . .* "

Pauline Newman

✓ **How did the large number of immigrants in the Northeast change the cities there?**

LIVING IN CITIES

Like New York, most cities across the United States have grown larger and more crowded over time. Cities have grown so much that today more than three-fourths of all Americans live in or near them. In the Northeast about nine out of every ten people live in or near cities.

Why do so many people choose to live in or near cities? Most people live there because of their jobs. In cities workers can get many kinds of jobs—both in manufacturing and in services. In the Northeast, New York City is a leading center for banking. More than 40 insurance companies are based in Hartford, Connecticut. There are more than 20 colleges and universities in and around Boston.

Cities are exciting places. They also offer many services to the people who live in or near them. For example, large hospitals can give special care when people are hurt or sick. Because most cities have many ethnic groups, people can enjoy different kinds of foods, dance, and music. They can visit the city's theaters and go to see sports teams play.

✓ **What kinds of things do cities offer the people who live in or near them?**

CITIES CHANGE

Cities in the Northeast, like cities everywhere, have grown in much the same way. The **central business district**, or downtown area, is in the center of a city. The central business district is often the oldest part of a city. It covers a small area but is very crowded. Buildings there are often close together.

In the past, the central business district was where almost everything in a city happened. Cars, trucks, and highways have changed that, however. Today many businesses are found in the outer parts of cities or in nearby suburbs. Shopping malls, movie theaters, and restaurants are

Large hospitals often have special equipment that can help doctors understand what is wrong with their patients.

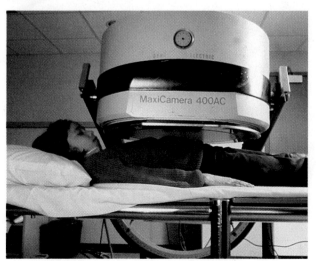

More people live in New York City than in any other city in the United States.

found there, too. Over time, more and more land around cities has been used for new buildings and highways. This spreading of urban areas and the growth of new centers of business and shopping is called **urban sprawl**.

 How are cities today different from cities of the past?

CITIES CONNECT

Nearly every large city has smaller cities and suburbs around it. These places around a large city are part of its metropolitan (meh•truh•PAH•luh•tuhn) area. A **metropolitan area** is a large city together with its suburbs.

A metropolitan area often stretches over state borders. New York City is in the state of New York, but it is close to Connecticut and New Jersey. People often call the area around New York City the Tri-State Region. *Tri-* means "three."

People who live in suburbs in New Jersey and Connecticut often feel like New Yorkers. Many of them work in New York City. They cheer for the city's sports teams. But people who live in New York City also depend on neighboring states. One of the three airports serving New York City is in Newark, New Jersey!

Trains help link people living in different cities in the Northeast. An engineer (right) operates this train from his seat at the front of the train.

New York City is at the center of the area that has the most people in the United States. Years ago there was empty land between New York City and other cities along the coast. Today those cities almost run into one another. In fact, it is sometimes hard to tell where one city ends and the next one begins. The rural areas near the cities are building up, too.

A long, wide string of cities already stretches more than 500 miles (800 km) from southern Maine to northern Virginia. Some of those cities are Boston, New York City, Philadelphia, Baltimore, and Washington, D.C. Together, they make up the largest megalopolis (meh•guh•LAH•puh•luhs) in the United States. A **megalopolis** is a huge urban region formed when two or more metropolitan areas grow together. The word *megalopolis* means "great city."

Today's transportation makes it quick and easy to get from place to place in the Northeast. Highways connect all the cities. Trains travel between Boston and Washington, D.C. Airlines also offer many short flights each day between major cities.

 **What is a megalopolis?**

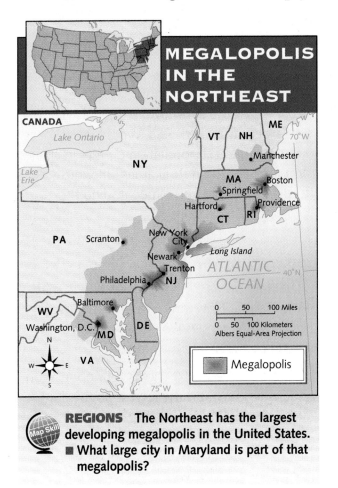

REGIONS The Northeast has the largest developing megalopolis in the United States. ■ What large city in Maryland is part of that megalopolis?

LSSON 2 REVIEW

Check Understanding

1. **Recall the Facts** How has urban sprawl changed cities?
2. **Focus on the Main Idea** How are cities in the Northeast like cities in other parts of the United States?

Think Critically

3. **Cause and Effect** How might urban sprawl affect the wildlife in an area?
4. **Link to You** Think about your city or one close to you. Are its businesses all in a central business district, or are there businesses in suburbs and in other areas as well?

Show What You Know

Map Activity On a sheet of paper, draw or trace a map of the Northeast region's coast. Mark and label all the cities named in this lesson. Label large bodies of water, too. Then use your map to explain to classmates why the Northeast is sometimes called a region of cities.

Use a Population Map

Why Is This Skill Important?

You may live in a large city, a suburb, or a small town, or you may live in a rural area where there are not many people. Each kind of place has a different population density (DEN•suh•tee). **Population density** tells how many people live in an area of a certain size. The size is usually 1 square mile or 1 square kilometer. A square mile is a square piece of land. Each of its four sides is 1 mile long. A square kilometer is a square piece of land with sides that are each 1 kilometer long.

The population density of your area may affect the way you live. Suppose that three people live on each square mile of land where you live. Your area would have a population density of three people per square mile. With only three people per square mile, there would be few people and lots of space around you. Now suppose that 10,000 people live on each square mile. With 10,000 people per square mile, the place would be very crowded.

Like resources, population is not spread evenly across the Earth. More people live in some places than in others. Would you expect to find the highest population density in cities, in small towns, or in rural areas? In which of those areas would you expect to find the lowest population density?

Understand the Process

The map on page 145 is a population map of the state of New York. A population map shows where people live. It also shows the population density of each place.

1. Find the map key. It shows four population densities. What is the lowest population density shown on the map? How is it marked on the map?

In cities many people are crowded together.

Few people live in the rural areas of Vermont.

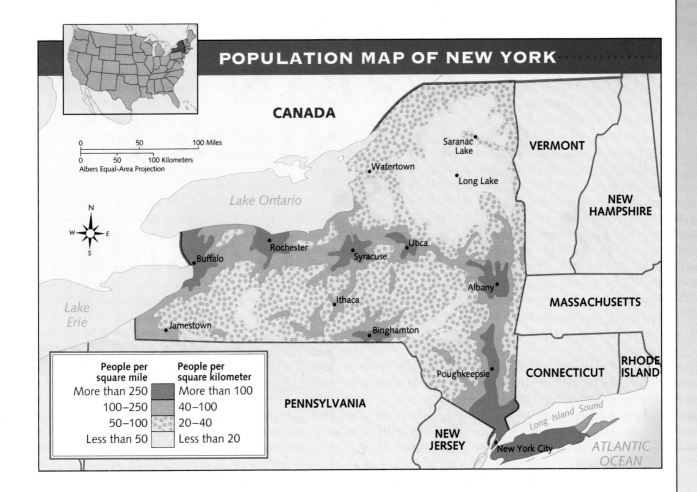

POPULATION MAP OF NEW YORK

2. Look at the map key again. What is the highest population density shown on the map? How is it marked on the map?

3. Find the city of Albany on the map. Albany, like New York's other large cities, has a population density of more than 250 people per square mile. Some of New York's cities, however, have much higher population densities. The population density of New York City is more than 20,000 people per square mile. How do you think such a high population density affects the lives of people living in New York City?

4. Now find the city of Jamestown. What is its population density?

5. A band of land with a population density of more than 100 people per square mile runs through the state of New York. Find the band on the map. It begins in western New York, along Lake Erie. Near what large coastal city does it end?

6. Notice that this map uses both colors and patterns to show population densities. Find the city of Watertown. What is its population density?

7. What part of New York has a very large area of land with the state's lowest population density?

Think and Apply

In an encyclopedia or an atlas, find a population map of your state. What is the population density where you live? In which parts of your state is the population density the highest? In which parts is it the lowest? In which areas of your state might you expect to find most large industries? Share your findings with family members.

URBAN CONVENIENCE OR RURAL CHARM?

Hamden, Connecticut, was once a little town near the city of New Haven, Connecticut. New Haven was on the edge of the New York City metropolitan area. Over time both New York City and New Haven grew larger. More and more people who worked in those cities moved to Hamden, so Hamden grew larger, too.

A building company told the people of Hamden that it wanted to build a new shopping center in their town. The plan was to build a 100-store mall. The company pointed out that the mall would bring a lot of money and new businesses to Hamden. That would mean more jobs for the people who lived nearby.

Some townspeople liked the idea, but others were against it. They were afraid that Hamden would be spoiled. They argued that a mall would bring too many cars into town. A mall might bring crime to the town, too. The new buildings and roads might even harm the environment.

CONNECTICUT

0   15   30 Miles
0   15   30 Kilometers
Albers Equal-Area Projection

N
W   E
S

MASSACHUSETTS

NEW YORK

★ Hartford

CONNECTICUT

Connecticut River

Hamden
New Haven

Bridgeport

RHODE ISLAND

Long Island Sound

New York City

NEW YORK

ATLANTIC OCEAN

LOCATION Hamden, Connecticut, is located near the city of New Haven.
■ About how far away is Hamden from New York City?

The problem Hamden faced was like the problems faced by other small towns in growing metropolitan areas. Long-time citizens often want to keep their town small and rural. They do not want to see new businesses, shopping malls, and housing developments built near them. Other citizens, however, feel that development would help their town's economy and make life there easier.

Writing letters to newspapers is one way that citizens can give their viewpoints. Many people in Hamden wrote such letters about the mall.

One person wrote, "People are concerned about the number of new cars on Hamden's streets, over 20,000 projected and between 30,000 and 40,000 cars a day coming to the Mall during the Christmas shopping season!"

A second person wrote, "I'd love to see Hamden build up with beauty like a pretty mall. We have nothing in Hamden. It's a ghost town. I go to the Connecticut Post [Mall]. I don't like driving there. It's too far. With the new mall maybe I can get a job."

A third person wrote, "I am in favor of the mall but would prefer it to be a smaller size than currently proposed."

The people of Hamden decided that a shopping center could be built. However, it would be much smaller than the mall that was first planned.

COMPARE
VIEWPOINTS

1. What viewpoint about the mall does the first writer hold? How do you know?
2. What viewpoint about the mall does the second writer hold? How do you know?
3. How is the viewpoint given by the third person different from the viewpoints given by the first two writers?

THINK
–AND–
APPLY

Find a letter to the editor in your newspaper. Cut out the letter, and tape it to a piece of paper. Then write a paragraph explaining the problem the letter is about and giving the writer's viewpoint.

BUILDING CITIZENSHIP

A large grocery store is one of several stores being built in Hamden's new shopping center.

CITIES FACE CHALLENGES

LESSON 3

*L**nk to Our World*

How do people work together to solve the problems they face?

Focus on the Main Idea
Read to find out about some of the many problems people in cities face today.

Preview Vocabulary
unemployment

Modern skyscrapers tower above historic Faneuil Hall in downtown Boston, Massachusetts.

People often choose to live in or near cities because of their work. They may also enjoy the things that cities offer. Yet cities present people with problems. People must learn how to live with those problems, or they must take action to solve them.

THE PROBLEMS OF CROWDING

The Northeast region's coast is crowded. More than 7 million people live in New York City, the largest city in the United States. About 12 million more people live in its metropolitan area. Millions more live in the busy metropolitan areas around Boston, Philadelphia, Baltimore, and Washington, D.C.

Most cities along the Northeast's coast are not very large in area. They are also closer to each other than cities in other parts of the country. Having so many people living in such a small area makes many urban problems worse.

Traffic is a big problem for cities in the Northeast. Many cities there are among the oldest in the United States. In cities like Boston, New York, and Philadelphia, skyscrapers rise next to buildings that are hundreds of

What?

Electric Cars and Trucks

To help reduce air pollution in busy cities, manufacturers are developing cars and trucks that can run on electric batteries instead of on gasoline. Such cars and trucks do not pollute the air. They are also quiet. They do not add to the noise in cities.

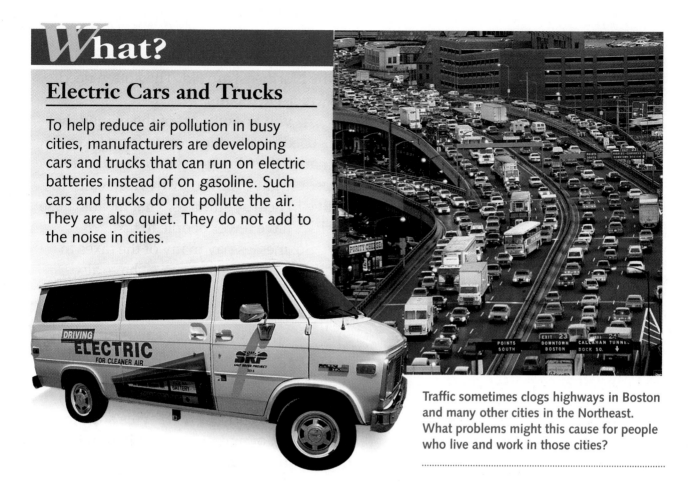

DRIVING **ELECTRIC** FOR CLEANER AIR

Traffic sometimes clogs highways in Boston and many other cities in the Northeast. What problems might this cause for people who live and work in those cities?

years old. The streets of these cities are often narrow. After all, they were built long ago for horses and carriages! They were never meant to handle the large numbers of cars and trucks that use them now.

When people are going to work or going home, traffic on city streets and highways becomes so bad that often cars, trucks, and buses cannot move. Horns honk and tempers rise.

Crowding makes pollution worse, too. The fumes from so many cars and trucks, along with smoke from homes and factories, pollutes the air. Sometimes the air becomes hazy and smells bad. Breathing such air is bad for people's health.

People in cities also throw away huge amounts of trash—paper, plastic, cans, and bottles. In fact, each person in the United States produces a little more than 4 pounds (almost 2 kg) of trash each day.

LEARNING FROM TABLES This table gives information about the five largest cities in the United States.

■ In what state is the second-largest city found?

LARGEST CITIES IN THE UNITED STATES

CITY	STATE	POPULATION*
New York	New York	7,311,966
Los Angeles	California	3,489,779
Chicago	Illinois	2,768,483
Houston	Texas	1,690,180
Philadelphia	Pennsylvania	1,552,572

*The most recent figures available

Dirty water from city streets and factories can pollute nearby rivers and harbors.

All this trash must be removed by city workers. If the trash were left on city streets, insects and rats would get into it. They could carry diseases to people.

People sometimes dump waste products from ships and factories into rivers and harbors near cities. Dirty water from city streets also runs into rivers and harbors. Laws now make people get rid of wastes in more healthful ways. Still, the water in many rivers and harbors is not clean.

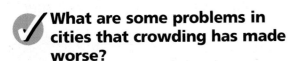 **What are some problems in cities that crowding has made worse?**

MONEY PROBLEMS

City governments provide many services to their citizens, such as police, schools, hospitals, and transportation. But city governments do not always have all the money that they need. The cost of running a large city is high. Water pipes, sewers, roads, and bridges in the cities of the Northeast are old. They often need expensive repairs.

As you know, most of the money that is used to run cities comes from taxes. In many cities, however, more and more people have moved away from cities to live in nearby suburbs. That means those cities have fewer people to tax.

Businesses pay many of the taxes in cities, but some businesses have also moved away from cities in the Northeast. They have moved to places outside the cities or to other states. These cities now have even less tax money to spend on services.

When a business leaves a city, jobs are lost along with the taxes. This adds to the problem of unemployment in the city. **Unemployment** is being without a job. It is hard for people without jobs to pay for good housing, to buy food, or to meet their other needs.

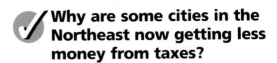 **Why are some cities in the Northeast now getting less money from taxes?**

WORKING TO SOLVE PROBLEMS

Poverty, crime, drugs, and violence are also problems in many cities and towns across the United States. One man who is working on a problem in his city is Emanuel (ee•MAN•yoo•uhl) Freeman.

Mr. Freeman grew up in Philadelphia, in a neighborhood called Germantown. He studied engineering and building in school and as a U.S. Marine. After Mr. Freeman got out of the Marines, he went back to his old neighborhood.

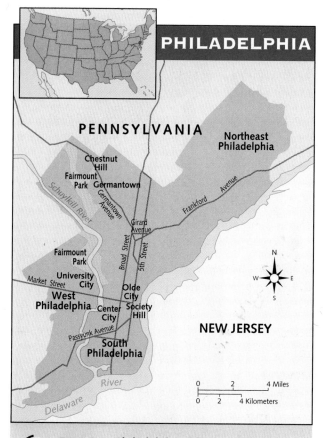

PHILADELPHIA

PENNSYLVANIA

Northeast Philadelphia

Chestnut Hill

Fairmount Park

Germantown

Germantown Avenue

Schuylkill River

Frankford Avenue

Girard Avenue

Broad Street

5th Street

Fairmount Park

University City

Market Street

West Philadelphia

Olde City

Center City

Society Hill

Passyunk Avenue

South Philadelphia

NEW JERSEY

Delaware River

0 2 4 Miles
0 2 4 Kilometers

N W E S

PLACE Philadelphia, like most cities, has several neighborhoods.
■ In what part of Philadelphia is the Germantown neighborhood located?

low-cost housing. He helped change the company so that people in Germantown could say what kind of housing they would like built and where. In 1989 he became the company's president.

Mr. Freeman's company buys old, rundown houses in Germantown and then repairs them. That helps make Germantown a better place to live. The company also bought an old factory and turned it into low-cost apartments for older people.

Mr. Freeman's company helps provide houses that people in Germantown can afford. It helps people learn how to become home owners. It also helps the people who will live in the houses find the jobs they need to pay for them.

Because of Emanuel Freeman's work, many families have been able to buy their own homes for the first time. Has Mr. Freeman been successful in making his

Mr. Freeman saw that there was a problem in his neighborhood. Many buildings there were run down. People were not taking care of the neighborhood.

Mr. Freeman first thought about the problem. Then he thought about different ways to solve it. Mr. Freeman knew that many people in Germantown could not afford to buy their own homes. So he decided that helping people buy their own homes was one of the best ways he could help his neighborhood.

In 1972 Mr. Freeman went to work for a company in Germantown that built

Emanuel Freeman became president of the Greater Germantown Housing Development Corporation in 1989.

neighborhood a better place to live? Mr. Freeman says, "Success is measured in part by the change in attitude people have to themselves and their neighborhood.... New development stimulates a sense of community pride."

✔ **How does Mr. Freeman's company help make Germantown a better place to live?**

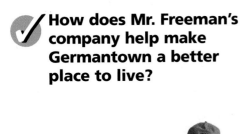

These rundown buildings (above) are being repaired so that people can live in them. It takes many skilled workers (left) to make such repairs.

LESSON 3 REVIEW

Check Understanding

1. **Recall the Facts**   What is the definition of unemployment?
2. **Focus on the Main Idea**   What are some of the problems people in cities face today?

Think Critically

3. **Personally Speaking**   Would you rather live in a city or someplace else? Give reasons for your choice.

4. **Link to You**   What are some problems where you live? How are people working to solve them?

Show What You Know

Art Activity   Choose a problem that cities face today. Think about how people add to that problem and what they might do about it. Then make a poster to get people to work on the problem.

How To

Solve a Problem

Why Is This Skill Important?

Think about some problem that you faced recently. Perhaps you had trouble making good grades in one of your classes at school. Perhaps you had trouble learning how to do something. Or perhaps you had trouble getting along with a brother or sister at home. How did you know you had a problem? Were you able to solve it? Did you wish you could have found a better way to solve the problem?

People everywhere have problems at some time. Learning how to recognize and solve problems is an important skill. Sometimes people can solve their own problems, but sometimes they need a little help from other people.

Remember What You Have Read

In the last lesson you read about a man named Emanuel Freeman. You learned that Mr. Freeman grew up in the part of Philadelphia called Germantown. After Mr. Freeman got out of the Marine Corps, he returned to his old neighborhood. But he looked at it with fresh eyes. Think again about the problem Mr. Freeman saw in his neighborhood and how he went about solving it.

1. What problem did Mr. Freeman see in his neighborhood?
2. Mr. Freeman thought about different solutions, or ways to solve the problem. What did he decide was one of the best ways he could help?
3. What did Mr. Freeman do to carry out his solution to the problem?
4. What does Mr. Freeman's company do to help people?
5. How has Mr. Freeman's solution helped solve Germantown's problem?

Understand the Process

You can use similar steps to help you recognize and solve problems.

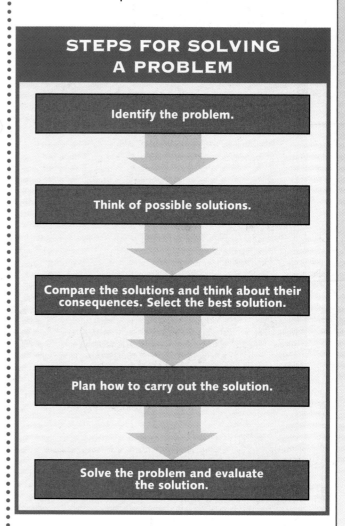

STEPS FOR SOLVING A PROBLEM

Identify the problem.

Think of possible solutions.

Compare the solutions and think about their consequences. Select the best solution.

Plan how to carry out the solution.

Solve the problem and evaluate the solution.

Think and Apply

Look around your school or your neighborhood. What problems do you see? Which one seems the most important to you? Use the steps in the flow chart above to think of ways to solve that problem. Share your solution with classmates, and consider their suggestions.

CONNECT MAIN IDEAS

Use this organizer to show that you understand how the chapter's main ideas are connected. First copy the organizer onto a separate sheet of paper. Then complete it by writing three examples for each main idea.

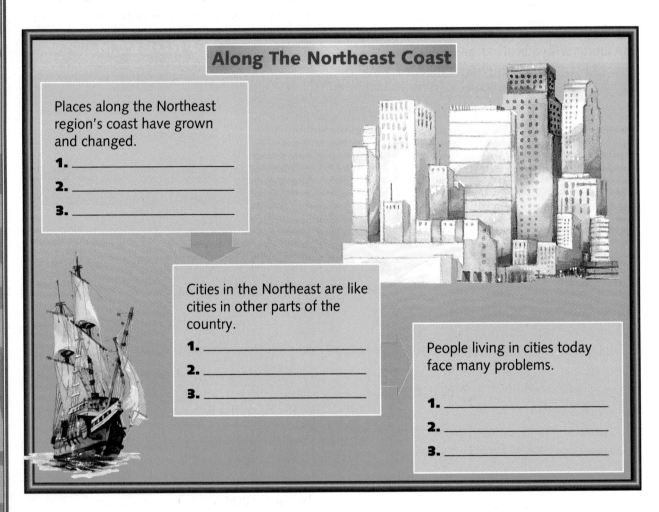

Along The Northeast Coast

Places along the Northeast region's coast have grown and changed.

1. _____
2. _____
3. _____

Cities in the Northeast are like cities in other parts of the country.

1. _____
2. _____
3. _____

People living in cities today face many problems.

1. _____
2. _____
3. _____

WRITE MORE ABOUT IT

1. **Express a Viewpoint** Imagine that you are an American Indian living in the Northeast when European settlers are building colonies there. Describe the changes that you see taking place, and explain how your life is changing. What do you think about those changes?

2. **Write a Report** Ellis Island is now a museum that tells about immigration. Look in the library for information about the changes that have taken place there. Then write a short report that describes how Ellis Island has changed and how it has stayed the same.

USE VOCABULARY

For each group of terms, write a sentence or two explaining how the terms are related.

1. cape, harbor, port

2. import, export

3. population, urban growth

4. central business district, urban sprawl

5. metropolitan area, megalopolis

CHECK UNDERSTANDING

1. Which explorer named New England? What physical features did he see along the coast?

2. Why did the Pilgrims start their own colony in North America?

3. What is a raw material?

4. How are ports important to international trade?

5. What caused cities in the Northeast to grow?

6. How have cars and highways helped change American cities?

7. What can happen when many businesses move away from a city?

THINK CRITICALLY

1. **Explore Viewpoints** Why do you think some people want to live in cities, while others prefer to live in the country or in small towns?

2. **Think More About It** Has urban growth made life in the United States better or worse? Are there both good and bad changes when cities grow larger?

3. **Personally Speaking** What would you like to do to make life better for the people in your city or town? Why?

APPLY SKILLS

How to Read a Cutaway Diagram
Draw a cutaway diagram that shows your classroom inside your school or a room inside your home. Add labels to your diagram.

How to Use a Population Map
Use the population map on page 145 to answer these questions.

1. What is the population density near the town of Long Lake?

2. Is the population density greater along the eastern shore of Lake Ontario or near the city of Binghamton?

How to Solve a Problem Think of a problem that you have. Then list the steps that you might follow to solve that problem.

READ MORE ABOUT IT

City Trains by Roger Yepsen. Macmillan. This fast-moving book looks at many kinds of city trains, from the first horse-drawn railcars to high-speed maglev trains.

Giants in the Land by Diana Appelbaum. Houghton Mifflin. This book tells the story of the great forests that once covered all of New England.

My Island Grandmother by Kathryn Lasky. Morrow Junior Books. Abbey spends a great summer with her grandmother, delighting in life on an island off the coast of Maine.

Town Life by Philip Parker. Thomson Learning. This interesting book investigates cities and the problems people who live in them face.

USING LAND AND WATER

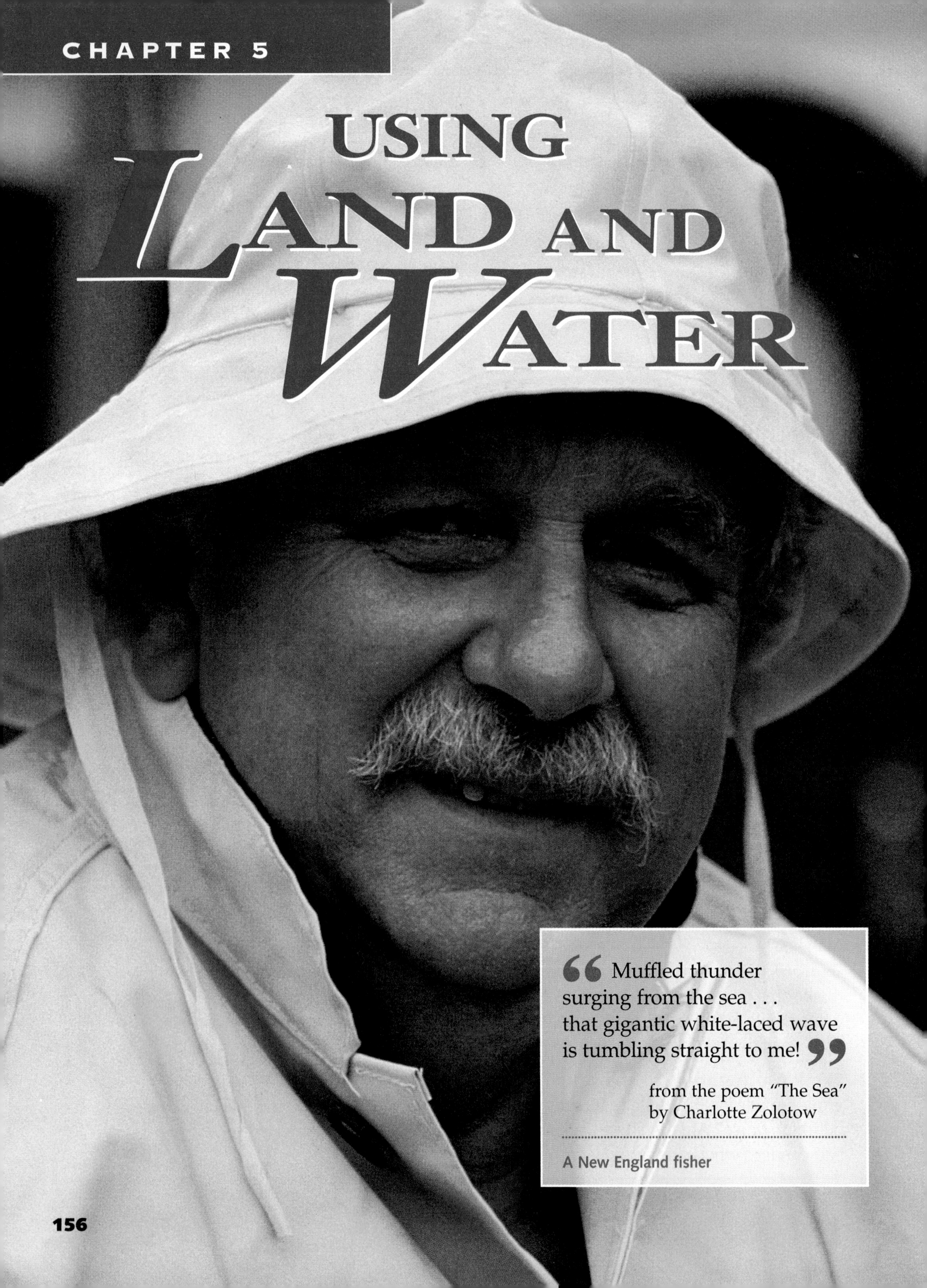

> 66 Muffled thunder surging from the sea . . . that gigantic white-laced wave is tumbling straight to me! 99
>
> from the poem "The Sea" by Charlotte Zolotow

A New England fisher

156

THE NEW ENGLAND COUNTRYSIDE

How does the geography of a region affect the way people live?

Focus on the Main Idea
Read to find out how landforms and natural resources affect how people in New England live.

Preview Vocabulary
**glacier
quarry
tradition**

A New England stone wall

Most people in New England live in busy metropolitan areas near the Atlantic coast. Yet New England is also known for its quiet countryside. People come from far away to visit New England's small towns, to enjoy its colorful autumn leaves, or to ski down its snowy mountainsides.

THE LAND

Inland from the Atlantic coast, New England is a region of broad valleys and rolling hills. Several low mountain ranges stretch across the region. They are part of the Appalachian Mountains.

The Green Mountains of Vermont form New England's western boundary. To the east, in Maine and New Hampshire, lie the White Mountains. The Connecticut River flows between those mountain ranges.

Thousands of years ago the Earth's climate turned very cold. Glaciers (GLAY•sherz) covered much of the land. A **glacier** is a huge, slow-moving mass of ice. As the glaciers moved across the land, they wore down mountains and carried away fertile soil.

After the glaciers had melted, many places in New England were left with poor, rocky soil. The soil was so rocky that early settlers had to clear away the stones before they could farm the land. They often used the stones to build walls around their fields. Today New England is famous for its stone walls. "Stone Wall," a poem by Ann Turner, tells about them.

> **"**A line across the field,
> a mound of rising snow,
> a hiding place of nuts,
> and chipmunk in his hole.
> Built with horse and arm,
> to keep the cows from harm,
> and now it keeps the field locked tight
> and me inside its bounds.**"**

✓ **What kind of soil covers much of New England?**

At harvesttime cranberry fields (above) are flooded and the berries are knocked off the vines. The berries float on the water, and workers collect them. To the right is an old wooden cranberry scoop.

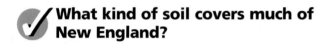

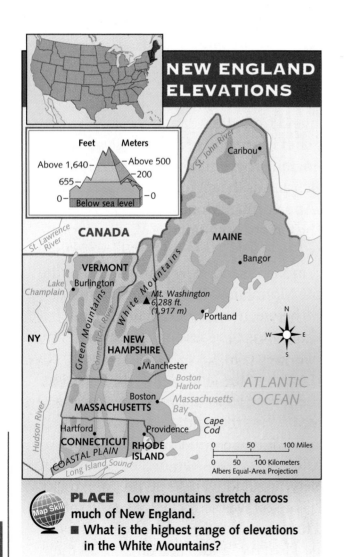

NEW ENGLAND ELEVATIONS

Feet — Meters
Above 1,640 — Above 500
655 — 200
0 — 0
Below sea level

St. John River
Caribou
CANADA
St. Lawrence River
MAINE
Bangor
VERMONT
Lake Champlain
Burlington
White Mountains
Green Mountains
Connecticut River
Mt. Washington
6,288 ft. (1,917 m)
Portland
NY
NEW HAMPSHIRE
Manchester
Boston Harbor
ATLANTIC OCEAN
Hudson River
Boston
Massachusetts Bay
MASSACHUSETTS
Cape Cod
Hartford
Providence
CONNECTICUT
RHODE ISLAND
COASTAL PLAIN
Long Island Sound

0   50   100 Miles
0 50 100 Kilometers
Albers Equal-Area Projection

PLACE Low mountains stretch across much of New England.
■ What is the highest range of elevations in the White Mountains?

NEW ENGLAND FARMS

Many crops do not grow well in New England's poor, rocky soil and cool climate. However, agriculture is important in every New England state. New England farmers simply raise the crops and animals that do well there.

Does your family eat cranberries at Thanksgiving? The cranberries may have come from Massachusetts, the leading cranberry grower. Maine is famous for its potatoes. Other leading crops grown in New England are blueberries, apples, corn, and oats.

Pasture grasses also grow well in New England's cool climate. Many farmers raise dairy cattle on those thick, green grasses. Their farms are just a short drive from the large cities along the coast, where a lot of milk, butter, and cheese is sold.

✓ **Why do New England farmers raise only certain crops?**

OTHER RESOURCES

New England farmers have learned how to farm well even with their poor, rocky soil. Some New Englanders, however, make their living from rocks.

Both New Hampshire and Vermont have a lot of marble, granite, and other kinds of stone used in buildings. In fact, Vermont has the largest granite quarries (KWAWR•eez) in the nation. A **quarry** is a large open pit cut into the ground to mine stone. Blocks of stone are cut from the sides of the quarry.

Other people make their living from the forests that cover much of New England. Logging has always been Maine's biggest industry. Wood cut from the state's many forests is used to make everything from lumber to paper products to toothpicks. Logging is an important industry in New Hampshire and Vermont, too.

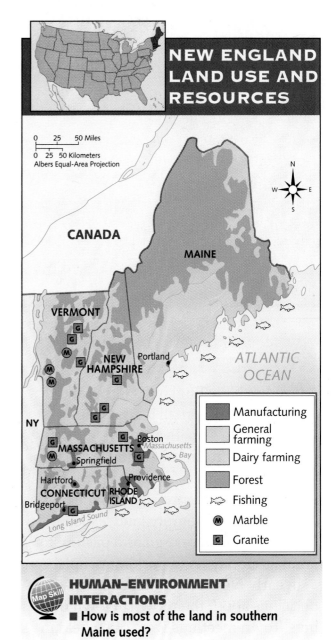

The granite from this quarry will be cut and polished before it is used. Granite is a hard stone that lasts for many years.

HUMAN–ENVIRONMENT INTERACTIONS

■ How is most of the land in southern Maine used?

Another industry in New England also uses trees. Each spring farmers and other workers take sap from sugar maple trees. Sap is the liquid that runs through the stems and roots of trees. The sap is boiled until most of the liquid is gone. What is left is sweet maple syrup—the kind that people put on pancakes. It takes more than 30 gallons (114 L) of sap to make 1 gallon (about 4 L) of syrup!

✓ **Besides farming the land, how else do people use resources?**

NEW ENGLAND TOWNS

Among New England's farms and forests are many small towns. These towns, and the smaller villages around them, are often laid out in much the same way. Houses, stores, and other buildings are built around empty land in the center of the town. This empty land, called the common, was once used as a pasture for animals. Today it is a park for people.

In early New England, people made decisions about their town at town meetings. Town meetings were often held in a church, called a meetinghouse, which stood at one end of the common.

In Craftsbury, Vermont, and in many other New England towns, the tradition of holding town meetings goes on. A **tradition** is a way or an idea that has been handed down from the past. Important decisions in Craftsbury are still made at a town meeting held every March. The meeting, which is now held at a school, is open to all the town's citizens. Between 100 and 250 people usually attend.

 How do many New England towns make decisions?

Many New England towns and villages are built around a large common. Craftsbury Common (above), in Vermont, is a popular place to visit, especially in the fall, when leaves turn bright colors.

 **L**ESSON 1 REVIEW

Check Understanding

1. **Recall the Facts**   What are some crops that grow well in New England's poor soil and cool climate?
2. **Focus on the Main Idea**   How do landforms and natural resources affect the way people in New England live?

Think Critically

3. **Cause and Effect**   How have glaciers affected the land in New England?
4. **Personally Speaking**   What would you like most about a vacation in New England? Explain.

Show What You Know

Map Activity   Draw a map showing what a typical New England town or village might look like. Show the common, meetinghouse, homes, stores, and other buildings. Add a map key to your map.

Tell Fact from Opinion

Why Is This Skill Important?

Each day you get information from many sources, such as books, television, newspapers, and other people. Whenever you get information, you must decide whether or not it is true. You must ask yourself if it can be trusted.

One thing that can help you do that is learning how to tell fact from opinion. A **fact** is a statement that can be checked and proved to be true. An **opinion** is a statement that tells what a person thinks or believes. It cannot be proved.

Understand the Process

Snow falls in New England during the winter. This sentence states a fact. You could prove that fact true by visiting New England in the winter, by looking in books, or by talking to weather forecasters.

To tell whether a statement is a fact, ask yourself these questions. If one or more of your answers is yes, the statement is probably a fact.

- Do I know this idea to be true from my own experience?
- Can the idea be proved true by testing?
- Is the idea from a book or another source I can trust?

I think winter is the most beautiful time of the year in New England. This sentence gives someone's opinion. There is no way to prove what is the most beautiful time

of the year in New England. A person who likes cold weather and snow may think New England is beautiful in the winter, but another person might like the summer more.

An opinion tells what a speaker or writer believes. Looking for these clues can help you know when a statement is an opinion.

- Certain key words, such as *I think, I believe, in my opinion,* and *I doubt* tell you that someone is about to give an opinion.
- Words such as *beautiful, wonderful, terrific,* and *terrible* are often part of an opinion.
- Because no one can know the future, any statement about the future is an opinion.
- Sayings, old or new, also give opinions. *My grandmother says you can never go to school too often because education helps make a good life.*

Opinions cannot be proved, but they can still be important. An opinion may be based on facts or experience. Thoughtful opinions can help people better understand the past or prepare for the future.

Think and Apply

A newspaper is a good place to find facts and opinions. Look through several newspapers. Find at least five statements of fact and five statements of opinion. Use a crayon or marker of one color to underline each fact, and use another color to underline each opinion.

BUILDING CITIZENSHIP

LESSON
2
LEARN
with
LITERATURE
Focus on Natural
Resources

by Brenda Z. Guiberson
illustrated by Megan Lloyd

Lobster Boat

The rich fishing places that lie off the coast of New England brought many of the first Europeans to North America. Fishing is still an important industry in New England and in other coastal areas of the Northeast. The fishing industry provides not only food, but also jobs for thousands of workers. Workers are needed to pull the catch from the water and to unload the boats at the docks. Other workers get the catch ready for market and take it to supermarkets and restaurants around the country.

Read now about one worker, Russ, and his nephew, Tommy, who work on a lobster boat named the *Nellie Jean*. As you read, think about why fishing is an important industry in the Northeast.

Soon the fog burns off and the bright blue-green of the ocean glistens in the sunlight. *Scree! Scree!* More sea gulls follow the *Nellie Jean* with noisy chatter. Russ lines up the boat with a distant white cliff to keep her headed in the right direction. "Uncle Russ!" Tommy shouts loud into the wind. "Are we going to move the traps out into deeper water?" Russ shakes his head. "Not yet. Most of the lobsters seem to be moving across the gravel bottom, right by the traps we put in last week."

Russ squints across the bright ocean as he guides the boat. Soon they pass a group of painted buoys that are tied to lobster traps under the sea. The red-and-white ones belong to the Jensen brothers. Old Sam paints his buoys with orange stripes. Tommy grins when he sees the ones painted yellow on top and red on the bottom. Everyone knows that these belong to the lobster crew of the *Nellie Jean*. Throttle back, out of gear. Russ nudges the boat alongside their closest buoy.

Tommy reaches out to hook the rope coming from the buoy. Russ slings it

buoys (BOO•eez) floating objects used to mark places in the water

around the automatic winch and turns on the switch. *Wirrrrr.* The winch grinds and groans, slowly pulling up a lobster trap that has been sitting on the gravel bottom one hundred feet below the sea. The dripping rope brings water, seaweed, and a tiny crab into the boat. *Scree! Scree!* Sea gulls come so close that Tommy feels a wing flap against his shoulder.

When the trap reaches the surface of the water, Tommy pulls it to the railing of the *Nellie Jean*. The trap is covered with furry sea growth and is slippery in his hands. *Click, click.* Reddish-black lobster claws reach out through the wires and a pair of lobster

antennas twitch in the salty sea air. "Looks like we got ourselves a big one," says Russ.

Tommy opens the back door of the trap and carefully grabs the lobster from behind. *Click, click* go the crusher and ripper claws. *Click! Clack-click!*

"Look at this female," says Tommy. "Loaded with eggs." Russ shows Tommy where to make a notch in her tail. "No one will keep her now," he says, "even when she isn't carrying eggs." Tommy puts the lobster back into the sea, where she will protect her eggs for months and months until they are ready to hatch.

Tommy reaches in for another lobster. "Too small," says Russ. *Click, click. Sssplash.* Another lobster goes back into the sea. Tommy takes out the last one. "Better measure it," says Russ. Tommy fits a brass gauge between the eye sockets and the end of the body shell. The lobster is three-and-a-half inches long and big enough to keep. Russ slips a thick rubber band over each claw. The lobster squirms and wiggles, but the claws do not open. This lobster goes into a bucket of seawater.

Tommy takes the old bait from the trap and throws it into the air. *Scree! Scree! Screeee!* Finally the noisy sea gulls get their breakfast. They swoop down and catch some of the soggy fish before it hits the water. Tommy uses the baiting iron to load new fish frames onto the bait string in the trap. "I'll check the depth finder," says Russ. "I don't want to drift away from that gravel bottom where all the lobsters seem to be traveling."

Russ watches the gauge and pulls hard on the steering wheel to make a

sharp turn. When he nods his head, Tommy pushes the freshly baited trap overboard.

The lobstermen move on from trap to trap. They work quickly and check twenty, then fifty, then more than a hundred traps. The buckets fill up with lobsters and sea gulls fill up with old bait. They find two traps that are damaged and replace them with new ones.

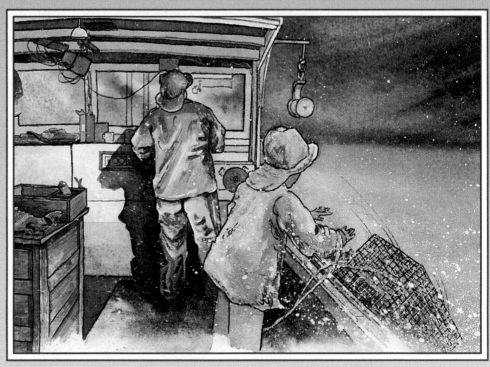

As the warm, sunny day turns blustery, Russ keeps a watchful eye on the darkening sky to the south.

On the way to another trap, Russ gets a call on the radio. "New weather report," says old Sam, who is fishing nearby. "That squall has changed its mind and is headed right this way." Tommy looks over to see the dark clouds moving in fast. Both of them pull on yellow slickers and long oil-cloth hats. Throttle full ahead, they start back to the harbor.

The United States, like most countries that border the sea, claims ownership over all fishing within about 230 miles (370 km) of its coast. To help conserve fish resources, there are laws about how many fish may be caught each year. Other laws tell which kinds of fish can be caught and the sizes they must be. Yet overfishing, along with increased pollution, is harming the future of the fishing industry in some areas.

Literature Review

1. Why is fishing an important industry in the Northeast?
2. Why is it important for Tommy and his uncle not to keep small lobsters?
3. Draw a picture showing how a lobster trap might look at the bottom of the sea. Add sea life to your picture.

OLD RESOURCES, NEW INDUSTRIES

Link to Our World

How can using resources lead to changes in a region?

Focus on the Main Idea
Read to find out how the Middle Atlantic states have changed because of the ways that people have used resources.

Preview Vocabulary
produce
truck farm
agricultural economy
industrial economy
finished product
waterway
competition

Strawberries are grown on truck farms in New Jersey.

The waters off the coast of New England were good places to fish. But settlers were sometimes unhappy about the poor, rocky soil they found on shore. In the Middle Atlantic states—New York, New Jersey, Pennsylvania, Delaware, and Maryland—settlers found mostly rich soil. William Penn, who founded Pennsylvania, said the land in his colony was "fast, fat earth." It was a place where farmers could do well.

RICH FARMLAND

As in much of New England, coastal areas in the Middle Atlantic states are crowded with cities. Many of those cities, such as New York, Philadelphia, and Baltimore, are centers of trade, services, and manufacturing. Away from the cities, however, much of the land is used for farming. This land helps feed the millions of people who live in cities along the coast.

Much of the land in the Middle Atlantic states is part of the Coastal Plain, the low land that stretches along the Atlantic Ocean. Crops grow well in the Coastal Plain's rich, sandy soil. **Produce** (PROH•doos), or fresh fruits and vegetables, grows very well.

Produce must get from farms to stores quickly before it spoils. So produce is often grown on farms close to the cities where it is sold. Such farms are called **truck farms** because their produce can be taken by trucks to nearby markets.

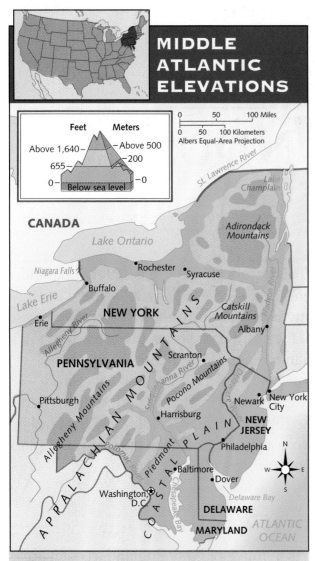

MIDDLE ATLANTIC ELEVATIONS

Feet | Meters
Above 1,640 — — Above 500
655 — — 200
0 — — 0
Below sea level

0 50 100 Miles
0 50 100 Kilometers
Albers Equal-Area Projection

St. Lawrence River

CANADA

Lake Ontario

Lake Champlain

Adirondack Mountains

Niagara Falls

Buffalo

Rochester

Syracuse

Lake Erie

Erie

NEW YORK

Catskill Mountains

Albany

Hudson River

Allegheny River

Scranton

PENNSYLVANIA

Susquehanna River

Pocono Mountains

Pittsburgh

Allegheny Mountains

Harrisburg

Newark

New York City

NEW JERSEY

Philadelphia

Baltimore

Dover

Washington, D.C.

Potomac River

Piedmont

COASTAL PLAIN

Chesapeake Bay

DELAWARE

Delaware Bay

MARYLAND

ATLANTIC OCEAN

APPALACHIAN MOUNTAINS

PLACE The Coastal Plain, the Piedmont, and the Appalachian Mountains are major landforms in the Middle Atlantic states.
■ Which city has a higher elevation, Philadelphia or Scranton?

This Amish farmer uses a horse-drawn machine to cut hay.

Inland from the Coastal Plain is the Piedmont, another region with mostly fertile soil. The Piedmont's rolling hills and broad valleys stretch through parts of several Middle Atlantic states.

The land in southeastern Pennsylvania is among the richest in the world. Because the land is so fertile, many farms there are small. A small field can produce a large crop of corn or wheat.

A group of people called the Amish (AH•mish) live in this part of the state of Pennsylvania. The Amish have an **agricultural economy**, or an economy in which people meet most of their needs by farming. The Amish raise their own food. They make most of the things they use.

Because of their religious beliefs, the Amish live very simply. They do not use electricity or telephones in their homes, and they do not use cars or tractors. Instead, they use simple tools, such as plows pulled by horses. They travel by horse and buggy.

✔ **How is much of the land in the Middle Atlantic states different from the land in New England?**

NEW INDUSTRIES

In the early years of the United States, most people had to make or grow much of what they needed to live. One person wrote that a familiar sight in the 1700s was "the American who, with the help of his wife and children, not only tilled his fields . . . but who also built his own dwelling, contrived his own tools, made his own shoes, and wove the coarse stuff of his own clothing." In fact, one leader described the early United States as "a vast scene of household manufacturing."

This glass factory in Pennsylvania was built along the Delaware River in the 1820s.

MIDDLE ATLANTIC LAND USE AND RESOURCES

0   75   150 Miles
0   75   150 Kilometers
Albers Equal-Area Projection

CANADA

Lake Ontario

Lake Erie

Rochester   Utica
Buffalo   Syracuse
Albany
Binghamton

Erie

Pittsburgh   PA   Allentown   New York City
Philadelphia   Trenton
ATLANTIC OCEAN

MD   Baltimore
WV   Washington, D.C.   DE   Delaware Bay

VA

Legend:
- Manufacturing
- General farming
- Dairy farming
- Forest
- Fruits and vegetables
- Coal
- Iron
- Oil or natural gas
- Zinc

PLACE The Appalachian Mountains have rich deposits of minerals and fuels.
■ What fuels are found in western Pennsylvania?

All that began to change in the 1800s. New cities and industries were springing up across the country. The United States was building an **industrial economy**, or an economy in which factories and machines manufacture most goods.

The first factories were built along rivers so that the rushing water could be used to run machines. Rivers also gave factories a way to ship their finished products to market. A **finished product** is a manufactured good made from raw materials.

Over time, railroads were built, and machines began to run on steam or electricity. Factories no longer had to be built next to rivers. Now they could be built nearer to the resources they used. Often that was in the Appalachians.

The Appalachian Mountains are rich in many of the resources that factories need. In the Middle Atlantic states, the Appalachians are made up of several smaller mountain ranges. There are the Allegheny Mountains in western Pennsylvania and Maryland, the Pocono (POH•kuh•noh) Mountains in eastern Pennsylvania, and the Adirondack (a•duh•RAHN•dak) and Catskill mountains in eastern New York.

✓ **How was the United States changing in the 1800s?**

Steel that is molten, or melted, is poured into blocks called ingots (above). Smoke from early steel mills (right) caused much pollution in Pittsburgh.

A CENTER OF INDUSTRY

Many new industries started in the Middle Atlantic states. The steel industry, for example, began in western Pennsylvania, near Pittsburgh. Steel is made by heating iron, coal, and limestone. Western Pennsylvania and nearby areas in Ohio and West Virginia had all three resources. They also had an important waterway—the Ohio River. A **waterway** is a body of water that boats can use.

In her book *No Star Nights*, Anna Egan Smucker tells about growing up in Pittsburgh.

66 We went to school across from the mill. The smokestacks towered above us and the smoke billowed out in great puffy clouds of red, orange, and yellow, but mostly the color of rust. Everything—houses, hedges, old cars—was a rusty red color. Everything but the little bits of graphite, and they glinted like silver in the dust. 99

As the United States grew, steel became more important. Railroad tracks, bridges, and many buildings and machines were built with steel. By the 1920s the United States was making nearly three-fifths of the world's steel. About half of that was made in the mills of Pennsylvania.

W ho?

Andrew Carnegie 1835–1919

Andrew Carnegie (KAR•nuh•gee) was a leader in the steel industry. Carnegie came from Scotland to live in Pittsburgh when he was 13 years old. When he was a young man, Carnegie learned about a better way to make steel. In time he became one of the richest people in the world. Carnegie gave much of his money to build libraries and schools.

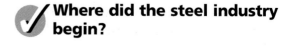 **Where did the steel industry begin?**

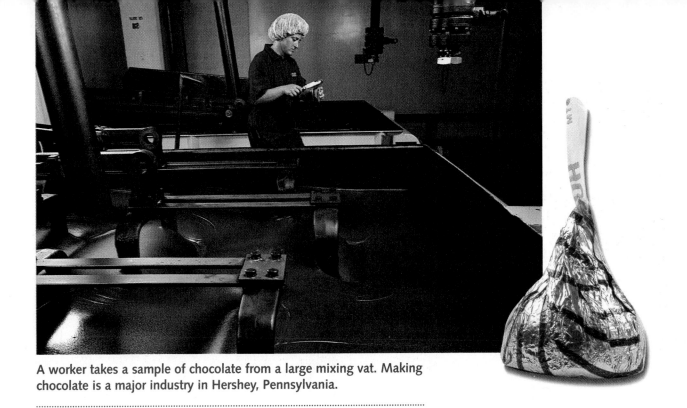

A worker takes a sample of chocolate from a large mixing vat. Making chocolate is a major industry in Hershey, Pennsylvania.

CHANGING INDUSTRIES

Steel mills in Pennsylvania no longer make as much steel as they once did. The raw materials needed to make steel are now more costly, and larger amounts of resources are found in other places. The steel industry also faces strong competition (kahm•puh•TIH•shuhn) from steelmakers in other countries. In business, **competition** is the contest among companies to sell the most products. Partly because of this competition, steel mills in many cities have closed.

Today manufacturing is less important in Pennsylvania and in the other Middle Atlantic states than it once was. However, the Middle Atlantic states are still leaders in manufacturing. Now they use their resources to make not only steel but also food products, chemicals, glass, electrical equipment, and machinery.

 **Why do Pennsylvania's steel mills now produce less steel?**

LESSON 3 REVIEW

Check Understanding

1. **Recall the Facts**   How is an agricultural economy different from an industrial economy?
2. **Focus on the Main Idea**   How have the Middle Atlantic states changed because of the ways that people have used resources?

Think Critically

3. **Think More About It**   Without fertile farmland nearby, could the Northeast's coastal cities have grown as large as they are? Explain your answer.
4. **Link to You**   How has work changed over time in your community or state?

Show What You Know

 **Writing Activity**   Write a paragraph or two telling how your life might be different today if the United States had not built an industrial economy.

Use a Line Graph to See Change

Why Is This Skill Important?

You have read that much less steel is made in Pennsylvania now than in the past. The numbers that show such changes are often very large and may be hard to understand just by reading them. Putting these numbers on a line graph makes them easier to understand. A **line graph** is a graph that uses a line to show changes over time.

Understand the Process

The line graph you see on this page shows the amount of steel that was produced in Pennsylvania between 1970 and 1995. The numbers on the left side of the graph give the amount of steel produced per year in millions of tons. Across the bottom of the graph are the years. As the red line moves across the graph, it shows the change that took place in each five-year period.

1. Find 1970 at the bottom of the graph. With your finger, trace the line above that date toward the top of the graph. When the 1970 line reaches the black dot, let your finger change direction. Now it should follow a straight line to the left side of the graph. The number that you see there will tell you how much steel was produced in 1970. About how many million tons were produced that year?

2. Now find 1995 at the bottom of the graph. Repeat the process. About how many million tons of steel were produced that year?

3. About how many million tons of steel were produced in 1990?

4. About how many million tons of steel were produced in 1980?

5. Look at the red line on the graph. What happened to the amount of steel produced

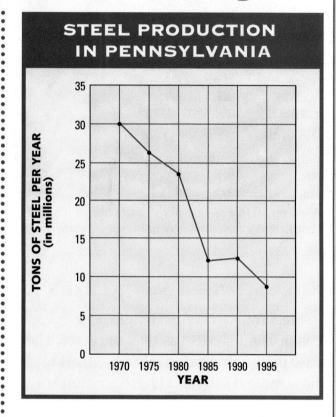

STEEL PRODUCTION IN PENNSYLVANIA

between 1970 and 1995? About how many more million tons of steel were produced in 1970 than in 1995?

6. In what five-year period did the largest change take place? Did the amount go up or down?

7. During one five-year period, the amount of steel produced rose a little. When did that happen?

Think and Apply

Think about the information you see on this graph. Then write a paragraph that describes the changes in steel production in Pennsylvania between 1970 and 1995. With a partner, use library books to research how and why those changes took place. Report your findings to your class.

LINKING WATERWAYS

LESSON 4

Link to Our World

How have people changed the land to allow better transportation among places?

Focus on the Main Idea
As you read, look for ways people have linked waterways in the Northeast.

Preview Vocabulary
**navigable river
rapid
canal
lock**

Large ships can travel on the Great Lakes.

The Atlantic coast of the Northeast region has many deep harbors, and many rivers flow across the land. To the west lie other large bodies of water—the Great Lakes. All these waterways have been important to the growth of the Northeast. But for many years they were not linked.

THE GREAT LAKES

Two of the five Great Lakes form part of the border of the Northeast region. Lake Ontario and Lake Erie lie along the western edge of New York. Lake Erie lies along the northwestern edge of Pennsylvania.

Along the shores of both lakes are low, rolling plains. Just as the land along the Coastal Plain is good for farming, so is the land along the Great Lakes. The cool, damp climate along the Great Lakes is very good for growing fruit. Apples, pears, and grapes are raised there.

Today the Great Lakes are an important waterway for the country. At one time, however, they were not as useful. Ships on the Great Lakes could not reach the Atlantic Ocean. There was no way to ship goods without also using some kind of land transportation.

Many navigable (NA•vih•guh•buhl) rivers flowed into the Great Lakes. A **navigable river** is a river that is deep and wide enough for ships to use. Many navigable rivers also flowed into the Atlantic Ocean. But the Appalachian Mountains lay between the rivers that flowed into the Great Lakes and those that flowed into the Atlantic Ocean.

Chapter 5 • **173**

Only one river, the St. Lawrence, flowed from the Great Lakes to the Atlantic Ocean. The St. Lawrence River, however, was not navigable along its whole length. Upstream there were rapids. A **rapid** is a rocky place in a river where a sudden drop in elevation causes fast-moving, dangerous water.

Ships could not even travel from one end of the Great Lakes to the other. Some of the lakes were joined by short rivers, but the water was not deep. Rapids often blocked ships. On the Niagara River, between Lake Ontario and Lake Erie, for example, the water dropped about 167 feet (51 m), forming Niagara Falls.

✔ **Why were ships on the Great Lakes not able to reach the Atlantic Ocean?**

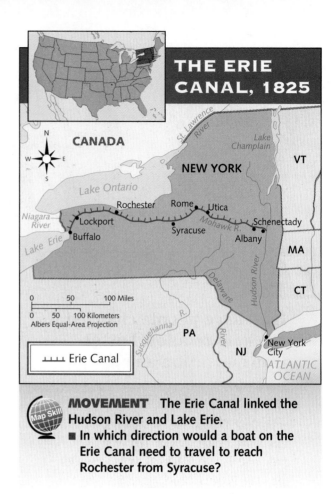

THE ERIE CANAL, 1825

MOVEMENT The Erie Canal linked the Hudson River and Lake Erie.
■ In which direction would a boat on the Erie Canal need to travel to reach Rochester from Syracuse?

FROM LAKE ERIE TO THE ATLANTIC

Before there were railroads, goods had to be moved either by ship or by horse and wagon. Moving goods by horse and wagon cost a lot. It was hard, slow work, too, because most roads were poor.

Many people wanted the Great Lakes to be linked with the Atlantic Ocean so that goods could be moved by ship. A group of people led by De Witt Clinton of New York City decided to build a canal to do just that. A **canal** is a waterway dug across land. The Erie Canal would connect the city of Buffalo, New York, on Lake Erie, with Albany, New York, on the Hudson River. From Albany, ships could sail down the Hudson to the Atlantic.

When the plan for the Erie Canal was shown to President Thomas Jefferson in 1809, he described it as "little short of madness." Other people laughed openly, calling it "Clinton's Ditch." Many people thought such a long canal could not be built. After all, workers would have to cut through more than 350 miles (563 km) of forests and hills.

Clinton knew that linking Lake Erie and the Hudson River would increase trade. And what coastal port would handle this trade and the money it would bring in? Why, New York City, of course.

When Clinton was elected governor of the state of New York in 1817, work started on the Erie Canal. Eight years later the canal was ready for business. It worked well from the start. Before the canal was built, a trip from New York City to Buffalo took up to six weeks. With the canal, the same trip took ten days! Shipping prices dropped from $100 a ton

When?

Sending Messages in 1825

Today television cameras report news almost instantly. When the Erie Canal opened in 1825, there were no televisions. To spread the news of the canal's opening, many cannons were set up. When the canal opened, the cannons were fired, one after another. It took 81 minutes to send the message between Buffalo and Sandy Hook, a distance of 500 miles (805 km).

to $10 a ton, and trade boomed. The Erie Canal showed that the Great Lakes and the Atlantic Ocean could be linked. It also gave settlers a better way to move west.

✓ **How did the Erie Canal affect trade?**

LINKING WATERWAYS TODAY

Today other waterways connect the Great Lakes with the Atlantic Ocean. One is the New York State Barge Canal System. Part of it follows the path of the Erie Canal. It connects Lake Champlain in northern New York, the Hudson River, Lake Ontario, and Lake Erie. Some ships still use this waterway. Most ships, however, now use a larger and newer waterway—the St. Lawrence Seaway.

The St. Lawrence Seaway was built by the United States and Canada. It stretches about 450 miles (724 km) from the eastern end of Lake Erie to Montreal. Montreal is a Canadian city on the St. Lawrence River.

On parts of the St. Lawrence Seaway, ships move through canals and locks. A **lock** is a part of a canal in which the water level can be raised or lowered. This brings the ship to the level of the next part of the canal. This must be done because the elevation of the land along the St. Lawrence Seaway changes.

The St. Lawrence Seaway links several inland ports on the Great Lakes with the Atlantic Ocean. Ships can use the

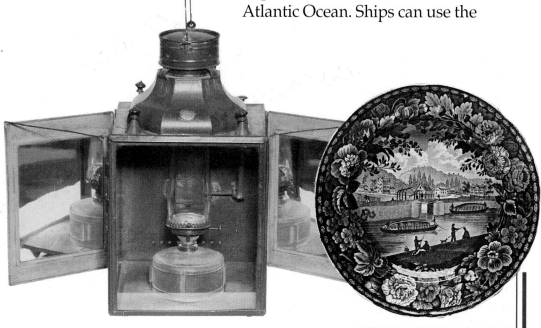

Boats, pulled by mules, traveled through the Erie Canal together, one after another. Lanterns like this one (right) were hung at the front of the first boat. The number of lanterns told how many boats were traveling together. This plate (far right) was made to celebrate the opening of the Erie Canal in 1825.

St. Lawrence Seaway, which includes the Welland Ship Canal built between Lake Ontario and Lake Erie, to take products made in cities along the Great Lakes to world markets. Other ships use the St. Lawrence Seaway to bring raw materials and imported goods to those same cities.

The St. Lawrence Seaway has helped make Buffalo and Rochester, in New York, and Erie, in Pennsylvania, important manufacturing centers. Buffalo is one of the largest producers of flour in the United States. Rochester produces cameras and film. Erie produces heavy machinery.

Locks like this one on the Welland Ship Canal (above) allow ships to move between the Great Lakes.

✓ **Why is the St. Lawrence Seaway important to cities along the Great Lakes?**

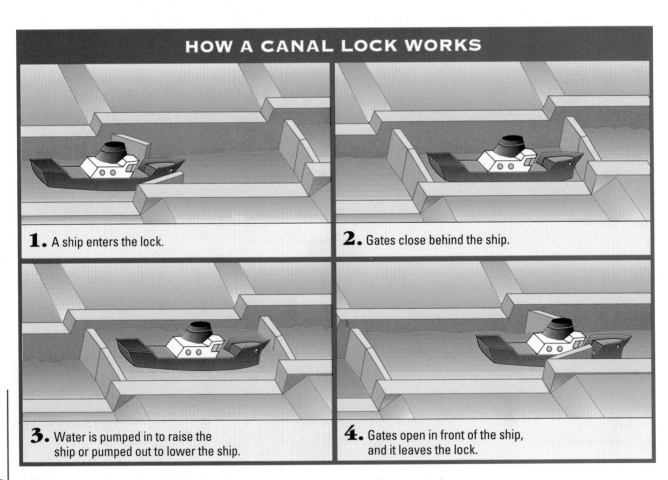

HOW A CANAL LOCK WORKS

1. A ship enters the lock.

2. Gates close behind the ship.

3. Water is pumped in to raise the ship or pumped out to lower the ship.

4. Gates open in front of the ship, and it leaves the lock.

LEARNING FROM DIAGRAMS This diagram shows how a ship is raised or lowered in a lock.
■ What causes a ship to rise when it is in a lock?

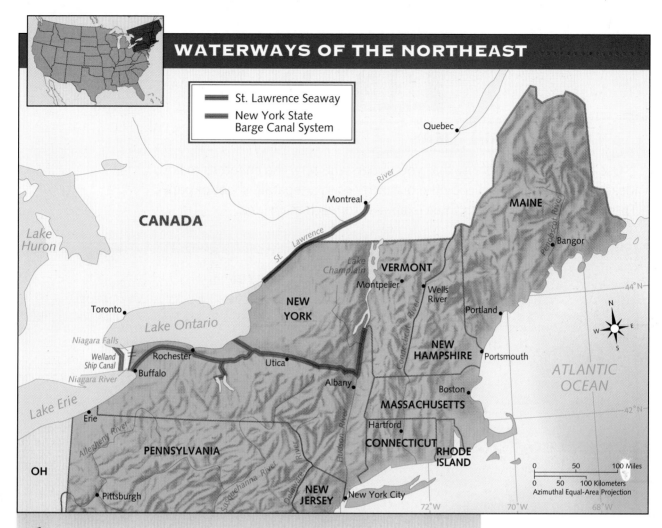

WATERWAYS OF THE NORTHEAST

Legend:
- St. Lawrence Seaway
- New York State Barge Canal System

 HUMAN–ENVIRONMENT INTERACTIONS People have built different waterways to link the Great Lakes and the Atlantic Ocean.
■ Which waterway was built to allow travel between the St. Lawrence River and Lake Erie?

LESSON 4 REVIEW

Check Understanding

1. Recall the Facts What was the first canal to link the Great Lakes with the Atlantic Ocean?

2. Focus on the Main Idea How have people linked waterways in the Northeast?

Think Critically

3. Cause and Effect How do you think the Erie Canal affected the growth of New York City?

4. Think More About It Why do you think people sometimes laugh at new ideas?

Show What You Know

Simulation Imagine that President Jefferson has asked you to explain the purpose of the Erie Canal to him. Plan an oral presentation that tells where the canal will be built and why De Witt Clinton wants to build it.

CONNECT MAIN IDEAS

Use this organizer to show that you understand how the chapter's main ideas are connected. First copy the organizer onto a separate sheet of paper. Then complete it by writing three examples for each main idea.

Using Land and Water

Geography Interaction Change

Landforms and natural resources affect how people in New England live.	The Middle Atlantic states have changed because of the ways that people have used resources.	People have linked waterways in the Northeast to allow better transportation.
1. _____	1. _____	1. _____
2. _____	2. _____	2. _____
3. _____	3. _____	3. _____

WRITE MORE ABOUT IT

1. **Write a Magazine Article**   Imagine that you have been asked by a magazine to write a short article about New England. Choose one topic that you would like to write about—perhaps the land, New England's resources, or how people earn their living. Then write two or three paragraphs about that topic.

2. **Write a Story**   Imagine that you work on a lobster boat that fishes in the waters off the coast of New England. Write a story that tells about what you do on the boat or about something that happens to you on the job.

3. **Write a Descriptive Paragraph**   Suppose that you are aboard a ship sailing through the St. Lawrence Seaway and the Great Lakes. Write a descriptive paragraph telling about your journey and what you see along the way.

USE VOCABULARY

Write a term from this list to complete each of the sentences that follow.

canal   glacier
competition   navigable river
finished product   tradition

1. A huge, slow-moving mass of ice is called a _____.

2. A _____ is a way or idea that has been handed down from the past.

3. A _____ is a manufactured good made from raw materials.

4. In business, _____ is a contest among companies to sell the most products.

5. A _____ is deep and wide enough for ships to use.

6. A _____ is a waterway dug across land.

CHECK UNDERSTANDING

1. What are town meetings?

2. How is farmland on the Coastal Plain of the Middle Atlantic states different from farmland in New England?

3. How is an agricultural economy different from an industrial economy?

4. Why were many factories built near the Appalachian Mountains?

5. Why were the Great Lakes less useful in the past than they are today?

THINK CRITICALLY

1. **Link to You** Farmers in New England plant crops that grow in cool climates and poor soils. How do people adapt to the geography of the place where you live?

2. **Cause and Effect** How can competition affect a business, its workers, and its customers?

3. **Personally Speaking** What do you think the world would be like today if people such as De Witt Clinton had listened to their critics and not tried out their new ideas?

APPLY SKILLS

How to Tell Fact from Opinion News reports give both facts and opinions. Listen to a news report. Write down three facts and three opinions that you hear.

How to Use a Line Graph to See Change Use the following information to make a line graph showing how the population of New York City changed between 1910 and 1990. Write the years across the bottom of your graph. On the left side, from bottom to top, mark each million between 1 million and 8 million.

Year	Population
1910	4,477,000
1950	7,892,000
1990	7,323,000

READ MORE ABOUT IT

Amish Home by Raymond Bial. Houghton Mifflin. This book tells about the Amish people and their beliefs.

A New England Scrapbook by Loretta Krupinski. HarperCollins. This collection of poems creates a scrapbook of the sights and sounds of New England.

Voices of the River by Jan Cheripko. Boyds Mills Press. On a canoe trip down the Delaware River, 14-year-old Matthew Smith discovers the river's history and beauty.

Making Their Mark in the Cities

Graffiti (gruh•FEE•tee)—you see it almost everywhere. You see words and symbols spray-painted on buildings, on bridges, and even on the sides of trucks and subway cars. City governments and private citizens spend millions of dollars each year to remove graffiti from public and private property.

Painting graffiti on someone else's property is against the law. When graffiti writers, or "taggers," are caught, they may have to pay fines or go to jail. In the city of Philadelphia, however, taggers are not always arrested. Instead many are sent to art school! The Philadelphia Anti-Graffiti Network is a city program that teaches young people to use their talents to improve the community, rather than spoil it. Taggers are put to work painting over graffiti and creating murals on walls all around the city. Says Jane Golden, the network's artistic director, "It's a place where these kids can make their mark."

Since the program began, taggers have completed more than 1,200 murals. Many of these murals show well-known people, and some celebrate the city's many cultures. As for the young artists, they are learning about their city and helping make it beautiful. Their skills have given them new interests and even new career choices.

Members of the Philadelphia Anti-Graffiti Network paint over the graffiti that covers the walls of buildings.

This mural was painted by the Philadelphia Anti-Graffiti Network. It shows a Native American family.

THINK AND APPLY

Thanks to the Anti-Graffiti Network, some of Philadelphia's neighborhoods have wonderful murals. With a partner, draw a mural for your neighborhood or city on a sheet of poster-board. Share your mural with other students in your school.

BUILDING CITIZENSHIP

Another mural in Philadelphia shows an African American family planting a garden.

STORY CLOTH

Study the pictures shown in this story cloth to help you review what you read about in Unit 2.

Summarize the Main Ideas

1. Settlers used the Northeast's resources to meet their needs. They built settlements along its many harbors. Over time many of those settlements became busy ports.

2. Cities have grown larger and more crowded over time. Cities have many problems, but they also offer many good things to people.

3. Glaciers left poor soil in many places in New England. Farmers in New England raise crops and animals that do well there. Away from the large coastal cities are many small villages.

4. Fishing is an important industry in New England and in other coastal areas of the Northeast.

5. The rich farmland in the Middle Atlantic states helps feed the millions of people who live in coastal cities. The Appalachian Mountains are rich in the resources that many factories need. Today, however, manufacturing in the region is less important than it was in the past.

6. People have built canals and other waterways to link the Great Lakes with the Atlantic Ocean.

Draw Another Scene Choose one of the industries of the Northeast described in Unit 2. Draw a picture that shows people at work in this industry. Tell where your scene should be placed in the story cloth.

COOPERATIVE LEARNING WORKSHOP

Remember

- Share your ideas.
- Cooperate with others to plan your work.
- Take responsibility for your work.
- Show your group's work to the class.
- Discuss what you learned by working together.

Activity 1
Write and Perform a Class Play

Write and perform a play about the settlement and growth of the Northeast. As a class, decide on the people and events you want to have in your play. Then form small groups. Each group will write one scene about a person, a group of people, or an important event. After the scenes are written, the groups should decide together the order in which the scenes will be presented. Choose roles, practice, and perform the play for invited guests from your school or the community.

Activity 2
Draw a Map

Work with the members of your group to draw an outline map of the Northeast on a large sheet of paper. Maps in your textbook and in encyclopedias and atlases can help you. Use two different colors to show the New England states and the Middle Atlantic states. Then add dots and labels to show where the region's largest cities are located. Also label large rivers and landforms. Draw symbols to show some of the region's major resources. Then point out places on the map as your group takes the rest of your class on a "tour" of the Northeast.

Activity 3
Draw a Mural

Work with group members to draw a mural of a Nashua village, an early New England colony, a New England village today, the central business district of a large city in the Northeast, or an Amish farm in Pennsylvania. Use your textbook, an encyclopedia, and books from the library for ideas. Present your mural to the class, and lead a discussion about the place you have shown.

USE VOCABULARY

Use each term in a sentence that helps explain its meaning.

1. cape
2. colony
3. raw material
4. international trade
5. prejudice
6. unemployment
7. produce
8. waterway
9. rapid
10. lock

CHECK UNDERSTANDING

1. Why did the Pilgrims think Plymouth Bay was a good place to build their colony?

2. How has urban sprawl changed cities?

3. Why does much of New England have poor, rocky soil?

4. How did the economy of the United States change in the early 1800s?

5. Why did factories no longer have to be built next to rivers in the 1800s?

6. How has competition from steelmakers in other countries affected steel mills in Pennsylvania?

7. Why was it important to link waterways in the Northeast?

THINK CRITICALLY

1. **Personally Speaking**   How do you think immigrants who lived in New York City tenements felt about the United States?

2. **Link to You**   Many towns and villages in New England still hold town meetings. What traditions do people in your community follow?

3. **Think More About It**   Railroads changed trade and manufacturing in the United States in the 1800s. What things are changing trade and manufacturing today?

APPLY GEOGRAPHY SKILLS

 How to Use a Population Map
Use the map below to answer these questions.

1. What is the population density near Newark?

2. What is the population density for Salem?

3. Do more people live in the northeastern or southeastern part of New Jersey?

POPULATION MAP OF NEW JERSEY

People per square mile	People per square kilometer
More than 1,000	More than 400
500–1,000	200–400
250–500	100–200
Less than 250	Less than 100

UNIT 3

THE SOUTHEAST

Alabama   **Arkansas**   **Florida**   **Georgia**   **Kentucky**   **Louisiana**

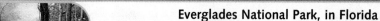

Everglades National Park, in Florida

Hot Springs
National
Park, in
Arkansas

The French Quarter, in
New Orleans, Louisiana

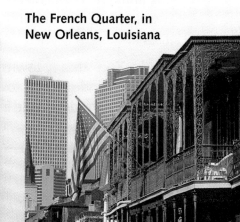

The Southeast is a large region. In fact, it is almost three times as large as the Northeast. It stretches inland from the Atlantic Ocean and the Gulf of Mexico, north to the Ohio River, and west to Arkansas and Louisiana.

The Southeast is also a changing region. Many people are moving there, and its states and cities are growing quickly. Yet the Southeast is a land of history and tradition. Like the Northeast, the Southeast has played an important part in the history of the United States.

← The space shuttle *Columbia* lifts off from Cape Canaveral, in Florida.

Mississippi   North Carolina   South Carolina   Tennessee   Virginia   West Virginia

Mount Mitchell, in North Carolina

Charleston, South Carolina

Mount Vernon, in Virginia

ALMANAC
The Southeast

Did You Know?

There are 12 states in the Southeast. Virginia, North Carolina, South Carolina, and Georgia are 4 of the 13 original states. Georgia is the largest state in the Southeast. Florida, however, has the most people.

STATE	CAPITAL	NICKNAME	POPULATION*	TEN LARGEST CITIES	LEADING PRODUCTS AND RESOURCES

THE SOUTHEAST STATES

STATE	CAPITAL	NICKNAME	POPULATION*	TEN LARGEST CITIES	LEADING PRODUCTS AND RESOURCES
Alabama (AL)	Montgomery	Heart of Dixie	4,361,000	1. Jacksonville, Florida	**Farming:** Beef cattle, citrus fruits, cotton, dairy cows, hogs, horses, peanuts, poultry, rice, soybeans, sugarcane, tobacco, vegetables
Arkansas (AR)	Little Rock	Land of Opportunity	2,513,000	2. Memphis, Tennessee	
Florida (FL)	Tallahassee	Sunshine State	14,663,000	3. Nashville-Davidson, Tennessee	
Georgia (GA)	Atlanta	Empire State of the South	7,324,000		
Kentucky (KY)	Frankfort	Bluegrass State	3,911,000		**Fishing:** Clams, crabs, fish, lobsters, scallops, shrimp
Louisiana (LA)	Baton Rouge	Pelican State	4,404,000	4. New Orleans, Louisiana	
Mississippi (MS)	Jackson	Magnolia State	2,700,000	5. Virginia Beach, Virginia	**Manufacturing:** Chemicals, dairy products, electrical equipment, furniture, glass, lumber, paper products, plastics, processed foods, textiles
North Carolina (NC)	Raleigh	Tar Heel State	7,347,000	6. Charlotte, North Carolina	
South Carolina (SC)	Columbia	Palmetto State	3,814,000	7. Atlanta, Georgia	
Tennessee (TN)	Nashville	Volunteer State	5,359,000	8. Miami, Florida	
Virginia (VA)	Richmond	Old Dominion	6,814,000	9. Tampa, Florida	**Mining:** Coal, iron, limestone, natural gas, oil, phosphates, zinc
West Virginia (WV)	Charleston	Mountain State	1,832,000	10. Louisville, Kentucky	

*The most recent figures available.

Most of the glass marbles manufactured in the United States are made in West Virginia.

The largest sculpture in the world is carved on the face of Stone Mountain, in Georgia. Stone Mountain is the largest mass of granite in North America.

STONE MOUNTAIN

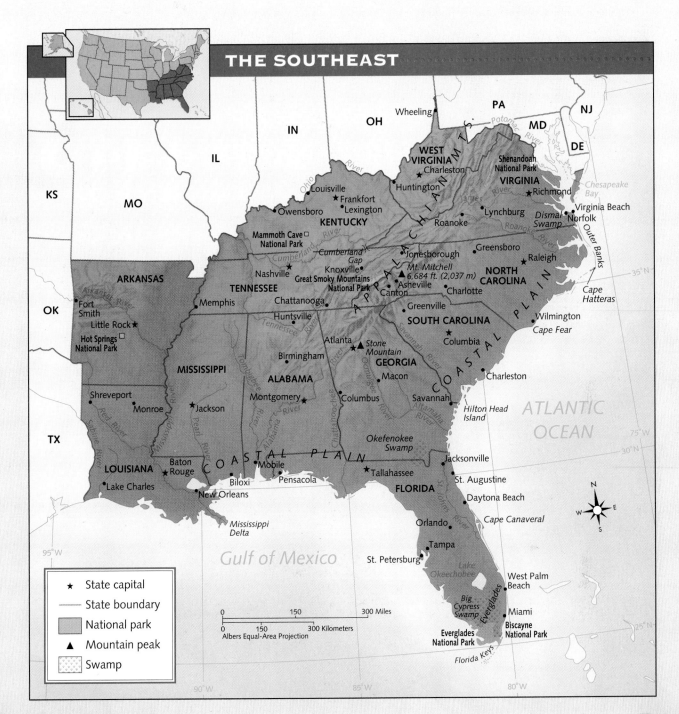

KS

MO

IN

OH

Wheeling

PA

NJ

MD

DE

IL

WEST
VIRGINIA
★ Charleston

Shenandoah
National Park

VIRGINIA
★ Richmond

Chesapeake
Bay

Huntington

Potomac River

Louisville

Frankfort
★

Lexington

KENTUCKY

Owensboro

Ohio River

Mammoth Cave ☐
National Park

Cumberland River

Lynchburg

Roanoke

Dismal
Swamp

Virginia Beach
Norfolk

Outer Banks

ARKANSAS

Fort
Smith

Little Rock ★

Hot Springs ☐
National Park

Arkansas River

Nashville

Memphis

TENNESSEE

Cumberland
Gap

Knoxville

Great Smoky Mountains
National Park

Chattanooga

Huntsville

Tennessee River

Jonesborough

Mt. Mitchell
6,684 ft. (2,037 m)

Asheville

Canton

James River

Roanoke River

Greensboro

Raleigh ★

35° N

NORTH
CAROLINA

Charlotte

Greenville

APPALACHIAN MTS.

COASTAL PLAIN

Cape
Hatteras

Wilmington

Cape Fear

OK

TX

MISSISSIPPI

ALABAMA

Birmingham

Montgomery ★

Columbus

Atlanta

Stone
Mountain

GEORGIA

Macon

SOUTH CAROLINA
★ Columbia

Charleston

Savannah

Hilton Head
Island

ATLANTIC
OCEAN

Shreveport

Monroe

Jackson ★

Red River

Tombigbee River

Alabama River

Chattahoochee River

Ocmulgee River

Altamaha River

Savannah River

LOUISIANA

Baton
Rouge ★

Lake Charles

New Orleans

Biloxi

Mobile

Pensacola

Mississippi River

Pearl River

Sabine River

COASTAL PLAIN

Okefenokee
Swamp

Tallahassee ★

FLORIDA

Jacksonville

St. Augustine

St. Johns River

Daytona Beach

Cape Canaveral

30° N

75° W

Mississippi
Delta

Gulf of Mexico

Orlando

Tampa

St. Petersburg

Lake
Okeechobee

West Palm
Beach

Big
Cypress
Swamp

Everglades

Miami

Biscayne
National Park

25° N

Everglades
National Park

Florida Keys

80° W

95° W

90° W

85° W

Legend:
- ★ State capital
- State boundary
- National park
- ▲ Mountain peak
- Swamp

0   150   300 Miles

0   150   300 Kilometers

Albers Equal-Area Projection

N
W   E
S

Mammoth
Cave, in
Kentucky,
is part of
the world's
largest known
cave system.

St. Augustine, Florida, is the oldest
permanent settlement built by
Europeans in what is today the
United States. It
was settled by the
Spanish in 1565.

The manatee is an
endangered sea mammal
found near Florida's coasts.

MISSION 2

ADVENTURE SPACE CAMP

BY ROSS BANKSON

Jennifer Hicks connects fuel lines in a simulator at the U.S. Space Camp.

Reprinted by permission of National Geographic World, the official magazine for Junior Members of the National Geographic Society.

George Fredenburg sits at the controls during a simulated space shuttle flight.

The United States space program is an important part of life in the Southeast region. Space shuttle flights begin at Cape Canaveral (kuh·NAV·ruhl), Florida. Huntsville, Alabama, is sometimes called Rocket City, U.S.A. In Huntsville, scientists design rockets and other spacecraft. Also in Huntsville is the United States Space Camp. The following magazine article describes how students who go there learn about space travel.

The flight had gone like clockwork. Now, its mission completed, the space shuttle *Endeavour* was streaking toward the runway. The crew was looking forward to a well-deserved rest. Suddenly a red warning light flashed.

"We blew a tire when we landed," explains mission specialist Jennifer Hicks, 12, of Jacksonville, Florida. "Most people would have slammed down the brakes. We had been well trained, though, so we applied the brakes slowly, then throttled down. We kept our cool and avoided disaster." Jennifer experienced her in-flight adventures without ever leaving the ground. She "flew" for two hours in a simulated, or imitation, space shuttle at U.S. Space Camp in Huntsville, Alabama.

New groups of students attend Space Camp every week from February through December. They are attracted by the camp's five-day, hands-on course in space technology. They come from across the United States and from countries as far away as Indonesia and South Africa. They share common interests: a love of math and science, and a wish to become pilots, engineers, or even astronauts.

The simulated space shuttle mission crowns the students' week. The mission involves a launch and landing. It also includes a task such as retrieving a satellite for repair. "You feel as if you're really doing the task," says George Fredenburg, 14, of Chevy Chase, Maryland. "The simulator is equipped just as an actual shuttle is. Ground Control is authentic. And the instructors keep throwing emergency situations at you."

Campers follow a busy schedule. Between wake-up at 6 a.m. and lights-out at 9:30 p.m., they attend lectures, view films, and tour a space flight center. They might work with simulators to experience added gravity. They also might work on model rockets, preparing them for launch. They visit a rocket park to learn what role different rockets have played in the United States space program.

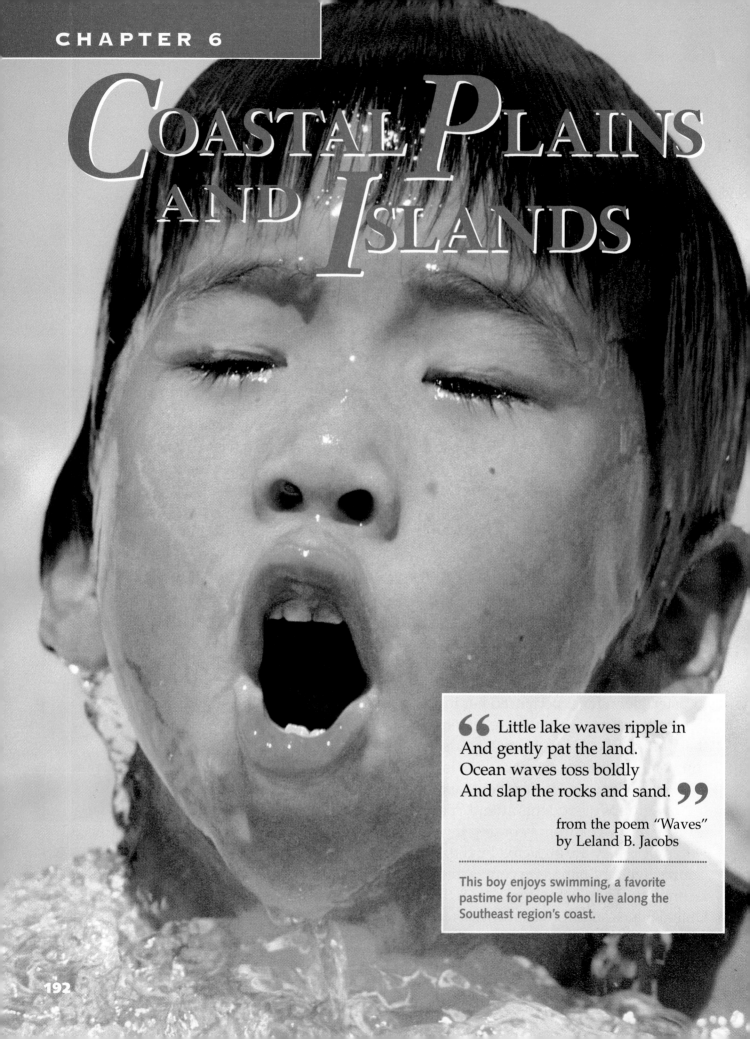

CHAPTER 6

COASTAL PLAINS AND ISLANDS

" Little lake waves ripple in
And gently pat the land.
Ocean waves toss boldly
And slap the rocks and sand. "

from the poem "Waves"
by Leland B. Jacobs

This boy enjoys swimming, a favorite
pastime for people who live along the
Southeast region's coast.

FARMING ON THE COASTAL PLAIN

Brown pelicans are among the many kinds of birds that live in coastal areas of the Southeast.

Link to Our World

Why are plains regions generally good places for farming?

Focus on the Main Idea
Read to find out what makes the Southeast an important farming region.

Preview Vocabulary
generation   **growing season**
marsh   **swamp**
plantation

The Southeast region has many large and important cities. However, it was the farmland of the Coastal Plain that first attracted people to the Southeast. This wide, fertile plain has helped make the region an important farming area.

THE COASTAL PLAIN

On a spring day more than 500 years ago, several Powhatan (pow•uh•TAN) women walked into a forest clearing. They used hoes to loosen the soil. Then they planted corn, beans, peas, squash, and pumpkins.

For generations (jeh•nuh•RAY•shuhnz) Powhatan women had been planting crops to help feed their families. A **generation** is the average time between the birth of parents and the birth of their children.

The Powhatan Indians lived close to the Atlantic Ocean in what is now the state of Virginia. Eastern Virginia, like much of the Southeast, has low, flat land. There are many rivers and oak and pine forests. This land is part of the Coastal Plain.

As the Coastal Plain stretches south from Virginia, it grows wider. Along the coast the plain is almost at sea level. Here fresh water from rivers mixes with salt water from the ocean. Large coastal marshes form. A **marsh** is low, wet land where cattails, tall grasses, and other similar plants grow.

✓ **What are some natural features found on the Coastal Plain in the Southeast region?**

EARLY FARMS IN THE SOUTHEAST

A farmer recently said, "America's greatest asset today is farmland and the people who will bend low to work it." The same thing could have been said more than 300 years ago. Farming has always been important to the United States. And the Southeast has always been an important farming region.

The first European settlers learned how rich the land was soon after they arrived. Charles Percy was one of them. In 1607 he and others started Jamestown, in what is now Virginia. Jamestown was the first permanent English colony built in North America. It was begun 13 years before the Pilgrims landed at Plymouth Bay.

Percy wrote that Jamestown was a place of "fair meadows and goodly tall trees, with such fresh waters running through the woods." He saw "vines in bigness of a man's thigh, running up to the tops of the trees."

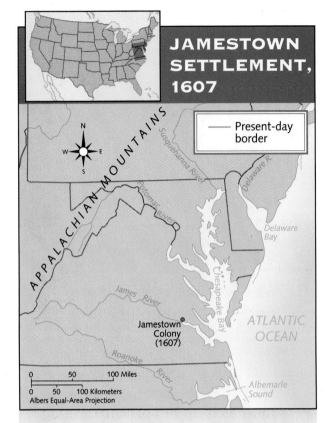

JAMESTOWN SETTLEMENT, 1607

— Present-day border

APPALACHIAN MOUNTAINS

Susquehanna River

Delaware R.

Potomac River

Delaware Bay

Chesapeake Bay

James River

Jamestown Colony (1607)

ATLANTIC OCEAN

Roanoke River

Albemarle Sound

0   50   100 Miles
0   50   100 Kilometers
Albers Equal-Area Projection

LOCATION Jamestown was built next to the James River.
■ Into what bay does the James River flow?

Percy and the other settlers knew they had to grow their own food. To farm the

People who visit Jamestown Festival Park, built near the original site of Jamestown, can see brass cooking pots used by early settlers and metal helmets worn by soldiers.

land, though, they first had to cut down many trees. This was because huge forests covered the Southeast. The forests were so big, wrote Percy, that the settlers could smell the "sweet perfume" of the trees even before they stepped off their ships.

Many other settlers came to America. In time, 13 English colonies spread north and south along the Atlantic coast. Settlers also began to move inland from the coast. Soon the Coastal Plain was covered with farms. Many kinds of crops were grown, including corn, tobacco, and squash. These were crops that Native Americans had shown the settlers how to grow.

It was easier to plow the Coastal Plain's flat land than the hilly, rocky land in New England. This meant that farms in the Southeast could be larger. Farmers used the land to raise food. However, they also grew such crops as tobacco and cotton. Those crops could be sold for money.

Some farmers became very rich. They started huge farms called **plantations**. Tobacco, cotton, and rice were the main crops grown on plantations. Many workers were needed to care for these crops. Most often those workers were slaves.

✓ **How did early settlers depend on the land?**

THE COASTAL PLAIN TODAY

It is early morning in southern Georgia. The sun is just beginning to peek over the nearby pecan trees. A farmer slowly climbs onto a tractor. He turns the key, and the engine roars to life.

The farmer will spend this day planting peanuts. Peanuts are an important crop in Georgia. They are also important in other states in the Southeast, such as Alabama, North Carolina, and Virginia. Peanuts became a leading crop there in the early 1900s. This happened after George Washington Carver had urged farmers to plant more peanuts.

Carver was a scientist who became well known for his work with peanuts. All over the country he talked about their many uses. He explained that growing peanuts could make the soil more fertile.

Peanuts need loose, sandy soil. They also need lots of sun and rain and a long growing season. A **growing season** is the time when the weather is warm enough for plants to grow.

The Coastal Plain in the Southeast is a good place to grow peanuts and many other crops. The land on the Coastal Plain is mostly flat or rolling. That makes it easier for farmers to plant and harvest their crops.

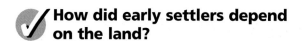

Who?

George Washington Carver 1864?–1943

George Washington Carver was an African American scientist. He became well known for his work with peanuts and ways to improve farming. Born a slave on a Missouri plantation, Carver went on to become a teacher at Tuskegee Institute in Alabama. This was a new college run by African Americans. At Tuskegee, Carver and his students worked to find new uses for peanuts. He also taught farmers how to conserve soil and grow better crops.

The Coastal Plain offers other good things for farmers, too. Most places have a long growing season and get plenty of rain. In most years 40 to 50 inches (102 to 127 cm) of rain fall on the Coastal Plain in the Southeast.

✓ **What good things does the Coastal Plain offer farmers in the Southeast?**

GROWING DIFFERENT CROPS

The Coastal Plain stretches over a very large area of the Southeast. Because of this, it differs from place to place. Along the southern Atlantic coast and the Gulf coast, summers are long and hot and winters are short and mild.

Farmers in both areas can grow many of the same crops that grow farther north. But the farmers can also grow crops that need a longer and warmer growing season, such as cotton and peanuts. Georgia grows more peanuts than any other state. Louisiana and Arkansas grow rice. Florida leads the states in growing sugarcane and citrus fruits. Sugarcane is a plant used to make sugar. Some citrus fruits are oranges, grapefruit, and lemons.

Farmers on the Coastal Plain in the Southeast do more than grow crops, however. They also raise many farm animals, such as beef cattle, dairy cows, and hogs. Poultry is raised on many farms, too. Arkansas, Georgia, Alabama, North Carolina, and Mississippi are all leading states for raising chickens. North Carolina raises more turkeys than any other state.

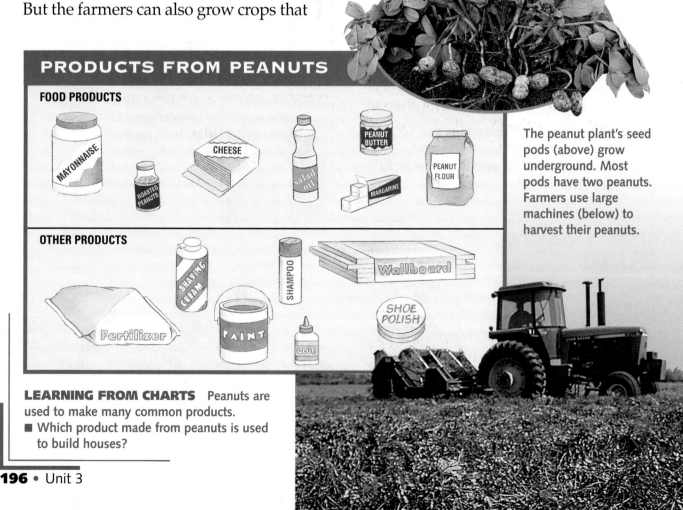

The peanut plant's seed pods (above) grow underground. Most pods have two peanuts. Farmers use large machines (below) to harvest their peanuts.

PRODUCTS FROM PEANUTS

FOOD PRODUCTS

MAYONNAISE · ROASTED PEANUTS · CHEESE · salad oil · PEANUT BUTTER · MARGARINE · PEANUT FLOUR

OTHER PRODUCTS

Fertilizer · SHAVING CREAM · PAINT · GLUE · SHAMPOO · Wallboard · SHOE POLISH

LEARNING FROM CHARTS Peanuts are used to make many common products.
■ Which product made from peanuts is used to build houses?

Okefenokee (oh•kee•fuh•NOH•kee) Swamp in Georgia and Florida, and the Big Cypress Swamp in Florida. Another large area of low, wet land, called the Everglades, covers much of southern Florida.

✓ **Why are farmers on the Coastal Plain able to grow so many kinds of crops?**

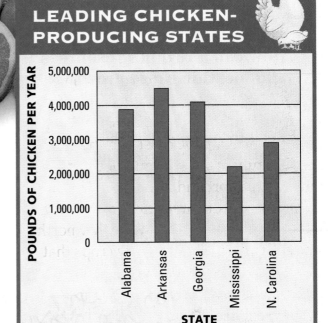

In Florida, oranges are harvested during the fall and winter months. This worker is putting oranges into a large bin that will later be loaded onto a truck.

As in all regions, parts of the Southeast are not good for farming. Swamps are found in some places. A **swamp** is a low, wet area where trees and bushes grow. The land in a swamp is covered by shallow water at least part of the year.

The largest and best-known swamps in the United States are all in the Southeast. Some of these are the Dismal Swamp in Virginia and North Carolina, the

LEARNING FROM GRAPHS All the leading chicken-producing states are in the Southeast.
■ Which state produces the most chickens?

LESSON 1 REVIEW

Check Understanding

1. Recall the Facts What is a growing season?

2. Focus on the Main Idea What makes the Southeast an important farming region?

Think Critically

3. Personally Speaking Do you agree with the farmer who said, "America's greatest asset today is farmland and the people who will bend low to work it"? Why or why not?

Show What You Know

Make a Collage Make a collage that shows some farm products of the Southeast. Use pictures from newspapers and magazines, or draw your own pictures.

LESSON 2

A GROWING REGION

Link to Our World

How can a region's resources and location cause growth?

Focus on the Main Idea
Read to find out how the Southeast's resources and location have caused it to grow more crowded.

Preview Vocabulary
food processing
textile
pulp
renewable
  resource

Sun Belt
tourist
tourism

Making peanut butter is a leading industry in Dawson, Georgia.

Farming is important on the Coastal Plain. Most people who live there, however, do not work on farms. Instead, they live and work in urban areas. In the Southeast, cities have been growing quickly.

INDUSTRIES AND AGRICULTURE

At one time agriculture was the leading industry in the Southeast. That has changed. Now other industries are more important to the Southeast's economy. Some of those industries, however, are related to agriculture. Food processing is one. **Food processing** is cooking, canning, or freezing food and preparing it for market. Workers in many cities in the Southeast process the food crops grown there. They make such products as peanut butter, sugar, and orange juice.

Other workers in the Southeast turn cotton into **textiles**, or cloth. In fact, the Southeast is at the center of the nation's textile industry. Textiles are used to make many kinds of products. Among them are clothing, towels, and sheets.

Another important industry in the Southeast depends on the region's great pine forests. Sawmills use pine trees to make boards and other wood products. The trees are also cut down to make pulp. **Pulp** is a soft mixture of ground-up wood chips and chemicals that is used to make paper.

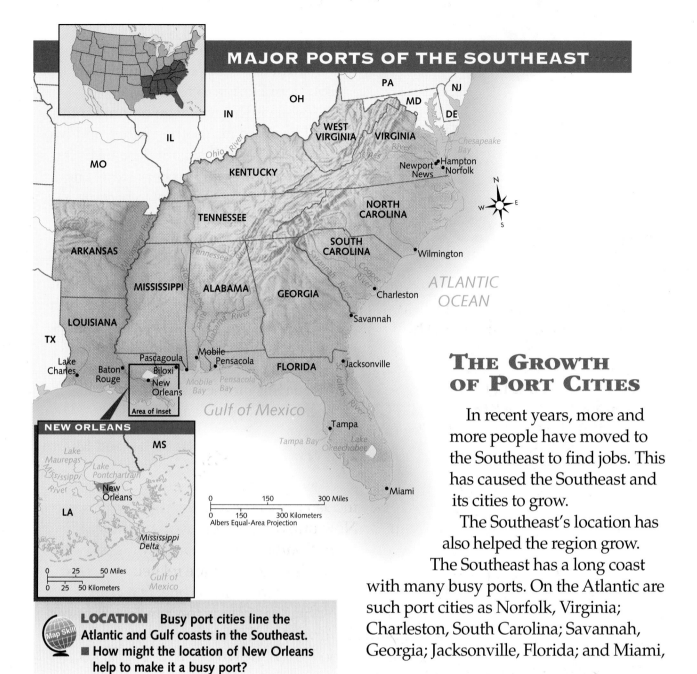

PA

OH

IN

IL

MO

WEST VIRGINIA

VIRGINIA

MD

NJ

DE

Ohio River

James River

Chesapeake Bay

KENTUCKY

Newport News • • Hampton
• Norfolk

TENNESSEE

NORTH CAROLINA

N
W • E
S

ARKANSAS

Tennessee River

SOUTH CAROLINA

Savannah River

Cooper River

• Wilmington

ATLANTIC OCEAN

MISSISSIPPI

ALABAMA

GEORGIA

• Charleston

LOUISIANA

• Savannah

TX

Lake Charles •

Baton Rouge •

Pascagoula •
• Biloxi
• New Orleans

Mobile •
• Pensacola

Mobile Bay

Pensacola Bay

FLORIDA

• Jacksonville

St. Johns River

Gulf of Mexico

Area of inset

• Tampa

Tampa Bay

Lake Okeechobee

• Miami

0   150   300 Miles
0   150   300 Kilometers
Albers Equal-Area Projection

NEW ORLEANS

MS

Lake Maurepas

Lake Pontchartrain

Mississippi River

• New Orleans

LA

Mississippi Delta

Gulf of Mexico

0   25   50 Miles
0   25   50 Kilometers

LOCATION Busy port cities line the Atlantic and Gulf coasts in the Southeast.
■ How might the location of New Orleans help to make it a busy port?

Map Skill

THE GROWTH OF PORT CITIES

In recent years, more and more people have moved to the Southeast to find jobs. This has caused the Southeast and its cities to grow.

The Southeast's location has also helped the region grow. The Southeast has a long coast with many busy ports. On the Atlantic are such port cities as Norfolk, Virginia; Charleston, South Carolina; Savannah, Georgia; Jacksonville, Florida; and Miami,

In many places in the Southeast, trees are raised as a crop. As trees are cut down for their wood, new ones are planted. People have learned that trees can be a renewable (rih•NOO•uh•buhl) resource. A **renewable resource** is a resource that can be used again or made again by people or nature.

✔ **What industries in the Southeast are related to agriculture?**

Ships must sail up the Mississippi River to reach New Orleans, the Southeast's busiest port.

Joshua lives in North Miami Beach, Florida. His grandparents came to the United States from countries in Latin America.

Florida. Large port cities along the Gulf of Mexico are Tampa, Florida; Mobile, Alabama; and New Orleans, Louisiana. All these cities are leading centers for manufacturing, services, and trade.

New Orleans is the busiest port in the Southeast. It lies along the Mississippi River about 100 miles (160 km) upstream from the Gulf of Mexico. About 5,000 ships dock in New Orleans each year.

Miami is another leading port in the Southeast. As with all port cities, trade has helped it grow. Because Miami is at the southern tip of the Florida peninsula, much of its trade is with countries in Latin America. Latin America includes all the countries in the Western Hemisphere south of the United States.

Trade is just one of the reasons Miami has grown. Immigration is another.

Thousands of immigrants from Latin America have moved to Miami and southern Florida in recent years.

Joshua is the grandson of immigrants. He lives with his mother, father, and two brothers in North Miami Beach. His father is a meat cutter in a grocery store. His mother is going to school to become a teacher.

Both of Joshua's grandparents on his father's side came to Florida from Cuba, an island nation in the Caribbean (kair•uh•BEE•uhn) Sea. This sea is southeast of Florida. His grandparents on his mother's side came to Florida from Colombia, a country in South America. Joshua, his brothers, and his parents speak both Spanish and English.

✓ **What things have helped Miami grow larger?**

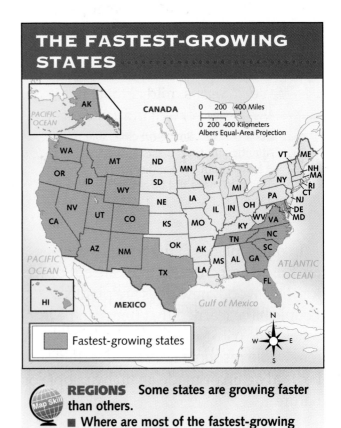

THE FASTEST-GROWING STATES

Fastest-growing states

REGIONS Some states are growing faster than others.
■ Where are most of the fastest-growing states located?

A MILD CLIMATE

Joshua's mother, Martha, says the climate is what she likes most about Florida. Other people like the Southeast's climate, too. Many people and businesses have moved to the region because of the mild climate.

The Southeast is part of the Sun Belt. The **Sun Belt** is a wide area of the United States that has a mild climate all year. The Sun Belt stretches from Virginia through the Southwest to California. Most places in the Sun Belt are growing much faster than most other parts of the country.

Among the many people moving to the Sun Belt are retired people, or older people who no longer work for pay or hold full-time jobs. Many other people in Sun Belt states have jobs in service industries that meet the needs of retired people.

The Southeast's mild climate has helped another service industry grow, too. Have you ever been to Orlando, Florida? Orlando is a favorite place for tourists to go. A **tourist** is someone who travels to a place for pleasure. The Orlando area is filled with things that are fun for tourists to do.

Tourists from all over the world go to Orlando, Miami, New Orleans, and other cities in the Southeast. Many people there work in tourism. **Tourism** is the selling of goods and services to tourists. Hotels, restaurants, and theme parks are all part of the tourism industry.

 **How has a mild climate helped the Southeast grow?**

Hotels stretch for miles along the coast of Miami Beach (above). Tourists and retired people come to fish, swim, and relax in the mild climate.

LESSON 2 REVIEW

Check Understanding

1. **Recall the Facts** Besides agriculture, what are two other important industries in the Southeast?
2. **Focus on the Main Idea** How have the Southeast's resources and location caused the region to grow more crowded?

Think Critically

3. **Link to You** How have resources and location affected the growth of your community?

Show What You Know

 **Map Activity** Draw a map of the Southeast and its coastline. Then label all the places named in this lesson. Use your map to explain why those places have grown so quickly.

Identify Causes and Their Effect

Why Is This Skill Important?

Suppose you wake up late and miss your school bus. Waking up late is the cause of your missing the bus. A **cause** is something that makes something else happen. Missing your bus is the effect of getting up late. An **effect** is what happens because of an earlier action.

Often an effect has more than one cause. Besides waking up late, you may also have read the comics before you ate breakfast and watched TV while you got dressed. Knowing all the causes of an effect can help you plan better next time. If you do not want to miss the bus again, you can get up earlier and get dressed before taking time to do other things.

Understanding causes and their effect can help you make better decisions. It can also help you understand why certain things have happened.

Remember What You Have Read

You have read about how the Southeast changed from a mostly agricultural region to a region with rapidly growing cities and many industries. Think about some of the causes for the Southeast's rapid growth.

1. How have the Southeast's industries caused growth?
2. How has the location of the Southeast caused growth?
3. How has the Southeast's climate caused growth?

Understand the Process

You can use the following steps to help you find all the causes of an effect.

- Look for the effect.
  The Southeast is growing rapidly.

- Look for all the causes of that effect.
  The Southeast's industries, location, and climate are causes of the region's rapid growth.
- Think about how these causes relate to each other and to the effect.
  Many tourists like to vacation in regions with mild climates. The Southeast's mild climate brings the region many tourists. Other people have moved to the Southeast to work in the tourism industry.

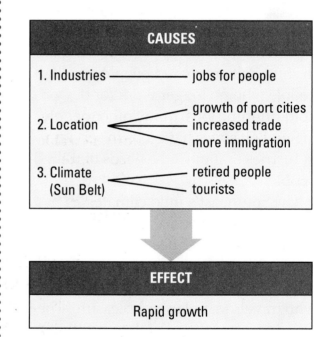

Think and Apply

Interview your parents, grandparents, or other adults about how the area in which you live has changed. Use the steps from Understand the Process to identify an effect, or a change that has happened, and all the causes for it. Share your findings with classmates.

LIFE ALONG THE GULF COAST

Link to Our World

How does a region's geography affect how people live and work?

Focus on the Main Idea
Read to find out how the geography of the Gulf coast affects the people who live there.

Preview Vocabulary
inlet
bayou
petroleum
crude oil
nonrenewable
resource
refinery
petrochemical
hurricane

People celebrating Mardi Gras wear brightly colored costumes.

Cities along the Gulf coast are centers of services, manufacturing, and trade. Offshore, fishing is an important industry. Under the land and water are two of the Southeast's most valuable resources—oil and natural gas.

A SPECIAL WAY OF LIFE

Land along the Gulf of Mexico is mostly low and flat. Often it is wet. The coast itself is made up of broad beaches, coastal marshes, and shallow inlets. An **inlet** is a narrow strip of water leading into the land from a larger body of water.

The Mississippi River is the largest river that flows into the Gulf of Mexico. At its mouth is a huge delta called the Mississippi Delta. Here the Mississippi River divides into several smaller channels. Each one has muddy islands and bayous (BY•ooz). A **bayou** is a slow-moving body of water.

A special way of life has grown up along those bayous. This is partly due to two groups who live there. They are the Creoles (KREE•ohlz) and the Cajuns (KAY•juhnz). The ancestors of the Creoles were early French and Spanish settlers. The Cajuns' ancestors were a group of French colonists who came to the Mississippi Delta from Canada.

These two groups have given much of southern Louisiana a French heritage. Today many Creoles and Cajuns speak both English and a form of French. They also celebrate Mardi Gras (MAHR•dee GRAH). This is a holiday their ancestors first brought to the area.

What?

Gumbo

Gumbo is a popular food in the Mississippi Delta. Gumbo began as a fish stew made by French settlers. Spanish settlers added hot sausage and peppers. Africans added vegetables, such as green peppers and okra. Africans also gave the stew its name. It was first called *gombo*. This is the word for okra in Bantu, a language of Africa.

The bayous helped keep the Creoles and the Cajuns separate from other people living in the area. Yet the Creoles and the Cajuns have been influenced by other people. Their language is now mixed with words from other languages. Zydeco (ZY•duh•koh) music is enjoyed in many places. It is a mix of French, Caribbean, and North American music.

✓ **What makes the way of life in southern Louisiana special?**

OIL ALONG THE COAST

The Mississippi Delta is part of a large area that produces oil. This area stretches all the way from Texas to Mississippi. In the state of Louisiana alone more than 22,000 wells pump oil, or **petroleum** (puh•TROH•lee•uhm), from the Earth.

In 1901 workers were busy drilling for oil at Spindletop, an oil field near the Texas and Louisiana border. Each day, the well went deeper. Then, on January 10, the ground began to shake. With a roar oil shot nearly 200 feet (61 m) into the sky.

Soon more wells were drilled along the Gulf coast. When the oil in a well was used up, people drilled new wells in other places. Those early wells spilled much of the crude oil they pumped. **Crude oil** is the name given to petroleum pumped from the ground.

People thought there was so much oil that it would never run out. They did not realize that oil is a nonrenewable resource. A **nonrenewable resource** is a resource that cannot be made again by nature or by people.

✓ **What is a nonrenewable resource?**

OIL AND NATURAL GAS IN THE UNITED STATES

0   200   400 Miles
0   200   400 Kilometers
Albers Equal-Area Projection

PACIFIC OCEAN
ALASKA
CANADA
ROCKY MOUNTAINS
APPALACHIAN MOUNTAINS
PACIFIC OCEAN
ATLANTIC OCEAN
HAWAII
MEXICO
Gulf of Mexico

■ Oil and natural-gas field

PLACE Many places in the United States have rich deposits of oil and natural gas.
■ Where are most of Louisiana's oil and natural-gas fields?

MAKING A LIVING

Along the Gulf coast, many workers earn their living in the oil industry. Some have jobs at oil wells. Others work at refineries. A **refinery** is a factory that turns crude oil into useful products such as gasoline and other fuels.

Some crude oil is used to make petrochemicals (peh•troh•KEH•mih•kuhlz). A **petrochemical** is a chemical made from oil. Petrochemicals are used in many products. Some of these products are plastics, tires, paints, and even some clothing and medicines.

The same forces in the Earth that made oil millions of years ago also produced natural gas. Many workers along the

Oil refineries, like this one in New Orleans, turn crude oil into fuels and other useful products.

LEARNING FROM CHARTS Many products are made from petroleum.
■ How does transportation depend on petroleum?

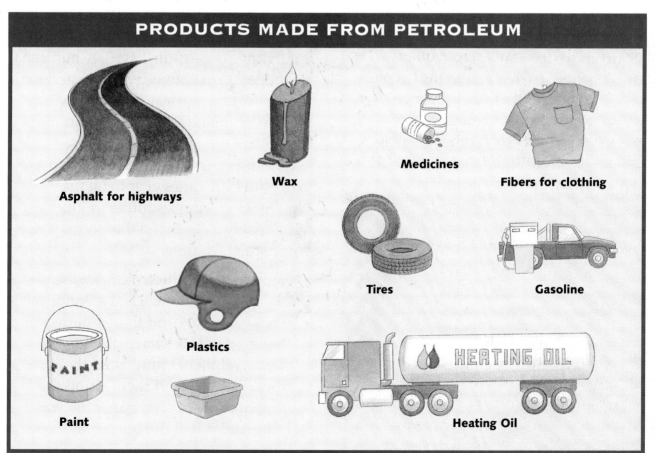

PRODUCTS MADE FROM PETROLEUM

Asphalt for highways

Wax

Medicines

Fibers for clothing

Tires

Gasoline

Plastics

Paint

HEATING OIL

Heating Oil

Gulf coast have jobs at gas wells. Other workers help build pipelines that take the gas to other places.

✔ **What kinds of jobs are linked to crude oil and natural gas?**

OFFSHORE DRILLING

In the early 1900s, oil and gas wells were always drilled on land. As more oil and gas were needed, however, people started to drill wells offshore, under the water.

Drilling offshore costs much more than drilling on land. Huge platforms, called rigs, must be built to hold the drilling equipment above the water. The workers and everything they use must be taken to and from the rig by boat or by helicopter.

One oil worker, Kim Bartlett, wrote about working on an oil rig in the Gulf of Mexico. To get to work, he took an eight-hour, 125-mile (201-km) boat ride to the oil rig. The rig's main deck was 70 feet (21 m) above the water. The only way for Bartlett to reach it was to ride in the

Huge platforms, called rigs, make offshore drilling possible. This rig stands off the Louisiana coast, in the Gulf of Mexico.

"basket." This was a small container hung from a crane on the rig. The crane raised and lowered the basket like an elevator. Bartlett told how he felt about riding in the basket.

❝It dangles aloft, seventy feet up, swinging back and forth in the gusting wind. . . . Have I really got to get on that thing? Is that really the only way to get from here up to there? I've asked the question a hundred times, in silence and aloud, always with the same answer: That's it, pardner. Just get on and hold on, and whatever happens, don't let go.❞

✔ **Why does offshore drilling cost more than drilling on land?**

TRAILS OF DESTRUCTION

Working on an oil rig in the Gulf of Mexico can be dangerous. Working in the Gulf can be even more dangerous during a hurricane (HUHR•uh•kayn). A **hurricane** is a huge storm with heavy rains and high winds. Near a hurricane's center, winds blow at 74 miles (119 km) per hour or more.

On August 24, 1992, one of the most powerful hurricanes ever to hit the United States struck southern Florida. Victor Sabdul described the storm, which was named Andrew.

❝It was about three o'clock when the lights went out. Then a window went behind us and things started flying. . . . Glass was exploding all over. And then, Plum! went the front door. . . . And then, Plum! the back door went. The hurricane was here. And it had the house all to itself.❞

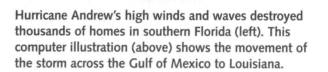

Hurricane Andrew's high winds and waves destroyed thousands of homes in southern Florida (left). This computer illustration (above) shows the movement of the storm across the Gulf of Mexico to Louisiana.

The Sabdul house, along with about 25,000 others, was destroyed. Another 60,000 homes were damaged. Winds of more than 160 miles (257 km) per hour blew down almost everything in their path. Altogether some 250 thousand people were left without homes.

Instead of ending its damage there, however, Andrew kept right on going. The storm blew across the Gulf of Mexico and slammed into Louisiana two days later. Huge waves flooded the coast.

Hurricane Andrew drove more than a million people in Louisiana from their homes. When the storm ended, though, they quickly began to clean up the mess, just as the people in Florida had done earlier. For many people, hurricanes are just part of life in the Southeast region.

 **What is a hurricane?**

LESSON 3 REVIEW

Check Understanding

1. Recall the Facts   What happens in a refinery?

2. Focus on the Main Idea   How does the geography of the Gulf coast affect the people who live there?

Think Critically

3. Think More About It   Why was Hurricane Andrew such a damaging storm?

Show What You Know

 Writing Activity   Divide a sheet of paper in half. On one half of your paper, list three ways in which geography affects workers and other people along the Gulf coast. On the other half, make a list that tells how geography affects the people where you live. Compare the lists and discuss any differences with classmates.

Read a Cross-Section Diagram

Why Is This Skill Important?

Have you ever looked closely at the trunk of a tree after the tree has been cut down? If you have, you probably saw circles, or rings, on the end that was cut. The rings were layers of wood. The layers of wood looked like rings because you were looking at a cross section of the tree. A **cross section** is a slice or piece cut straight across something.

The drawing on the next page is a cross-section diagram of an offshore oil rig. A **cross-section diagram** is a drawing that shows what you would see if you could slice through something and then look at the cut surface. Reading a cross-section diagram can help you understand what something looks like on the inside. It can also help you understand how something works.

Most trees grow a layer of wood each year. Each ring in a trunk represents one year in a tree's life.

How Oil Formed

Millions of years ago, oceans covered most of the Earth's surface. As tiny sea organisms (AWR•guh•nih•zuhmz) died, their remains sank to the bottoms of the oceans. Mud and sand washed into the oceans and covered the organisms. Over time, layers of mud and sand hardened into rock. The layers of rock pressed down on the organisms' remains, turning them into oil. Sometimes workers must drill through hundreds of feet of rock before they reach oil.

Oil is often found in layers of porous (PAWR•uhs) rock. Porous rock has tiny holes in it. These holes hold oil the way a sponge holds water. Above and below the porous rock are layers of nonporous rock that the oil cannot soak through.

Understand the Process

1. Find the platform in the cross-section diagram. The platform holds the derrick and the drilling equipment high above the water. What keeps the platform above the water?
2. Several layers of rock lie beneath the sand on the ocean floor. Find the oil that lies trapped in the rock. What natural resource is found on top of the oil?
3. To reach the oil, a large drill bit, called a rotary bit, digs a hole through the layers of rock. As the hole is being dug, workers add more and more drill pipe to the rotary bit.

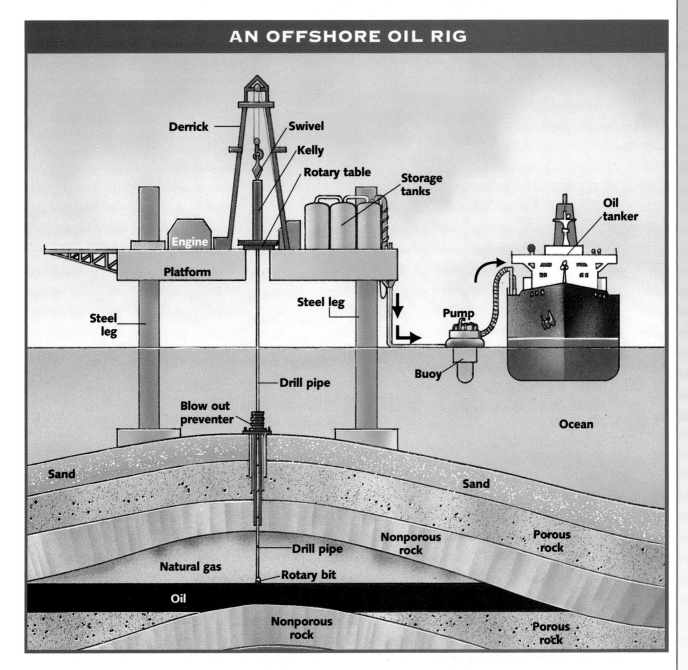

AN OFFSHORE OIL RIG

Derrick

Swivel

Kelly

Rotary table

Storage tanks

Oil tanker

Engine

Platform

Steel leg

Pump

Steel leg

Drill pipe

Buoy

Blow out preventer

Ocean

Sand

Sand

Nonporous rock

Porous rock

Drill pipe

Natural gas

Rotary bit

Oil

Nonporous rock

Porous rock

At the top of the drill pipe is another piece of pipe called the kelly. What does the kelly rest on?

4. Find the engine, which sits on the platform. The engine is connected to the rotary table. When the engine turns, it spins the rotary table. This causes the kelly to turn. What other parts of the drill also turn?

5. When workers reach the oil, they remove the drill pipe and rotary bit. In place of these go other pipes that bring up the oil. The oil then goes into the storage tanks. What happens to the oil after that?

Think and Apply

Find a cross-section diagram in an encyclopedia or a library book, or draw your own. Use the diagram to tell classmates about the object shown. Explain what the object looks like on the inside or how it works.

LESSON 4

ISLANDS AND PEOPLE

Link to Our World

How can an island environment affect people's lives?

Focus on the Main Idea
As you read this lesson, compare the challenges that people face on different islands off the Southeast region's coast.

Preview Vocabulary
barrier island   tropics
mainland   territory
legend   commonwealth
strait
coral
reef

Blackbeard's real name was Edward Teach.

Hurricanes sometimes hit coastal areas in the Southeast. However, the climate along both the Atlantic and Gulf coasts is generally mild. Near both coasts are many islands that also have mild, sunny climates. Each of those islands is different. Yet the people who live there face many of the same challenges.

ISLANDS ALONG THE COAST

Barrier islands line much of the Atlantic and Gulf coasts of the Southeast region. **Barrier islands** are low, narrow islands that are near a coast. They are made up of sand, silt, and gravel carried there by rivers or ocean waves.

Barrier islands help block ocean winds and waves from reaching the mainland. The **mainland** is the continent, or part of a continent, nearest to an island. Barrier islands protect the mainland during stormy weather.

Some barrier islands, like those off the coast of North Carolina, have wild and windy weather. Those islands, called the Outer Banks, are hit by powerful storms every year. Hundreds of ships have wrecked and sunk in the choppy waters off those islands.

One group of people who went to the Outer Banks long ago were pirates. One of the most feared of those pirates was called Blackbeard. A legend says that Blackbeard's stolen treasures are still buried somewhere on the islands. A **legend** is a story that has come down

This lighthouse in Key West, Florida, once signaled ships that land was near. Today, it is a popular place for tourists to visit.

from the past. Parts of the story may or may not be true.

Some barrier islands, such as the Sea Islands of Georgia, are vacation areas. One of the most popular vacation areas is Hilton Head Island, off the coast of South Carolina. Other barrier islands have large cities on them. In Florida the cities of Daytona Beach and Miami Beach are on barrier islands.

✓ **What are barrier islands?**

THE FLORIDA KEYS

Islands of another kind rise from the blue-green waters at the tip of the Florida peninsula. They are the Florida Keys, a chain of islands that stretches about 150 miles (241 km) along the north side of the Straits of Florida. A **strait** is a narrow channel that connects two larger bodies of water. The Straits of Florida connect the Atlantic Ocean and the Gulf of Mexico.

The Florida Keys are coral islands. **Coral** is a stony material formed by the skeletons of tiny sea animals. Over time coral can build up to form a low island.

Key West, the largest city on the Florida Keys, has about 25,000 people. It is on the island of Key West, about 100 miles (160 km) southwest of the mainland. Except for cities in Hawaii, Key West is the most southern city in the United States.

✓ **How did the Florida Keys form?**

Corals are known for their bright colors.

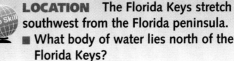

THE FLORIDA KEYS

FLORIDA
Lake Okeechobee
Big Cypress Swamp
Everglades
Key Largo
Gulf of Mexico
Sugarloaf Key
Florida Bay
Florida Keys
Key West
Straits of Florida
ATLANTIC OCEAN
CUBA

0   50   100 Miles
0   50   100 Kilometers
Albers Equal-Area Projection

LOCATION The Florida Keys stretch southwest from the Florida peninsula.
■ What body of water lies north of the Florida Keys?

A LINK TO THE MAINLAND

During the 1800s some people in Key West made their living by fishing for shrimp and sponges. However, most people recovered goods from sunken ships. The ships had sunk after hitting sharp coral reefs in the Straits of Florida. A **reef** is a ridge of rocks, sand, or coral near the surface of the sea.

Key West's warm climate brought tourists, but the city was hard to reach. The only way to get there was by boat. That changed in the early 1900s, though. A rich man named Henry Flagler built a railroad across the Florida Keys from Miami to Key West.

Before the railroad, people in Key West traded more with Cuba than they did with the United States. After all, Cuba is just 90 miles (145 km) from Key West! The railroad, however, made trade with the mainland much easier. Many more tourists could reach Key West, too, so the city grew larger.

In 1935 Key West's link to the mainland was destroyed in one day. A powerful hurricane hit the Florida Keys. Ocean waves washed away much of the railroad.

By 1938 Key West was once again linked to the mainland. The new link was the Overseas Highway, the world's longest oceangoing highway. It is more than 100 miles (160 km) long and has more than 40 bridges. One bridge stretches for 7 miles (11 km)!

Today Key West has a booming tourist industry. But Key West is now facing the kinds of problems that growth brings to island cities. One of the biggest problems is space. Key West is only about 1 mile (less than 2 km) wide. Buildings now reach to the water's edge. The city is especially crowded during the winter months, when many tourists visit. This crowding causes pollution that is harming nearby coral reefs.

Until it was destroyed by a hurricane in 1935, a railroad (below) linked Key West to the Florida mainland. The 7-Mile Bridge (right) is the longest bridge on the Overseas Highway.

Climate Zones

The tilt of the Earth as it moves around the sun causes climate zones. Climate zones are wide bands that circle the Earth. Most of the places in a climate zone have about the same climate. Most places in the tropic zone, for example, have a warm climate. Places in the polar zones have a cold climate. Places in between, in the temperate zones, have a warm climate for part of the year and a cold climate for part of the year.

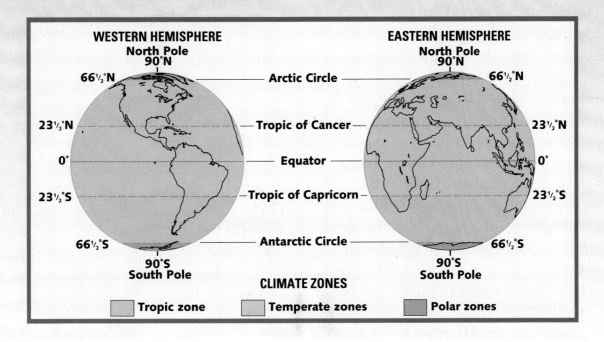

Getting enough fresh water, food, and electricity to Key West is another problem. A 130-mile (209-km) pipeline now carries 12 million gallons (45 million L) of fresh water from the Florida mainland to Key West every day. But that water costs five times what it costs on the mainland. Most of the food that people in Key West use must be brought by truck from the mainland. So it often costs more, too. The electricity that people in Key West use reaches the city from the mainland through undersea cables.

 What are some of the problems that people in Key West must face?

PUERTO RICO

Other islands in the Southeast region lie far off the coast. The only way to reach those islands is by ship or airplane. One of those islands is Puerto Rico (PWAIR•tuh REE•koh), which means "rich port" in Spanish. Puerto Rico is about 1,000 miles (1,609 km) southeast of Florida. It is in the **tropics**, a band of warm climate that circles the Earth near the equator.

Puerto Rico is made up of the peaks of a mountain range that formed under the ocean millions of years ago. Unlike barrier or coral islands, Puerto Rico has steep mountains and deep valleys. All along its coast is a wide, fertile plain.

Christopher Columbus landed on Puerto Rico in 1493. Spanish settlers soon followed. They brought to the island the language, religion, and laws of Spain. In 1898, however, after a war between Spain and the United States, Puerto Rico became a territory (TAIR•uh•tohr•ee) of the United States. A **territory** is a place owned and governed by a country.

The people of Puerto Rico were later made citizens of the United States. This meant they could freely move to the United States mainland. Then, in 1952, Puerto Rico became a commonwealth. A **commonwealth** is a territory that governs itself. As a commonwealth, Puerto Rico has close ties to the United States, but it has its own government. Unlike other citizens, however, people in Puerto Rico do not have a representative who can vote in Congress. Also, they do not get to vote for President.

What is it like to live in Puerto Rico? Puerto Rico has a mix of Spanish and American customs. The main language is Spanish. The island is crowded, and most

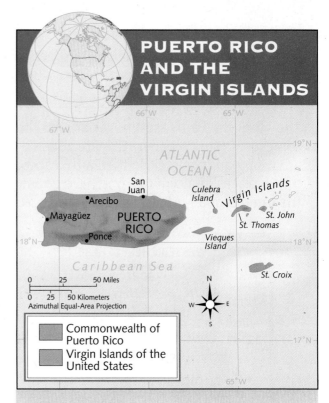

LOCATION Puerto Rico and the Virgin Islands lie between the Atlantic Ocean and the Caribbean Sea.

■ Which city in Puerto Rico lies nearest to the line of latitude 18°N? Which city lies nearest to the line of longitude 66°W?

El Morro Fortress stands at the entrance to the Bay of San Juan in Puerto Rico. Spanish soldiers built this fort between 1539 and 1787.

Large cruise ships (above) bring thousands of tourists to St. Thomas each year. The island's outdoor markets (right) are a favorite place for tourists to shop.

people live in or near cities along the coast. San Juan (SAN WAHN) is Puerto Rico's capital and largest city. It has large buildings, shopping centers, factories, and rush-hour traffic jams.

 **How is Puerto Rico different from barrier and coral islands?**

THE VIRGIN ISLANDS

The Virgin Islands of the United States are about 60 miles (97 km) east of Puerto Rico. Like Puerto Rico, these islands are the peaks of ancient mountains. The three largest islands are St. Croix (SAYNT KROY), St. Thomas, and St. John.

The Virgin Islands of the United States are a U.S. territory. The United States bought them from Denmark in 1917. Like Puerto Ricans, the people of the Virgin Islands are citizens of the United States.

The Virgin Islands are crowded places. There is not enough fresh water on the islands to meet the needs of all the people who live or visit there. Most fresh water and food must be imported.

 **Why must the Virgin Islands import fresh water?**

L SSON 4 REVIEW

Check Understanding

1. **Recall the Facts** How do barrier islands help protect the mainland?
2. **Focus on the Main Idea** What are some challenges that people face on the islands off the Southeast region's coast?

Think Critically

3. **Personally Speaking** What would you like most about living on an island? What would you like least?

Show What You Know

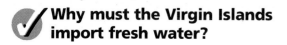 **Art Activity** Choose one of the islands described in this lesson. Then make a travel brochure that describes the island. Draw a picture for your brochure, and write a caption that tells what the picture shows about the island.

CONNECT MAIN IDEAS

Use this organizer to show that you understand how the chapter's main ideas are connected. First copy the organizer onto a separate sheet of paper. Then complete it by writing the main idea of each lesson.

Farming on the
Coastal Plain

_____

_____

_____

A Growing
Region

_____

_____

_____

Coastal Plains
and
Islands

Life Along
the Gulf Coast

_____

_____

_____

Islands and
People

_____

_____

_____

WRITE MORE ABOUT IT

1. **Write a Persuasive Letter** Write a letter to your principal to explain why you should be chosen to go to the United States Space Camp. Tell why you want to go, what you would learn there, and how you would spend your days.

2. **Write a Descriptive Paragraph** Imagine that you and your family have just moved to a state on the Coastal Plain of the Southeast region. Write a paragraph that describes some features you

see near your new home. Tell how the people who live on the Coastal Plain might earn a living.

3. **Write a Story** Legend says that Blackbeard's treasures are still buried on the Outer Banks, the barrier islands that lie off the coast of North Carolina. Write a story about pirates, stolen treasure, and shipwrecks on the Outer Banks. In your story, show that you understand the geography of these islands.

USE VOCABULARY

Write the term that correctly matches each definition.

bayou   strait
generation   Sun Belt
growing season territory
refinery   textile

1. the average time between the birth of parents and the birth of their children

2. the time when the weather is warm enough for plants to grow

3. cloth

4. a wide area of the United States that has a mild climate all year

5. a slow-moving body of water

6. a factory that turns crude oil into useful products

7. a narrow channel that connects two larger bodies of water

8. a place owned and governed by a country

CHECK UNDERSTANDING

1. Why are farmers on the Coastal Plain of the Southeast able to grow many kinds of crops?

2. How has the Southeast's economy changed?

3. Which two groups give much of southern Louisiana a French heritage? How have those groups been influenced by other people?

4. How is a renewable resource different from a nonrenewable resource?

5. How is the geography of Puerto Rico different from the geography of a barrier island?

THINK CRITICALLY

1. **Cause and Effect** How can living on an island affect people?

2. **Personally Speaking** Tourism is an important industry in the Southeast. Would you like to visit there? Why?

3. **Think More About It** How do the rights of citizens in Puerto Rico differ from the rights of other American citizens?

4. **Explore Viewpoints** How do you think the people who live in Key West feel about tourists?

APPLY SKILLS

How to Identify Causes and Their Effect Think about something that has happened to you at school, such as earning a good grade or making a new friend. List the causes for that effect.

How to Read a Cross-Section Diagram
Use the cross-section diagram on page 209 to answer these questions.

1. What does the derrick do?

2. What turns the rotary table?

READ MORE ABOUT IT

Everglades by Jean Craighead George. HarperCollins. This book describes how people have changed the Everglades.

Mardi Gras! by Suzanne M. Coil. Macmillan. This book tells all about the Mardi Gras and its history.

The Private World of Smith Island by Sally Foster. Cobblehill. Life on Smith Island, in Chesapeake Bay, is described by the people who live there.

HIGHLANDS AND MOUNTAINS

> 66 Almost Heaven,
> West Virginia,
> Blue Ridge Mountains,
> Shenandoah River.
> Life is old there,
> older than the trees,
> Younger than the mountains,
> growing like a breeze. 99
>
> from the song
> "Take Me Home, Country Roads,"
> written by John Denver,
> Bill Danoff, and Taffy Danoff

This woman has lived in the Appalachian Mountains of West Virginia for most of her life.

USING A RIVER'S ENERGY

*L*nk to Our World

How can people change rivers to meet their needs?

Focus on the Main Idea
Read to find out how people in the Southeast have changed rivers to meet their needs.

Preview Vocabulary
**fall line
pass
waterpower
reservoir
hydroelectric power**

The Fall Line on the Potomac River, near Washington, D.C.

Rivers provide water for people. They also help supply the power for industries and cities. Before people can use rivers, however, they must often change them in some way.

THE FALL LINE

Many of the Southeast's oldest cities began near the mouths of the broad, deep rivers that flow across the region. Settlers later followed those rivers upstream, where they cleared land for new farms and towns. Some people used the rivers to take them even farther inland, toward the Appalachian Mountains. Boats could not take them all the way, however. On every river, waterfalls blocked the way.

Many rivers in the Southeast flow from the Appalachian Mountains across the Piedmont to the Coastal Plain. Where the Piedmont meets the Coastal Plain, the elevation of the land drops suddenly. This causes waterfalls to form on the rivers. The place where those waterfalls form is called the Fall Line. A **fall line** is the place where rivers drop from higher to lower land.

Settlers who went beyond the Fall Line had to carry their supplies overland, around the waterfalls. Then, to cross the mountains, they had to find passes through them. A **pass** is a low place between mountains.

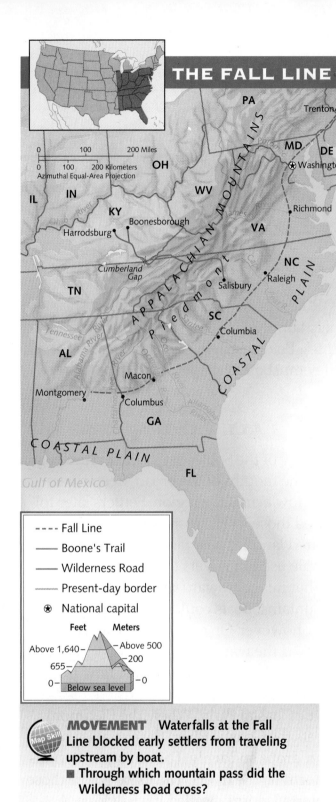

THE FALL LINE

Fall Line
Boone's Trail
Wilderness Road
Present-day border
National capital

Feet   Meters
Above 1,640 — Above 500
655 —   200
0 —   0
Below sea level

MOVEMENT Waterfalls at the Fall Line blocked early settlers from traveling upstream by boat.
■ Through which mountain pass did the Wilderness Road cross?

One of the first pioneers who searched for a pass was Daniel Boone. From traders, Boone had heard about a fertile land west of the mountains. Boone had also heard that an Indian trail led there. With the help of a friend, Boone found the

trail. He followed it across the Appalachians through a mountain pass called the Cumberland Gap.

Boone later helped make a narrow road to what is now the state of Kentucky. This road was called the Wilderness Road. One pioneer said that when the road was finished, "thousands of men, women, and children came . . . , forming a continuous stream of human beings, horses, and cattle . . . , all moving onward along a lonely and houseless path."

✓ **Why do waterfalls form along the Fall Line?**

USING FALL LINE RIVERS

Many people went on to places west of the mountains. However, some settled at the Fall Line. Those settlers knew they could make a good living there. After all, people who lived upstream from the falls would need goods. They would also need help getting their products to ships below the falls. The ships would take the products to markets in cities along the coast.

Other people settled at the Fall Line because they knew how to use the energy, or waterpower, of the falls. **Waterpower** is the power produced by rushing water. People used waterpower to run machines in mills and other factories.

To use waterpower, people built waterwheels. Water from a river was made to flow over the waterwheel, which caused the wheel to turn. The wheel then could run machines connected to it.

HOW A WATERWHEEL WORKS

Flow from river

Waterwheel

Direction waterwheel turns

Post that turns mill machines

Mill

This mill in Pigeon Forge, Tennessee, still uses waterpower to grind corn into meal.

YELLOW CORN MEAL
STONE GROUND WITH WATER POWER
NET WT. 32 OZS. (2 LBS.)

LEARNING FROM DIAGRAMS
People used waterpower to run early mills.
■ What turns the mill machines?

Cities along the Fall Line grew very quickly. The waterfalls gave businesses a way to run their machines. The rivers gave them a way to ship their products downstream to market. Many cities in the Southeast grew up along the Fall Line. Some of them are Richmond, Virginia; Raleigh, North Carolina; Columbia, South Carolina; Macon, Georgia; and Montgomery, Alabama.

✓ **How did people use rivers along the Fall Line?**

PEOPLE CHANGE RIVERS

Rivers provide waterpower. Yet people need rivers in other ways, too. Think about all the ways you and other people use water each day. If we did not have a good supply of water, our lives would be very different.

Water, like most other kinds of natural resources, is not distributed equally all over the Earth. To make sure they have enough water, people sometimes build dams across rivers. Dams form reservoirs (REH•zuh•vwahrz) behind them. A **reservoir** is a lake that stores water held back by a dam. People and industries use the water stored in reservoirs.

Dams help make electricity, too. Water from reservoirs can be used to turn the large machines that make electricity. **Hydroelectric power** is electricity made by waterpower. This is an important source of electricity in much of the Southeast.

The Tennessee River and its tributaries used to flood often. To help control the floods, the national government set up the Tennessee Valley Authority, or TVA. The TVA built many dams. It also built power plants to make electricity. Having this good source of electricity brought more industries and jobs to the Southeast.

Building dams is one way people change rivers, but they change them in other ways, too. People build bridges over them and levees beside them. People also make rivers deeper so that ships can travel on them. People sometimes pollute rivers, too. They do this by dumping waste into them or by allowing harmful chemicals to wash into them.

How do people sometimes change rivers?

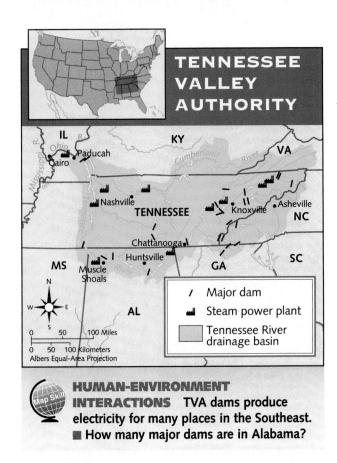

TENNESSEE VALLEY AUTHORITY

Legend	
/	Major dam
⌐	Steam power plant
▨	Tennessee River drainage basin

0   50   100 Miles
0   50   100 Kilometers
Albers Equal-Area Projection

HUMAN-ENVIRONMENT INTERACTIONS TVA dams produce electricity for many places in the Southeast.
■ How many major dams are in Alabama?

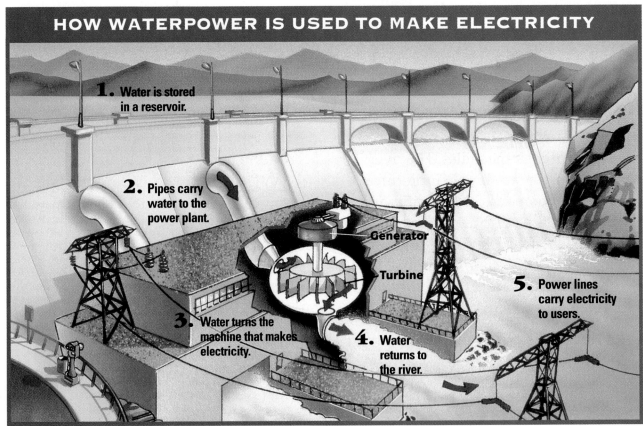

HOW WATERPOWER IS USED TO MAKE ELECTRICITY

1. Water is stored in a reservoir.
2. Pipes carry water to the power plant.
3. Water turns the machine that makes electricity.
4. Water returns to the river.
5. Power lines carry electricity to users.

Generator
Turbine

LEARNING FROM DIAGRAMS Water rushing through dams provides the waterpower needed to make electricity.
■ What two machines are used to make electricity?

Modern pulp washers (above) help to conserve water in paper mills. This symbol (right) lets people know that products have been made with recycled materials.

INDUSTRIES AND RIVERS

Industries need a lot of water to manufacture most goods. For example, it takes about 250 tons of water to make just 1 ton of paper. To make one Sunday newspaper takes almost 150 gallons (560 L) of water. That is enough to fill about three bathtubs.

One company has been making paper at its mill in Canton, North Carolina, since 1908. It uses water from the Pigeon River. David Craft, the company's Director of Public Affairs, says the river's water is important in making paper. "The first raw material that we see coming into Canton is the wood chip, which is a postage-stamp-size chip that is either pine or hardwood. And we take that wood and wash it."

It may not seem that washing wood chips would use a lot of water. But the company uses a lot of wood chips—enough to make about 1,500 tons of paper a day. The company makes about one-fourth of all the paper for envelopes in the United States. It also makes one out of every three milk cartons.

To make all that paper, the company uses about 29 million gallons (about 110 million L) of water each day. After the water has been used, it is cleaned and put

back into the Pigeon River. For many years, however, water from the paper mill flowed back into the river without being cleaned. That added to pollution in the river. Today, the company's ways have changed. As Mr. Craft explains, "Like many companies that use rivers for manufacturing, we began to install processes to minimize water pollution in the early 1960s. Now we are coming to the end of a $300 million expenditure . . . that is resulting in extremely significant improvements in water quality."

The company now makes recycled paper, too. Making recycled paper uses less water and fewer wood chips than making new paper. So, using recycled paper helps save natural resources.

✓ **How do industries sometimes depend on rivers?**

LESSON 1 REVIEW

Check Understanding

1. **Recall the Facts**   How are rivers important to manufacturing?
2. **Focus on the Main Idea**   How have people in the Southeast changed rivers to meet their needs?

Think Critically

3. **Link to You**   How might your life be different if the United States did not have so many rivers?

Show What You Know

Art Activity   Work with classmates to paint a mural showing some ways in which people change rivers.

Should More DAMS Be BUILT?

People have been building dams across rivers in the Southeast for many years. Along just the Chattahoochee (cha•tuh•HOO•chee) River and its tributaries, there are 16 dams. The Chattahoochee River flows southwest across Georgia. Then it forms part of Georgia's border with Alabama. From there it flows through Florida, where it is known as the Apalachicola (a•puh•la•chih•KOH•luh) River.

Buford Dam was built across the Chattahoochee River in the 1950s. Like many dams, it was built to help control floods and to make electricity. Most people in Georgia were happy when the dam was built. They liked the reservoir, Lake Sidney Lanier (luh•NIR), that formed behind it. Today Lake Sidney Lanier is enjoyed as a recreation area.

Buford Dam, like many dams in the Southeast, was built by the Army Corps (KAWR) of Engineers. In 1978 the Corps made plans to begin another dam along the Chattahoochee River. It was to be built near the city of Atlanta. Atlanta is downstream from Buford Dam.

CHATTAHOOCHEE RIVER

TENNESSEE

NORTH CAROLINA

Buford Dam

Gainesville

Lake Sidney Lanier

Atlanta

West Point Lake

ALABAMA

Lake Harding

Columbus

GEORGIA

SOUTH CAROLINA

Walter F. George Lake

Lake Seminole

ATLANTIC OCEAN

Apalachicola R.

Tallahassee

FLORIDA

0   50   100 Miles

0   50   100 Kilometers
Albers Equal-Area Projection

/ Major dam

LOCATION The Chattahoochee River forms part of the border between Georgia and Alabama.
■ Which Georgia city shown on the map is located closest to Buford Dam and Lake Sidney Lanier?

Arguments for Building a Dam

When electricity is produced by Buford Dam, huge amounts of water go into the Chattahoochee. The Army Corps of Engineers said that a new dam would hold back some of this water and even out its flow through the river. A new dam, the Corps said, would also give the Atlanta metropolitan area more water. That area does need more water. By 2010 it will use about 529 million gallons (2 billion L) of water each day!

Arguments Against a New Dam

Many people do not want new dams. "People like lakes but they don't like dams," said one person who helps build dams. People worry about how dams affect the environment.

Some people told the Army Corps of Engineers that a new dam on the Chattahoochee River was not needed. They said that some of the water stored in Lake Sidney Lanier could be given to Atlanta.

A New Plan

The Army Corps of Engineers changed its plan. Instead of building a new dam, the Corps would increase the flow of water through Buford Dam by 160 million gallons (606 million L) each day.

Many people, however, do not like that plan. They worry that it would cause lower water levels in Lake Sidney Lanier. This would affect fishing and boating.

Many people downstream fear that the Atlanta area would use more than its share of the water. This could mean too little water for boating or for making electricity. They also fear that the water reaching them would be more polluted. The Army Corps of Engineers and the states of Georgia, Alabama, and Florida have agreed to study the problem some more.

The Chattahoochee River in northern Georgia

COMPARE
VIEWPOINTS

1. What did people have to say against a new dam?
2. Why are many people who live near Lake Sidney Lanier against the Army Corps of Engineers' new plan?
3. Why are many people downstream also against the plan?

THINK
–AND–
APPLY

Think of some problem that separates people in your community. In writing, tell what the problem is. Also give your own point of view. Then list some things that support your point of view. Is there anything that might make you change your mind? Explain.

BUILDING CITIZENSHIP

THE GROWTH OF PIEDMONT CITIES

*L*nk to Our World

What can help a city grow?

Focus on the Main Idea
Read to find out why many cities in the Piedmont have grown so quickly.

Preview Vocabulary
state legislature
governor

Atlanta is Georgia's capital and largest city. Downtown Atlanta (below) has many modern skyscrapers.

Many of the Southeast's largest cities are in the Piedmont. As you know, this is the area between the Fall Line and the Appalachian Mountains. Some of the cities are on the Fall Line. Others are among the region's many hills and forests. All of the cities, however, are growing quickly.

GROWING INDUSTRIES, GROWING CITIES

The Piedmont is rich in minerals. It has many forests and good farmland. Many of the Southeast's factories are in large cities in the Piedmont, such as Charlotte, North Carolina, and Atlanta, Georgia. Both of these cities are also leading transportation centers for the Southeast region.

Richmond, Virginia, is like many other Piedmont cities. Richmond is at the Fall Line on the James River. Today Richmond is a large and growing city. It is also the capital of Virginia.

Richmond's location on the Fall Line made it an important place for trade. Early settlers took furs and crops—mostly corn and tobacco—to Richmond to be sold. From there the goods were taken down the James River to the coast.

Early industries in Piedmont cities depended on the region's natural resources or on the crops grown there. Many industries still depend on the same resources or crops. Richmond, for example, is a leading producer of tobacco products.

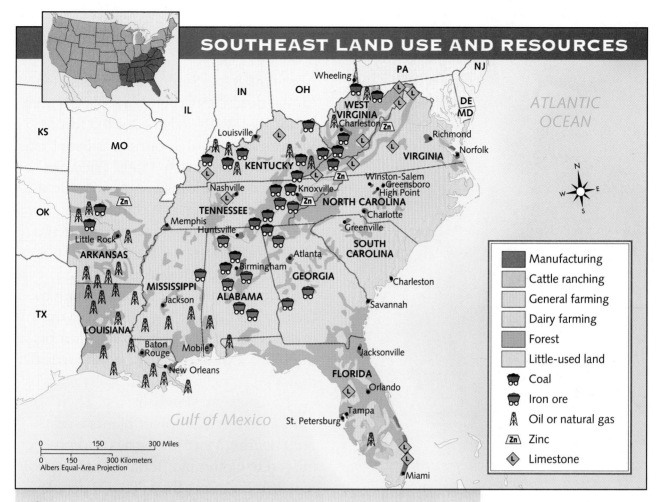

SOUTHEAST LAND USE AND RESOURCES

Manufacturing
Cattle ranching
General farming
Dairy farming
Forest
Little-used land
Coal
Iron ore
Oil or natural gas
Zn Zinc
Limestone

0   150   300 Miles
0   150   300 Kilometers
Albers Equal-Area Projection

HUMAN-ENVIRONMENT INTERACTIONS The Piedmont is a leading manufacturing area in the Southeast.
■ In what part of North Carolina is most manufacturing found?

Textiles, furniture, lumber, and paper are leading products made in Piedmont cities. Greensboro, North Carolina, has one of the largest denim factories in the world. Denim is the cloth used to make blue jeans. Making furniture is an important industry in High Point, North Carolina, and in Montgomery, Alabama.

The Piedmont, like the rest of the Southeast, is part of the Sun Belt. As people have moved

Much of the denim used in blue jeans is made from cotton that is grown on farms in the Southeast region.

to the Sun Belt, Piedmont cities have grown much larger. Important new industries have also helped the cities grow. Among the new industries are services, chemicals, electronics, and scientific research. Near Raleigh alone more than 60 companies and government offices do scientific research.

✓ **What are some leading products made in Piedmont cities?**

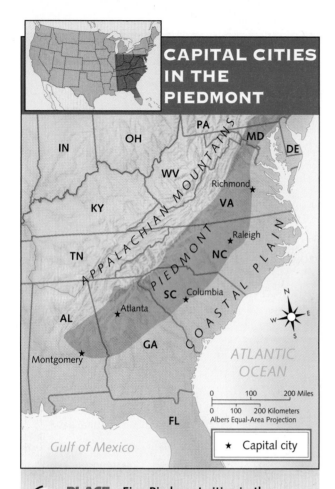

CAPITAL CITIES IN THE PIEDMONT

PLACE Five Piedmont cities in the Southeast are state capitals.
■ Which Piedmont city is the capital of North Carolina?

STATE CAPITALS

Five Piedmont cities in the Southeast are state capitals. They include Richmond, Virginia; Atlanta, Georgia; and Raleigh, North Carolina. Montgomery, Alabama; and Columbia, South Carolina, are state capitals, too.

Being a state capital helps a city to grow in many ways. State governments provide jobs for workers. Many companies also have offices in state capitals. Business people like being close to the government leaders and offices that affect their work. They also use the many services that are available in capital cities. These include communications, banking, and hotel services.

The mayor of South Carolina's state capital describes Columbia as "a city rich in tradition with a vision for the future." Visitors to Columbia can see houses that were built in the early 1800s. They can also see new buildings rising into the sky.

Columbia began as a trading center on the Fall Line. Farmers raised cotton and other crops on nearby farms. They took their crops to Columbia to be sold.

Cotton has always been important to the city's economy. The first textile mills in the Southeast were built in Columbia in the 1800s. Columbia later had the world's first all-electric textile mill.

The city grew slowly at first. Then dams and nuclear power plants were built nearby. More industries and people moved to Columbia. Today the metropolitan area has more than 500,000 people.

✓ **How does being a state capital help a city grow?**

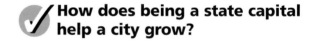

South Carolina's capitol building is called the State House. It stands in downtown Columbia, the state's capital and largest city.

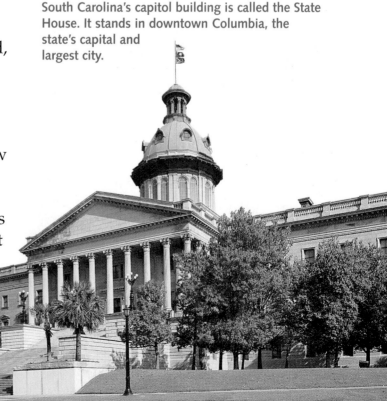

The South Carolina state legislature is called the General Assembly. Like Congress, it is divided into two parts— the House of Representatives (above) and the Senate.

STATE GOVERNMENT

Like the federal government in Washington, D.C., state governments have a constitution. They also have three branches. The legislative branch of state government is the **state legislature** (LEH•juhs•lay•cher). The voters in a state elect representatives to the state legislature.

The state legislature makes laws for all the people of the state. These laws affect highways, schools, state parks, and many other things. The legislature decides how much people will pay in state taxes. It also decides how the state's money will be spent.

In most cases, new laws must be signed by the governor. The **governor** is the head of the state executive branch. The

executive branch sees that all state laws are carried out.

The courts make up the third branch of state government—the judicial branch. State courts make sure that state laws are fair. State courts also judge people accused of breaking state laws. Many state laws have to do with crime. If people are caught breaking these laws, the courts must decide how the people will be punished.

What branch of state government makes the laws for a state?

LESSON 2 REVIEW

Check Understanding

1. **Recall the Facts**   How has being a state capital helped some Piedmont cities grow?
2. **Focus on the Main Idea**   Why are many cities in the Piedmont growing quickly?

Think Critically

3. **Think More About It**   Look at the map on page 228. Why do you think five states in the Southeast chose Piedmont cities as their capitals?
4. **Link to You**   What is your state's capital? Why do you think it is located where it is?

Show What You Know

Simulation Activity
Imagine that you are running for election to your state legislature. Make a list of some things state governments do. Then use the list to make a speech about what you would do if you were elected. Tell classmates how those things might affect growth in your state or community.

Compare Distances on Maps

Why Is This Skill Important?

Have you ever helped the members of your family plan a long trip? If so, you may have wanted to know how far you had to travel. You could have used the map scale on a map to find out.

As you know, a map scale helps you find out how far one place is from another. The map scale shows you that a certain distance on the map stands for a longer, real distance on the Earth.

No map is as large as the part of the Earth it shows. Depending on the size of the land area they show, some maps need to be made smaller than others. This means that different maps are drawn to different scales.

Understand the Process

Look at the two maps on these pages. Both maps show South Carolina. On Map A, however, South Carolina looks larger than it does on Map B. That is because the maps have different scales.

1. Find the map scale on Map A. Use a ruler to measure the exact length of the scale bar. What distance does 1 inch stand for?
2. Find Columbia and Charleston on Map A. Use your ruler to measure the distance between these two cities. Then find how many miles that distance stands for on the map scale. About how many miles is it from Columbia to Charleston?

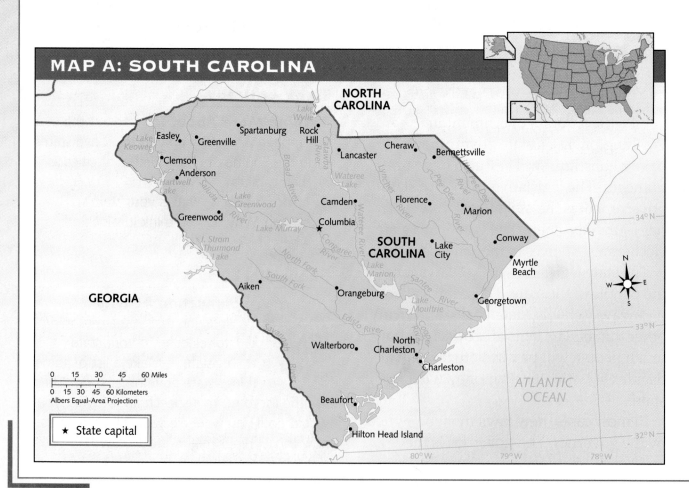

MAP A: SOUTH CAROLINA

MAP B: SOUTH CAROLINA

TENNESSEE

NORTH CAROLINA

Raleigh★

Charlotte

Greenville   Spartanburg

Columbia

SOUTH CAROLINA

Wilmington

34°N

Myrtle Beach

Atlanta

ALABAMA

GEORGIA

Lake Marion
Lake Moultrie

Macon

Charleston

ATLANTIC OCEAN

32°N

Montgomery

Savannah

★ State capital

0   30   60   90   120 Miles
0   30   60   90   120 Kilometers
Albers Equal-Area Projection

81°W   79°W   77°W   75°W

Instead of using a ruler to measure the distance between places on a map, you can use a strip of paper and a pencil. Place the paper below the map scale and mark the distances in either miles or kilometers. Move the strip of paper to the left and keep marking equal distances. Then write the correct number of miles or kilometers next to each mark. To measure distances in miles, your strip of paper for Map A should look like this.

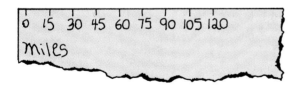

0   15   30   45   60   75   90   105   120
miles

3. Place the strip of paper between Columbia and Charleston on Map A, making sure the zero is on the dot for Columbia. About how many miles is it from Columbia to Charleston?

4. Now find the map scale on Map B. How many miles does 1 inch stand for? Using either a ruler or another marked strip of paper, find the distance between Columbia and Charleston. How does the distance between the two cities on this map compare with the distance on Map A?

Even though these two maps are drawn to different scales, you can use either map to find the distance between any two cities shown. Real distances on the Earth do not change. The scale used for a map depends on the amount of information that needs to be shown. Map A is drawn to a larger scale, so it can show you more details about South Carolina than Map B can. Map B would be very crowded if it showed the same information as Map A.

Think and Apply

Look through your textbook to find two different maps that show the same state or region. Compare the scales on the two maps, and measure the distance between any two places shown on both maps. Is the distance the same? What kinds of things are shown on one map but not on the other? Why is it useful to draw maps to different scales?

APPALACHIA
The Voices of Sleeping Birds

written by Cynthia Rylant   illustrated by Barry Moser

In the southern Appalachian Mountains is a region that people call Appalachia (a·puh·LAY·chuh). It has no exact borders, but it covers all of West Virginia and parts of several other states in the Southeast. In her book *Appalachia*, Cynthia Rylant describes the region as she remembers it. She grew up in Raleigh County, West Virginia, during the 1960s. As you read from *Appalachia*, think about how mountains have affected ways of life there.

In a certain part of the country called Appalachia you will find dogs named Prince or King living in little towns with names like Coal City and Sally's Backbone. These dogs run free, being country dogs, and their legs are full of muscles from running rabbits up mountains or from following boys who push old bikes against the hill roads they call hollows. These are mostly good dogs and can be trusted.

The owners of these dogs who live in Appalachia have names like Mamie and Boyd and Oley, and they probably have lived in Appalachia all of their lives. Many of them were born in coal camps in tiny houses which stood on poles and on the sides of which you could draw a face with your finger because coal dust had settled on their walls like snow. The owners of these dogs grew up more used to trees than sky and inside of them had this feeling of mystery about the rest of the world they couldn't see because the mountains came up so close to them and blocked their view like a person standing in a doorway. They weren't sure about going beyond these mountains, going until the land becomes flat or ocean, and so they stayed where they knew for sure how the sun would come up in the morning and set again at night.

The owners of these good dogs work pretty hard. Many of them are coal miners because the mountains in Appalachia are full of coal which people want and if you are brave enough to travel two miles down into solid dark earth to get it, somebody

will pay you money for your trouble.
The men and women who mine
the coal probably had fathers and
grandfathers who were miners before
them. Maybe some thought they
didn't have any other choice but to be
a miner, living in between or on the
sides of these mountains, and seeing
no way to go off and become doctors
or teachers and having no wish to
become soldiers.

Those who do go off, who find some
way to become doctors or teachers,
nearly always come back to the part
of Appalachia where they grew up.
They're never good at explaining why.
Some will say they had brothers and
sisters still here and they missed them.
But most will shake their heads and have a look on their faces
like the look you see on dogs who wander home after being lost
for a couple of weeks and who search out the corner of the yard
they knew they had to find again before they could get a good
sleep.

Those who don't live in Appalachia
and don't understand it sometimes
make the mistake of calling these
people "hillbillies." It isn't a good word
for them. They probably would prefer
"Appalachians." Like everyone else,
they're sensitive about words.

The houses in Appalachia are as different as houses anywhere. Some are
wood and some are brick. Some have
real flowers in pots on the porch and
some have plastic ones. Some have
shiny new cars parked in their drive-
ways and some have only the parts of
old cars parked in theirs. Most have
running water inside the house, with

sinks in the kitchens, washing machines in their basements, and pretty blue bathrooms. But a few still have no water pipes inside their houses and they carry their water from an old well or creek over the hill and they wash themselves in metal tubs and build themselves wooden toilets in their back yards, which most of them call "outhouses."

Inside their homes you will see photographs on the walls, mostly of their children or their families from long ago. And you will see pretty things they have made hanging on these walls: clocks carved from wood, sometimes in the shape of their state, or wreaths made from corn husks. Some will have pictures they bought at the department store when they went into town.

In their bedrooms there are usually one or two or three quilts somebody in the family made. In the winter these are on the bed, but usually not on top. And in the summer they stay folded up on shelves in small dark closets which smell of old wood and moth balls.

The good old dogs who live in Appalachia are not allowed on these beds and most of them are not allowed in the house at all. They have their own houses.

Literature Review

1. How do you think the Appalachian Mountains have affected ways of life in Appalachia?
2. How does Appalachia compare with where you live?
3. Write a story that describes the land around your community and how it affects what people do there.

Understand Point of View

Why Is This Skill Important?

Artists and photographers share their feelings and beliefs, just as writers do. If you learn to look for an artist's point of view, you will have a better idea of why the artist took the photo or painted the picture. Then you may learn more about the picture's meaning.

Understand the Process

Look again at the picture on page 232. It is a painting by Barry Moser that is used to illustrate the book *Appalachia*. Now look at the photograph of Appalachia on this page. Like Moser's painting, it tells something about life in Appalachia in the 1960s. Follow these steps to help you think more about the two artists' points of view.

1. *Think about how a work of art makes you feel.* Your own feelings can help you better understand the artist's point of view. Look at Moser's painting of the children walking along the dirt road. How do its warm colors make you feel about life in Appalachia?

2. *Study the details to help you understand the artist's point of view.* What details in Moser's painting tell you about the weather? How might your feelings change if the painting showed a rainstorm and a muddy road?

3. *Decide what point of view the artist wants to show you.* Look at the photograph again. What does this photograph show about life in Appalachia?

4. *Think about how the work of art shows the artist's point of view.* What feelings about Appalachia is the photographer sharing with you? How is that point of view different from the one shown in Moser's painting?

Think and Apply

Look for a photograph or painting that gives you strong feelings. You can use books, magazines, or newspapers to find a picture. Describe how the picture makes you feel. What did the artist show you to make you feel as you do? What do you think the artist's point of view is?

A hill settlement near Pikeville, Kentucky, in the 1960s

WORKING IN APPALACHIA

LESSON 4

Link to Our World

Why is mining important to people who live in mountain regions?

Focus on the Main Idea
Read to find out how people in Appalachia depend on their environment to earn a living.

Preview Vocabulary
reclaim
ore

There are few large cities in Appalachia. This region also has less manufacturing than some other places. Yet Appalachia is rich in natural resources that people depend on.

MINING COAL

Who was the first person to learn that coal gives off heat when it is burned? No one knows. But people have used coal for hundreds of years to heat buildings and to run machines.

Most of the coal mined in the United States today is used as a fuel to make electricity. In fact, about half of our electricity is made by power plants that burn coal. Coal is burned to heat water, which forms steam. The steam is used to run the machines that make electricity.

Much of the coal mined in the United States comes from Appalachia. When coal lies near the Earth's surface, it is fairly easy for miners to reach. They remove the soil and rocks covering the coal. Then giant shovels can pick up the coal.

Because these surface mines strip away the soil, they are sometimes called strip mines. In the past, strip mines spoiled many places in Appalachia. When all the coal was gone, mining companies left the mines and moved on. Because trees or grass had been removed, the land quickly eroded. Today, however, mining companies must **reclaim** the land, or put it back to its natural condition. The strip mines must be filled in with soil and the land must be replanted.

Coal miners often wear helmets that have lamps attached to them.

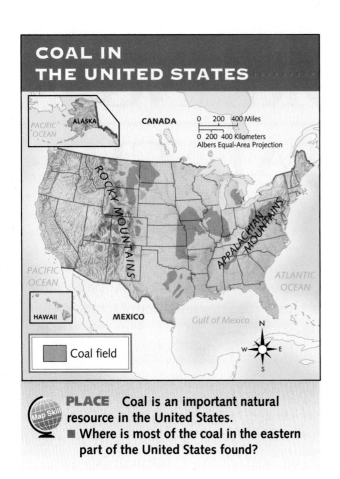

COAL IN THE UNITED STATES

0 200 400 Miles
0 200 400 Kilometers
Albers Equal-Area Projection

ALASKA
CANADA
PACIFIC OCEAN
ROCKY MOUNTAINS
APPALACHIAN MOUNTAINS
PACIFIC OCEAN
ATLANTIC OCEAN
HAWAII
MEXICO
Gulf of Mexico

Coal field

PLACE Coal is an important natural resource in the United States.
■ Where is most of the coal in the eastern part of the United States found?

When coal is buried far below the Earth's surface, mines must be dug deep in the ground. Usually two large shafts, or holes, are dug. One is used to let in the miners and the tools they need. The other is used to take out the coal. To get the coal, miners dig low tunnels out from the shafts. As coal is removed, the tunnels grow longer. Sometimes they stretch for miles. So the coal must be loaded onto shuttle cars or conveyor belts to carry it to the shafts.

It takes courage to work in an underground mine. The miners ride an elevator down a shaft early in the morning and do not see the sun all day. One West Virginia miner said, "Let me tell you, it's like crawlin' under your kitchen table on your hands and knees eight hours a day, settin' roof bolts and timbers, draggin' 50-pound sacks of rock dust and shovelin' coal."

LEARNING FROM DIAGRAMS In the Appalachian Mountains, coal often lies deep underground. This diagram shows how that coal is sometimes mined.
■ How do miners reach the coal?

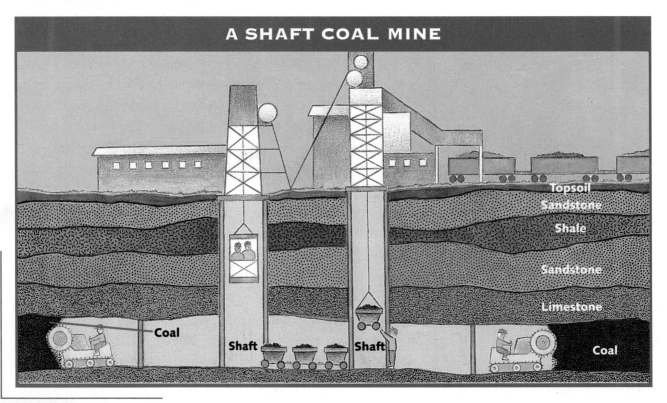

A SHAFT COAL MINE

Topsoil
Sandstone
Shale
Sandstone
Limestone
Coal
Shaft
Shaft
Coal

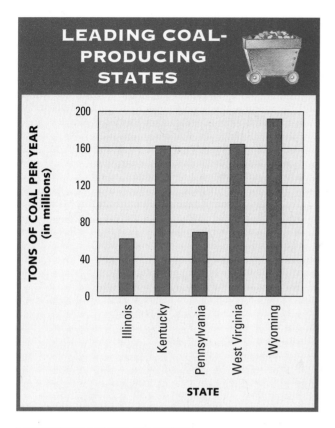

LEADING COAL-PRODUCING STATES

TONS OF COAL PER YEAR (in millions)

STATE

Illinois, Kentucky, Pennsylvania, West Virginia, Wyoming

LEARNING FROM GRAPHS
■ Which state in the Southeast produces more coal, Kentucky or West Virginia?

Machines, such as this continuous miner, are used to dig coal from the wall of a mine. Using this machine, a miner can dig as much as 12 tons of coal a minute.

The first underground mines were worked by hand. Today machines do much of the work. They dig the coal and haul it out of the mines. With machines a miner of today can produce three times as much coal as a miner working 40 years ago.

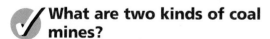 **What are two kinds of coal mines?**

OTHER INDUSTRIES

Mining coal is just one way that people in Appalachia earn their living. Other workers mine limestone, zinc, and iron ore. An **ore** is rock that contains one or more kinds of minerals.

The rugged land in Appalachia makes farming hard. Yet many people earn their living by farming. Tobacco and corn are leading crops. Some farmers raise apples to sell as fresh fruit or for making cider.

Many people work in the lumber industry and in small factories. The region's maple, walnut, and oak trees are good for making furniture. They are used by furniture factories in nearby Piedmont cities.

As in many other parts of the Southeast region, tourism is a growing industry in Appalachia. The Appalachian Mountains are a wonderful place for people who like being outdoors. The Great Smoky Mountains National Park in Tennessee and North Carolina is the country's most-visited national park. Thousands of visitors go there each year to enjoy the views and to walk on mountain trails. People who like music can find much to enjoy in

The Appalachian National Scenic Trail

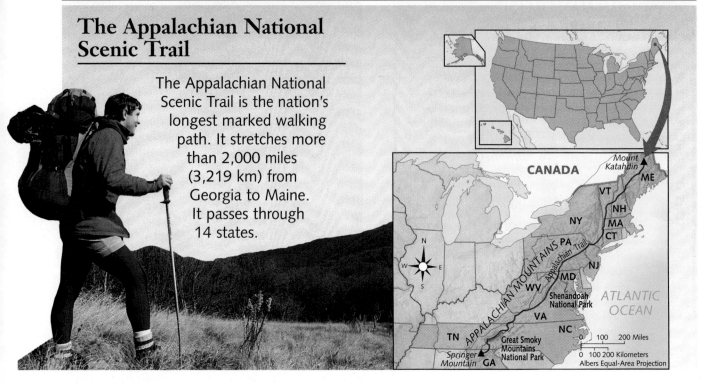

The Appalachian National Scenic Trail is the nation's longest marked walking path. It stretches more than 2,000 miles (3,219 km) from Georgia to Maine. It passes through 14 states.

Appalachia, too. Appalachia is where country music began.

 Besides coal mining, what other kinds of industries are in Appalachia?

CRAFTS AND FESTIVALS

Before Appalachia had modern transportation, travel there was not easy. So people had to make much of what they needed. They made cloth from the wool of their own sheep. They grew all their own food. Many even made their own musical instruments. Today many people like the handmade quilts, woven cloth, wood carvings, and other crafts made in the traditional Appalachian way.

These things are sold in some stores. They are also sold at festivals held in Appalachia. At these festivals people can enjoy Appalachian music, foods, and crafts. Many festivals celebrate a time of the year, such as the flowering of the dogwood blossoms in the spring or the apple harvest in the autumn.

Playing country music is a popular pastime at Appalachian festivals. Banjos, guitars, and fiddles, like these, are common musical instruments in Appalachia.

Appalachian craftspeople are admired for their skill. These corn-husk dolls (above) were made in West Virginia. Lucy George (right), a Cherokee Indian from North Carolina, weaves beautiful baskets.

Do you like to tell stories with your friends? Nearly everyone likes to listen to someone tell a good story. Just imagine spending a whole weekend listening to some of the best storytellers in the United States. That is what happens each fall at the National Storytelling Festival in Jonesborough, Tennessee.

The storytellers come from all around the country. In tents set up just for them, they tell all kinds of amazing stories. At the "Swappin' Ground" anyone can stand up and tell a story.

It is no accident that the National Story-telling Festival is held in the town of Jonesborough. This town is in the middle of Appalachia. Many of the country's best storytellers come from Appalachia. Storytelling there is a tradition.

 **Where are Appalachian crafts sometimes sold?**

LESSON 4 REVIEW

Check Understanding

1. **Recall the Facts** How is most of the coal mined in the United States used?
2. **Focus on the Main Idea** How do people in Appalachia depend on their environment to earn their living?

Think Critically

3. **Cause and Effect** Why did making things by hand become a tradition in Appalachia?

Show What You Know

 **Writing Activity** Write a descriptive paragraph telling what working as a coal miner might be like. Describe the mine. Tell how you feel as an elevator takes you under the ground.

REVIEW

CONNECT MAIN IDEAS

Use this organizer to show that you understand how the chapter's main ideas are connected. First copy the organizer onto a separate sheet of paper. Then complete it by writing three examples for each main idea.

Highlands and Mountains

Rivers

Appalachia

The Piedmont

People in the Southeast have changed rivers to meet their needs.

1. _____
2. _____
3. _____

Many cities in the Piedmont have grown quickly.

1. _____
2. _____
3. _____

People in Appalachia depend on their environment to earn a living.

1. _____
2. _____
3. _____

WRITE MORE ABOUT IT

1. **Write a Diary Entry**   Imagine that you and your family are pioneers. You are traveling upstream on one of the many rivers that flow across the Coastal Plain in the Southeast region. When you reach the Fall Line, you must decide whether to settle there or go on. State your decision and the reasons for it in a diary entry.

2. **Write a Report**   Use encyclopedias and books from the library to find out more about your state's government and its elected leaders. Then write your findings in a report. Share your report with classmates.

3. **Write a Story**   Imagine that you are planning to attend the National Storytelling Festival in Jonesborough, Tennessee. Write a story to share at the "Swappin' Ground." Your story should take place in Appalachia.

USE VOCABULARY

For each group of underlined words in the sentences, write the term that has the same meaning. Choose terms from the list.

governor
hydroelectric power
pass

reservoir
state legislature
waterpower

1. Before settlers could begin to cross the Appalachians, they had to find a <u>low place between mountains</u>.

2. Settlers used <u>the power produced by rushing water</u> to run machines in factories.

3. <u>A lake that stores water held back by a dam</u> is used by people and industries.

4. Electricity made by <u>waterpower</u> is an important source of electricity.

5. Voters in each state elect representatives to the <u>branch of state government that makes laws</u>.

6. In most cases, new state laws must be signed by the <u>head of the state executive branch</u>.

CHECK UNDERSTANDING

1. How did Daniel Boone make travel easier for early settlers?

2. How did settlers use rivers at the Fall Line?

3. How does making and using recycled paper help save natural resources?

4. What are the three branches of state government? What is the main job of each branch?

5. How are surface mines different from underground mines?

6. What must mining companies do to reclaim the land?

THINK CRITICALLY

1. **Cause and Effect** How can being a state capital cause a city to grow?

2. **Link to You** Do you or members of your family make crafts in a traditional way? Does your family have other traditions? How are these traditions important to you and your family?

APPLY SKILLS

How to Compare Distances on Maps Use the maps on pages 230 and 231 to answer these questions.

1. About how many miles is it from Rock Hill to Spartanburg? Which map did you use? Why?

2. About how far is it from Columbia, South Carolina, to Montgomery, Alabama? Which map did you use? Why?

How to Understand Point of View
Find a painting or photograph that you like. Tell what it shows and describe the artist's point of view.

READ MORE ABOUT IT

Pioneer Children of Appalachia by Joan Anderson. Clarion. This book tells the story of the pioneers who settled Appalachia in the 1800s.

Sweet Creek Holler by Ruth White. Farrar, Straus & Giroux. Ginny grows up in a small community in Appalachia.

When I Was Young in the Mountains by Cynthia Rylant. Dutton. The author recalls spending time with her grandparents at their mountain home in Appalachia.

Taking Action
for the
Environment

For one group of students in Fort Myers, Florida, a class project turned out to be much more than that. It changed a whole community, and it helped save an important part of the natural environment of the Southeast.

The Monday Group is a class that has been meeting twice a month since 1969 to learn about the environment. In 1980 members of the class led a citywide effort to keep the Six-Mile Cypress Swamp from being developed by builders. First, the students collected citizens' names on a petition, or a written request. This showed that many people wanted to save the 2,500-acre swamp. Next, the students presented their petition to county leaders. Then they talked to voters, asking them to agree to a tax that would raise enough money to buy and take care of the swamp.

Today the Monday Group works on other projects, but class members still talk about the swamp. It reminds them of how much a small group of people, working together, can do.

THINK AND APPLY

Think about something in your community that should be preserved, or saved for the future. Or think about a problem in your community. In a small group, brainstorm some ways that you and your class might be able to help. Write a plan of action, and share your plan with community leaders.

BUILDING CITIZENSHIP

Other students now use Six-Mile Cypress Swamp as a "classroom," where they can study wildlife and learn about the environment firsthand.

STORY CLOTH

Study the pictures shown in this story cloth to help you review what you read about in Unit 3.

Summarize the Main Ideas

1. The Coastal Plain in the Southeast is an important farming area in the United States.

2. Both location and resources have helped places in the Southeast grow quickly.

3. The geography of the Gulf coast affects the people who live there and the work that they do.

4. People on islands face special challenges.

5. People change rivers to meet their needs.

6. Piedmont cities are centers of industry and government in the Southeast.

7. Many people in Appalachia depend on their environment to make their living.

Write a Brochure   Look closely at the scenes shown in the story cloth. Then write a travel brochure about the Southeast based on what you see in the scenes. Include your own drawings to add interest to the brochure. Display your brochure on a class bulletin board along with the brochures of your classmates.

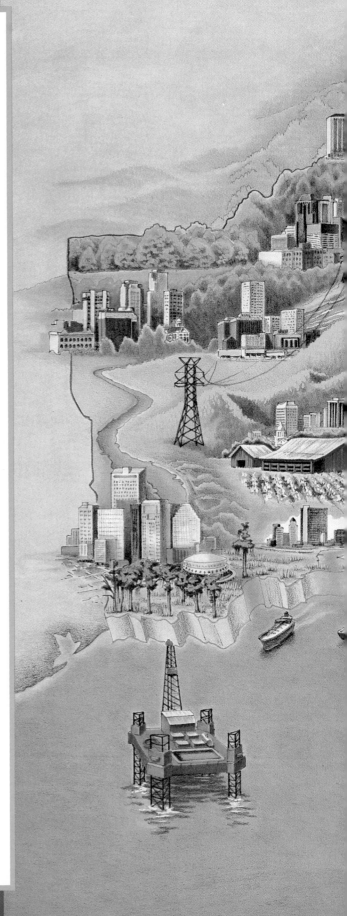

COOPERATIVE LEARNING WORKSHOP

Remember

- Share your ideas.
- Cooperate with others to plan your work.
- Take responsibility for your work.
- Show your group's work to the class.
- Discuss what you learned by working together.

Activity 1
Make a Collage

To better understand how people depend on natural resources, work in a group to make a collage. First, divide a large sheet of paper into two parts. Label one part *Renewable Resources* and the other part *Nonrenewable Resources*. Then, draw pictures or cut out magazine and newspaper photographs that show people using both kinds of resources. Paste your pictures onto the paper under the correct heading. Display the collage, and talk to your classmates about ways people can conserve natural resources.

Activity 2
Draw a Map

Work in a group to draw an outline map of the Southeast on a large sheet of paper. Maps in your textbook and in encyclopedias and atlases can help you. Add dots and labels to your map to show where the region's largest cities are located. Also label large bodies of water and large landforms. Draw symbols to show the region's major resources. Then point out places on the map as your group takes the rest of the class on a "tour" of the Southeast.

Activity 3
Hold a Class Fair

With your class, plan a fair that celebrates the arts and crafts of Appalachia. Decide what things to include in your fair, such as quilting and weaving, country music, musical instruments, or Appalachian cooking. Then your class should form small groups. Each group should research a topic and make a display about it. All the groups should decide together how the displays will be presented to the whole class and invited guests.

USE VOCABULARY

Use each term in a sentence that helps explain its meaning.

1. marsh
2. food processing
3. tourist
4. crude oil
5. petrochemical
6. barrier island
7. mainland
8. tropics
9. reclaim
10. ore

CHECK UNDERSTANDING

1. Why was Jamestown important?

2. Why are farms in the Southeast often larger than farms in New England?

3. How does a long growing season affect farming in the Southeast?

4. How is food processing in the Southeast related to agriculture?

5. Which port in the Southeast is the busiest? Why?

6. Why are food and water often more expensive in Key West than in other cities in Florida?

7. How do people change rivers?

8. Why are many cities in the Piedmont growing quickly?

9. How is most of the coal from U.S. coal mines used?

THINK CRITICALLY

1. **Cause and Effect** Why did important lumber and paper industries develop in the Southeast?

2. **Explore Viewpoints** Why is it important for a factory owner to think about the effect of his or her factory on the environment?

3. **Think More About It** Why do you think state governments have three branches?

4. **Link to You** What are some products from the Southeast that you or members of your family depend on?

5. **Personally Speaking** Which city or area of the Southeast would you most like to live in or visit? Explain your answer.

APPLY GEOGRAPHY SKILLS

 How to Compare Distances on Maps Use the map of Georgia and the inset map of Atlanta to answer these questions.

1. How far is Atlanta from Macon? Which map did you use to find this distance?

2. Which map would you use to find the distance from Smyrna to Decatur? Explain.

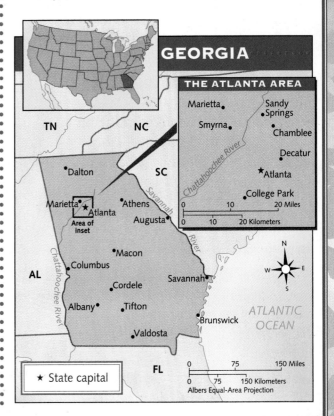

GEORGIA

THE ATLANTA AREA

Marietta • Sandy Springs
Smyrna • Chamblee
Decatur
★ Atlanta
College Park

0   10   20 Miles
0 10 20 Kilometers

TN   NC

• Dalton   SC

Marietta • ★ Atlanta
Area of inset
• Athens
Augusta •
Savannah River

Chattahoochee River
AL
• Macon
• Columbus
• Cordele   Savannah •
• Albany   • Tifton
Brunswick •
ATLANTIC OCEAN
• Valdosta

★ State capital   FL

0   75   150 Miles
0   75   150 Kilometers
Albers Equal-Area Projection

UNIT 4

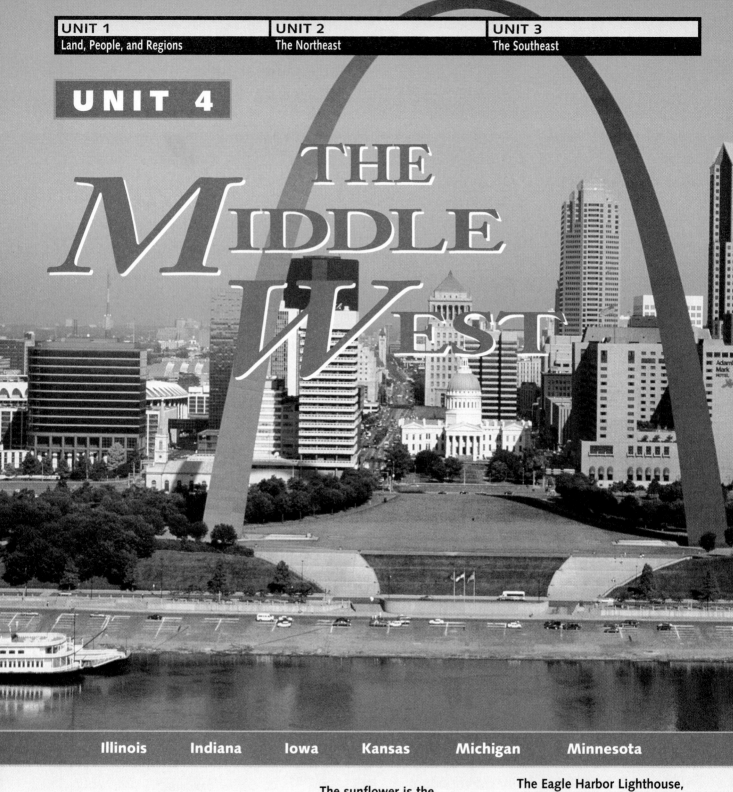

THE *M*IDDLE *W*EST

Illinois   Indiana   Iowa   Kansas   Michigan   Minnesota

The sunflower is the state flower of Kansas.

The Eagle Harbor Lighthouse, on Lake Superior, in Michigan

A race car from the Indianapolis Motor Speedway, in Indianapolis, Indiana

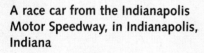

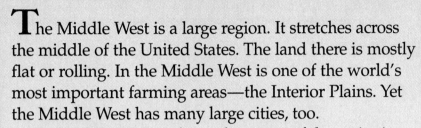

The Middle West is a large region. It stretches across the middle of the United States. The land there is mostly flat or rolling. In the Middle West is one of the world's most important farming areas—the Interior Plains. Yet the Middle West has many large cities, too.

The Middle West is also at the center of the nation's transportation system. Busy highways and railways crisscross much of the region. Mighty rivers flow across the land. The major rivers are the Mississippi, the Ohio, and the Missouri. These rivers and the Great Lakes help connect many places in the United States.

← **The Gateway Arch rises above the Mississippi River in St. Louis, Missouri.**

Missouri   Nebraska   North Dakota   Ohio   South Dakota   Wisconsin

Chimney Rock, in Nebraska

The Football Hall of Fame, in Canton, Ohio

Mount Rushmore, in South Dakota

ALMANAC
The Middle West

Did You Know?

Twelve states make up the Middle West. Sometimes those states are divided into two smaller regions—the Plains states and the Great Lakes states. All six Great Lakes states border a Great Lake.

STATE	CAPITAL	NICKNAME	POPULATION*	TEN LARGEST CITIES	LEADING PRODUCTS AND RESOURCES
THE GREAT LAKES STATES				1. Chicago, Illinois	**Farming:** Beef cattle, beets, corn, dairy cows, grain sorghum, hay, hogs, oats, poultry, sheep, soybeans, sunflower seeds, wheat
Illinois (IL)	Springfield	Prairie State	11,989,000	2. Detroit, Michigan	
Indiana (IN)	Indianapolis	Hoosier State	5,920,000	3. Indianapolis, Indiana	
Michigan (MI)	Lansing	Wolverine State	9,656,000	4. Columbus, Ohio	
Minnesota (MN)	St. Paul	North Star State	4,706,000	5. Milwaukee, Wisconsin	**Manufacturing:** Automobiles, books, chemicals, dairy products, electrical equipment, machinery, metal products, packaged meats, paper products, processed foods
Ohio (OH)	Columbus	Buckeye State	11,318,000	6. Cleveland, Ohio	
Wisconsin (WI)	Madison	Badger State	5,256,000	7. Kansas City, Missouri	
THE PLAINS STATES				8. St. Louis, Missouri	
Iowa (IA)	Des Moines	Hawkeye State	2,893,000	9. Minneapolis, Minnesota	
Kansas (KS)	Topeka	Sunflower State	2,652,000	10. Cincinnati, Ohio	**Mining:** Coal, copper, crushed stone, gold, iron, lead, limestone, natural gas, oil
Missouri (MO)	Jefferson City	Show Me State	5,347,000		
Nebraska (NE)	Lincoln	Cornhusker State	1,670,000		
North Dakota (ND)	Bismarck	Peace Garden State	639,000		
South Dakota (SD)	Pierre	Mount Rushmore State	750,000		

*The most recent figures available

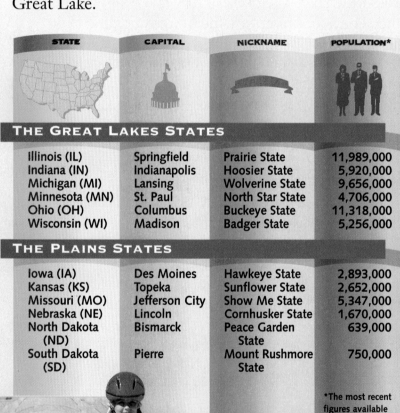

The National Museum of Roller Skating is in Lincoln, Nebraska. It is the only museum in the world just for roller skating.

Ice-cream cones were first served at the 1904 Louisiana Purchase Exposition World's Fair in St. Louis, Missouri.

252 • Unit 4

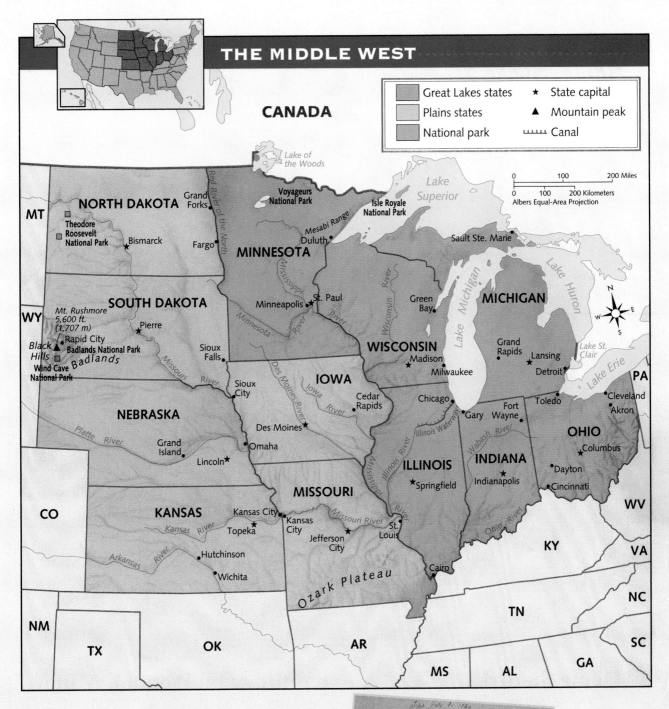

Great Lakes states   ★ State capital
Plains states   ▲ Mountain peak
National park   ⊔⊔⊔⊔ Canal

0   100   200 Miles
0   100   200 Kilometers
Albers Equal-Area Projection

CANADA

Lake of the Woods

MT

NORTH DAKOTA
Grand Forks
Theodore Roosevelt National Park
Bismarck
Fargo

Red River of the North

Voyageurs National Park

Lake Superior

Isle Royale National Park

Mesabi Range
Duluth

Sault Ste. Marie

MINNESOTA

Mississippi River

WY

Mt. Rushmore
5,600 ft. (1,707 m)
SOUTH DAKOTA
Pierre
Black Hills
Rapid City
Badlands National Park
Wind Cave National Park
Badlands

Minnesota River

Minneapolis   St. Paul

Sioux Falls

Missouri River

Green Bay

Lake Michigan

MICHIGAN

Grand Rapids
Lansing
Detroit

Lake Huron

Lake St. Clair

N
W   E
S

WISCONSIN
Madison
Milwaukee

Wisconsin River

Des Moines River

Sioux City

IOWA
Cedar Rapids
Iowa River

NEBRASKA
Grand Island
Lincoln
Omaha
Des Moines

Platte River

Chicago
Gary
Fort Wayne

Illinois Waterway
Illinois River

Lake Erie

PA

Toledo
Cleveland
Akron

CO

KANSAS
Kansas City
Topeka
Kansas City
Jefferson City
St. Louis

Kansas River

Missouri River

MISSOURI

Mississippi River

ILLINOIS
Springfield

INDIANA
Indianapolis

Wabash River

OHIO
Columbus
Dayton
Cincinnati

WV

Hutchinson
Wichita

Arkansas River

Ozark Plateau

Cairo

Ohio River

KY

VA

NM

TX

OK

AR

TN

MS   AL   GA

NC

SC

SIWINOWE Kesibwi.
PALAKO WAHOSTOTA NAKOTE KESIBO.—WISELIBI. 1841.
BAPTIST MISSION PRESS
J. LYKINS EDITOR.   NOVEMBER, 1841.

The first newspaper in North America to be printed entirely in an Indian language was the *Siwinowe Kesibwi*, or "Shawnee Sun." It was first printed in Kansas in 1835.

In 1869 the Cincinnati Red Stockings, now the Cincinnati Reds, became the first professional baseball team.

H E A R T L A N D

by Diane Siebert   paintings by Wendell Minor

The Midwest. Middle America. These are two other names
that people often use for the Middle West. Because it is in the
very heart of the country, the Middle West region has still
another name. It is sometimes called the Heartland of America.
Read now from a poem that tells about America's Heartland.

I am the Heartland,
Great and wide.
I sing of hope.
I sing of pride.
I am the land where wheat fields grow
In golden waves that ebb and flow;
Where cornfields stretched across the plains
Lie green between the country lanes.

I am the Heartland,
Shaped and lined
By rivers, great and small, that wind
Past farms, whose barns and silos stand
Like treasures in my fertile hand.

I am the Heartland.
I can feel
Machines of iron, tools of steel,
Creating farmlands, square by square—
A quilt of life I proudly wear:
A patchwork quilt laid gently down
In hues of yellow, green, and brown
As tractors, plows, and planters go
Across my fields and, row by row,
Prepare the earth and plant the seeds
That grow to meet a nation's needs.
A patchwork quilt whose seams are etched
By miles of wood and wire stretched
Around the barns and pastures where
The smell of livestock fills the air.
These are the farms where hogs are bred,
The farms where chicks are hatched and fed;
The farms where dairy cows are raised,
The farms where cattle herds are grazed;
The farms with horses, farms with sheep—
Upon myself, all these I keep.

silos (SY•lohz)
towers in which
feed for animals
is stored

livestock
animals
raised for
profit

I am the Heartland.
On this soil
Live those who through the seasons toil:
The farmer, with his spirit strong;
The farmer, working hard and long,
The feed-and-seed-store cap in place,
Pulled down to shield a weathered face—
A face whose every crease and line
Can tell a tale, and help define
A lifetime spent beneath the sun,
A life of work that's never done.

elevators large towers used to store grain

I am the Heartland.
On these plains
Rise elevators filled with grains.
They mark the towns where people walk
To see their neighbors, just to talk;
Where farmers go to get supplies
And sit a spell to analyze
The going price of corn and beans,
The rising cost of new machines;
Where steps are meant for shelling peas,
And kids build houses in the trees.

I am the Heartland.
In my song
Are cities beating, steady strong,
With footsteps from a million feet
And sounds of traffic in the street;
Where giant mills and stockyards sprawl,
And neon-lighted shadows fall
From windowed walls of brick that rise
Toward the clouds, to scrape the skies;
Where highways meet and rails converge;
Where farm and city rhythms merge
To form a vital bond between
The concrete and the fields of green.

stockyards
places with large
pens for livestock
waiting to be
shipped to
market

    The Heartland is an important farming area, but most people
live in cities. There they do many kinds of jobs. Many work
in transportation industries. They help move goods on the
Heartland's railroads, highways, and waterways. Others work
in factories. Most people, however, have service jobs, just like
the people who live in other regions of the United States.

THE INTERIOR PLAINS

> 66 We come and go, but the land is always here. And the people who love it and understand it are the people who own it—for a little while. 99
>
> from the book *O Pioneers!* by Willa Cather, 1913

This farmer from the Middle West is examining his corn crop.

FARMING ON THE PLAINS

Link to Our World

How does climate affect farming?

Focus on the Main Idea
Read to find out how different amounts of precipitation affect the kinds of crops grown on the Interior Plains.

Preview Vocabulary
prairie
drought
blizzard
hailstorm
tornado

On the Interior Plains, farm children often help care for livestock.

The Interior Plains stretch across most of the Middle West region, which includes both the Great Lakes states and the Plains states. The fertile, rolling land in those states helps make the Middle West a good place for farming. Farmers in different parts of the Middle West, however, grow different kinds of crops.

TWO PLAINS REGIONS

Because the Interior Plains cover such a large area, they are often divided into two smaller regions. The eastern region is called the Central Plains. The western region is called the Great Plains. The Central Plains begin in Ohio and end west of the Mississippi River. The Great Plains stretch from there to the Rocky Mountains.

Look at the map on page 260. The main difference between the Central Plains and the Great Plains is the amount of precipitation. Most places on the Central Plains usually receive from 20 to 40 inches (51 to 102 cm) of precipitation each year. The Great Plains are much drier. Most places there receive less than 20 inches (51 cm) of precipitation each year. Long ago, banks sometimes refused to loan money to farmers who lived on the Great Plains. Bankers feared that the dry climate would make it impossible for farmers to grow enough crops to earn a living and pay back their loans.

Before pioneers plowed the land, much of the Interior Plains was a prairie (PRAIR•ee). A **prairie** is an

PRECIPITATION IN THE UNITED STATES

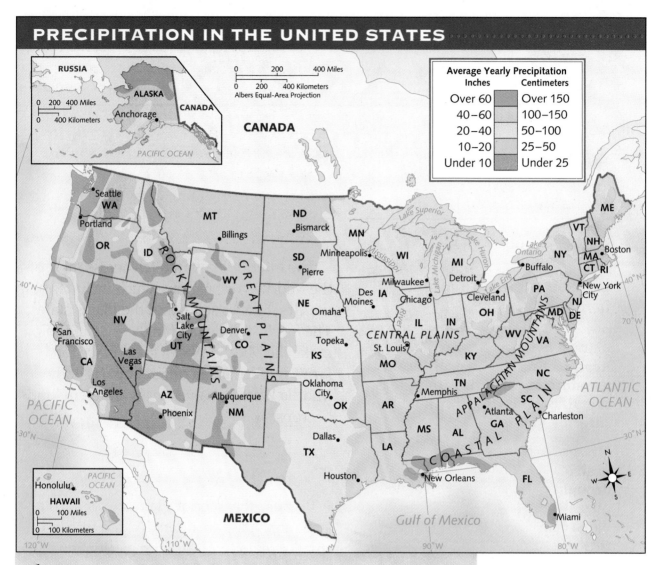

Average Yearly Precipitation

Inches	Centimeters
Over 60	Over 150
40–60	100–150
20–40	50–100
10–20	25–50
Under 10	Under 25

REGIONS The Great Plains are much drier than the Central Plains.
■ About how much precipitation does Des Moines, Iowa, receive each year? Is that city on the Great Plains or the Central Plains?

area of flat or rolling land covered mostly by grasses and wildflowers. On the Great Plains, prairie grasses grew short and stubby.

With more precipitation on the Central Plains, the prairie grasses there grew tall and thick. The first pioneers to see this tall-grass prairie described it as a "sea of grass." In some places the grasses rose above the heads of the pioneers.

Those grasses helped make the soil very dark and fertile. The roots of the grasses reached deep into the ground. When the grasses died, they rotted and left behind matter that enriched the soil.

Today most of the tall-grass prairie is gone. In its place are cities and farms. Yet the dark, fertile soil remains. In some areas the soil is so dark that it appears black. Farms in the Central Plains get plenty of rain and have warm summer temperatures. These things help make the Central Plains a leading farming area.

 What is the main difference between the Central Plains and the Great Plains?

CORN AND THE CENTRAL PLAINS

Farmers on the Central Plains grow many crops, such as wheat, soybeans, and oats. Corn, however, is the leading crop in most years. The rich soil and warm, humid summers are ideal for growing corn.

About three-fourths of all the corn grown in the United States is from the Central Plains. In fact, almost half of all the corn grown in the world is raised there. Iowa, Illinois, and Nebraska are the three leading corn-producing states.

Some of the corn grown on the Central Plains is sweet corn. This is the kind that people can eat right off the cob. Most of the corn, though, is dent corn. It makes good feed for livestock.

LEARNING FROM GRAPHS The soil and the climate in all these states are good for growing corn.
■ Which state raised more than 1,800 million bushels of corn?

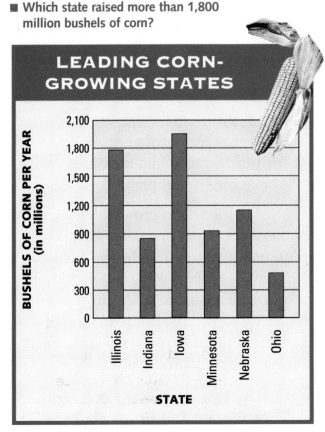

LEADING CORN-GROWING STATES

Livestock raised on the Central Plains includes cattle, hogs, and chickens. To the north, where the climate is cooler, the grasslands are especially good for raising dairy cattle. Wisconsin and Minnesota are both important dairy states.

About half of all the dent corn raised on the Central Plains is fed to livestock. Farmers often can make more money by feeding the corn to livestock and then selling the livestock than they can by selling the corn directly.

Large amounts of corn are also used in other ways. Corn is an important part of such foods as breakfast cereals, margarine, and syrup. Corn is also used to make building materials, paints, fuels, and paper goods.

✓ Why is corn important to the Central Plains?

WHEAT AND THE GREAT PLAINS

Corn does not grow as well on the Great Plains. It needs from 18 to 25 inches (46 to 64 cm) of rain during the growing season. Most parts of the Great Plains receive less rain than that during the whole year.

In some years there is enough rain for growing corn. But in other years there are droughts (DROWTS). A **drought** is a time of little or no rain. During a drought, crops often die. A drought can last for months or even years.

Because most parts of the Great Plains are dry, few trees grow there. In the past only short prairie grasses covered the ground. Today miles of wheat fields cover the region. Kansas and North Dakota are the leading wheat-producing states.

HOW WHEAT BECOMES BREAD

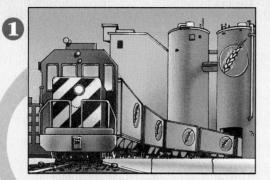
1 Wheat is delivered to a flour mill.

2 Mill workers grind wheat into flour.

3 Flour is delivered to a bakery.

4 Bakery workers make bread.

LEARNING FROM FLOW CHARTS This flow chart shows how wheat is made into bread.
■ What happens after workers grind the wheat?

Farmers use large machines, called combines (KAHM•bynz), to harvest wheat. A combine can cut the wheat and separate the grain from the stems in one step.

Wheat can grow in less fertile soil than corn can. It also needs less water than corn does. So wheat grows well in the drier climate of the Great Plains.

As wheat becomes ripe, it turns amber, or golden, in color. Just before harvest the wheat fields are a beautiful sight. For as far as the eye can see, wheat sways in the wind. The song "America, the Beautiful" describes this sight.

❝O beautiful for spacious skies,
For amber waves of grain,
For purple mountain majesties
Above the fruited plain!❞

Most of the wheat grown on the Great Plains is used to make flour. That is why the Great Plains is sometimes called the Nation's Breadbasket. Another kind of wheat, called durum (DER•uhm) wheat, is also grown on the northern Great Plains. It is used to make pasta products, such as spaghetti and macaroni.

 Why is more wheat than corn grown on the Great Plains?

DANGER ON THE PLAINS

Farmers on the Interior Plains must watch the weather closely. A whole year's crop can be wiped out by a single storm. Livestock can be hurt or killed.

The flat, treeless land of the Great Plains offers little protection from strong winds. In the winter, howling winds from the north sometimes cause blizzards. A **blizzard** is a snowstorm driven by strong, freezing winds.

Another frozen danger comes in the form of hailstorms. A **hailstorm** drops hail, or lumps of ice, that can damage or destroy crops.

Students all over the United States have fire drills at school. On the Interior Plains, students also have tornado drills. A **tornado** is a funnel-shaped, spinning windstorm. Tornadoes are sometimes called cyclones or twisters.

Tornadoes are the Earth's strongest winds. At the center of a tornado, the wind can blow at more than 200 miles (322 km) per hour. Some tornadoes have been known to reach speeds of 500 miles (805 km) per hour! Most tornadoes last for

Much of the Interior Plains is known as "Tornado Alley" because many tornadoes form there. This tornado is blowing across Nebraska.

less than an hour, but they can do terrible damage.

 Why can storms be especially bad for farmers?

LESSON 1 REVIEW

Check Understanding

1. **Recall the Facts** Why does corn grow well on the Central Plains?
2. **Focus on the Main Idea** How do different amounts of precipitation affect the kinds of crops grown on the Interior Plains?

Think Critically

3. **Link to You** How might a drought on the Interior Plains affect you and your family?

Show What You Know

Writing Activity Suppose you have been visiting farms on both the Central Plains and the Great Plains. Farmers on the Great Plains want to know how their farms are different from farms on the Central Plains. Write them a letter describing some of the differences you have seen during your visits. Compare your letter to letters written by classmates.

Read Pictographs

Why Is This Skill Important?

Have you ever been asked to compare two things? As you know, a graph is a drawing that helps you compare numbers. The graph below compares the amounts of wheat grown in five states in the Middle West region. Instead of using numbers, however, this graph uses symbols.

A graph that uses symbols to stand for numbers is called a **pictograph**. A pictograph always has a key that tells how much each symbol stands for. To read a pictograph, you must use both the key and the symbols.

Understand the Process

Follow these steps to understand the symbols used on this pictograph.

1. Look at the key. How much does each symbol 🌾 stand for?

2. Find South Dakota. There are two whole symbols beside it.

3. Figure out how much wheat two whole symbols stand for. If one symbol stands for 50 million bushels of wheat, how much wheat do two whole symbols stand for?

4. Find South Dakota again. There is about one-fifth of another symbol. This stands for about 10 million bushels.

5. Add the two amounts to figure out about how much wheat is raised altogether. About how much wheat is raised in South Dakota?

Think And Apply

Find Kansas on the pictograph. About how much wheat is raised there? Think about what you have learned about the Interior Plains. Why do you think much more wheat is raised in Kansas than in Illinois?

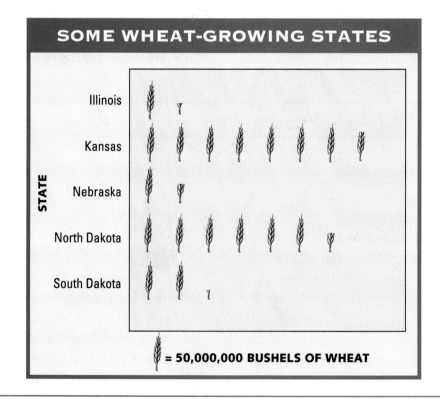

SOME WHEAT-GROWING STATES

STATE

Illinois

Kansas

Nebraska

North Dakota

South Dakota

🌾 = 50,000,000 BUSHELS OF WHEAT

Lesson 2 AMBER WAVES OF GRAIN

Link to Our World

How do people sometimes adapt their ways of life to new environments?

Focus on the Main Idea
As you read, look for changes people made so they could live on and farm the Great Plains.

Preview Vocabulary
sod
self-sufficient
fertilizer
urbanization

Early settlers on the Great Plains sometimes used iron plows, like this one, to prepare their fields for planting crops.

Wheat fields did not always blanket the Great Plains. In fact, early maps labeled this area the Great American Desert. To run farms and live there, people had to adapt to the dry, treeless land.

NEW HOMES IN A NEW LAND

Mattie Huffman was a young woman when she and her family arrived at their new farm in Kansas in 1875. An old house stood alone on the prairie. Mattie was surprised to find the door locked. What was there for anyone to steal?

When Mattie's father turned the key and opened the door, she saw why it had been locked. An iron plow was inside. The plow was very important to their lives. It was needed to till the soil, or prepare it for planting. Without the plow, no crops could be planted on the grass-covered prairie.

Mattie and her family were lucky to have a house already standing on their farm. Most settlers had to build their own. Many houses, however, were not built with wood. Few trees grew on the Great Plains. In fact, trees were so scarce that the Plains Indians had to go all the way to the Rocky Mountains to get long wooden poles for their shelters.

Settlers had to use the building materials that their new environment offered. They had to change the kind of shelter they called home. Instead of using lumber, most settlers built their houses out of sod. **Sod** is a layer of soil held together by the roots of grasses. It took about an acre of sod to make a one-room soddy, as sod houses were called.

To build a soddy, family members first had to cut blocks of sod from the prairie. Then, they piled the sod, like bricks, to form walls. For the wooden doors and window frames, families had to bring lumber with them or do without.

Next, family members built the roof. Most families laid strips of sod over cornstalks or brush. Others brought lumber to build a wooden frame for the roof. Finally, dirt and mud were forced into cracks between the sod blocks. This helped keep wind out of the soddy.

Sod houses had some good points. In the summer they stayed cool, like a cave. In the winter their thick walls kept the houses warm inside. And sod houses did not burn easily. This was important on the prairie, where there were sometimes dangerous grass fires.

Soddies had bad points, too. They were damp and dirty, of course. But the biggest problem was creepy-crawly things, such as insects and small animals. One woman wrote, "I remember it—bugs and snakes and mice were always dropping down from the ceiling. . . . Mama used to hang sheets over the tables and beds so that things wouldn't fall on them."

✓ **Why did settlers on the Great Plains have to learn new ways of building?**

A LONELY LIFE

Pioneers on the Great Plains had to be brave. To begin their new lives, they had to make a long, hard journey. From cities in the East, it could take six weeks just to reach the Great Plains.

Think of being six weeks away from everything you knew, from everything you grew up with! Think of how lonely

Many pioneer families on the Great Plains lived in sod houses. In 1888 the Moses Speese family (below) lived in this sod house in Nebraska. The windmill standing behind the house was used to pump water from a well.

you might feel. Many pioneers could not take the lonely life on the prairie and went back home. One saying of the time was

> 66 Ten miles to the nearest water,
> Twenty miles to the nearest tree,
> Thirty miles to the nearest house.
> Gone back East to the factory. 99

Farms on the Great Plains were often a long way from a town and stores. Even the closest neighbors could be miles away. Because of this, pioneer families had to be self-sufficient. **Self-sufficient** means doing almost everything for yourself, with no help from other people.

✓ **Why did pioneer families need to be self-sufficient?**

CHANGES COME TO FARMING

Farmers on the Great Plains needed a crop that would grow well in a dry climate. They found that crop when Russian Mennonites (MEH•nuh•nyts) moved to the Great Plains in the late 1800s. This group came from an even drier plains region in Russia.

The Russian Mennonites brought with them a new kind of wheat. It was a winter wheat that grew well in dry climates. Winter wheat was planted in the fall and harvested the following summer.

Growing winter wheat was an important change in farming on the Great Plains. Several inventions from years before had also changed farming.

Wheat and other grain crops once had to be cut by hand. Using hand tools, farmers could harvest no more than 2 to 3 acres of wheat each day. Cyrus McCormick changed that. In 1831 he built a machine, called a reaper, to cut down the plants.

When?

Preserving Food in the 1800s

In the 1800s, most people had to preserve their own foods. Meats were either dried in the sun or smoked over a fire to keep them from spoiling. Fruits and vegetables were kept in glass jars, which had to be sealed and then boiled in water. Other foods were stored in heavy stone jars called crocks. Today people can buy most foods at grocery stores. Workers in food-processing plants preserve the foods.

Using a reaper, a farmer could harvest as many as 10 acres of wheat each day.

Once the plants had been cut down, farmers had to thresh, or separate, the grain from the stems. In 1834 two brothers, Hiram and John Pitts, built a machine to do that. Threshing machines saved farmers many days of hard work.

Iron plows, like the one owned by Mattie's family, were not very good at turning over the prairie's thick sod. Teams of oxen had to struggle just to pull the plow through the earth. Iron plows had a rough surface. The soil stuck to it. Every few minutes, the farmers had to stop and clean the plow.

In 1837 an American inventor named John Deere made a steel plow. Steel cut through sod better, and the soil did not

Inventor John Deere shows how his steel plow works. Why would an improved plow be important to farmers on the Great Plains?

stick to its smooth surface. Steel plows made tilling the prairie soil much easier, although for a long time they were too expensive for many farmers, like Mattie's father, to afford.

In 1855 James Oliver of Indiana built another kind of plow that was even better at cutting through the sod of the Great Plains. With reapers, threshers, and improved plows, farmers could till and plant more land. This meant they got bigger harvests.

✓ **How did new farm machines and improved plows change farming?**

CHANGES CONTINUE

Farming methods keep changing. Today most farming is done with large machines. Many farmers add fertilizers (FER•tuhl•eye•zerz) to the soil. **Fertilizer** is matter added to the soil to help crops grow. Some farmers use chemical sprays to fight weeds and insects. Also, scientists have improved many kinds of plants. These improved plants grow faster and produce more food than older kinds.

When crop dusting, a plane (above) sprays a field with chemicals to kill insects. This scientist (right) is testing chemicals used to kill weeds.

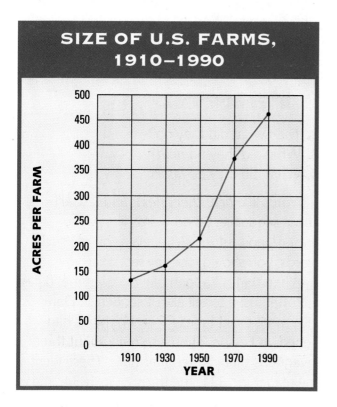

SIZE OF U.S. FARMS, 1910–1990

ACRES PER FARM vs **YEAR**

LEARNING FROM GRAPHS The size of the average American farm has grown since 1910.
■ Which 20-year period shows the biggest increase in the size of farms?

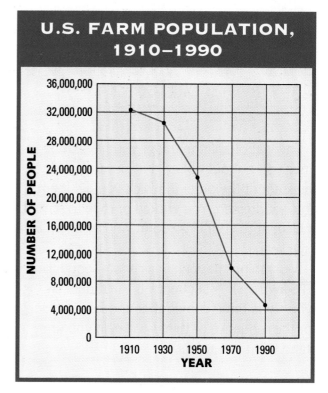

U.S. FARM POPULATION, 1910–1990

NUMBER OF PEOPLE vs **YEAR**

LEARNING FROM GRAPHS Fewer people now live on farms than in the past.
■ About how many fewer people lived on farms in 1990 than in 1970?

All these changes have improved harvests. Farmers are now able to raise more crops on each acre of land. Individual farmers can plant more land, too. Most farms in the United States today are more than three times as big as they were in 1900. Many are owned by large businesses. However, fewer people are now farmers. Out of every 100 people in the United States today, less than 3 live and work on farms.

As people have left farms, urbanization (er•buh•nuh•ZAY•shuhn) has been happening. **Urbanization** is the spread of city life. Cities in the United States have grown rapidly.

✓ **How has the number of people who earn their living on farms changed?**

LESSON 2 REVIEW

Check Understanding

1. **Recall the Facts** Why did pioneers on the Great Plains build soddies?
2. **Focus on the Main Idea** What changes did people make so they could live on and farm the Great Plains?

Think Critically

3. **Link to You** What changes might you face if you moved to a new region?

Show What You Know

Writing Activity Imagine that you are a pioneer living in a soddy on the Great Plains. Write a diary entry describing your life.

How To

Identify Time Patterns

Why Is This Skill Important?

Think about all the things you have done since you got out of bed this morning. Also think about the order in which you did them. You got dressed. You walked or rode to school. You went to your classroom. You sat down in your seat.

Most things happen in a certain sequence (SEE•kwuhns). A **sequence** is the order in which one thing comes after another. Looking for the sequence of things will help you understand what you read.

Remember What You Have Read

In Lesson 2 you read about how pioneer families on the Great Plains used sod to build their houses. To build a soddy, the families had to do things in the right sequence.

1. What was the *first* thing pioneers had to do to build a soddy?

This soddy was built in Custer County, in Nebraska. The land in Custer County is part of the Great Plains.

2. *Then* what did they do?
3. What did they do *next*?
4. What did they do *last*?

Words like *first, then, next,* and *last* tell about sequence. So do words like *past, present,* and *future.* Whenever you see such words, you should look for sequence.

When things happen over a long time, dates are often used to tell about sequence. Dates give more exact times for when things happened. In Lesson 2 you also read about three inventions that changed farming. These were the reaper in 1831, the thresher in 1834, and the steel plow in 1837. The date with each invention told you the sequence in which they were built.

Understand the Process

Here are some things you can do to identify sequence as you read.

- Think about the order, or sequence, in which things happen.
- Look for words that tell about sequence.
- Look for dates that tell about sequence. You may find years or just months or days of the week.

Think and Apply

Think about some things you have done, either today or over a longer time. Then write a paragraph that tells about them.  Be sure to use either words or dates to help your readers understand the sequence in which things happened.

FARMS, RANCHES, AND CITIES

Link to Our World

How do people who live in cities and on farms and ranches depend on one another?

Focus on the Main Idea
Read to find out how products from the Middle West have added to people's interdependence.

Preview Vocabulary
**entrepreneur   supply
free enterprise   meat packing
demand**

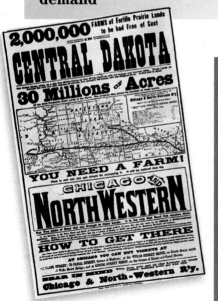

This railroad poster from the 1870s advertises free land to people willing to move to the area that is now South Dakota.

Cities are very different from places in rural areas. However, people who live and work in cities and on farms and ranches share something. They all depend on one another.

LINKING FARMS AND CITIES

For years farmers east of the Mississippi River sent their goods by train to markets in cities. People in cities depended on farmers to sell them food. Many factories in the cities depended on other farm products. They needed raw materials, such as cotton, wool, and leather, from farms. They used those raw materials to make goods.

Farmers, in turn, depended on workers in the cities. Without city workers, farmers would not have had manufactured goods and other supplies. Trains brought these things to the farms from factories in the cities.

Over time, railroad tracks spread west through the Great Plains. Building railroad tracks on the prairie was much easier than building them in the East. On the prairie, there were fewer hills or trees to get in the way, and there were no cities to connect. However, the steam engines that pulled the trains needed water, so railroad tracks usually followed rivers. As the railroads spread west, new cities sprang up along the tracks. Among them were Omaha, Nebraska, and Topeka, Kansas.

 How did trains link farms and cities?

RANCHING ON THE GREAT PLAINS

Railroads connected the Great Plains with cities in other parts of the country. But they did much more. Railroads also helped an important ranching industry to grow on the Great Plains.

In what is today southern Texas and northern Mexico, ranchers had been raising cattle for many years. Thousands of longhorn cattle roamed the grasslands there. Longhorns came from cattle Spanish settlers had brought to the Americas.

When the Spanish first came to the Americas, there were no cattle or horses here. Christopher Columbus brought some with him to the Caribbean. Later, Spanish settlers brought cattle and horses to Mexico. From there, cattle ranching spread northward into Texas and the southern Great Plains.

People in cities in the East were eager to buy beef, and they were willing to pay a lot of money for it. In the East, ranchers could get ten times as much money for their cattle as they could get in Texas.

However, there was no good way to get the cattle from Texas to the East. That changed once the railroads reached the Great Plains.

In Abilene, Kansas, a cattle trader named Joseph McCoy built stockyards near the new railroad. Then, in 1867, he sent word to Texas that he would buy herds of cattle. In great cattle drives, ranchers moved their cattle to McCoy's stockyards. From there the cattle were loaded into railroad cars and shipped to markets in Chicago and other cities.

Several cattle trails led from Texas through Oklahoma north to the railroads in Kansas, Nebraska, and Missouri.

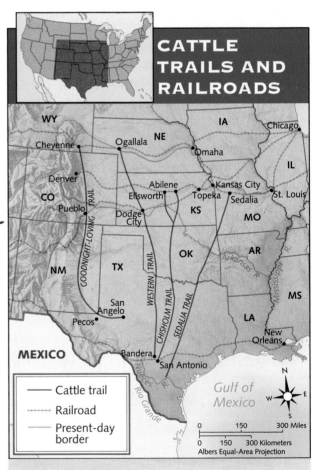

CATTLE TRAILS AND RAILROADS

— Cattle trail
······· Railroad
— Present-day border

0   150   300 Miles
0   150   300 Kilometers
Albers Equal-Area Projection

 MOVEMENT To reach the railroads, ranchers moved their cattle north from Texas in great cattle drives.
■ Which cattle trail led to Abilene, Kansas?

Longhorn cattle have long, sharp horns. During the late 1800s, ranchers moved millions of these cattle from Texas to stockyards in Kansas, Missouri, and Nebraska.

Who?

Nat Love (1854–1921)

Nat Love was one of the thousands of cowhands who worked in the great cattle drives from Texas. Love was born a slave in Tennessee, but he moved west to Dodge City, Kansas, after the Civil War. There he became an expert rider and roper. Love worked in cattle drives until 1889.

Dodge City, Kansas, in 1878

The most famous of these trails was the Chisholm (CHIH•zuhm) Trail. It went to Abilene and Ellsworth, Kansas. Other trails led to Sedalia, Missouri; Dodge City, Kansas; and Ogallala (oh•guh•LAHL•uh), Nebraska.

Cattle ranching spread north across the Great Plains. Today ranching is a leading industry in all the Great Plains states. Ranching is most important where the land is too rough or too dry for farming. Both cattle and sheep graze there.

✓ How did railroads help the cattle industry?

BUILDING NEW BUSINESSES

Other businesses grew on the Great Plains, too. Some were started by farmers. Mills in the East did not like to grind the hard winter wheat that grew so well on the Great Plains. So farmers on the Great Plains built their own flour mills.

In the United States, a person is free to become an entrepreneur (ahn•truh•pruh•NER). An **entrepreneur** is a person who sets up a new business. Having the right to start a new business is an important part of free enterprise. **Free enterprise** is a kind of economy in which people own and run their own businesses with only some control by the government.

In some countries, governments tell owners exactly how they must run their businesses. Governments tell them what to make and how much to charge. In the United States, however, business owners decide those things mostly on their own.

A free enterprise economy means freedom to do well in business. It also means freedom to fail. A Great Plains farmer who tries to grow oranges will fail because orange trees cannot live through the region's cold winters. A business owner who specializes in iron plows will not stay in business, either. There is little demand for iron plows today. A **demand** is a desire for a good or service by people who are willing to pay for it.

To do well, a business must offer goods or services that people want to buy. A good or service that a business offers for sale is called a **supply**. The cattle that a rancher offers for sale are a supply. The service of grinding wheat in exchange for money is a kind of supply, too.

The supply of a good or service usually rises or falls to meet the demand. This means a business will produce more of something if customers want to buy a lot of it. If customers do not want to buy very much of something, a business will produce less of it.

 In a free enterprise economy, who makes most of the decisions about a business?

BUSINESSES AND TRANSPORTATION

The Middle West is rich in natural resources. Large forests cover much of northern Michigan, Wisconsin, and Minnesota. Minnesota also has one of the largest iron ore deposits in the world. South Dakota has the largest gold mine in the country, and Missouri is a leading producer of lead. Several states in the Middle West region have large amounts of coal and oil.

Cities in the Middle West have many of the same kinds of businesses as cities in other regions. Other businesses are in the Middle West because they use products that nearby farmers and ranchers supply. These businesses do not have to pay for

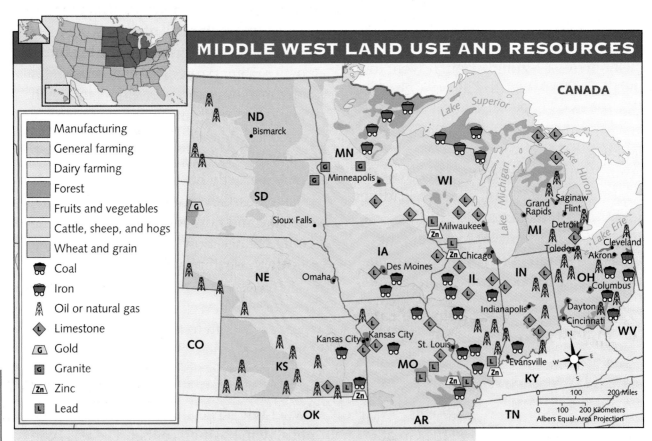

MIDDLE WEST LAND USE AND RESOURCES

Manufacturing
General farming
Dairy farming
Forest
Fruits and vegetables
Cattle, sheep, and hogs
Wheat and grain
Coal
Iron
Oil or natural gas
Limestone
Gold
Granite
Zinc
Lead

HUMAN-ENVIRONMENT INTERACTIONS People in the Middle West use the land in many ways.
■ What is the main land use for most of North Dakota?

shipping the products over long distances. Flour mills, for example, are in several cities in the Middle West. In other cities workers use corn and wheat to make cereals.

The raising of cattle has helped another important industry grow in the Middle West region—meat packing. **Meat packing** is the preparing of meat for market. It is a leading business in several states. Among them are Iowa, Kansas, South Dakota, and Missouri.

Other industries in the Middle West supply products that ranchers and farmers need. Makers of farm machinery and supplies started factories in the Middle West to be near farmers. Today those industries are still adding to the economies of such states as Iowa and Nebraska.

Regardless of their locations, all businesses need transportation to deliver goods and services. As in the past, railroads still connect ranches and farms to

An early advertisement (left) for a flour mill in Minneapolis, Minnesota. Farm machinery (above) is manufactured in several states in the Middle West.

cities. Today, however, people can choose other forms of transportation. Many send goods to markets on roads. Every day, trucks use the nearly 4 million miles (more than 6 million km) of roads in the United States to deliver goods to markets.

✔ **Why are certain businesses likely to be in cities in the Middle West?**

L*SSON 3 REVIEW*

Check Understanding

1. Recall the Facts How were railroads important to the early cattle industry in the Middle West?

2. Focus on the Main Idea How have products from the Middle West added to people's interdependence?

Think Critically

3. Cause and Effect How did railroads cause cattle ranchers and people in cities in the East to become more dependent on one another?

4. Personally Speaking Why does a free enterprise economy give you more choices about what to buy and where to buy it?

Show What You Know

Listing Activity Divide a sheet of paper into two halves. Label one half *Farms and Ranches.* Label the other half *Cities.* On the first half, list ways farmers and ranchers depend on people in cities. On the second half, list ways people in cities depend on farms and ranches.

Follow Routes on a Road Map

Why Is This Skill Important?

"Look at the road map. I need to know where to turn." Have you ever heard these words on a car trip with your family or friends? At some time nearly everyone has to use a road map. A road map shows routes between places. A **route** is a path from one place to another.

Road maps give other important information, too. They show the locations of many cities and towns. They also show physical features, such as mountains, major bodies of water, and forests. Many road maps show where to find parks, museums, and other points of interest.

Kinds of Highways

Road maps use different colors to show the different kinds of highways that connect places. The number of each highway is printed inside a symbol. Each kind of symbol also stands for one kind of highway. Knowing the different kinds of highways helps you choose good routes.

Look at the map key for the road map of Kansas on page 277. A heavy blue line shows an interstate highway. *Inter* means "between or among." An **interstate highway** is a highway that goes through more than one state. Interstate highways are wide, divided highways that connect large cities. They usually do not have stoplights, so people can use them to travel long distances quickly.

Interstate highways that run east and west, like Interstate 70, have even numbers. Interstate highways that run north and south have odd numbers.

The map key shows other kinds of highways, too. Like an interstate highway, a United States highway goes from state to state. However, United States highways often have stoplights and lower speed limits. They may or may not be divided highways, but they usually are wider than state highways. State highways connect places in one state.

This map key shows another kind of highway, called a toll highway. A toll highway, or **toll road**, is a road that drivers must pay to use. The toll road shown on the Kansas road map is called the Kansas Turnpike. Parts of Interstate Highways 35, 335, and 70 use the same route as the Kansas Turnpike.

Understand the Process

Suppose a truck driver needs to take wheat flour from a mill in Hutchinson to a market in Salina. What route should the driver take? Use

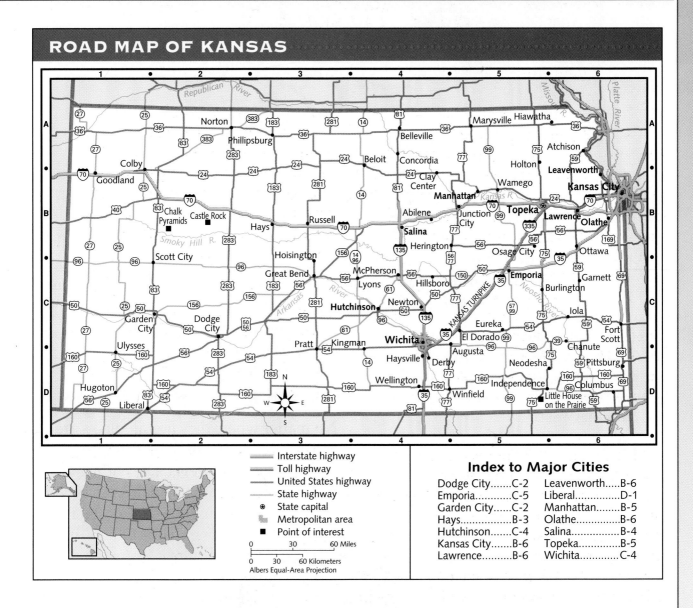

ROAD MAP OF KANSAS

Interstate highway
Toll highway
United States highway
State highway
⊛ **State capital**
▨ **Metropolitan area**
■ **Point of interest**

0   30   60 Miles
0   30   60 Kilometers
Albers Equal-Area Projection

Index to Major Cities

the road map to find the highways and the directions. Follow the numbered steps.

1. Use the map index and grid to find Hutchinson and Salina.

2. Find the highways that connect the two cities.

3. Choose the best route if there is more than one. The best route may be the shortest one, the one that uses wider highways, or the one that has fewer stops.

4. Name each highway to be used and the direction to be taken. The map's compass rose will help you name the direction.

5. Describe the route. What highway should the truck driver use to leave Hutchinson? In which direction should he or she go? What highway should the driver use then? In which direction should he or she go?

Think and Apply

Find two places on the map. On paper, describe a route that connects those places. Be sure to name the highways and the direction to be traveled on each one. Give your paper to a classmate. See if your classmate can follow the route you described.

PLAINS AROUND THE WORLD

LESSON 4

Link to Our World

How are plains regions around the world alike and how are they different?

Focus on the Main Idea
Read to find out how the Pampa of Argentina is similar to and different from the plains of the Middle West.

Preview Vocabulary
gaucho
estancia

A rhea—an ostrichlike bird that lives in the plains regions of South America

Plains stretch across much of the Middle West region of the United States. They hug the Atlantic and Gulf coasts, too. Plains are also found in many other places around the world. In fact, plains are the Earth's most common landform.

OTHER PLAINS REGIONS

No matter where they are, all plains are broad, mostly flat lands. Not all plains regions are alike, however. Depending on their location and climate, plains can be very different. Some plains, like the Coastal Plain in the United States, lie along coasts. Others, like the Central Plains and the Great Plains, stretch through a continent's interior. The soil of some plains is fertile. In other places it is poor and rocky. Some plains have thick forests, while others have almost no trees.

People everywhere have found ways to use the resources and physical features of plains. In the United States, people mostly use plains for farming and ranching. But many of the largest cities in the United States are built on plains, too.

In many other parts of the world, plains are also places for farms, ranches, and cities. In fact, most of the world's plains are used to grow food. Many of the world's largest cities are also on plains.

✓ **How do people around the world use plains regions?**

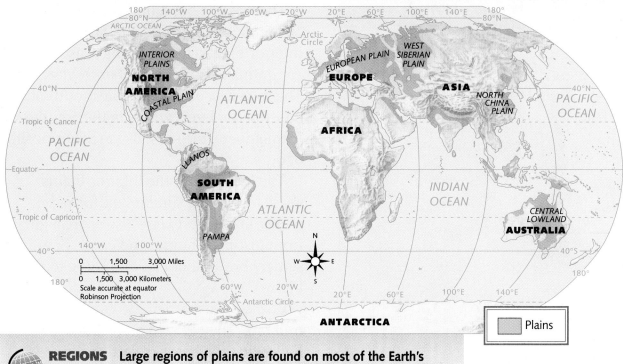

Plains

REGIONS **Large regions of plains are found on most of the Earth's continents.**

■ **What two large plains regions are in South America? What large plain covers much of Europe?**

THE PAMPA

A girl wakes early to the sounds of the ranch coming to life. She rises and looks out her window. For as far as she can see, a sea of grass stretches west across a broad plain. This plain is the Pampa. The Pampa is in the country of Argentina, in South America. In Spanish, the word *pampa* means "level land."

Like the Coastal Plain in the United States, Argentina's Pampa stretches inland from the Atlantic Ocean. Then it spreads west for hundreds of miles toward the Andes Mountains. In 1912 an American scientist named W. J. Holland traveled across the Pampa. He

wrote, "I have crossed the prairies of Minnesota and the Dakotas, of Kansas and Nebraska . . . but in none of them have I seen such absolutely level lands."

Summers on the Pampa are hot, and winters are generally mild. Places on the Pampa receive different amounts of rain. The amount of rain decreases from east to west. In the east moist air blows in from the Atlantic Ocean. This causes a humid climate. To the west the Andes Mountains block moist Pacific winds from reaching the Pampa. Like the Interior Plains of the United States, the western half of the Pampa is much drier than the eastern half.

> ❝ *IN NONE OF THEM HAVE I seen such absolutely level lands.* ❞
>
> W. J. Holland, 1912

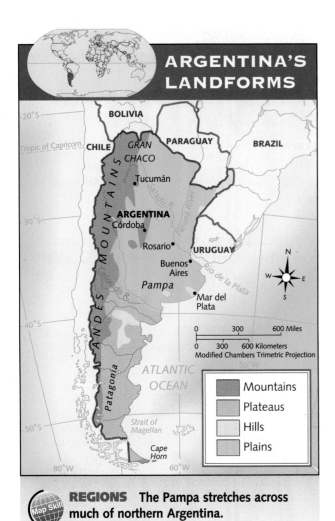

ARGENTINA'S LANDFORMS

BOLIVIA

CHILE

GRAN CHACO

PARAGUAY

BRAZIL

Tucumán

ARGENTINA

Córdoba

Rosario

URUGUAY

Buenos Aires

Pampa

Mar del Plata

Rio de la Plata

20°S

Tropic of Capricorn

30°S

40°S

50°S

ANDES MOUNTAINS

Colorado R.

Córdoba R.

Salado R.

Paraná River

Patagonia

ATLANTIC OCEAN

Strait of Magellan

Cape Horn

80°W

60°W

50°W

0   300   600 Miles

0   300   600 Kilometers

Modified Chambers Trimetric Projection

N E S W

Mountains
Plateaus
Hills
Plains

REGIONS The Pampa stretches across much of northern Argentina.
■ What landform marks the Pampa's western border?

Map Skill

The western Pampa is too dry for many trees to grow. Instead, short grasses cover the ground. This is grazing land for cattle and sheep.

✓ **How does the Pampa's climate change from east to west?**

FARMING AND RANCHING

If you were crossing the Pampa, you might think you were in the Heartland of the United States. Like the Interior Plains, the Pampa has some of the world's richest soil. Wheat is the leading crop on the western Pampa, where the land is drier. Corn grows well on the eastern Pampa.

Much of this wheat and corn is exported to other countries.

There is one big difference between farming on the Pampa and farming on the Interior Plains. The growing season in Argentina is from December to March. This is because Argentina lies south of the equator. Everywhere in the Southern Hemisphere, the seasons are the opposite of ours.

The Pampa and the Interior Plains share more than similar landforms, climates, and crops. They also share a gift from history—horses and cattle. Spanish settlers brought horses and cattle to the Pampa, too.

Cattle once roamed the Pampa by the millions. They grazed on its thick grasses. Following the herds of cattle rode the gauchos (GOW•chohz). **Gauchos** were skilled riders who lived on the open land of the Pampa. They hunted the cattle for food and hides.

Today, gauchos live and work as ranch hands. Most gauchos wear baggy pants, high leather boots, and bright scarves around their necks.

Horses are raised on many estancias, like this one near San Antonio de Areco, Argentina. Most estancias are smaller than they were in the past, but some still cover thousands of acres.

In the late 1700s government leaders began to give away large areas of land on the Pampa to their powerful friends. Along with the land went the cattle on it. The new owners started **estancias** (es•TAHN•see•ahs), or large ranches. The estancias covered thousands of acres. Gauchos were no longer free to ride the Pampa in search of cattle.

Today estancia owners hire gauchos to care for their cattle. Gauchos are now ranch hands. They often live with their families in small houses on the estancias, instead of on open land. Their way of life has changed. However, gauchos remain an important part of Argentina's heritage. Poems and songs about the gauchos tell of the free life on the Pampa in days gone by.

Cattle ranching is an important part of Argentina's economy, too. Cattle have been raised on the Pampa for hundreds of years. With the invention of refrigerated ships in the late 1800s, beef became one of Argentina's chief exports. Refrigerated

ships made it possible to ship meat over long distances. Today Argentina's cattle herds help feed the world.

Buenos Aires (BWAY•nahs AIR•eez) is Argentina's capital and largest city. It has always served as a main port for shipping exports. Both meat packing and food processing are leading industries in Buenos Aires.

 How is farming on the Pampa different from farming on the Interior Plains?

LESSON 4 REVIEW

Check Understanding

1. **Recall the Facts**   How are plains around the world important to people?
2. **Focus on the Main Idea**   How is the Pampa of Argentina similar to and different from the plains in the Middle West?

Think Critically

3. **Cause and Effect**   Different parts of the Pampa receive different amounts of precipitation. How has this affected the ways people use the land?
4. **Link to You**   Argentina's seasons are the opposite of ours. How might having opposite seasons affect when you or other people in your state do things?

Show What You Know

 Art Activity   Draw a picture showing different ways in which people in Argentina use the Pampa. Then write a caption for your picture. In the caption, tell how the uses of the Pampa are like or unlike the uses of the Interior Plains in the United States. Share your finished picture with classmates.

REVIEW

CONNECT MAIN IDEAS

Use this organizer to show that you understand how the chapter's main ideas are connected. First copy the organizer onto a separate sheet of paper. Then complete it by writing two sentences about each main idea.

The Interior Plains

The amount of precipitation affects the kinds of crops grown on the Interior Plains.

1. _____
2. _____

People made changes so they could live on and farm the Great Plains.

1. _____
2. _____

Products from the Middle West have added to people's interdependence.

1. _____
2. _____

Plains Around the World
The Pampa of Argentina is similar to and different from the plains of the Middle West.

1. _____
2. _____

WRITE MORE ABOUT IT

1. **Compare Past and Present**   Imagine that you climb aboard a time machine and travel back to the 1800s. Tell how farms and farming methods that you see are different from farms and farming methods today.

2. **Explain What You Would Have Done**   Railroad companies gave away land on the Great Plains to get more people to settle there. Write a paragraph explaining why you would or would not have accepted a railroad's offer of free land.

USE VOCABULARY

For each group of terms, write a sentence or two that explains how the terms are related.

1. prairie, sod
2. drought, blizzard, tornado
3. entrepreneur, free enterprise
4. demand, supply
5. gaucho, estancia

CHECK UNDERSTANDING

1. Which region usually receives less rain, the Central Plains or the Great Plains?
2. What makes the Central Plains a good place to grow corn?
3. Why did many settlers on the Great Plains use sod to build their homes?
4. Why did pioneer families need to be self-sufficient?
5. Why do farmers often add fertilizers to the soil?
6. What is urbanization?
7. Why are plains regions important to many people around the world?

THINK CRITICALLY

1. **Link to You**   How does your family depend on farms on the Interior Plains?
2. **Think More About It**   Why might it be more difficult for people to be self-sufficient today than in the past?
3. **Cause and Effect**   How did the invention of the reaper, thresher, and steel plow affect American farms?

APPLY SKILLS

How to Read Pictographs   Use the pictograph on page 264 to answer these questions.

1. Which state grows more wheat, North Dakota or South Dakota?
2. About how much wheat is grown in Nebraska?

How to Identify Time Patterns   Find a newspaper article that tells about a sequence of events. Cut out the article, and paste it onto a sheet of paper. Then circle any words or dates that helped you identify the sequence. Under the article, list the events in the order in which they took place.

How to Follow Routes on a Road Map   Using a road map of your state, describe a route from your city or town to the state capital. If you live in the state capital, describe a route from your city to another city in your state.

READ MORE ABOUT IT

Dakota Dugout by Ann Turner. Macmillan. This book tells what it was like to live in a sod house on the prairie.

Justin and the Best Biscuits in the World by Mildred Pitts Walter. Lothrop, Lee & Shepard. Justin spends the summer on Grandpa's ranch in Kansas and learns about African American cowhands of the past.

On the Pampas by María Christina Brusca. Henry Holt. A girl spends her summer vacation at her grandparents' estancia.

Thrashin' Time: Harvest Days in the Dakotas by David Weitzman. David R. Godine. A young boy tells about his family's farm.

GREAT WATERWAYS
SHAPE NATIONS

> **"** I heard the singing of the Mississippi
> when Abe Lincoln went down to
> New Orleans, and I've seen its muddy
> bosom turn all golden in the sunset.
> I've known rivers:
> Ancient, dusky rivers.
> My soul has grown deep like the rivers. **"**
>
> from *Selected Poems*
> by Langston Hughes, 1926

A riverboat captain on the Mississippi River

ALONG THE
GREAT LAKES

LESSON 1

Link to Our World

Why do large cities and industries often develop along waterways?

Focus on the Main Idea
Read to find out why many large cities and industries have grown up along the Great Lakes.

Preview Vocabulary
**capital resource
factors of production
mass production
assembly line**

The 110-story Sears Tower, in Chicago, is the country's tallest building.

Few places in the world have as many navigable rivers and lakes as the Middle West region of the United States. Many large cities and industries have grown up along those waterways. The waterways offer transportation routes for the region's natural resources and products. They have helped the Middle West become a leading center of manufacturing.

GREAT LAKES PORTS

Thousands of years ago a giant glacier pushed south over the middle part of North America. It made hills flat and filled in valleys with rich soil. The weight of the glacier also formed five huge holes in the ground. As the glacier melted, water filled in the holes and formed the Great Lakes. Four of these lakes—Erie, Huron, Michigan, and Superior—border on states in the Middle West.

Many streams and rivers flow into the Great Lakes. Long ago, ports were started at the mouths of some of the larger rivers. Over time many of those ports became large cities. On Lake Erie are Cleveland and Toledo, both in Ohio. On Lake Michigan are Gary, Indiana; Chicago, Illinois; and Milwaukee, Wisconsin. Duluth, Minnesota, is a large port on Lake Superior.

The Great Lakes make up one of the most important inland waterways in North America. Some Great Lakes ports lie more than 1,000 miles (1,609 km) from the Atlantic Ocean, but ships from these ports can reach the

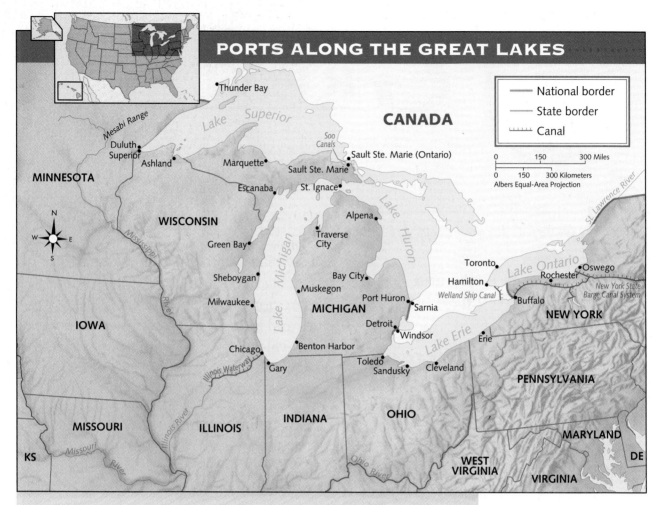

HUMAN-ENVIRONMENT INTERACTIONS Before the Illinois Waterway was built, ships could not reach the Mississippi River system from the Great Lakes.

■ How has the Illinois Waterway improved transportation?

Atlantic through the St. Lawrence Seaway or the New York State Barge Canal.

Small ships traveling to and from the Great Lakes have another way of reaching the ocean. A canal called the Illinois Waterway links Lake Michigan and the Illinois River, which flows into the Mississippi River. Using the Illinois Waterway, ships can carry goods between ports on the Great Lakes and those on the Gulf of Mexico.

✓ **Which two waterways link the Mississippi River and Lake Michigan?**

CENTERS OF INDUSTRY

The good transportation provided by the Great Lakes has brought many industries to cities along their shores. The region has become one of the largest industrial areas of the United States.

Factories in cities along the Great Lakes manufacture all kinds of products. Some of them process foods from corn and mill flour from wheat. Ships on the Great Lakes carry corn, wheat, and other grains from farms in the Middle West to food-processing plants and flour mills in cities along the lakes.

Places near the Great Lakes have many of the natural resources that industries need, such as coal and iron ore. Those resources first brought many industries to cities along the lakes. One of those industries was steel production.

As you know, the steel industry started in western Pennsylvania. However, large deposits of iron ore were later discovered west of Lake Superior. The largest deposits were in Minnesota's Mesabi (muh·SAH·bee) Range. To be nearer to those resources, the steel industry spread to cities along the Great Lakes. Ships carried iron ore from the Mesabi Range to steel mills in such cities as Chicago and Cleveland. Coal and limestone, two other resources needed to make steel, came from Illinois, Indiana, and other nearby states. Those resources were taken to the mills on railroad cars.

✓ **What brought many industries to cities along the Great Lakes?**

INDUSTRIES NEED MANY RESOURCES

In 1905 a large company was looking for a place to build a new steel mill. The company wanted to build its mill on the shore of Lake Michigan, close to Chicago. There the mill would be near important waterways and railroads.

To manufacture steel or any other product, a business uses three different kinds of resources. It must have natural resources, such as water, minerals, and fuel. It must have human resources, or workers. It must also have capital resources. **Capital resources** are the money, buildings, machines, and tools needed to run a business.

In 1907 these workers, along with hundreds of others, helped build the city of Gary, Indiana. Why was Gary built?

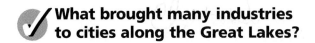

Before deciding where to build the new mill, the company had to think about all the factors of production. The **factors of production** are the natural, human, and capital resources that a business needs to produce goods or services.

The place the company chose for its new steel mill was in northwest Indiana. The land was near natural resources, but there were no workers because there was no city. So the company built the city of Gary. Many people moved to Gary to find jobs in the new mill.

As in Pittsburgh, steel mills in Gary and in other cities along the Great Lakes no longer make as much steel as they once did. However, making steel is still an important industry in many places near the Great Lakes. Indiana, Ohio, Michigan, and Illinois are all important steel-producing states.

✓ **What three kinds of resources does a business need to manufacture products?**

INDUSTRIES CONNECT

Sometimes one industry helps other industries grow in the same area. That happened with automobiles and steel. The steel mills along the Great Lakes supplied automobile makers with the steel they needed.

Detroit, Michigan, became the center of the automobile industry—the "automobile capital of the world." One reason for this was Detroit's location on the Detroit River. All ships sailing between Lake Huron and Lake Erie must use this river.

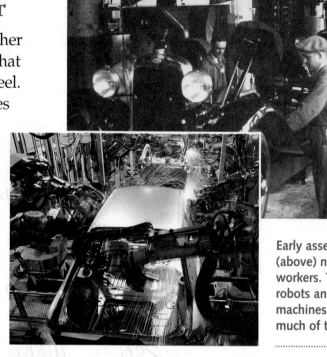

Early assembly lines (above) needed many workers. Today, robots and other machines (left) do much of the work.

THE DETROIT AREA

0   40   80 Miles
0   40   80 Kilometers
Albers Equal-Area Projection

Lake Huron

MICHIGAN   Bay City

Grand River   Flint

St. Clair River

CANADA

Detroit   Lake St. Clair
Windsor
Detroit River

Lake Erie

Toledo

Cleveland

INDIANA   Maumee River

OHIO   —— National border
—— State border

LOCATION Detroit is the largest city in the state of Michigan.
■ How has Detroit's location on the Detroit River helped the city to grow?

The Detroit River connects Lake Erie with a smaller lake called Lake St. Clair. Another river connects Lake St. Clair with Lake Huron. The rivers and lakes made it easy to ship steel and other products to Detroit. Today the Detroit River is one of the busiest waterways in the United States. And the Detroit area produces more automobiles than anywhere else in the United States.

The automobile industry grew rapidly. Factories began to use mass production to manufacture cars. In **mass production** many goods that are alike can be made quickly and cheaply. Machines help with the work.

Products made by mass production are the same. For example, cars of the same model and year look the same, except for color. Their parts are the same, too. The parts from one car will fit on another car of the same model and year.

Mass production made the assembly line possible. An **assembly line** is a line of workers along which a product moves as it is put together one step at a time. In most automobile assembly plants today, a computer-controlled assembly line moves an unfinished car past workers and machines. Each worker or machine does a special job or adds certain parts to each car. Like cars, most manufactured goods today are made on assembly lines.

 What made the assembly line possible?

Who?

Henry Ford
1863–1947

Henry Ford wanted to build automobiles that large numbers of people could afford to buy. Instead of making cars one at a time, as had been done, Ford used an assembly line to produce automobiles faster and cheaper. Ford sold millions of his Model T cars, which people called the Tin Lizzie. Workers on Ford's assembly line could build a Model T in less than two hours. Soon, as Ford had dreamed, many people owned their own cars.

The Model T Ford was the first car to be built on an assembly line. This 1920 Model T Runabout reached a maximum speed of 40 miles (64 km) per hour and sold for $550.

LESSON 1 REVIEW

Check Understanding

1. **Recall the Facts**   How are the Great Lakes important to transportation?
2. **Focus on the Main Idea**   Why did many large cities and industries grow up along the Great Lakes?

Think Critically

3. **Think More About It**   How has mass production helped make more products available to people?
4. **Cause and Effect**   What caused the Great Lakes to form?

Show What You Know

Map Activity   Draw a map showing the four Great Lakes that border on states in the Middle West. Label the lakes and the states that border on them. Label the Mesabi Range in Minnesota. Then label these cities—Duluth, Gary, Detroit, and Cleveland. Use one color to trace the route that a ship might follow between Duluth and Gary. Then use different colors to trace routes between Duluth and Detroit and between Duluth and Cleveland.

Chapter 9 • **289**

Link to Our World

How do rivers help connect people and places?

Focus on the Main Idea
As you read, look for ways the Mississippi River system has been used as a transportation and trade route.

Preview Vocabulary
shaman
migration
flatboat
barge

Legend says that a staff with carved ears of corn, like the one above, was carried by the Chickasaw Indians when they first came to live along the Mississippi River.

Rivers have always been important to travel and trade. Long ago, American Indians traveled up and down rivers in canoes to trade goods in faraway places. Colonists from Europe later used the same rivers to travel inland from their first settlements. Today people still use rivers as trade routes between different parts of the United States.

THE MISSISSIPPI RIVER SYSTEM

There is a story about the ancestors of the Choctaw and Chickasaw Indians. Long ago, it is said, their ancestors camped along the Mississippi River. Their **shaman** (SHAH•muhn), or spiritual leader, said, "No man can know the story of the river. It belongs to the time when there were no men upon the earth. Therefore, do I give it the name of *Misha Sipokni*—beyond the ages, the father of all its kind."

No one knows if this legend is true. Still, "father of all its kind" seems to be a good way to describe the mighty Mississippi River. It is North America's largest river. In fact, the Mississippi is so large that a raindrop falling into the river at its source will not reach the Gulf of Mexico for 60 days!

Like the Great Lakes, the Mississippi River is one of the country's most important inland waterways. On the Mississippi, small ships can go all the way from Minneapolis, Minnesota, to the Gulf of Mexico. That is more than 1,800 miles (2,897 km)! Large ships that sail

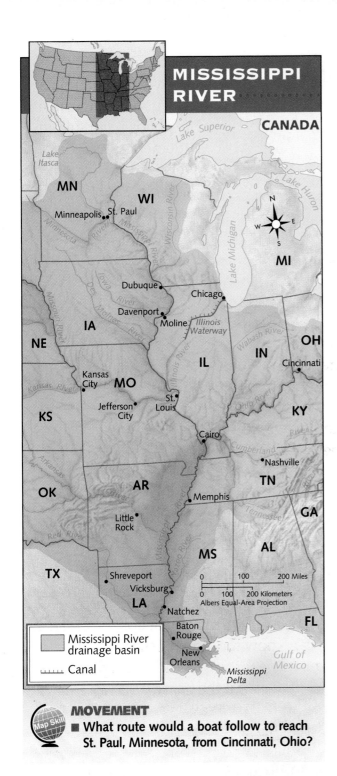

MISSISSIPPI RIVER

MOVEMENT
Map Skill
■ What route would a boat follow to reach St. Paul, Minnesota, from Cincinnati, Ohio?

the oceans can go up the Mississippi River as far as Baton Rouge (BA•tuhn ROOZH), Louisiana.

The Mississippi River and its tributaries form an important transportation route through America's Heartland. Before the Mississippi River reaches Cairo, Illinois, the Missouri and Illinois rivers flow into

it. Then, at Cairo, the Ohio River joins it. There the Mississippi River is the widest, almost 1 mile (nearly 2 km) across. Downstream it is joined by still other navigable rivers.

✓ **How is the Mississippi River important to transportation?**

USING RIVER HIGHWAYS

Early America did not look like what you see out your window today. Thick forests and rugged mountains made it hard to travel by land. Even where there were roads, they were often just narrow, muddy paths.

As you know, rivers carried early settlers inland from the Atlantic coast toward the Appalachian Mountains. After pioneers crossed those mountains, they used rivers on the other side to go even farther inland. The Ohio, Mississippi, and Missouri rivers became water highways for a huge westward migration. A **migration** is the movement of many people who leave one country or region to settle in another.

After pioneers crossed the Appalachian Mountains, it was hard for them to get supplies. There were no rivers that directly linked them to the cities along the Atlantic coast. Supplies had to be carried over the mountains or in canoes up the Mississippi River from New Orleans.

Pioneer families needed a way to carry a lot of supplies with them. When they reached the Ohio River at Pittsburgh, they often boarded flatboats. A **flatboat** was a large raft made of boards that were tied together. Flatboats could carry pioneer families and their things all the way from Pittsburgh to New Orleans or to any place in between.

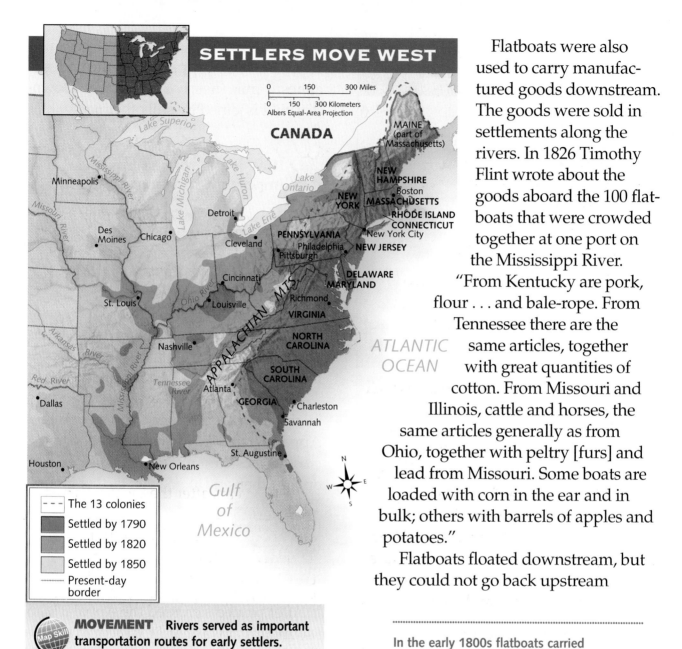

SETTLERS MOVE WEST

CANADA

MAINE
(part of
Massachusetts)

NEW HAMPSHIRE
Boston
NEW YORK   MASSACHUSETTS
RHODE ISLAND
CONNECTICUT
New York City
PENNSYLVANIA
Philadelphia   NEW JERSEY
Pittsburgh

DELAWARE
MARYLAND
Richmond
VIRGINIA

NORTH
CAROLINA

SOUTH
CAROLINA

GEORGIA   Charleston
Savannah

St. Augustine

Minneapolis

Detroit

Des
Moines   Chicago
Cleveland

Cincinnati

St. Louis   Louisville

Nashville   APPALACHIAN MTS.

Atlanta

Dallas

Houston   New Orleans

Lake Superior
Mississippi River
Missouri River
Lake Michigan
Lake Huron
Lake Ontario
Lake Erie
Ohio River
Arkansas River
Red River
Tennessee River
Mississippi River

ATLANTIC
OCEAN

Gulf
of
Mexico

0   150   300 Miles
0   150   300 Kilometers
Albers Equal-Area Projection

N S E W (compass rose)

The 13 colonies (dashed)
Settled by 1790
Settled by 1820
Settled by 1850
Present-day border

MOVEMENT Rivers served as important transportation routes for early settlers.
■ By what year was the land along the Ohio River settled?

Flatboats were also used to carry manufactured goods downstream. The goods were sold in settlements along the rivers. In 1826 Timothy Flint wrote about the goods aboard the 100 flatboats that were crowded together at one port on the Mississippi River.

"From Kentucky are pork, flour . . . and bale-rope. From Tennessee there are the same articles, together with great quantities of cotton. From Missouri and Illinois, cattle and horses, the same articles generally as from Ohio, together with peltry [furs] and lead from Missouri. Some boats are loaded with corn in the ear and in bulk; others with barrels of apples and potatoes."

Flatboats floated downstream, but they could not go back upstream

Flatboats were of different sizes. Some were 20 feet (6 m) wide and 50 to 100 feet (15 to 30 m) long. Flatboats were sometimes called arks. Like Noah's ark in the Bible, they carried everything a family had. One person who traveled on a flatboat in 1788 described it as "pretty close crowded having 27 men on board— 5 horses—2 cows—2 Calfs—7 hogs—and 9 dogs besides 8 tons of baggage."

In the early 1800s flatboats carried thousands of pioneers to new settlements in the Middle West. Why did flatboats provide one-way transportation only?

against the current. After their trip downstream they were usually broken up and their lumber was sold. New Orleans had many sidewalks made from this steady supply of wood.

 How did pioneers who crossed the Appalachian Mountains use rivers?

RIVER TRAVEL CHANGES

Keelboats soon joined flatboats on the rivers. Keelboats were pointed at both ends and sometimes used a sail. Unlike flatboats, they could be sailed or poled upstream. This meant that people and goods could be moved upstream as well as downstream.

In the summer of 1807, there was a major change in river travel. Robert Fulton took the *Clermont* on its first trip up the Hudson River from New York City. The *Clermont* was the first money-making steamboat. It was powered by a steam engine that turned a large paddle wheel. As the paddle wheel turned in the water, it caused the steamboat to move.

*W*ho?

Samuel Clemens 1835–1910

Samuel Clemens was a well-known American writer. He wrote many stories and books about the two years he piloted steamboats on the Mississippi River. His stories were often funny, but some made fun of important people. To keep from getting in trouble, he signed his stories with the name *Mark Twain*. Clemens had heard the term *mark twain* used many times on the river. It was shouted out whenever the river was getting too shallow for a steamboat to pass safely.

Just 13 years after the *Clermont's* first trip, steamboats were carrying passengers and goods on most of the country's navigable rivers. Many steamboats were on the Ohio and the Mississippi. With steamboats, river trips that had taken months

Steamboats such as the *Delta Queen*, shown here, still travel the Mississippi River and its major tributaries. Instead of moving goods and products, however, most steamboats now carry people on pleasure trips.

took only a few days. The improved transportation led to more trade. Cities and industries along rivers grew rapidly. St. Louis, Missouri, and Cincinnati, Ohio, both became major river ports.

✓ How did steamboats change river travel?

USING RIVERS TODAY

The Mississippi River system is just as important today in moving goods from one region of the country to another. Instead of steamboats, however, barges now carry most cargo. A **barge** is a large, flat-bottomed boat used on rivers and other inland waterways. Barges are a good way to move raw materials and other heavy goods.

The Mississippi River alone carries more than half the freight transported on inland waterways in the United States. Barges on the Mississippi carry crops grown on farms in the Middle West. They carry coal from Appalachia and the southern Great Lakes states. They also carry petroleum and petrochemicals from the Gulf coast.

Often, several barges are joined to form units called tows. These long tows are then pushed or pulled up or down a river by tugboats.

Large cities have grown up along the Mississippi River system to make use of its good transportation. Many are centers for manufacturing, services, and transportation. One of these cities is St. Louis. It is about 10 miles (16 km) south of where the Missouri River joins the Mississippi. Because of its location, St. Louis is one of the busiest ports on the Mississippi River. It is also a transportation center for trucking and railroads.

✓ What carries most cargo up and down rivers today?

LSSON 2 REVIEW

Check Understanding

1. **Recall the Facts**   Why is the Mississippi River such an important inland waterway?
2. **Focus on the Main Idea**   What are some ways the Mississippi River system has been used as a transportation and trade route?

Think Critically

3. **Think More About It**   What might happen to the price of food and other goods if the Mississippi River system could not be used?

Show What You Know

Simulation Activity
Imagine that you and your family are pioneers. You are about to board a flatboat in Pittsburgh for a trip down the Ohio River to your new home in Illinois. You must choose ten things to take. List in order of their importance the ten things you will take. Explain to classmates why these things are important.

LESSON 3

RIVERS AROUND THE WORLD

Link to Our World

How are rivers around the world alike and how are they different?

Focus on the Main Idea
Read to compare and contrast the ways that people in different places use rivers.

Preview Vocabulary
irrigation
paddy
rain forest

This ancient painting shows early Egyptian farmers harvesting a field.

Like many people in the United States, people in other countries often choose to live along rivers. They farm the fertile flood-plains, or they live and work in cities along the rivers. They also use rivers to transport their goods. Yet all rivers in the world are different, and people around the world use rivers in their own ways.

THE NILE RIVER

The Nile is the longest river in the world. Its 4,187-mile (6,738-km) journey begins in the mountains of East Central Africa, near the equator. From there, it flows north through several countries. At the end of its journey, in the country of Egypt, the Nile empties into the Mediterranean (meh•duh•tuh•RAY•nee•uhn) Sea. Like the Mississippi River, the Nile has formed a large delta at its mouth.

The Nile is the most important source of fresh water in all of Egypt. Along the river's banks lies the fertile and green Nile Valley. Away from the river, however, the land is mostly desert. In fact, this land is part of the Sahara (suh•HAIR•uh), the world's largest desert.

Most of Egypt's people are crowded into the Nile Valley and the Nile Delta. Because both areas have fertile land, many people earn their living by farming. "This is the best place on earth," says Ahmed, an Egyptian *fellah* (FEH•luh), or farmer. "Soil, water, sun—we can grow anything!"

However, Egyptian farmers must water their fields by irrigation. **Irrigation** is the use of canals, ditches, or pipes to move water to dry areas. In Egypt, farms are watered by more than 50,000 miles (80,450 km) of irrigation ditches. Farmers raise such crops as cotton, rice, and sugarcane. Even in Cairo, Egypt's capital, many people earn their living from industries related to farming.

For thousands of years, Egyptian farmers depended on floods. The floods watered the fields and left behind silt, which made the soil fertile. Each summer, after the Nile flooded, farmers planted their seeds. They threw them down on the ground and let cattle walk on the seeds to push them into the soil. The farmers also trapped water from the floods by digging basins in the ground. That water was used to irrigate fields during the growing season.

Today the Aswan High Dam stops the Nile from flooding. However, the water stored behind the dam has allowed farmers to irrigate millions of acres of new

farmland. Farmers in Egypt can now plant year-round, too.

Why is the Nile River important to Egypt?

THE RHINE RIVER

The Rhine River is in Europe. It forms part of the borders of several countries before flowing through Germany and the Netherlands. In the Netherlands the Rhine empties into the North Sea at the city of Rotterdam, one of the world's busiest ports. The North Sea is part of the Atlantic Ocean.

The Rhine River is like many navigable rivers in the United States. It connects inland cities to an ocean port. However, the cities on the Rhine are in several different countries.

Industries in those countries use the Rhine River to transport both raw materials and finished products. Each day, long lines of barges travel the river. They carry goods to and from busy river ports and trading centers. All of this makes the Rhine River the most important inland waterway in Europe.

People traveling up and down the Rhine River see some of Europe's most beautiful sights. Along many parts of their trip, they pass by old castles that were built on hills above the river hundreds of years ago. They also pass by many large factories and busy cities. Some of Europe's largest and most important cities are along the Rhine and its tributaries.

Why is the Rhine River Europe's most important inland waterway?

Many kinds of fruits and vegetables are sold at outdoor markets in Egypt. This man sells produce at a market in Cairo, Egypt's capital.

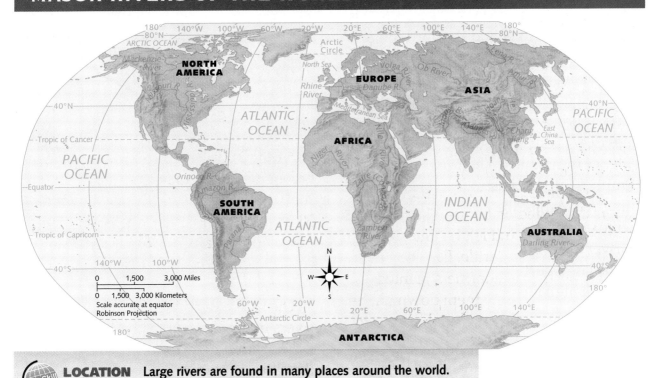

THE GANGES RIVER

The Ganges River is in southern Asia. For much of its course, the Ganges flows across the country of India. Millions of people in India live along the river.

Like the soil along the Nile, the soil along the Ganges is fertile. Along the Ganges, however, there is usually more rain. Still, farmers use a lot of water from the river to irrigate their fields.

The Ganges is like other rivers in many ways. However, it also is very different. For Hindus, people who follow the religion of Hinduism, the Ganges is a holy river. Each year thousands of Hindus go to the Ganges to bathe in its waters. They believe the river's waters will purify and heal them. Others go there to die. To help the worshippers reach the water, Hindu temples along the river have ghats (GAWTS), or stairs, leading down to the water's edge. "The Ganges is more than a river," says one man. "It is a . . . force that holds 5,000 years of history, culture, and tradition."

 What makes the Ganges different from many other rivers?

Stairs, called ghats, help worshippers reach the waters of the Ganges River in Varanasi, India.

Chapter 9 • **297**

THE CHANG JIANG

The Chang Jiang (CHAHNG jee•AHNG) is China's longest river and the third-longest river in the world. The name *Chang Jiang* means "long river." The Chang Jiang starts high in the mountains of southern China. It flows more than 3,400 miles (5,471 km) through the center of the country. Then it empties into the East China Sea, part of the Pacific Ocean. Near the river's mouth lies the large port city of Shanghai (shang•HY). It is China's largest city.

About one-fifth of the world's people live in China. This is more than in any other country. About half of China's people live along the Chang Jiang. In fact, more people live near this river than in all the United States!

Many cities and factories lie along the Chang Jiang. Along much of its course, the Chang Jiang is deep enough for large ships to use. It connects China's interior to the sea.

Farmers use the fertile land on the Chang Jiang's floodplain to grow crops. Miles and miles of rice fields, or **paddies**, stretch out from the banks of the river. Cotton, wheat, and other crops also grow along the river.

 How do people use the land along the Chang Jiang?

Rice grows best in land covered with shallow water, so water from the Chang Jiang is used to flood nearby rice paddies. Rice is the most important food crop grown in China.

THE AMAZON RIVER

The Amazon River in South America is huge. At some places the river is so wide that a person on one bank cannot see the other side. The Nile River is longer, but the Amazon carries 17 times more water. In fact, the Amazon carries more water than any other river in the world. It carries more than the Nile, the Rhine, and the Mississippi rivers put together.

The Amazon begins in the country of Peru. It then flows east across Brazil, South America's largest country. Hundreds of tributaries feed the river before it empties into the Atlantic Ocean. Ships that sail the oceans can go up the Amazon from the Atlantic for about 2,300 miles (3,701 km). That is nearly as far as from New York City to Los Angeles, California.

Much of the land in the Amazon River basin is low and wet. Many areas receive more than 100 inches (254 cm) of rain a

Where?

The Amazon Rain Forest

The Amazon River flows through the largest rain forest in the world. The Amazon rain forest covers about one-third of South America. Most of it lies in the country of Brazil. The Amazon rain forest has more kinds of trees than any other place on Earth. It also has many kinds of animals.

Plant life in the Amazon rain forest is so thick that the only way to travel in many places is by river.

year. Because most of the land lies near the equator, it also is hot all year.

The hot, humid climate along the Amazon River has produced the world's largest rain forest. A **rain forest** is a warm, wet area where tall trees, vines, and other plants grow close together. Some trees in the rain forest grow as tall as 200 feet (61 m)—about the height of a 15-story building. One tour guide explains, "You can walk . . . for six months and still be in the rain forest."

Few people live along the Amazon River. For many people, the climate is just too hot and humid. Still, there are some

small cities and ports along the river. From these places raw materials, such as rubber, wood, and gold, can be transported downstream.

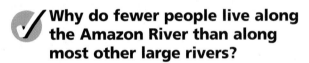 **Why do fewer people live along the Amazon River than along most other large rivers?**

LESSON 3 REVIEW

Check Understanding

1. **Recall the Facts**   What is the world's longest river?
2. **Focus on the Main Idea**   How do people in different countries use rivers?

Think Critically

3. **Think More About It**   Why is irrigation important in countries like Egypt?

Show What You Know

Writing Activity   Suppose you are visiting a place along one of the rivers described in this lesson. Make a postcard that shows a scene along the river. Then, on the back, describe what you have seen on your visit.

How To

Use a Table to Group Information

Why Is This Skill Important?

How many different ways can you think of to describe yourself? Your descriptions might include your height, your weight, or your age. You could also describe yourself by making comparisons with some other people you know. You could see how many are taller or shorter than you are.

When you make comparisons, a table is a good way to show the information. A table lets you compare numbers, facts, and other information quickly. Before you can show information in any table, however, you must decide how you want to **classify** it, or group it. You must present the information according to some pattern.

Understand the Process

The two tables on this page give information about some of the world's major rivers. Both tables give the same information, but they classify it in different ways.

1. Study Table A. Which river listed in the table is the longest? How long is it? Which river is the shortest? As you can see, Table A lists the rivers in order, from longest to shortest.

2. Now study Table B. Table B gives the same information as Table A, but the information has been classified differently. How are the rivers listed in Table B?

3. Which table makes it easier to find information about a certain river? Which table makes it easier to compare rivers by length? Explain your answers.

TABLE A: THE WORLD'S MAJOR RIVERS

RIVER	LENGTH		CONTINENT
	in miles	in kilometers	
Nile	4,187	6,738	Africa
Amazon	4,000	6,437	South America
Chang Jiang	3,434	5,526	Asia
Mississippi	2,348	3,779	North America
Volga	2,293	3,690	Europe
Darling	1,702	2,739	Australia
Ganges	1,557	2,506	Asia
Rhine	820	1,320	Europe

TABLE B: THE WORLD'S MAJOR RIVERS

RIVER	LENGTH		CONTINENT
	in miles	in kilometers	
Amazon	4,000	6,437	South America
Chang Jiang	3,434	5,526	Asia
Darling	1,702	2,739	Australia
Ganges	1,557	2,506	Asia
Mississippi	2,348	3,779	North America
Nile	4,187	6,738	Africa
Rhine	820	1,320	Europe
Volga	2,293	3,690	Europe

Think and Apply

Make a table in which the same information about rivers is grouped by continents. List the continents in alphabetical order. Then explain how this table would be useful in comparing information. Share your table with members of your family.

AMAZON BOY

written and illustrated by Ted Lewin

People depend on the Amazon River and its rain forest for food and for such raw materials as wood, rubber, and minerals. Rain-forest plants and trees give off huge amounts of oxygen into the air that people breathe. Many changes, however, have come to the region. Lakes have been made. Highways have been built. Mineral resources are being mined. Large parts of the rain forest have now been cleared for ranching and farming. Much of that land has been cleared by burning the trees.

The soil in the rain forest is poor. The heavy rains carry away the materials that would make the soil rich. People can farm the land for only a few years before it is no longer good for raising crops. Then they clear more land. Many people fear that clearing too much land will destroy the rain forest. As you read this story about Paulo, a boy who lives close to the Amazon River, think about how people depend on the rain forest and how they are changing it.

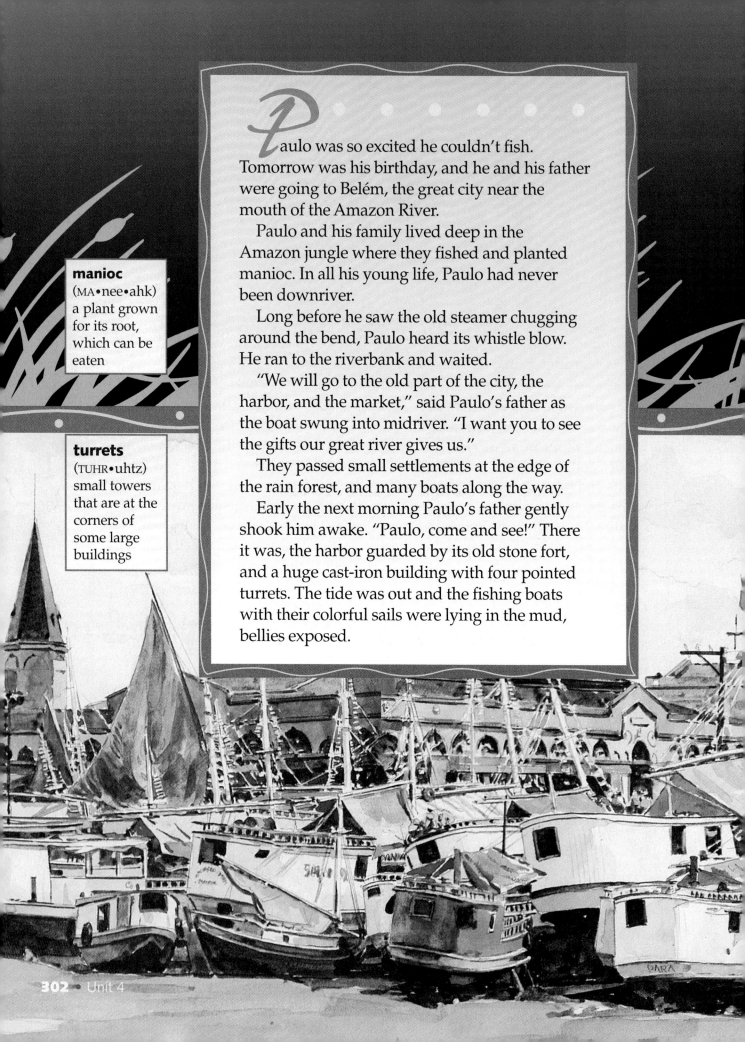

manioc
(MA•nee•ahk)
a plant grown
for its root,
which can be
eaten

turrets
(TUHR•uhtz)
small towers
that are at the
corners of
some large
buildings

aulo was so excited he couldn't fish. Tomorrow was his birthday, and he and his father were going to Belém, the great city near the mouth of the Amazon River.

Paulo and his family lived deep in the Amazon jungle where they fished and planted manioc. In all his young life, Paulo had never been downriver.

Long before he saw the old steamer chugging around the bend, Paulo heard its whistle blow. He ran to the riverbank and waited.

"We will go to the old part of the city, the harbor, and the market," said Paulo's father as the boat swung into midriver. "I want you to see the gifts our great river gives us."

They passed small settlements at the edge of the rain forest, and many boats along the way.

Early the next morning Paulo's father gently shook him awake. "Paulo, come and see!" There it was, the harbor guarded by its old stone fort, and a huge cast-iron building with four pointed turrets. The tide was out and the fishing boats with their colorful sails were lying in the mud, bellies exposed.

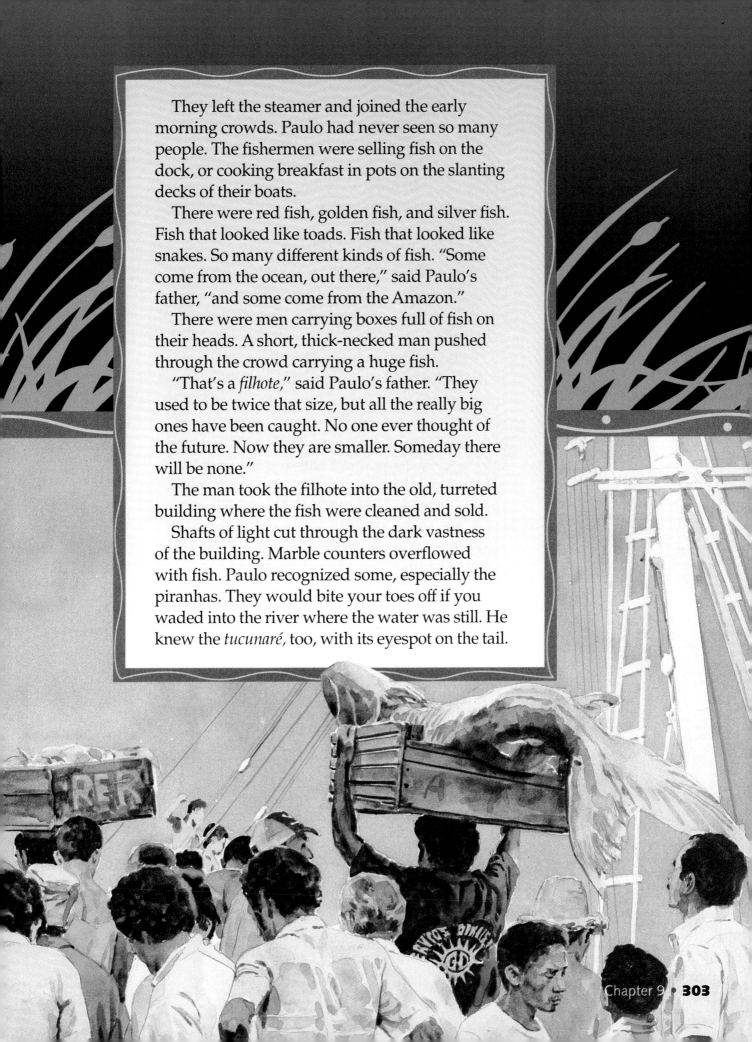

They left the steamer and joined the early morning crowds. Paulo had never seen so many people. The fishermen were selling fish on the dock, or cooking breakfast in pots on the slanting decks of their boats.

There were red fish, golden fish, and silver fish. Fish that looked like toads. Fish that looked like snakes. So many different kinds of fish. "Some come from the ocean, out there," said Paulo's father, "and some come from the Amazon."

There were men carrying boxes full of fish on their heads. A short, thick-necked man pushed through the crowd carrying a huge fish.

"That's a *filhote*," said Paulo's father. "They used to be twice that size, but all the really big ones have been caught. No one ever thought of the future. Now they are smaller. Someday there will be none."

The man took the filhote into the old, turreted building where the fish were cleaned and sold.

Shafts of light cut through the dark vastness of the building. Marble counters overflowed with fish. Paulo recognized some, especially the piranhas. They would bite your toes off if you waded into the river where the water was still. He knew the *tucunaré,* too, with its eyespot on the tail.

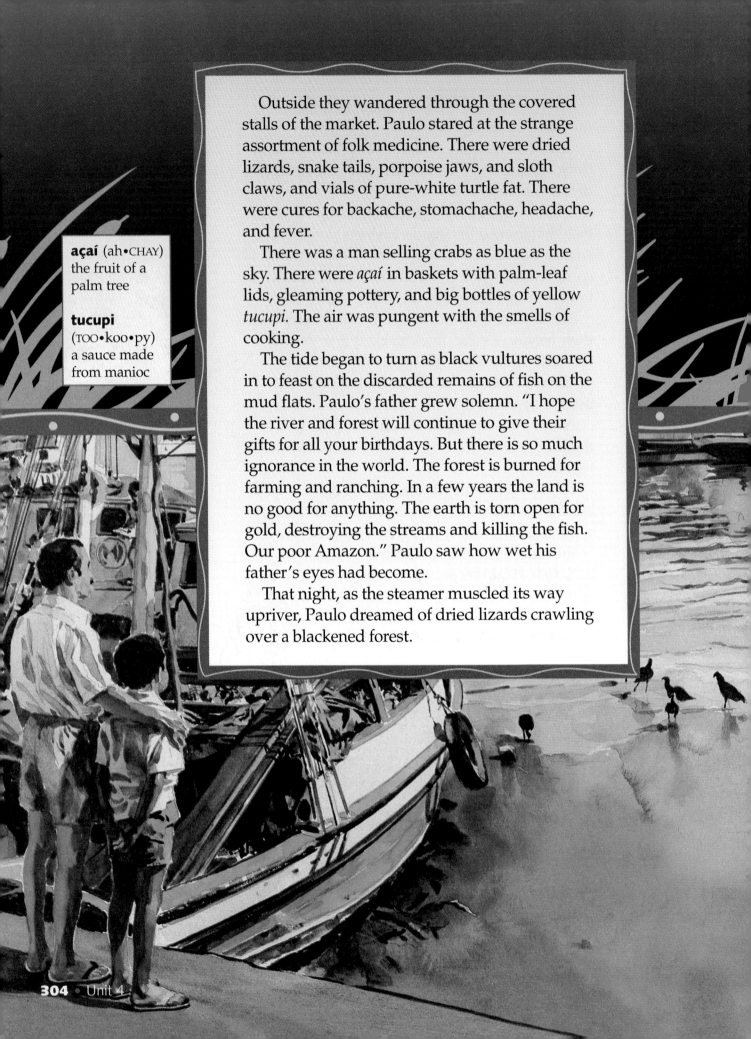

açaí (ah•CHAY)
the fruit of a
palm tree

tucupi
(TOO•koo•py)
a sauce made
from manioc

Outside they wandered through the covered
stalls of the market. Paulo stared at the strange
assortment of folk medicine. There were dried
lizards, snake tails, porpoise jaws, and sloth
claws, and vials of pure-white turtle fat. There
were cures for backache, stomachache, headache,
and fever.

There was a man selling crabs as blue as the
sky. There were *açaí* in baskets with palm-leaf
lids, gleaming pottery, and big bottles of yellow
tucupi. The air was pungent with the smells of
cooking.

The tide began to turn as black vultures soared
in to feast on the discarded remains of fish on the
mud flats. Paulo's father grew solemn. "I hope
the river and forest will continue to give their
gifts for all your birthdays. But there is so much
ignorance in the world. The forest is burned for
farming and ranching. In a few years the land is
no good for anything. The earth is torn open for
gold, destroying the streams and killing the fish.
Our poor Amazon." Paulo saw how wet his
father's eyes had become.

That night, as the steamer muscled its way
upriver, Paulo dreamed of dried lizards crawling
over a blackened forest.

Early the next morning, Paulo went fishing. Before long he realized his canoe was being pulled upstream. His fishing line was as taut as a bowstring.

Hand over hand, he pulled in the line until he saw in the water a filhote bigger than his canoe. "We will be rich!" cried Paulo. "My father and I will take you to Belém and sell you at the market. It will take three big men to carry you on their heads!"

He looked down at the great, whiskered face in the water, and suddenly remembered his father's solemn words. He reached down and gently removed the hook. The fish slid back into the gloom.

"Good-bye and good luck, great fish," said Paulo.

Literature Review

1. How do people depend on the rain forest, and how are they changing it?
2. Do you think Paulo made the right decision when he let the fish go? Why or why not?
3. Write a story about how people where you live are changing the environment.

CONNECT MAIN IDEAS

Use this organizer to show that you understand how the chapter's main ideas are connected. First copy the organizer onto a separate sheet of paper. Then complete it by writing details about the main ideas and about each river.

Great Waterways Shape Nations

Along the Great Lakes
Many large cities and industries have grown up along the Great Lakes.

_____

_____

_____

River Transportation
The Mississippi River system has been used for transportation and trade routes.

_____

_____

_____

The Nile River

_____

_____

Rivers Around the World
People in different places use rivers in different ways.

The Amazon River

_____

_____

The Rhine River

_____

_____

The Chang Jiang

_____

_____

The Ganges River

_____

_____

WRITE MORE ABOUT IT

1. **Write a Diary Entry**   Imagine that you are a pioneer traveling down the Ohio River on a flatboat. Write a diary entry that tells about one day of your trip. Tell what it is like to travel on a flatboat.

2. **Write a Newspaper Article**   Suppose that you are a newspaper reporter visiting Henry Ford's new automobile factory. Write a short article that describes how workers there put the cars together.

USE VOCABULARY

Write a term from this list to complete each of the sentences that follow.

assembly line   irrigation
barge   mass production
capital resources   migration

1. _____ are the money, buildings, machines, and tools needed to run a business.

2. In _____, many goods that are alike can be made quickly and cheaply.

3. An _____ is a line of workers along which a product moves as it is put together one step at a time.

4. A _____ is the movement of many people who leave one country or region to settle in another.

5. A _____ is a large, flat-bottomed boat used on rivers or other inland waterways.

6. Many Egyptian farmers must water their fields by _____, or by using canals, ditches, or pipes to move water to dry areas.

CHECK UNDERSTANDING

1. How were the Great Lakes formed?

2. How can ships sailing from ports along the Great Lakes reach the Atlantic Ocean?

3. What are the factors of production?

4. How did steamboats affect the growth of cities and industries along rivers?

5. What is the world's longest river?

6. How is the Rhine River like many navigable rivers in the United States?

7. Along which river is the world's largest rain forest found?

THINK CRITICALLY

1. **Link to You**   Many cities in the Middle West grew because they were near major waterways. What things have helped your community grow?

2. **Think More About It**   How might the United States be different today if Henry Ford had not started to use assembly lines for building cars?

3. **Personally Speaking**   Imagine that you are Paulo, the boy who lives close to the Amazon River. Would you let the great fish go free? Explain your answer.

APPLY SKILLS

How to Use a Table to Group Information   Look in almanacs and encyclopedias to find information about the Great Lakes. Find the total area of each lake, its length and width, and its depth. Then use this information to make a table. Compare your table with those of classmates. Is the information classified in the same way, or is it classified differently?

READ MORE ABOUT IT

The Barge Book by Jerry Bushey. Carolrhoda. A crew pilots a barge down the Mississippi River from Minneapolis to New Orleans.

River by Judith Heide Gilliland. Clarion. This book describes the Amazon, the mightiest river in the world.

Tugboats in Action by Timothy R. Burke. Albert Whitman. This book, written by a tugboat engineer and captain, describes the important and difficult work of a Great Lakes tugboat.

RELEVANT

The Nation's Breadbasket to the Rescue

Farmers in the United States produce more food than any other farmers in the world. Each one can raise enough to feed more than 80 people! In the Middle West, farmers grow huge amounts of corn, wheat, and other crops. On the Great Plains alone, so much wheat is grown that this area is sometimes called the Nation's Breadbasket.

The Great Plains could also be called the World's Breadbasket. Time and time again the United States has been asked to help suffering people around the world. The help our country sends almost always includes food. The United States produces enough food to share with people of other countries when natural disasters, such as floods or droughts, happen.

Bread is an important food for these Kurdish children, who live in a refugee camp near the Turkey-Iraq border.

THINK AND APPLY

From news reports, find out where the United States is sending food and why. Then think about what you can do to help people in your city or state who do not get enough to eat. Make a list of ideas, and share it with your classmates.

BUILDING CITIZENSHIP

People in the country of Zaire (above) carry sacks of corn sent to them by the United States after a drought struck their homeland. Workers in this shelter (left) help feed homeless people in the United States.

STORY CLOTH

Study the pictures shown in this story cloth to help you review what you read about in Unit 4.

Summarize the Main Ideas

1. The varying amounts of precipitation the region receives affects the kinds of crops grown on the Interior Plains. Corn is the leading crop on the Central Plains. Wheat is the leading crop on the Great Plains, which are drier.

2. To live on and farm the dry lands of the Great Plains, people changed their ways of life. Ways of farming are still changing today.

3. In the past and in the present, products from the Middle West region have added to the interdependence among people in the United States.

4. Many large cities and industries have grown up along the Great Lakes. That area is a center of industry today.

5. The Mississippi River system is used for transportation and trade routes. Large cities grew up along these rivers.

Write Descriptions Choose three scenes in the story cloth, and write a brief caption, or descriptive sentence, about each one. Each caption should tell *who, what, where,* and *when* about the scene.

Tell a Day-in-the-Life Story Pick one scene shown in the story cloth. Then imagine a person who might be part of that scene. Make up a story you might tell about a day in the life of that person.

UNIT 4
REVIEW

Remember

- Share your ideas.
- Cooperate with others to plan your work.
- Take responsibility for your work.
- Show your group's work to the class.
- Discuss what you learned by working together.

Activity 1
Make a Diorama

Work in a group to make a diorama about pioneer life on the Great Plains. Show a soddy and the kinds of work that pioneers had to do, such as plowing the thick prairie grasses. Also show one of the dangers that pioneers faced, such as blizzards, tornadoes, or hailstorms. Display your finished diorama in the classroom, and point to different parts of it as you talk to your classmates about pioneer life on the Great Plains.

Activity 2
Draw a Map

Work in a group to draw an outline map of the Middle West on a large sheet of paper. Maps in your textbook and in encyclopedias and atlases can help you. Use two different colors to show the Great Lakes states and the Plains states. Add dots and labels to your map to show where the region's largest cities are located. Also label large bodies of water and large landforms, such as the Central Plains and the Great Plains. Draw symbols to show the region's major resources or products. Then point out places on your map as your group takes the rest of the class on a "tour" of the Middle West.

Activity 3
Draw a Mural

Work in a group to draw a large mural that shows scenes from the Middle West. The scenes might be of well-known places, or they might show different kinds of activities in that region. Use pictures from your textbook and from library books for ideas. Then fasten a large sheet of paper to a wall in your classroom. Use pencils to sketch the scenes, and use paint, crayons, or markers to color them. Each group member should write facts about a place or an activity shown in the scene. Present the mural and the facts to your class.

USE VOCABULARY

Use each term in a sentence that helps explain its meaning.

1. self-sufficient
2. fertilizer
3. urbanization
4. free enterprise
5. mass production
6. shaman
7. irrigation
8. rain forest

CHECK UNDERSTANDING

1. How do different amounts of precipitation on the Central Plains and the Great Plains affect farming?

2. How are most farms today different from most farms in the past?

3. How is a demand different from a supply?

4. How are most of the world's plains regions used?

5. What caused the steel industry to spread to cities along the Great Lakes?

6. What is China's longest river?

7. Why do few people live along the Amazon River?

THINK CRITICALLY

1. **Think More About It** In the early 1800s most people in the Middle West lived on farms or in rural areas. Today most people in the Middle West live in urban areas. How has this change affected the region?

2. **Personally Speaking** If you could choose to visit the Nile River, the Rhine River, the Ganges River, the Chang Jiang, or the Amazon River, which would you choose? Why?

APPLY GEOGRAPHY SKILLS

How to Follow Routes on a Road Map The road map below shows some highways in central Indiana. Use the map to answer these questions.

1. Which interstate highway would you use to travel from Indianapolis to Columbus?

2. Which United States highway leads from Indianapolis to Rushville?

3. Suppose that you wanted to travel from Muncie to Greenfield. Describe the route you would follow.

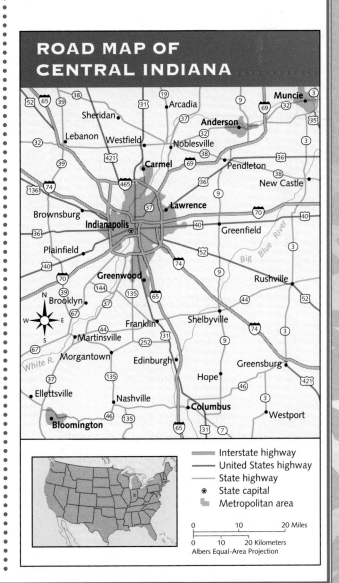

ROAD MAP OF CENTRAL INDIANA

- Interstate highway
- United States highway
- State highway
- ✪ State capital
- Metropolitan area

0   10   20 Miles
0   10   20 Kilometers
Albers Equal-Area Projection

UNIT 5

THE SOUTHWEST

Arizona　　　　　　　　　　　**New Mexico**

The Sonoran Desert, in Arizona

Canyon de Chelly, in Arizona

Carlsbad Caverns National Park, in New Mexico

UNIT 4
The Middle West

UNIT 5
The Southwest

UNIT 6
The West

The Southwest region is a land of wide open spaces. It is a land of cattle ranches and dusty trails. However, the Southwest also has large cities, busy highways, and rapidly growing industries.

Much of the Southwest is dry land or desert. Yet the Southwest has many other kinds of land. Its geography is not the same from place to place. Under the region's sunny skies are thick pine forests and mountains capped with snow. There are also humid plains, fertile river valleys, and rocky canyons.

← **Grand Canyon National Park, in Arizona**

Oklahoma

Texas

The Oklahoma State Capitol, in Oklahoma City, Oklahoma

The Alamo, in San Antonio, Texas

Dallas, Texas

ALMANAC

The Southwest

Did You Know?

The Southwest region is made up of four large states—Arizona, New Mexico, Oklahoma, and Texas. It stretches west from the Gulf Coast of Texas to the Colorado River in Arizona. Mexico borders the region on the south.

STATE	CAPITAL	NICKNAME	POPULATION*	TEN LARGEST CITIES	LEADING PRODUCTS AND RESOURCES

THE SOUTHWEST STATES

Arizona (AZ)	Phoenix	Grand Canyon State	4,223,000	
New Mexico (NM)	Santa Fe	Land of Enchantment	1,737,000	
Oklahoma (OK)	Oklahoma City	Sooner State	3,313,000	
Texas (TX)	Austin	Lone Star State	19,180,000	

1. Houston, Texas
2. Dallas, Texas
3. Phoenix, Arizona
4. San Antonio, Texas
5. El Paso, Texas
6. Austin, Texas
7. Fort Worth, Texas
8. Oklahoma City, Oklahoma
9. Tucson, Arizona
10. Albuquerque, New Mexico

Farming:
Beef cattle, citrus fruits, cotton, dairy cows, grain sorghum, hay, melons, rice, sheep, vegetables, wheat

Fishing:
Crabs, fish, oysters, shrimp

Manufacturing:
Chemicals, dairy products, electrical equipment, machinery, metal products, petroleum products, processed foods

Mining:
Coal, copper, natural gas, oil, potash, silver, uranium

*The most recent figures available.

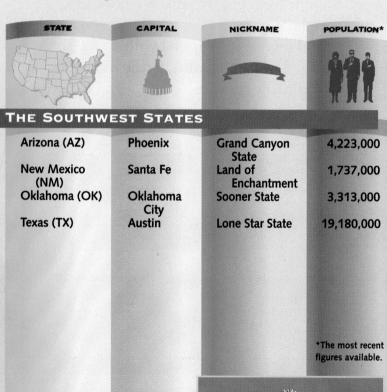

One desert plant, an agave (uh•GAH•vee), lives from 10 to 15 years. Then it blooms once and dies. When it starts to bloom, the plant's stalk can grow as much as 16 inches (41 cm) in 24 hours.

There are more telescopes near Tucson, Arizona, than anywhere else in the world. The clear desert air there makes it easier to study the stars.

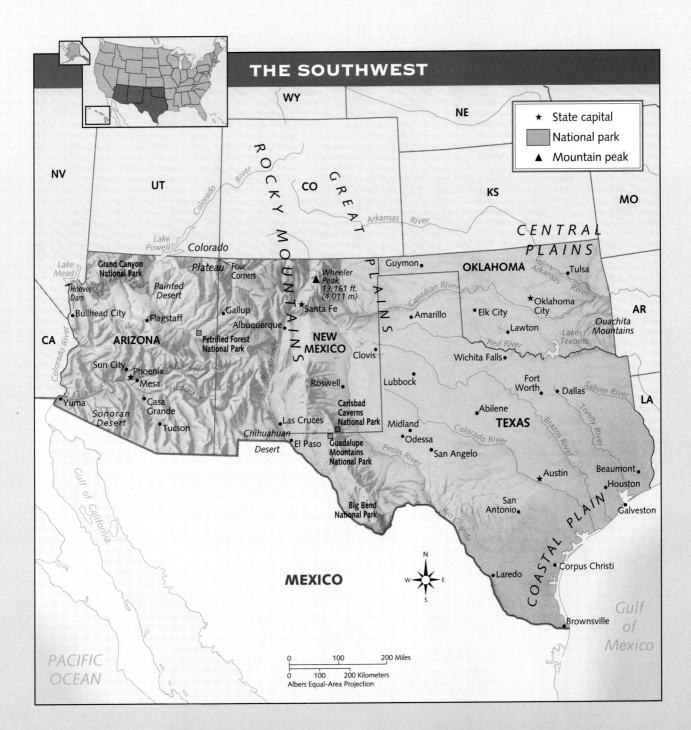

THE SOUTHWEST

Legend:
- ★ State capital
- ☐ National park
- ▲ Mountain peak

WY

NE

NV

UT

CO

GREAT

KS

MO

ROCKY MOUNTAINS

Colorado River

Arkansas River

CENTRAL PLAINS

Lake Powell

Colorado

Lake Mead

Grand Canyon National Park

Plateau

Four Corners

Wheeler Peak 13,161 ft. (4,011 m)

Guymon

OKLAHOMA

Tulsa

Arkansas River

Hoover Dam

Painted Desert

★ Santa Fe

Canadian River

Oklahoma City

AR

Bullhead City

Flagstaff

Gallup

Albuquerque

NEW MEXICO

Amarillo

Elk City

Lawton

Ouachita Mountains

CA

ARIZONA

Petrified Forest National Park

Clovis

Wichita Falls

Lake Texoma

Red River

Colorado River

Sun City

Phoenix

Mesa

Gila River

Roswell

Lubbock

Fort Worth

Dallas

Sabine River

LA

Yuma

Casa Grande

Las Cruces

Carlsbad Caverns National Park

Midland

Abilene

TEXAS

Tucson

Sonoran Desert

Chihuahuan Desert

El Paso

Guadalupe Mountains National Park

Odessa

San Angelo

Colorado River

Brazos River

Trinity River

Pecos River

Beaumont

Houston

Gulf of California

Big Bend National Park

Austin

San Antonio

Galveston

MEXICO

N W E S

Laredo

Rio Grande

COASTAL PLAIN

Corpus Christi

Gulf of Mexico

PACIFIC OCEAN

Brownsville

0   100   200 Miles
0   100   200 Kilometers
Albers Equal-Area Projection

FIRE DANGER

EXTREME

TODAY!

PREVENT FOREST FIRES
DEPT. OF ENVIRONMENTAL RESOURCES

There was a real Smokey Bear. He was a brown bear cub rescued from a forest fire in New Mexico's Lincoln National Forest. Today a state park in New Mexico is named for him.

The Four Corners is the only place in the United States where four states meet at a single point. The states are Arizona, Colorado, New Mexico, and Utah.

Estevan

from
Black Heroes of the Wild West
written by Ruth Pelz
illustrated by Wayne Still

The first Europeans to explore the Southwest came from Spain. They were looking for gold. An old Spanish legend told about seven lost cities—cities of gold! For many years people in Mexico had heard stories about seven great cities that lay to the north. Could those be the seven lost cities? Spanish leaders decided to find out.

The year was 1539. A large group of people was walking across the Arizona desert. In the lead was a tall, powerful black man named Estevan. He wore turquoise and gold jewelry and brightly colored feathers. Two sleek greyhounds trotted beside him, and as many as 300 Indians followed behind.

turquoise
(TER·koyz)
a mineral that is blue, bluish green, or greenish gray

They all were headed north. They were searching for seven cities, seven wonderful cities that legends had told them about.

Estevan did not live to finish his journey. But this man, who was searching for a legend, became a legend himself. It is not hard to understand why. His life was as full of adventures as any hero you may read about.

These adventures began in 1527. In that year, Estevan, who was born in Africa, was brought to America as a slave. He and his Spanish master were bound for Florida. They were to help explore that area for the king of Spain.

For weeks they marched with 300 other men through thick jungles and terrible swamps. The weather was hot and steamy. The men had little food. Mosquitoes, poisonous snakes, and deadly diseases were everywhere. In some places Indians attacked the travelers.

Many men died. The others decided to build wooden rafts and float out to sea. They would try to sail to Spanish settlements in Mexico.

They didn't make it. When they were near the present border of Texas and Louisiana, a terrible storm came up. All the rafts were wrecked or lost. Estevan and the other survivors were captured. They were made to work for the Indian tribes nearby.

They remained with their captors for more than five years. Life was so hard that soon only four were left alive, Estevan, his master, and two other Spaniards. They lived with different tribes, but they all thought about how they might join together and escape.

captors
people who hold others against their will

At last they had their chance. Each autumn the tribes gathered to harvest a kind of wild fruit called prickly pears. On the night of the full moon, the four men crept away to a planned meeting place. They were free!

Now the most amazing adventure of all began. Here they were, all alone on the Texas plain. They had no maps, of course, no food, no tools, and no shelter. They hoped to reach the closest Spanish settlement, but they did not even know where it was.

All they had was their experience. In years of living with the Indians, they had learned much about their way of life. They had learned how to survive. Estevan, who had a special talent for this, had learned several Indian languages. All of this would be very important to the travelers.

Hurrying to go as far as they could before winter began, the men headed west. They soon arrived at a village of friendly Indians. Some members of the village approached them and said, "We have heard that you are medicine men. Will you please try to cure our sick?"

The four travelers knew only a little about healing. Still, they had seen Indian medicine men at work before. They decided they must try. Amazingly, they were able to help many people get well. News of their successes traveled from tribe to tribe. As the men continued their journey, they received a warm welcome from other Indian villages along the way.

In each place, Estevan spoke with the people. He asked them about the lands and villages nearby. He asked about the best trails to follow. He helped the Spanish learn about lands and people that no one other than the native people had ever seen before.

On and on they continued, over deserts and mountains, through green valleys and back into deserts. They walked for more than a year and more than 1,000 miles! Finally, one day in March, 1536, they found what they had been seeking. They met a group of Spanish soldiers. Their journey had ended!

Estevan's full name was Estevanico (ehs•tay•vahn•EE•koh). He was also called Estéban. His early travels across the Southwest helped prepare him to guide the people who were searching for the seven lost cities. Although the seven cities were never found, other explorers continued to search for them.

A CHANGING LANDSCAPE

> 66 These hills have caught the lightning in its flight,
> Caught colors from the skies of day and night
> And shine with shattered stars and suns; they hold
> Dyed yellow, red and purple, blue and gold. 99
>
> from the poem "The Painted Hills of Arizona"
> by Edwin Curran

This boy lives in the Southwest.

THE *L*AND AND ITS *R*ESOURCES

*L*nk to Our World

How can the physical features of a region change from place to place?

Focus on the Main Idea
Read this lesson to compare and contrast the different landforms, climates, and resources in the Southwest.

Preview Vocabulary
mesa
rain shadow

The Spanish explorer Francisco Vásquez de Coronado hoped to find the seven cities of gold.

In 1540 the Spanish explorer Francisco Vásquez de Coronado (kawr•oh•NAH•doh) left Mexico and began a long search for the seven cities of gold. With him were more than 300 Spaniards, several Africans, and more than 1,000 American Indians. Coronado spent more than two years exploring the Southwest. There were no seven cities of gold, but Coronado learned much about this amazing region.

A REGION OF VARIETY

Different places in the Southwest have very different climates and landforms. In the western part of the region, the land is mostly dry. When Coronado and his followers reached this area of present-day Arizona, they could find little food or water. With their supplies running low, the members of the group turned northeast. They went into present-day New Mexico. There they could see the tall, snow-capped Rocky Mountains in the distance. The group spent the winter camped beside the Rio Grande.

In the spring Coronado led the group through what is today Texas and Oklahoma. Again the land changed. "There is nowhere a stone, a hill, a tree, or a bush," wrote one person. "Many fellows were lost at this time who went out hunting . . . not knowing how to get back to where they started from." Everywhere they looked, the land was the same. It was a flat, grass-covered plain with

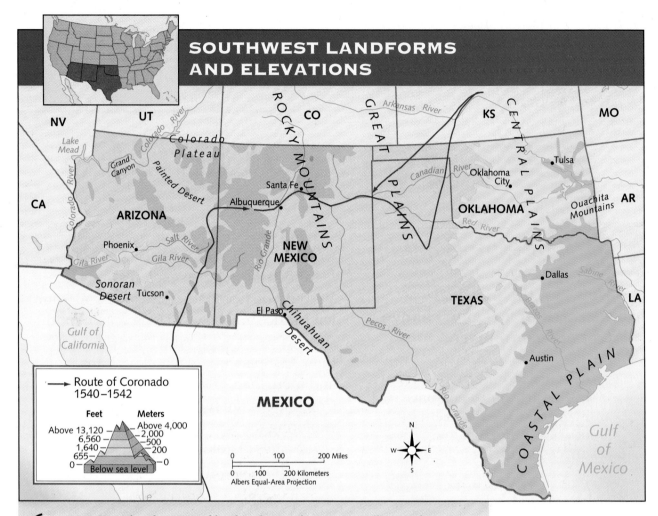

SOUTHWEST LANDFORMS AND ELEVATIONS

PLACE The elevation of land in the Southwest generally rises from east to west, but there are areas with high elevations throughout the region.
■ What mountains are in southeastern Oklahoma?

few trees. Disappointed and without any gold, Coronado returned to Mexico.

Had Coronado traveled farther to the east, he would have seen the land change again. In eastern Oklahoma and Texas, the land is mostly hilly, and the climate is wet enough for trees to grow. Southeastern Oklahoma even has low mountains.

The Southwest has many landforms. The elevation of the land, however, generally rises from east to west. Going from east to west, the climate also gets drier.

✓ **How do land elevation and climate in the Southwest change from east to west?**

A REGION OF PLAINS

The lowest lands in the Southwest are along the Texas Gulf coast. They are part of the Coastal Plain. The climate is usually warm and moist, and the soil is fertile. Low barrier islands lie offshore.

Inland from the coast are pine and hardwood forests. Workers cut down the trees to make lumber and paper products. In nearby fields farmers grow wheat, rice, and other grain crops. They also grow cotton. More cotton is raised in Texas than in any other state.

In the southern part of the Coastal Plain, near where the Rio Grande flows into the Gulf of Mexico, the weather is warm most of the winter. All year, farmers there can grow many kinds of vegetables and fruits, including citrus fruits.

Other large plains are northwest of the Coastal Plain. Part of the Central Plains stretch south through central Oklahoma and into Texas. This part of the Southwest has many farms and ranches.

Low hills separate the Coastal Plain from the Southwest's third major plains region—the Great Plains. The Great Plains cover parts of Oklahoma, Texas, and New Mexico. As the Great Plains stretch west to the Rocky Mountains, the land gets higher. In some places it is more than 5,000 feet (1,524 m) above sea level. Because the land is so high, this part of the Great Plains is sometimes called the High Plains.

Cattle and sheep graze on the short grasses that grow on the High Plains. This area has some of the world's best land for raising cattle. It helps make Texas

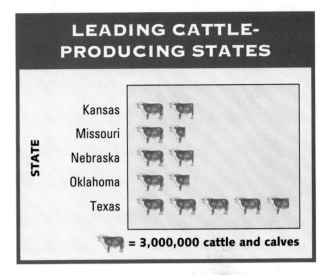

LEADING CATTLE-PRODUCING STATES

STATE	
Kansas	🐄🐄
Missouri	🐄🐄
Nebraska	🐄🐄
Oklahoma	🐄🐄
Texas	🐄🐄🐄🐄🐄

🐄 = 3,000,000 cattle and calves

LEARNING FROM GRAPHS Each year ranchers in Texas raise more than 14 million cattle and calves.
■ Which two states shown on the graph raise about the same number of cattle and calves?

the country's leading cattle-producing state. Although beef cattle are their largest source of income, farmers on the High Plains also grow such crops as wheat, grain sorghum, and cotton.

✓ **Which three major plains regions are found in the Southwest?**

Cowhands often ride horses as they move herds of cattle (right). Spurs attached to the cowhands' boots (below) allow the cowhands to guide and control their horses while keeping their hands free to work.

Mesas, like the Great Mesa (above) in Arizona's Monument Valley, are common landforms in some parts of the Southwest. Slowly, over millions of years, running water eroded most of the land, leaving these huge landforms behind.

MOUNTAINS AND PLATEAUS

The highest parts of the Southwest are the Rocky Mountains and the Colorado Plateau. The Rocky Mountains stretch into northern New Mexico. The Colorado Plateau begins at the western edge of the Rocky Mountains. It covers much of northern New Mexico and Arizona. The land on this huge, high plateau is mostly flat, but there are steep bluffs and some mountains.

About 100 years ago a pioneer and miner named John Hance started the first services for tourists in the area. When a visitor asked him why his index finger was missing, Hance said, "I plumb wore it off pointing at the scenery!"

Hance liked to tell this tall tale. Still, like many other tall tales, his was about something real. The Colorado Plateau is famous for its landforms. There are wide valleys, sharp cliffs, and broad mesas (MAY•sahz). A **mesa** is a hill or small plateau with a flat top and steep sides. *Mesa* is the Spanish word for *table*.

The landforms on the Colorado Plateau have been shaped over millions of years. They were formed mainly by water erosion. The Colorado River and its tributaries have cut many beautiful canyons into the land. The largest of these is the Grand Canyon. In other places running water has formed rocks into strange shapes. In Monument Valley, along the Arizona–Utah border, large pointed rocks rise from the desert floor.

 What shaped the landforms on the Colorado Plateau?

DESERTS

Much of the Colorado Plateau receives only 10 to 20 inches (25 to 51 cm) of rain each year. Farther south and west, however, the land is even drier. Most places there get less than 10 inches (25 cm) of rain a year. This land is desert.

Most desert areas in the Southwest formed because of the mountains far to the west. Those mountains keep moist air from reaching the deserts. When clouds of moist air from the Pacific Ocean blow against the mountains, the wind pushes the clouds up the side of the mountains. As the clouds rise, the air becomes cooler. Cool air cannot hold as much moisture as warm air. So the clouds drop most of their rain or snow on that side of the mountains. By the time the air reaches the other side of the mountains, little moisture remains. Places there receive little precipitation. They lie in the **rain shadow**, or the drier side of the mountains.

Two large deserts in the Southwest are the Sonoran (soh•NOHR•ahn) Desert and the Chihuahuan (chee•WAH•wahn) Desert. The Sonoran Desert covers parts of both Arizona and California. The Chihuahuan Desert lies in New Mexico and western Texas. Both deserts stretch south into Mexico.

Another desert in the Southwest is the Painted Desert in northern Arizona. One early visitor wrote that this desert was "paved with rainbows . . . fallen to earth and turned to stone." The light on the desert and the minerals in the soil combine to "paint" the land in bands of bright colors. As sunlight hits the rocks, they shine blue, red, yellow, green, and purple.

Many interesting plants and animals live in the deserts of the Southwest. Each plant or animal has developed ways to live in the dry, hot environment. One well-known desert plant is the cactus.

THE RAIN SHADOW

Winds

1.

2.

3.

4.

5.

Dry lands or deserts

Ocean

1. Air picks up moisture from the ocean.

2. Moist air forms clouds, which blow across the coast.

3. Winds push clouds up the mountains.

4. Cooler temperatures cause rain or snow.

5. Remaining clouds have little moisture.

LEARNING FROM DIAGRAMS Places in a rain shadow receive little precipitation.
■ What happens after winds push clouds up the mountains?

The cactus plant stores water in its thick stem. When the land is dry, the cactus lives on the stored water. Sharp spines keep most animals from eating the plant.

More than 1,000 kinds of cactuses grow in deserts in the United States. About 50 of them grow in the Sonoran Desert. One of these is the giant saguaro (sah•WAHR•oh) cactus. A saguaro can grow to a height of 60 feet (18 m) and can weigh as much as 10 tons! More than three-fourths of a saguaro's weight comes from the water it stores.

✓ **How can mountains cause deserts to form?**

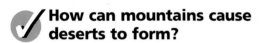

The giant saguaro, the largest kind of cactus in the United States, grows only in the Sonoran Desert. Insects and birds, such as this Gila woodpecker, gather nectar during May and June from saguaro blossoms.

What?

The Petrified Forest

A strange forest is found in Arizona's Painted Desert. The trees in this forest are all dead, and they lie flat on the ground. They are petrified. This means their wood has been replaced by stone! These large trees were buried in mud, sand, or ash millions of years ago. Water carried minerals into the buried trees. The minerals filled the wood cells as the cells decayed, so the trees became stone.

MINERALS AND FUELS

Deserts are full of interesting plants and animals. They are also full of valuable minerals. Mines in both Arizona and New Mexico produce silver and copper. Arizona alone produces more than half the copper mined in the United States. Potash, another mineral mined in the Southwest, is used to make fertilizers.

All the states in the Southwest are rich in the minerals and fuels that supply energy. In fact, many of the resources used to produce energy in the United States come from the Southwest. Uranium is a mineral used as a fuel for nuclear power plants. It is mined in Arizona, New Mexico, and Texas. Coal is also mined in Texas. Texas, Oklahoma, and New Mexico are all leading producers of petroleum and natural gas. Texas produces more natural gas than any other state.

✓ **Where do many of the energy resources used in the United States come from?**

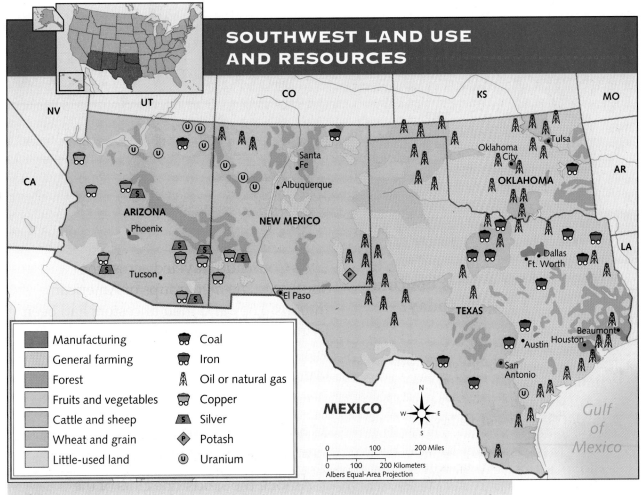

SOUTHWEST LAND USE AND RESOURCES

UT | CO | KS | MO

NV

CA

ARIZONA
Phoenix
Tucson

Santa Fe
Albuquerque

NEW MEXICO

El Paso

MEXICO

OKLAHOMA
Oklahoma City
Tulsa

AR

Dallas
Ft. Worth

LA

TEXAS

Austin Houston
San Antonio
Beaumont

Gulf of Mexico

Legend:

Manufacturing	Coal
General farming	Iron
Forest	Oil or natural gas
Fruits and vegetables	Copper
Cattle and sheep	Silver
Wheat and grain	Potash
Little-used land	Uranium

N
W   E
S

0   100   200 Miles
0 100 200 Kilometers
Albers Equal-Area Projection

HUMAN-ENVIRONMENT INTERACTIONS People throughout the United States depend on the Southwest for minerals and fuels that supply energy.
■ In which states is uranium mined?

LESSON 1 REVIEW

Check Understanding

1. **Recall the Facts**   How is the climate in eastern Texas different from the climate in western Arizona?

2. **Focus on the Main Idea**   How are the landforms, climates, and natural resources in the Southwestern states alike? How are they different?

Think Critically

3. **Link to You**   What are some ways in which you or someone you know uses the natural resources of the Southwest?

4. **Personally Speaking**   Which part of the Southwest would you most like to visit or live in? Give reasons for your answer.

Show What You Know

Write a Descriptive Poem or Song   Choose one of the landforms in the Southwest. Then write a poem or song that describes the land, climate, and resources found there. Share your poem or song with a classmate, or read it aloud to the whole class.

LESSON 2

THE SOUTHWEST LONG AGO

L nk to Our World

How do past events continue to affect a region today?

Focus on the Main Idea
As you read this lesson, look for Indian, Spanish, and Mexican ways from the past that live on in the Southwest today.

Preview Vocabulary
adobe
mission
society
reservation

This Anasazi petroglyph (PEH•truh•glif), or rock carving, shows a bighorn sheep. The Anasazi may have hunted these animals for food and wool.

As Coronado traveled across the Southwest, he met groups of American Indians. They and their ancestors had been living in the Southwest for thousands of years. However, other people would soon bring many changes to the region.

EARLY PEOPLES OF THE SOUTHWEST

Among the sandstone cliffs of the Southwest are the deserted towns of the Anasazi (ah•nuh•SAH•zee)—the Ancient Ones. The Anasazi built their towns near what is today called the Four Corners. That is where Arizona, Colorado, New Mexico, and Utah meet. The Anasazi built their homes on the mesas, on the canyon floors, and in the canyon walls. Their homes were like apartment buildings, with rooms built on top of other rooms.

The Anasazi were farmers. However, a long drought made it impossible for them to grow enough food. So they left their homes to settle in other parts of the Southwest. Many settled in the Rio Grande valley in present-day New Mexico. They were probably the ancestors of the Pueblo (PWEH•bloh) Indians who live there today.

The early Pueblos lived in villages that the Spanish called *pueblos*. In Spanish, *pueblo* means "village." Large pueblos were five or six stories high and had more than 800 rooms.

For nearly 1,000 years Indians of the Tano-Tigua tribe have lived in this pueblo near Taos, New Mexico.

All the buildings in a pueblo were connected, but they had no doors on the ground floor. To get inside, the Pueblos had to climb up ladders. Then whenever their enemies came near, the Pueblos just pulled up the ladders!

Few trees grow in the area's dry climate, so the Pueblos built their villages out of stone or adobe (ah•DOH•bay). **Adobe** is sun-dried clay brick. Thick adobe walls kept pueblo buildings warm in winter and cool in summer.

Near their villages the Pueblos grew cotton, squash, beans, and corn. The corn they grew was different from the corn that farmers grow today. It had very long roots that could reach deep into the soil for water. The Pueblos planted seeds deep in the ground, where the soil was wetter. They also dug ditches from the Rio Grande to irrigate their fields.

✔ **Why did the Pueblos use stone or adobe to build their villages?**

SANTA FE

Many groups of Indians lived in the Southwest. Spain, however, claimed all the land. The Spanish called the entire area New Mexico. By 1610, Spanish settlers were busy building the city of Santa Fe (SAN•tah FAY).

Santa Fe was founded between the Pecos River and the Rio Grande. It was built to be the capital of Spanish New Mexico. Today Santa Fe is the capital of the state of New Mexico. It is the oldest capital city in the United States.

Near Santa Fe were dozens of missions. A **mission** was a settlement started by

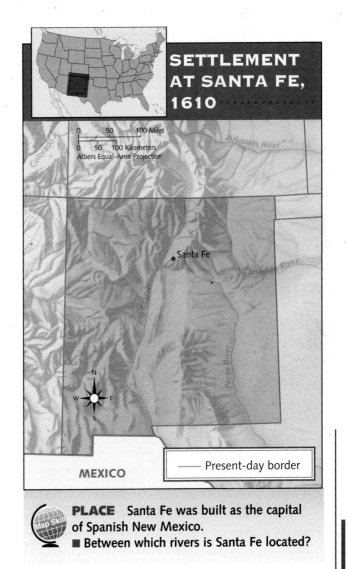

SETTLEMENT AT SANTA FE, 1610

Present-day border

MEXICO

PLACE Santa Fe was built as the capital of Spanish New Mexico.
■ Between which rivers is Santa Fe located?

Catholic priests who had gone to New Mexico to teach the Indians about Christianity. Besides their religion, the priests took Spanish customs and the Spanish language to the Southwest. They also took fruit trees, cattle, sheep, and horses.

Most missions were similar. They had a church, a school, and workshops. Often there was a wall around the mission. Outside were fields where the Indians raised crops and livestock.

Most missions also had a fort. Its soldiers kept the mission safe from attack. They also enforced Spanish ways. The Indians did not always welcome the missions. Often the Indians were made to work at the missions against their will.

The Spanish built missions throughout the Southwest. Over time the missions became the center of Spanish society. A society is a group of people who have many things in common. After missions were started, colonists settled on nearby lands. Farms, ranches, and cities grew up around the missions.

 **Why was Santa Fe built?**

STRUGGLES FOR INDEPENDENCE

Spain could not hold on to its land in North America. In 1821 Mexico fought a war against Spain and won its independence. Mexico took over all the Spanish lands in the Southwest.

Then even more people settled in the Southwest, especially in Texas. Some of those new settlers were immigrants from Europe. Others were from the United States.

At first the Mexican government welcomed settlers from the United States. By 1835, however, nearly 28,000 Americans

This engraving shows the Mexican army attacking the Alamo in 1836. Although greatly outnumbered, the Texans fought bravely.

were living in Texas. There were so many that the Mexican government became worried that it would lose control of Texas. It tried to stop any more Americans from moving there. It made the Americans who were already in Texas obey Mexican laws and pay more taxes.

Many people in Texas did not like the new Mexican laws. They decided to break away from Mexico and start their own country. To stop them, Mexican leaders sent about 5,000 soldiers into Texas. In the city of San Antonio, fewer than 200 Texans went to an old mission called the Alamo and turned it into a fort.

Thousands of soldiers from the Mexican army attacked the Alamo. For nearly two weeks the Texans inside the Alamo fought the Mexican army. When the battle was over, however, all the men in the Alamo were dead.

The news of the bravery at the Alamo spread across Texas. Soon other Texans joined the fight against Mexico. Their leader was Sam Houston (HYOO•stuhn). Under the battle cry Remember the Alamo! the Texans defeated the Mexican army in 1836. Texas became an independent country. Then, in 1845, Texas became a part of the United States.

✓ **Why did people in Texas decide to break away from Mexico?**

THE LAND RUSH

The areas that now make up Arizona, New Mexico, and Texas were settled slowly over many years. One part of Oklahoma, however, was settled in a day!

For many years the federal government allowed only Indians to live on the land that is today Oklahoma. In the late 1800s, however, the government decided that almost 2 million acres of land in Indian Territory, as it was called, would be opened to new settlement. Beginning at noon on April 22, 1889, land was to be given away to anyone willing to live on it for five years. The first person to reach and claim each 160-acre piece of land would receive it.

On the morning of April 22, between 50,000 and 100,000 men and women waited at the starting line. At exactly twelve o'clock the starting signal was given. The rush for land was on!

People raced to get the land they wanted. Some people rode away on horses. Some rode in covered wagons. Some even ran. All that day people rushed to claim good land. In just a few hours, every inch of land was taken.

What most settlers did not know, however, was that some people had not waited for the race to begin. The night before, they had slipped across the starting line and claimed land early. The people who sneaked onto the land ahead of time were called Sooners. This earned Oklahoma the nickname Sooner State.

✓ **Why did so many people settle in Oklahoma at the same time?**

PEOPLE OF THE SOUTHWEST

Today the states of the Southwest have a mix of people and cultures. Mexico, for example, has added much to the region's heritage. More than half the people of some cities in the Southwest trace their roots to Mexico. In all parts of the Southwest are buildings built by settlers from Mexico. Many modern buildings in the Southwest have also been built using early Spanish and Indian building

These pots were made by Keresan Indians of the Acoma Pueblo, near Albuquerque, New Mexico. How can making traditional crafts help to keep a people's way of life alive?

The Inter-Tribal Ceremonial is held each year in Gallup, New Mexico. Native Americans wear traditional dress in the parade that starts this event.

styles. Like the old missions, they have flat roofs and thick adobe walls.

More American Indians live in the Southwest than in any other region of the United States. Many live and work in cities and towns in the Southwest. Others live on reservations. A **reservation** is land set aside by the government for use by Indians. On reservations, Indians govern themselves. In the state of Arizona alone, more than 250,000 Indians live on reservations. The Navajo reservation is the largest in the United States. It lies in Arizona, New Mexico, and Utah.

Like other Americans, Indians on reservations farm and run businesses. They also face many of the same problems that other Americans face. They try to keep their ancient arts and customs alive, too. They make traditional goods, such as weavings, silver and turquoise jewelry, and pottery. Their children learn Indian languages as well as English in school.

How do Indians keep their ancient arts and customs alive?

LESSON 2 REVIEW

Check Understanding

1. **Recall the Facts**   How were missions important to the settlement of the Southwest?
2. **Focus on the Main Idea**   What Indian, Spanish, and Mexican ways from the past live on in the Southwest today?

Think Critically

3. **Link to You**   Which Indian groups live nearest to you?

Show What You Know

Mural Activity   Find pictures of early Indian, Spanish, and Mexican clothing, buildings, and crafts in the Southwest. Use your textbook as well as encyclopedias and library books. Then on a large sheet of paper, draw scenes from early life in the Southwest. Label your mural *The Southwest Long Ago.*

Read a Vertical Time Line

Why Is This Skill Important?

As you know, a time line shows events that happened over a certain period of time. Most time lines run horizontally, or across the page from left to right. Other time lines, however, are vertical. A vertical time line lists events from top to bottom.

Understand the Process

Look at the vertical time line on this page. The earliest date on a vertical time line is at the top. The latest date is at the bottom.

Time lines can show different periods of time. This time line shows 100 years, from 1800 to 1900. A period of 100 years is called a **century.** You can say that this time line shows the 1800s, the years from 1800 to 1899.

A century can be divided into ten decades. A **decade** is a period of 10 years. The years from 1830 to 1839, for example, are a decade that you can call the 1830s. On this time line ten decades are shown in all.

Now use the time line to answer the following questions about Santa Fe's history.

1. In what year was Santa Fe's first newspaper published?
2. How many years after the start of the Mexican-American War did New Mexico become a U.S. territory?
3. Which could you have done first in Santa Fe, ride in a stagecoach or ride on a train?

Think and Apply

Make a vertical time line that shows one century of your state's history. Mark the decades on your time line, and then list the important events that happened during those years. Use encyclopedias and library books to help you find events and their dates.

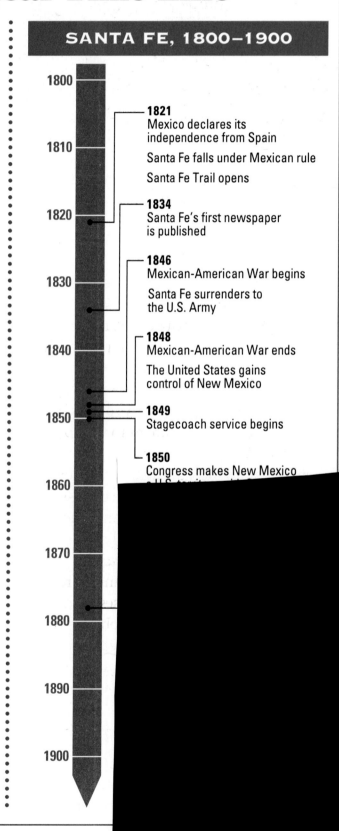

SANTA FE, 1800–1900

1800

1810

1821
Mexico declares its independence from Spain

Santa Fe falls under Mexican rule

Santa Fe Trail opens

1820
1834
Santa Fe's first newspaper is published

1846
Mexican-American War begins

1830
Santa Fe surrenders to the U.S. Army

1848
Mexican-American War ends

1840
The United States gains control of New Mexico

1849
Stagecoach service begins

1850
1850
Congress makes New Mexico

1860

1870

1880

1890

1900

A CHANGING REGION

Link to Our World

How can population growth change a region?

Focus on the Main Idea
As you read this lesson, look for reasons that cities in the Southwest have grown so fast.

Preview Vocabulary
dredge
aerospace

Riding horses is a popular pastime for some children who live in the Southwest.

The Southwest is known as a land of wide open spaces. There is good reason for this. Some ranches are so large that a person can ride horseback in a straight line all day without leaving the ranch!

Yet the Southwest is fast becoming a region of large cities. It is part of the Sun Belt. Its mild climate and rich natural resources have attracted many new people and industries. Many cities in the region have grown very quickly. In fact, four of the ten largest cities in the United States are in the Southwest. They are Houston, Texas; Dallas, Texas; Phoenix (FEE•niks), Arizona; and San Antonio, Texas.

A GULF COAST CITY

Houston is one of the fastest-growing cities in the Southwest. Its population has roughly doubled in the past 20 years. Today Houston is the largest city in the Southwest and the fourth-largest city in the United States.

Trade has played an important part in the city's growth. Houston lies on the Coastal Plain, about 50 miles (80 km) from the Gulf of Mexico. It was built on a shallow waterway called Buffalo Bayou.

During the 1800s only small boats could sail up the Buffalo Bayou to Houston, so city leaders decided to dredge it. To **dredge** is to dig out the bottom and sides to make a waterway deeper and wider. When the work was finished in 1914, the part of the bayou that linked Houston to Galveston Bay and the Gulf of Mexico was named the

MOVEMENT The Houston Ship Channel allows oceangoing ships, such as oil tankers, to unload near the city.
■ In which directions would a ship need to sail to reach Houston from Galveston Bay?

Houston Ship Channel. As the writer Will Rogers once said, "Houston is the only city that dared to dig a ditch to the sea."

The Houston Ship Channel helped make Houston a busy port. Today only New York City and New Orleans handle more cargo than Houston. Trains and trucks carry goods to and from the many ships that dock in Houston each year.

Oil played a very important part in Houston's growth, too. In the late 1800s and early 1900s, huge amounts of oil were

discovered in the Southwest. Thousands of people went there hoping to make money in the oil boom. Houston and other towns in Texas, such as Galveston and Dallas, grew quickly. So did Oklahoma City and Tulsa, two cities in the neighboring state of Oklahoma.

Large ships called oil tankers used the Houston Ship Channel to carry petroleum products to and from the many refineries built in Houston. Today Houston is the largest center for refining oil in the United

> **66 HOUSTON IS THE ONLY CITY** *that dared to dig a ditch to the sea.* **99**
>
> Will Rogers

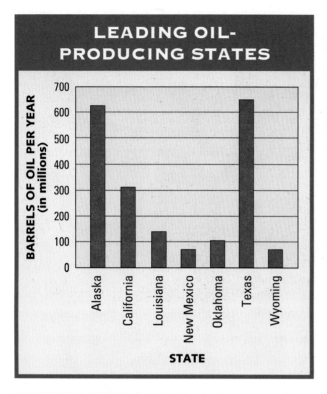

LEADING OIL-PRODUCING STATES

BARRELS OF OIL PER YEAR (in millions)

700
600
500
400
300
200
100
0

Alaska | California | Louisiana | New Mexico | Oklahoma | Texas | Wyoming

STATE

LEARNING FROM GRAPHS Only Texas produces more oil than Alaska.
■ About how much more oil does Alaska produce than California?

States. The Houston area also leads the nation in the production of petrochemicals.

The city has other important industries, too. The Lyndon B. Johnson Space Center has made Houston a leading center for the aerospace (AIR•oh•spays) industry. **Aerospace** is the technology used to build and test equipment for air and space travel. Workers at the center oversee all space shuttles during flight. Astronauts also train there.

 What two things played an important part in Houston's growth?

GROWTH IN THE DESERT

In 1867 a group of people settled in the Sonoran Desert, near the Salt River. They used water from the Salt River to irrigate their fields. Three years later the settlers built a new town, which they named Phoenix.

Like Houston and many other cities in the Southwest, Phoenix is growing quickly. In 1950 Phoenix was ranked ninety-ninth in size among cities in the United States. By the early 1990s it ranked eighth. More than half the people in Arizona live in or near Phoenix.

Before Phoenix could grow, however, it needed water. Huge pipes and canals were built to carry water to the city. Now Phoenix is an important trading center in the Southwest. Irrigation has turned the desert soil into valuable farmland. Having a supply of water has brought new industries to the city.

The city's climate has been important to its growth, too. Phoenix has more than 300 days of sunshine a year. The summers are very hot, but air-conditioning has made living there easier. The winter months are warm and pleasant. This

Horses and buggies were common sights on the streets of Phoenix, Arizona, in the early 1900s.

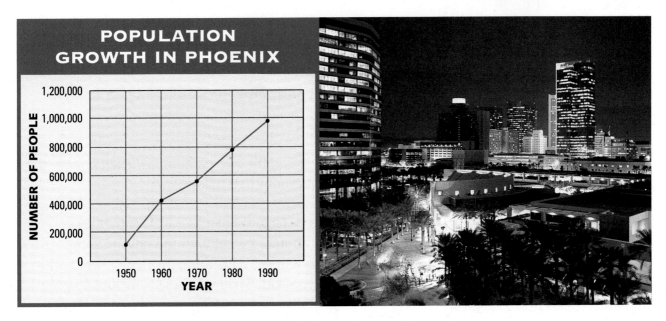

POPULATION GROWTH IN PHOENIX

NUMBER OF PEOPLE (y-axis): 0, 200,000, 400,000, 600,000, 800,000, 1,000,000, 1,200,000

YEAR (x-axis): 1950, 1960, 1970, 1980, 1990

LEARNING FROM GRAPHS The population of Phoenix has steadily grown larger. As in other large cities of the Southwest, tall buildings are now part of the Phoenix skyline.

■ About how many more people lived in Phoenix in 1990 than in 1950?

pleasant climate has done much to attract workers, businesses, retired people, and tourists.

So much growth coming so quickly has caused problems, however. Schools and highways are crowded. Growth has also led to major air pollution problems. A yellow-brown cloud now hangs over Phoenix on many winter mornings.

One of the biggest problems caused by growth has been supplying water for all the people. Water has always been scarce in the Southwest. Some people worry that there may not be enough water to meet the needs of this growing region.

 **What problems has rapid growth caused in Phoenix?**

LESSON 3 REVIEW

Check Understanding

1. **Recall the Facts** Why did many people move to the Southwest in the late 1800s and early 1900s?

2. **Focus on the Main Idea** Why have many cities in the Southwest grown so fast?

Think Critically

3. **Cause and Effect** How did the Houston Ship Channel affect Houston's growth?

4. **Link to You** What things have helped your community grow?

Show What You Know

 Writing Activity Choose either Phoenix or Houston. Then write a short story telling how water has affected that city's growth. Compare your story with those of classmates.

Tell Primary from Secondary Sources

Why Is This Skill Important?

Learning how to tell primary sources from secondary sources is an important social studies skill. A **primary source** is firsthand information from someone who saw an event or took part in it. A **secondary source** is a description of an event from someone who did not directly observe it.

Primary sources, which include photographs, recordings, diaries, journals, and letters, can give you firsthand information. But you still must study primary sources carefully. People who are close to an event may have strong feelings about it, and that may affect what they report. Primary sources often include people's opinions and their personal feelings.

Secondary sources include newspaper stories, magazine articles, and biographies and other books. They are written after an event by people who did not take part in it. Many secondary sources are references you can use quickly and easily. For secondary sources to be accurate, however, the people who write them must study many primary sources. You can check the accuracy of secondary sources by reading primary sources for yourself.

Understand the Process

Early settlers near Phoenix built canals to bring water to their crops. Both of the paragraphs that follow give information about these early canals. The first paragraph is from a diary written by Sadie Martin. She lived on a ranch near Phoenix with her husband and children in the late 1800s. The second paragraph is from a book written long after the canals were built.

Read the two paragraphs. Then answer the questions that follow.

> **"**Now that Father and Mother were home, I went with the boys to camp and we were gone for two or three weeks. They were all so anxious to get the water turned on in the canal so we could get things started to growing on the ranch. Everything depended on the success of the canal.**"**

> **"**Some of the first irrigation . . . was in the Salt River Valley. The men simply pooled their labor [work] to build small dams and dig canals that generally followed the old Indian canals, especially on the south bank. The men who did the work then shared the water.**"**

1. Which paragraph gives more facts? Which paragraph gives an opinion?
2. Which of the paragraphs is a secondary source? How do you know?
3. Which of the paragraphs is a primary source? How do you know?

Notice the language used in the primary source. The language can be a clue that something is a primary source. Primary sources often include opinions and words such as *I* or *we*.

Think and Apply

Look through your textbook or books from the library. Find three examples of primary sources. Explain how you were able to tell that each one is a primary source.

BUILDING CITIZENSHIP

SHARING A RIVER

LESSON 4

Link to Our World

How can a natural resource cause people both to work together and to disagree?

Focus on the Main Idea
Read to find out how the Rio Grande has caused the United States and Mexico both to work together and to disagree.

Preview Vocabulary
arid
conflict
compromise
runoff

Giant sprinklers help farmers grow cotton in the dry soil of the Southwest.

Water is scarce in many places in the fast-growing Southwest, including the Rio Grande valley. The people who live along the Rio Grande depend on the river for their water. So they often work together to protect the river. At other times, however, they may not agree on the best ways to use the river.

MEETING WATER NEEDS

The Rio Grande was named by early Spanish explorers. In Spanish, *rio grande* means "large river." The people of Mexico call the river Rio Bravo, or "bold river."

Near its mouth the Rio Grande flows through the warm, moist Coastal Plain. Upstream, however, the river cuts through mesas and high plateaus. Much of that land is **arid**, or dry. People there depend on the Rio Grande's water for drinking and for farming and industry.

To the people who live in the upper Rio Grande valley, getting enough water has always been a problem. One person there wrote, "So seldom is there water, never is there enough water." Yet when there are heavy winter snows in the mountains and gentle summer rains, water does its magic. "There will be corn, wheat, apples, apricots, and alfalfa, the horses will be sleek, and in the fall fat lambs and calves will go to

HUMAN-ENVIRONMENT INTERACTIONS

Farmers in the arid Rio Grande valley use the river's water to irrigate their fields.

■ Which two reservoirs along the United States–Mexico border help provide water for people to use?

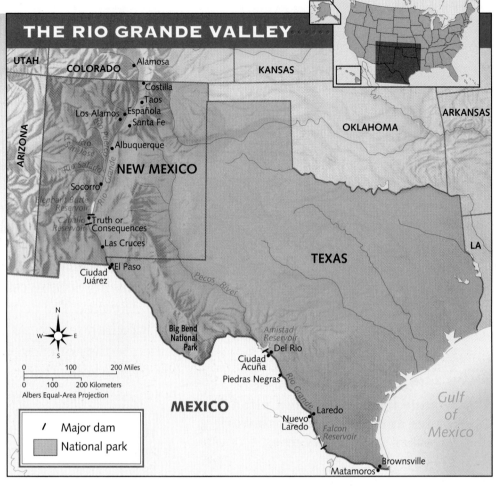

THE RIO GRANDE VALLEY

UTAH
COLORADO
Alamosa
Costilla
Taos
Los Alamos • Española
Santa Fe
Albuquerque
NEW MEXICO
ARIZONA
Socorro
Elephant Butte Reservoir
Caballo Reservoir
Truth or Consequences
Las Cruces
El Paso
Ciudad Juárez
Big Bend National Park

KANSAS
ARKANSAS
OKLAHOMA
TEXAS
LA
Pecos River
Amistad Reservoir
Del Rio
Ciudad Acuña
Piedras Negras
Rio Grande
Laredo
Nuevo Laredo
Falcon Reservoir
Gulf of Mexico
Brownsville
Matamoros

MEXICO

N W E S

0   100   200 Miles
0   100   200 Kilometers
Albers Equal-Area Projection

/ Major dam
National park

market and the drying strings of chili will make masses of scarlet against the warm brown walls of the adobe farmhouses." It is when the water runs out and harvests are poor that conflict sometimes begins. A **conflict** is a disagreement between two or more people or groups.

Farmers in the Rio Grande valley use the river's water to irrigate their fields. When farmers in Colorado use water for their fields, less water reaches New Mexico. In New Mexico, farmers also use the water. So much water is used in Colorado and New Mexico that people in El Paso, Texas, sometimes see a dry riverbed. El Paso is located where New Mexico and Texas meet the country of Mexico.

People downstream often blame people upstream for using too much water. To

make sure there is more water downstream, the national government has built dams across the Rio Grande. Water stored behind those dams can be used for irrigation and by people and industries. During dry times some of the water can be released into the river.

The water used upstream affects many people in Mexico, too. At Ciudad Juárez (SEE•u•dahd HWAR•ays), across the river from El Paso, Mexican farmers also irrigate their land. To protect Mexico's use of the river, the United States has agreed that a certain amount of water must reach Mexico.

To help solve their water problems, the United States and Mexico have worked together to build other dams on the Rio Grande. For example, the two countries built Falcon Reservoir about 50 miles

(80 km) downstream from Laredo, Texas. Water from this reservoir is used to irrigate citrus groves and vegetable and cotton fields on both sides of the river.

✓ **How have the United States and Mexico worked together to solve their water problems?**

BORDER CONFLICTS

The Rio Grande forms a natural border between the United States and Mexico. But rivers sometimes change course. That happened to the Rio Grande in the 1860s. After some small floods, the river's channel moved south. Land that had been a part of Mexico was now to the north of the Rio Grande. Mexico said the land still belonged to it. The United States, however, said the land had become part of the state of Texas.

The two countries were in conflict over which owned this small piece of land, called El Chamizal (SHAM•ih•zal). Neither side was willing to give up its claim to the land. So the conflict dragged on for almost 100 years. Finally, Mexico and the United States agreed to a

This plaque, on a bridge between Laredo, Texas, and Nuevo (noo•AY•voh) Laredo in Mexico, marks the border between the United States and the Republic of Mexico.

compromise. In a **compromise**, each side in a conflict gives up some of what it wants in order to make an agreement. The United States agreed to give El Chamizal back to Mexico. In return, Mexico gave

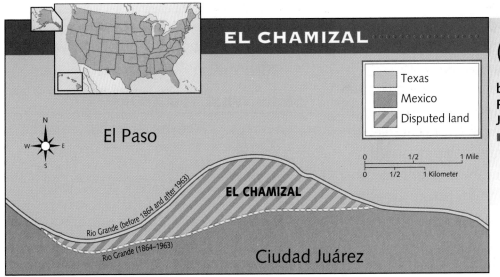

EL CHAMIZAL

El Paso

Texas
Mexico
Disputed land

0   1/2   1 Mile
0   1/2   1 Kilometer

Rio Grande (before 1864 and after 1963)

EL CHAMIZAL

Rio Grande (1864–1963)

Ciudad Juárez

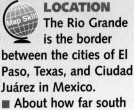

LOCATION The Rio Grande is the border between the cities of El Paso, Texas, and Ciudad Juárez in Mexico.
■ About how far south did the Rio Grande's channel move in 1864?

the United States some land on the north side of the original channel.

Under the compromise, the river was moved back north. This meant that all the land south of the river would once again belong to Mexico. All the land north of the river would belong to the United States. To make sure that the river would not change course again, the new riverbed was lined with concrete.

 What caused Mexico and the United States to disagree over their border?

COOPERATING IN OTHER WAYS

The conflict over the border was settled, but other problems remain. Every day cities and industries dump millions of gallons of waste into the Rio Grande. Runoff from irrigation and rainwater carries chemicals used on nearby farms into the river. **Runoff** is surface water that does not soak into the ground. Those things have made the Rio Grande one of North America's most polluted rivers.

Pollution affects people living on both sides of the river. The United States and Mexico are working together to try to reduce the river's pollution. Both countries plan to build more wastewater treatment plants along the Rio Grande.

Sharing the Rio Grande means that the United States and Mexico must cooperate in other ways. Increased trade between the two countries has caused rapid growth in the Rio Grande valley. Both countries must cooperate as they plan for future growth.

 What are the United States and Mexico doing about pollution in the Rio Grande?

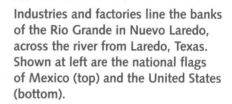

Industries and factories line the banks of the Rio Grande in Nuevo Laredo, across the river from Laredo, Texas. Shown at left are the national flags of Mexico (top) and the United States (bottom).

 **L**ESSON 4 REVIEW

Check Understanding

1. **Recall the Facts**   Why has too little water always been a problem in the upper Rio Grande valley?
2. **Focus on the Main Idea**   How has the Rio Grande caused the United States and Mexico both to work together and to disagree?

Think Critically

3. **Think More About It**   Why must the countries on both sides of a river work together to protect it?

Show What You Know

Writing Activity   Imagine that you are a newspaper reporter. You have been asked to describe how the United States and Mexico finally ended their border conflict over El Chamizal. In your report, tell how each side had to compromise to reach an agreement.

HowTo

Resolve Conflict by Compromise

Why Is This Skill Important?

Most people work well together when they agree. However, people sometimes have different ideas about how things should be done. That can lead to conflict.

There are many ways to resolve, or settle, conflict. For example, you can keep your opinions to yourself and walk away from the conflict. You can tell the other person what you think and try to get him or her to agree with you. You can also compromise.

As you know, a compromise is an agreement in which each side gives up something it wants in order to agree. Knowing how to compromise is one way in which people can settle their disagreements peacefully.

Remember What You Have Read

Being able to compromise is important for countries, too. The Rio Grande had been a natural boundary between the United States and Mexico for many years, but in the 1860s the river changed because of flooding. When the flood waters drained away, the river's channel had moved farther south. Land that had been south of the river, in Mexico, was now north of the river, in Texas.

The two countries could not agree on which nation owned this land, called *El Chamizal*. After nearly a century of conflict, Mexico and the United States agreed to a compromise. Think again about what happened.

1. What did each country have to do in order to make the compromise work?

2. What did the United States give up? What did Mexico give up?

3. What did the two countries do to make sure that a similar conflict would not happen in the future?

Understand the Process

To resolve a conflict by compromise, you can follow the steps below. They are similar to the ones that worked for the United States and Mexico.

- Identify what is causing the conflict.
- Tell the people on the other side what you want.
- Decide which things are most important to you.
- Present a plan for a possible compromise. Let the people on the other side present their plan.
- Talk about any differences in the two plans.
- Present a second plan for a compromise, giving up one of the things that is not most important to you. Look for a solution that allows each side to have much of what it wants.
- Continue talking until you agree on a compromise. If people on either side become angry, take a break so they can calm down before talking more.
- Plan your compromise so that it will work over time.

Think and Apply

Suppose the school board wants students in your school to wear uniforms. The students think they should be able to wear what they want. Work with a classmate. One of you should take the side of the school board, and the other the side of the students. Use the steps in Understand the Process to work out a compromise to resolve the conflict. Compare your compromise with those of other students. Which ones do you think would work best? Why?

CHAPTER 10
REVIEW

CONNECT MAIN IDEAS

Use this organizer to show that you understand how the chapter's main ideas are connected. First copy the organizer onto a separate sheet of paper. Then complete it by writing a sentence or two to summarize the main idea of each lesson.

A Changing Landscape

The Land and Its Resources

_____
_____
_____

Sharing a River

_____
_____
_____

The Southwest Long Ago

_____
_____
_____

A Changing Region

_____
_____
_____

WRITE MORE ABOUT IT

1. **Write a Diary Entry** Imagine that you are traveling with the explorer Coronado in search of the seven cities of gold. Write a diary entry describing the climates and landforms you have seen on your trip.

2. **Write About Conflict** Write a paragraph describing something that causes conflict in your community or state. Tell how people are trying to resolve that conflict through compromise.

USE VOCABULARY

Use the terms from the list to complete the paragraphs that follow. Use each term once.

adobe   missions
arid   rain shadow
conflict   runoff
mesas   society

The Southwest has different landforms. There are plains, mountains, and ___(1)___. Many places in the Southwest are dry because they lie in the ___(2)___ of the mountains. Early peoples in these dry areas often built their houses out of ___(3)___.

Spain once claimed all the land in the Southwest. Catholic priests built settlements called ___(4)___, where they taught the Indians about Christianity. These settlements soon became the center of Spanish ___(5)___.

Meeting water needs is still a challenge in the ___(6)___, or dry, areas of the Southwest. A shortage of water sometimes leads to ___(7)___, or disagreement, among people. ___(8)___ from irrigation can carry chemicals into rivers and pollute them.

CHECK UNDERSTANDING

1. How does the climate in the Southwest change from east to west?

2. Where are the lowest lands in the Southwest? Where are the highest lands?

3. What caused desert areas to form in the Southwest?

4. Why did the Mexican government try to stop Americans from moving to Texas?

5. What waterway connects Houston with the Gulf of Mexico?

6. What did Phoenix need in order to grow?

THINK CRITICALLY

1. **Personally Speaking**   Do you think holding a race was a fair way to open up Oklahoma to new settlement? Explain.

2. **Think More About It**   Why must the United States and Mexico work together to reduce pollution in the Rio Grande?

APPLY SKILLS

How to Read a Vertical Time Line   Use the time line on page 335 to answer these questions.

1. When did the Santa Fe Trail open?

2. How many years after the Mexican-American War ended did stagecoach service to Santa Fe begin?

How to Tell Primary from Secondary Sources   Answer these questions.

1. Is a description of an event in a history book a primary or a secondary source?

2. Is a diary entry by someone who saw an event a primary or a secondary source?

How to Resolve Conflict by Compromise   Think about a conflict you have with a friend or family member. Then list the steps that you might follow to resolve that conflict by compromise.

READ MORE ABOUT IT

Cherokee Summer by Diane Hoyt-Goldsmith. Holiday House. Bridget, a Cherokee Indian who lives in Oklahoma, shares her personal history as well as the history of her tribe.

Desert Giant by Barbara Bash. Little, Brown. This book gives many interesting facts about the saguaro cactuses that grow in Arizona.

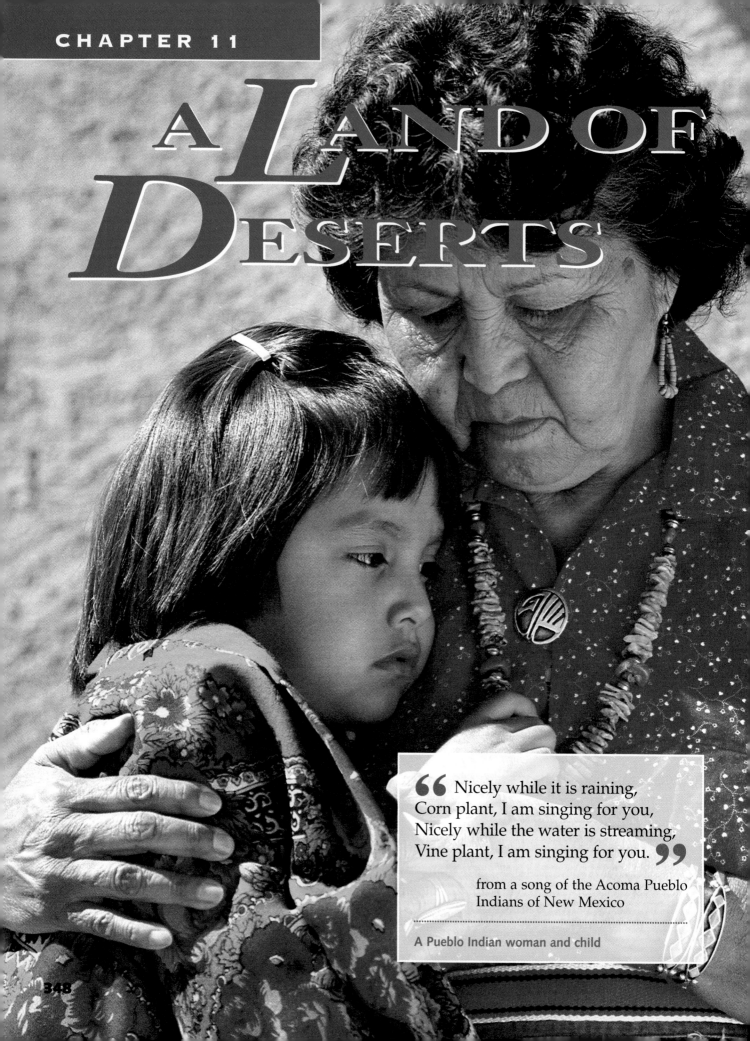

A LAND OF DESERTS

66 Nicely while it is raining,
Corn plant, I am singing for you,
Nicely while the water is streaming,
Vine plant, I am singing for you. 99

from a song of the Acoma Pueblo
Indians of New Mexico

A Pueblo Indian woman and child

WATER CHANGES DESERTS

Link to Our World

How can being able to get more of a resource affect an area's development?

Focus on the Main Idea
Read to find out how bringing more water to the deserts of the Southwest has changed them.

Preview Vocabulary
nomad
cloudburst
arroyo
aqueduct
migrant worker

This Hohokam jar, shaped like a human, was probably used for some kind of religious ceremony.

Deserts cover large areas of the Southwest. Those deserts have rich deposits of minerals. Often their soil is fertile. Before people could settle in deserts and use those natural resources, however, they first had to find a way to get enough water. But bringing water to deserts brought other changes, too.

CHANGES LONG AGO

At one time the only people who lived in deserts were nomads. A **nomad** is a person who has no permanent home but keeps moving from place to place. The deserts were too dry for people to stay in one place and grow crops. Instead, when water or food ran out, they moved to another place. Over time, however, Indians in the Hohokam (hoh•HOH•kahm) culture began to build settlements in the desert. They had learned that irrigation was the secret of living there.

The Hohokam settled in the Sonoran Desert about 2,000 years ago. They built their homes in the valleys of the Gila (HEE•lah) and Salt rivers near present-day Phoenix. Using only wooden sticks and poles, they dug miles of irrigation canals. The canals carried water to the Hohokam settlements and to hundreds of square miles of desert land. In fact, the canals carried water to nearly one-third of what is today the state of Arizona. In their irrigated fields the Hohokam grew cotton, beans, squash, and corn.

This illustration shows several Indians in the Hohokam culture digging canals and building dams to irrigate their field of maize. *Maize* is an Indian word for "corn."

About 500 years ago the Hohokam culture disappeared. No one knows why this happened. But their canals remained. Later, other Indian groups settled in the same area. Like the Hohokam, they used canals to carry water to their villages and fields.

✓ **How were the Hohokam able to build settlements in the desert?**

WATER IN THE DESERT

Deserts are very dry places, but there are streams and even a few rivers. For much of the year, however, those streams and rivers have no water flowing in them. Water flows only when mountain snows melt in the spring or after it has rained.

Most places in the desert receive rain only a few times a year. When it does rain, however, storms can be strong. Some places might get half of their yearly precipitation in just one cloudburst. A **cloudburst** is a sudden, heavy rain.

When a cloudburst happens, not all of the rain can soak into the hard, sun-baked desert ground. Instead, the runoff fills nearby streams and rivers. Some of the water races across the land, following the paths of ancient arroyos (ah•ROH•yohz). An **arroyo** is a deep, water-carved gully or ditch. Sometimes there is enough water to cause a powerful flash flood. Because a flash flood happens suddenly, without warning, it can be very dangerous to people. In fact, more people are killed in deserts by flash floods than by thirst!

A few low places in deserts almost always have water. They are often near rivers or natural springs. Such places are called water holes. Many desert animals depend on water holes for their water. Early desert travelers also depended on these places for water. They often camped or set up trading posts near water holes.

✓ **When might you expect to see water in a desert stream or river?**

NEW SOURCES OF WATER

When Arizona's first senator spoke before Congress in the early 1900s, he said, "The baby state I represent has a great potential. All we need is water and some good people." Over time many people moved to Arizona. The problem that remained was getting enough water.

To meet the growing demand for water, people began to change the desert environment. They built dams across the few large rivers in the desert Southwest. The dams formed reservoirs to supply water to the region's growing cities and for irrigation. Aqueducts (A•kwuh•duhktz) carry the water to the places it is needed. An **aqueduct** is a large pipe or canal built to carry water.

The largest of these dams is Hoover Dam. It was built across the Colorado River on the border between Arizona and Nevada. Hoover Dam is 1,244 feet (379 m) long and stands about as tall as a 54-story building. It provides electricity to cities in Arizona, Nevada, and California. Behind Hoover Dam lies Lake Mead, one of the world's largest reservoirs.

People in the desert Southwest also depend on wells for their water. Today's technology allows people to pump groundwater from deep beneath the Earth's surface. But there are problems with using groundwater. In moist climates rain quickly replaces the groundwater that people pump out. In many desert areas, however, people use groundwater much faster than nature can put it back. In Arizona, groundwater was once being used twice as fast as it was being

Hoover Dam formed Lake Mead.

Where?

Hoover Dam

Hoover Dam is located in the Black Canyon of the Colorado River, about 25 miles (40 km) from Las Vegas, Nevada. It is one of the world's highest concrete dams. Enough concrete to pave a two-lane highway from New York City to San Francisco, California, was used to build Hoover Dam. At its base the dam is 660 feet (201 m) thick.

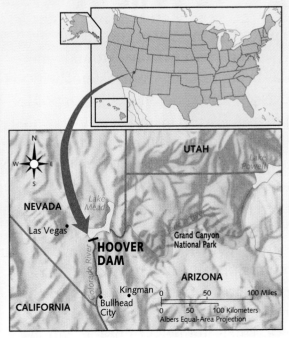

THE CENTRAL ARIZONA PROJECT

NEVADA

UTAH
Lake Powell

CO

Lake Mead

Grand Canyon

Colorado River

ARIZONA

Verde River

NEW MEXICO

CALIFORNIA

Lake Havasu

Granite Reef Aqueduct

Colorado

Phoenix•

Salt River

Gila River

Gila River

Tucson Aqueduct

San Pedro River

Tucson•

MEXICO

N W E S

— Central Arizona Project
↘ Dam

0   75   150 Miles
0   75   150 Kilometers
Albers Equal-Area Projection

HUMAN-ENVIRONMENT INTERACTIONS The Central Arizona Project was built to carry more water to the Phoenix and Tucson metropolitan areas.
■ Which reservoir supplies water for the Central Arizona Project?

replaced. In the city of Tucson (TOO•sahn), in southeastern Arizona, groundwater was being used up even faster. The water levels in some Tucson wells dropped as much as 110 feet (34 m) in just ten years!

This heavy use of groundwater left empty spaces beneath the Earth's surface, and in some places the land sank. A 120-square-mile (311-square-km) area between Phoenix and Tucson sank more than 7 feet (2 m). In other places large cracks appeared in the ground.

To help people use less groundwater, the Central Arizona Project was built. It uses canals, tunnels, pumping stations,

and pipelines to carry water from a reservoir on the Colorado River to places in the desert. The Central Arizona Project has brought more water to people who live and work in such desert cities as Phoenix and Tucson.

How do people in the desert Southwest get most of their water?

USING WATER IN THE DESERT

Having more water means that more people can live in and visit the desert Southwest. Today many places there are booming. Many cities and industries are growing rapidly.

Water has made the desert Southwest an important center of agriculture, too. Desert farms produce large amounts of

HOW MUCH WATER?

USE	AMOUNT
Brushing teeth	1 to 2 gallons (4 to 8 L)
Flushing a toilet	5 to 7 gallons (19 to 26 L)
Running a dishwasher	9 to 12 gallons (34 to 45 L)
Taking a shower	15 to 30 gallons (57 to 114 L)
Washing dishes by hand	20 to 30 gallons (76 to 114 L)

- The average amount of water used by one person in a day is 123 gallons (466 L).
- The average amount of water used by a household in a year is 110,000 gallons (416,394 L).

LEARNING FROM TABLES This table gives the average amount of water used for each activity.
■ About how much water does a person use when taking a shower?

cotton, lettuce, citrus fruits, and other crops. Many of those crops are harvested by migrant workers. A **migrant worker** is someone who moves from farm to farm with the seasons, harvesting crops.

Making sure there is enough water to meet everyone's needs is still a problem, however. The laws that govern how people use water are being changed to try to better meet the growing demands. In Arizona, for example, five water management areas have been formed. Leaders in each area decide how much water cities and farms should use. By the year 2025 they want Arizonans to use no more groundwater than the amount that is put back by nature.

Each water management area has also thought of ways to get people to conserve water. People are now being paid to put in toilets that use less water. Awards are given to people who use desert plants in their yards instead of grass that needs to be watered often. Are these working? One official says, "We're getting there!"

✓ **Why can more people live in and visit the desert Southwest today?**

LESSON 1 REVIEW

Check Understanding

1. **Recall the Facts** What did the Hohokam learn was the secret to being able to build settlements in the desert?

2. **Focus on the Main Idea** How has bringing more water to the deserts of the Southwest changed them?

Think Critically

3. **Explore Viewpoints** John Wesley Powell, an early explorer of the Colorado River, said, "In the whole region, land as mere land is of no value. What is really valuable is the water privilege." What do you think he meant?

4. **Link to You** What are some ways that you and members of your family might conserve water?

Show What You Know

Art Activity Suppose that you have been asked by the leaders of one of Arizona's five water management areas to design a poster. The poster should remind people of the importance of conserving water. Draw a poster that shows some of the ways people can conserve water. Then display your poster in your classroom.

YOURS or MINE?

The Colorado River is the main source of water for much of Arizona. Some of the river's water also goes to California and Nevada. But these three states have very different ideas about how the water should be used.

Years ago California, Nevada, and Arizona agreed that each state would have a certain amount of water to use. Those amounts have not changed in more than 30 years. But the three states have changed a lot. Many more people now live there, and all the states are using more water.

California was the first state to need more than its share of the river's water. When that happened, however, there was still plenty left. That was because Arizona could not use all of its share of the water. Arizona had no way to get all of its water from the river to all the places where it could be used, so California was allowed to use much of the extra water.

Arizona still does not use all of its share of the water. However, the Central Arizona Project has made it possible for the state to do so. Arizona wants to make sure that its share of the water will be there in the future, when its growing population will need it. People in California worry about what will happen when there is no longer any extra water for them to use.

THE LOWER COLORADO RIVER BASIN

UTAH

COLORADO

NEVADA

Colorado River

Lake Powell

Las Vegas

Lake Mead

Hoover Dam

Grand Canyon

Little Colorado River

Bullhead City

ARIZONA

NEW MEXICO

Lake Havasu

CALIFORNIA

Verde River

Central Arizona Project

Salt River

Phoenix

Colorado River

Gila River

Gila River

San Pedro River

Yuma

Tucson

Gulf of California

MEXICO

0   75   150 Miles

0   75   150 Kilometers
Albers Equal-Area Projection

PLACE The Colorado River supplies water to people living in California, Nevada, and Arizona.
■ What tributary flows into the Colorado River north of Yuma, Arizona?

Nevada has grown very quickly, too. In fact, the desert city of Las Vegas is one of the fastest-growing cities in the United States. Nevada will soon use all of its share of the water from the Colorado River.

Now it is hard for the states to agree on how water from the Colorado River should be shared. Recently, people from each state have come up with new ideas about how to use the water.

Some people in California think that less water should be kept in Lake Mead, the largest reservoir on the Colorado River. Then more water could be put into the river for people downstream to use. However, there would be less water saved up for times of drought.

Some people in Nevada think that a three-state commission (kuh•MIH•shuhn) should be set up. Each of the three states would have one vote. Together they would decide how the Colorado's water would be used. They would decide when extra water could be sold and at what cost.

Patricia Mulroy works for the Southern Nevada Water Authority. She says that if Arizona, California, and Nevada cooperate, there will be enough water to "meet any supply challenges that lie ahead."

People in Arizona, however, worry that Nevada and California might vote to take away the extra water that now belongs to Arizona. Rita Pearson works for the Arizona Department of Water Resources. She says, "Arizona cannot afford to permanently lose any of its entitlement [share] to out-of-state interests. . . . Its Colorado River entitlement is the state's largest renewable water supply, and soon enough it will need every ounce of it."

Instead, people in Arizona want their state to set up a "water bank." Through this bank Arizona would sell any extra water that it had each year. But the state would still keep its rights to all its share.

Farmland along the Colorado River

1. Find Lake Mead on the map on page 354. Why do some people in California want to put more water from Lake Mead into the Colorado River?
2. Why does Patricia Mulroy say there should be a three-state commission?
3. What does Rita Pearson think about the idea of a three-state commission? How do you know?

THINK
–AND–
APPLY

Think of another way for California, Nevada, and Arizona to meet their needs for more water.

BUILDING CITIZENSHIP

Then, on a sheet of paper, explain how that idea might affect the people in each of the three states. How do you think the people in each state might feel about your idea? Why?

ALEJANDRO'S GIFT

by Richard E. Albert   illustrated by Sylvia Long

Many different animals live side by side in the same part of a desert. Like all other living things, they need water, but water is scarce in a desert. All the animals depend on the same source for their water. Often that is a nearby water hole. Read now about Alejandro (ah•lay•HAHN•droh), a man who lives alone in the desert. As you read, think about how Alejandro changes the desert and how the changes he makes affect both him and the desert environment.

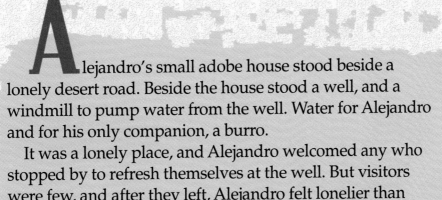

lejandro's small adobe house stood beside a lonely desert road. Beside the house stood a well, and a windmill to pump water from the well. Water for Alejandro and for his only companion, a burro.

It was a lonely place, and Alejandro welcomed any who stopped by to refresh themselves at the well. But visitors were few, and after they left, Alejandro felt lonelier than before.

To more easily endure the lonely hours, Alejandro planted a garden. A garden filled with carrots, beans, and large brown onions.

Tomatoes and corn.

Melons, squash, and small red peppers.

Most mornings found Alejandro tending the garden, watching it grow. These were times he cherished, and he often stayed for hours, working until driven indoors by the desert heat.

The days went by, one after another with little change, until one morning when there was an unexpected visitor. This visitor came not from the desert road, but from the desert itself.

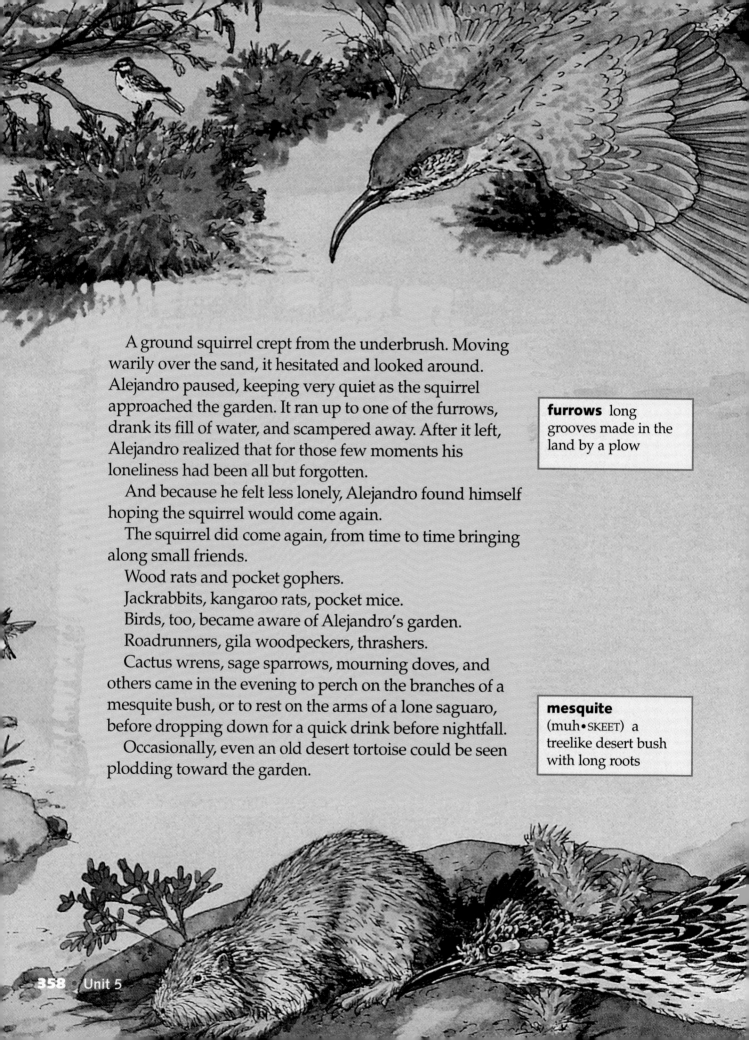

A ground squirrel crept from the underbrush. Moving warily over the sand, it hesitated and looked around. Alejandro paused, keeping very quiet as the squirrel approached the garden. It ran up to one of the furrows, drank its fill of water, and scampered away. After it left, Alejandro realized that for those few moments his loneliness had been all but forgotten.

And because he felt less lonely, Alejandro found himself hoping the squirrel would come again.

The squirrel did come again, from time to time bringing along small friends.

Wood rats and pocket gophers.

Jackrabbits, kangaroo rats, pocket mice.

Birds, too, became aware of Alejandro's garden.

Roadrunners, gila woodpeckers, thrashers.

Cactus wrens, sage sparrows, mourning doves, and others came in the evening to perch on the branches of a mesquite bush, or to rest on the arms of a lone saguaro, before dropping down for a quick drink before nightfall.

Occasionally, even an old desert tortoise could be seen plodding toward the garden.

furrows long grooves made in the land by a plow

mesquite (muh•SKEET) a treelike desert bush with long roots

Suddenly, Alejandro found that time was passing more quickly. He was rarely lonely. He had only to look up from his hoe, or from wherever he might be at any moment, to find a small friend nearby.

For a while this was all that mattered to Alejandro, but after a time he wasn't so sure. He began asking himself if there was something more important than just making himself less lonely. It took Alejandro little time to see there was.

He began to realize that his tiny desert friends came to his garden not for company, but for water. And he found himself thinking of the other animals in the desert.

Animals like the coyote and the desert gray fox.

The bobcats, the skunks, the badgers, the long-nosed coatis.

The peccaries, sometimes called *javelinas*, the short-tempered wild pigs of the desert.

The antlered mule deer, the does, and the fawns.

Finding enough water was not a problem. With his windmill and well, Alejandro could supply ample water for any and all. Getting it to those who needed it was something else.

The something else, Alejandro decided, was a desert water hole.

coatis
(kuh•WAH•teez)
animals related to the raccoon but with a longer body and a long snout

Without delay, Alejandro started digging. It was tiring work, taking many days in the hot desert sun. But the thought of giving water to so many thirsty desert dwellers more than made up for the drudgery. And when it was filled, Alejandro was pleased with the gift he had made for his desert friends.

drudgery dull, hard, unpleasant work

Literature Review

1. How did Alejandro change the desert? How did those changes affect both him and the desert environment?
2. Do you think you would get lonely if you lived alone in the desert? Why or why not?
3. Use encyclopedias and library books to find out more about the animals that came to visit Alejandro. Then write a short report about one of the animals. Draw a picture to go with your report. Share your report with classmates.

TUCSON: DESERT CITY

LESSON 3

Link to Our World

How are cities in the desert Southwest similar to and different from other cities?

Focus on the Main Idea
Read to compare and contrast the desert city of Tucson, Arizona, with other cities in the United States.

Preview Vocabulary

city manager   candidate
budget   ballot
municipal court   campaign
general election

Mission San Xavier del Bac, near Tucson, Arizona, is often called the White Dove of the Desert.

Tucson lies in the Santa Cruz River valley in the Sonoran Desert. While Tucson's desert location makes it special in some ways, the city has a lot in common with other cities in the United States. In fact, Tucson's buildings and streets look much like those in other large cities. One group of builders who visited the city reported that "with few exceptions . . . the buildings seem interchangeable with those in Rochester, N.Y., or Knoxville, Tenn."

A VARIED HISTORY

Like the Phoenix area, the land near present-day Tucson was first settled by the Hohokam. The Hohokam were likely the ancestors of the Tohono O'odham (tah•HOH•noh oh•OH•dham), an Indian group that lives in the Tucson area today. *Tohono O'odham* means "Desert People." Their reservation is the second-largest one in the United States.

Many different Indian groups live in the Tucson area. To show the importance of its Indian heritage, the city of Tucson asked a 100-year-old Hopi shaman to bless the new city hall when the building was finished.

The first Spanish settlement in the Tucson area was the Mission San Xavier (HAH•vee•er) del Bac. It was started in the late 1600s by a Spanish priest named Father Kino (KEE•noh). Just 15 miles (24 km) north of the mission was a small Indian village.

The Spanish spelled the Indian name for the village *Tucqui Son*. Father Kino described the land near Tucqui Son as "the richest soil in the whole fertile Santa Cruz Valley." The Spanish later built a fort at the village, which grew into the city of Tucson.

Tucson came under Mexican rule after Mexico won its independence from Spain in 1821. Then, in 1853, Tucson became part of the United States. The United States bought the area where Tucson is located from Mexico following a war between the two countries.

Tucson's Spanish and Mexican past is still an important part of the city's culture.

Many Mexican holidays are celebrated in Tucson. These dancers, dressed in traditional costumes, are taking part in a Cinco de Mayo celebration.

Like old Spanish buildings, many new buildings and houses in Tucson have tile roofs. Some have thick adobe walls. Tucson even has a shopping area built to look like a Mexican village.

As in other cities in the Southwest, many families in Tucson trace their roots to both Mexico and the United States. So people often celebrate the holidays of both countries. In fact, Mexican Independence Day is celebrated in Tucson with nearly the same excitement as the Fourth of July. Each September 15, *mariachis* (mar•ee•AH•cheez), or Mexican street bands, and large crowds of people gather to celebrate Mexico's freedom from Spain. One person from Tucson described the festival. "The *mariachis* play and sing, people dance. . . . Many wear traditional Mexican costumes, and for one evening Tucson looks and sounds much as it must have when it was a tiny walled *presidio* [fort]."

Another Mexican holiday celebrated in Tucson is Cinco de Mayo. In Spanish, *Cinco de Mayo* means "fifth of May." On that day in 1862, a group of Mexicans defeated a large, French army that had invaded Mexico.

 Why do many people in Tucson celebrate the holidays of both Mexico and the United States?

A MODERN DESERT CITY

At about the same time that Tucson became part of the United States, the city's climate began to change. No one is sure why, but the climate became much drier. The fertile lands near Tucson that Father Kino wrote about became desert.

At the Arizona–Sonora Desert Museum, visitors can see desert birds, such as the turkey vulture (above) and the kestrel (right).

Tucson's climate is hot for much of the year, so many houses there have cooling systems. Many houses also have solar panels on their roofs. These panels use the sun's energy to heat water.

Like other cities in the Southwest, Tucson has grown rapidly in recent years. In fact, the number of people living in the city grew by almost one-fourth between 1980 and 1990. Today the Tucson metropolitan area has more than 600,000 people.

Tucson has many of the same features as other large cities. It has busy streets and highways. It has a public transportation system that can take people all over the city. It has a central business district with tall buildings and a large convention center. Banks and shopping centers and a university—the University of Arizona— lie near the city's center.

Because Tucson is a desert city, visitors see many things that they cannot see in cities in other parts of the country. For example, a number of mostly dry arroyos cut across the city. Cactuses and other desert plants, such as mesquites, grow beside them.

One of the most popular places for any visitor to the city is the Arizona–Sonora Desert Museum. Part of this special museum is a zoo. It shows desert animals and plants in their natural surroundings.

The people of Tucson are proud of their desert environment. Most try to adapt to the desert rather than change it. One way they do that is in the way they landscape their yards. As in other desert cities, many people in Tucson do not grow grass in their yards. In fact, some neighborhoods do not even allow it! Instead, people use colored rocks and sand to make interesting designs in their yards.

Many people in Tucson use cactuses and other native desert plants, along with colorful rocks and sand, to landscape their yards.

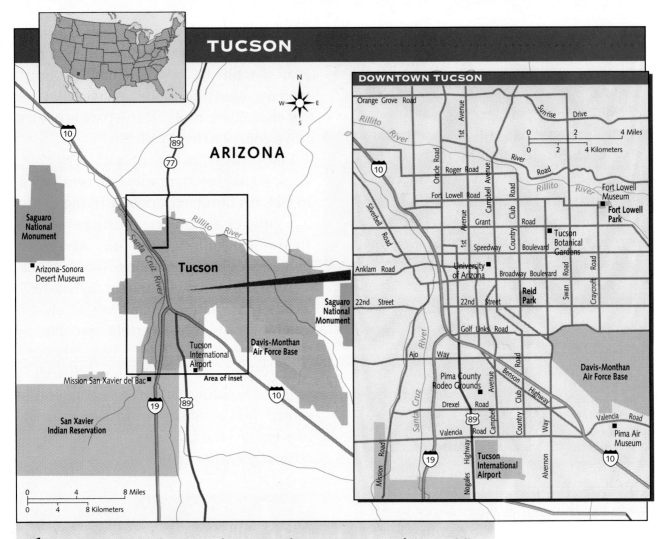

DOWNTOWN TUCSON

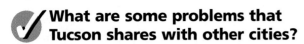

MOVEMENT Tucson is a busy city with many interesting places to visit.
■ Which roads would you use to go from the Tucson Botanical Gardens to Fort Lowell Park? In which direction would you travel on each road?

Tucson also faces many of the same problems as other large cities. Its schools are crowded, and sometimes there are not enough good jobs for all its people. The city has also had problems with crime and with air and water pollution.

✓ **What are some problems that Tucson shares with other cities?**

CITY GOVERNMENT

Like other cities, Tucson has a city government. The city government works to solve Tucson's problems and to provide services to its people. The six members of

the city council make the laws for Tucson. The mayor runs the council meetings and represents the city on special occasions.

Together the members of the city council and the mayor choose the city manager. A **city manager** is a person who is hired to run a city. The city manager hires city workers and oversees all the day-to-day operations of the city government. The city manager makes sure that all community services, such as the fire and police departments, are running smoothly. The city manager also prepares a yearly budget for the city. A **budget** is a plan for spending and saving money.

Like Tucson, many other large cities in the United States have both a mayor and a city manager. Some cities, however, do not have a city manager. Instead, the mayor runs the city.

Tucson's city council and mayor also choose judges to serve on the municipal (myu•NIH•suh•puhl), or city, court. A **municipal court** decides the cases of people accused of breaking city laws. These laws often have to do with traffic, parking, and other things important to the smooth working of a community.

The mayor and the members of the city council are elected by the people of Tucson in a general election. A **general election** is an election in which the voters choose the people who will represent them in government.

The people who are running for office in an election are called **candidates**. Usually there are two or more candidates for each office. So that voters can make a choice on election day, the names of all the candidates running for an office are listed on the ballot. A **ballot** is a sheet of paper or some other method used to mark a secret vote.

Most candidates have campaigns to get people to vote for them. During a **campaign** a candidate runs advertisements on television, displays signs, makes speeches, and talks with voters.

✓ **Who chooses Tucson's city manager?**

The city of Tucson has its own seal (left). Tucson is also the county seat of Pima County. The Pima County Justice Court Building (below) is in downtown Tucson.

LESSON 3 REVIEW

Check Understanding

1. **Recall the Facts**   What is the difference between a city council, a city manager, and a mayor?
2. **Focus on the Main Idea**   How is Tucson similar to and how is it different from other cities in the United States?

Think Critically

3. **Link to You**   How is the government in your community like Tucson's city government? How is it different?

Show What You Know

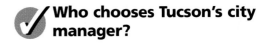

Diorama Activity   Think about how some houses and yards in Tucson are different from those in other parts of the United States. Then make a diorama showing what a house and yard in Tucson might look like. Build your diorama in an empty box turned on its side.

Use a Time Zone Map

Why Is This Skill Important?

Imagine that it is 7:00 A.M. on a winter day. You are having breakfast at home in New York City when you realize that today is your grandmother's birthday. Your grandmother lives in Tucson, and you want to call her to wish her a happy birthday. Is this a good time to call, or should you wait until after school?

Because the Earth turns on its axis, the sun does not shine on all the Earth at once. When it is daytime where you live, it may still be dark in other places. For this reason, people who live in different parts of the world set their clocks to different times. Daylight has not yet come to Tucson when it is 7:00 A.M. in New York City. So the people in Tucson must set their clocks to a time two hours earlier. Your grandmother probably would not want you to wake her at 5:00 A.M.—the time in Tucson—even to wish her a happy birthday!

To figure out the time anywhere in the United States, you can use a time zone map like the one on page 367. A **time zone** is a region in which people use the same clock time. Knowing how to use a time zone map can help you figure out times in other parts of the country. If you live in New York City, you can figure

out what time you would arrive on a trip to Los Angeles, when to place a phone order with a company in Chicago, or when to call Grandma in Tucson.

Looking at Time Zones

People divide the Earth into 24 time zones—one for each hour of the day. The United States has six of these time zones—the eastern time zone, the central time zone, the mountain time zone, the Pacific time zone, the Alaska time zone, and the Hawaii-Aleutian time zone.

The Earth rotates from west to east, so time zones east of you always have a later time than your time zone has. Time zones west of you always have an earlier time than your time zone has. Because New York City is in a time zone east of Tucson, the time in New York City is later than the time in Tucson.

Understand the Process

1. Find St. Louis, Missouri, on the time zone map. In what time zone is St. Louis?

2. Find the clock face above the central time zone. What time does the clock show?

3. Now find New York City. It is in the eastern time zone. What time does the clock above the eastern time zone show? When it is 9:00 A.M. in the central time zone,

As the sun rises above the eastern horizon, daybreak arrives in Arizona's Sonoran Desert.

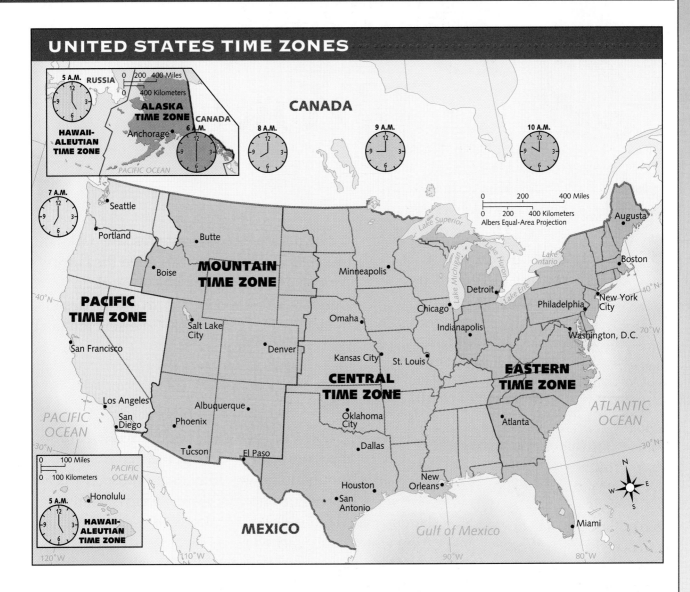

UNITED STATES TIME ZONES

it is 10:00 A.M. in the eastern time zone. Moving east, you must add one hour for each time zone you cross.

4. Now find Denver. It is in the mountain time zone. What time does the clock above the mountain time zone show? When it is 9:00 A.M. in the central time zone, it is 8:00 A.M. in the mountain time zone. Moving west, you must subtract one hour for each time zone you pass. What time is it in the Pacific time zone? in the Alaska time zone? in the Hawaii-Aleutian time zone?

5. Imagine that you are in San Francisco, California. Is it earlier, later, or the same time as in Chicago, Illinois?

6. If it is 4:00 P.M. in Dallas, Texas, what time is it in Boise, Idaho? in Atlanta, Georgia?

Think and Apply

On the map, locate the area where you live. Look at a watch or a classroom clock. What time is it in your time zone? Now figure out the time for each of these cities.

Seattle, Washington
Honolulu, Hawaii
Anchorage, Alaska
Minneapolis, Minnesota
Boston, Massachusetts

DESERTS OF THE WORLD

LESSON 4

Link to Our World

How are people in other desert regions affected by their environment?

Focus on the Main Idea
Read to find out how deserts everywhere and the ways that people use them are both alike and different.

Preview Vocabulary
sand dune
oasis

This snake, a horned adder, is a native of the desert regions of southwestern Africa.

The deserts of the Southwest are part of a much larger desert region called the North American Desert. The North American Desert is just one of the Earth's large deserts. In fact, deserts cover about one-seventh of all the land on Earth.

DIFFERENT DESERTS

Like the deserts of the Southwest, some of the world's deserts lie in the rain shadows of mountain ranges. Others are caused by cold ocean currents that flow next to coastal lands. Some land is desert because it is too far away from water to be reached by moist air. Still other places are deserts because of their locations north or south of the equator.

When people hear the word *desert*, they usually think of a place that is hot and sandy. However, not all deserts are alike. In fact, the only feature that all deserts have in common is a dry climate.

The driest desert in the world is the Atacama (a•tah•KAH•mah) Desert in South America. Even though this desert hugs the Pacific coast, it averages less than one-half inch of rain a year. The air there is cooled as it blows across the cold ocean currents. Most of the air's moisture turns to a thick fog that often covers the Atacama Desert.

Temperatures in deserts vary greatly. Even deserts that have hot temperatures during the day often have much lower temperatures at night. The world's largest

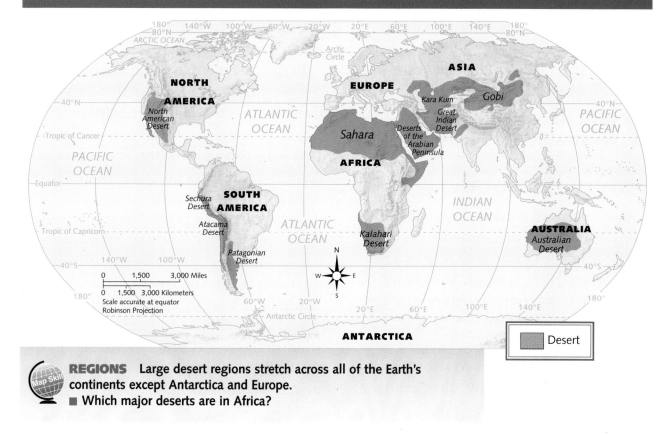

REGIONS Large desert regions stretch across all of the Earth's continents except Antarctica and Europe.
■ Which major deserts are in Africa?

desert is the Sahara in northern Africa. During the day, temperatures in the Sahara can reach 130°F (54°C) in the shade. At night, however, the temperature can drop by as much as 80°F (27°C).

Other deserts are always cold. Some places near the North and South poles are deserts. The air there is too cold to hold much moisture, so little precipitation falls. The Gobi, a desert in central Asia, is also cold for much of the year. It is hot only during the summer.

The Gobi lies on a high plateau. Its soil is rocky. Like most other deserts, the Gobi has few sandy places. In fact, sand

As this herder drives his camels, he wears heavy clothing to protect himself against the Gobi's cold winter climate.

Chapter 11 • **369**

covers less than one-fifth of most deserts. Yet the sandy parts of deserts can have interesting landscapes. This is because blowing sand often forms hill-like mounds called **sand dunes**. Sand dunes can be hundreds of feet high.

✓ **What do all deserts have in common?**

DESERT RESOURCES

Water is scarce in every desert. Water often can be found only near an oasis (oh•AY•suhs). An **oasis** is an area in a desert where there is water. Most of the water at an oasis comes from springs that flow underground.

About 90 oases dot the Sahara. People there grow grains such as wheat and barley. They may also grow olives, nuts, dates, and figs. Citrus fruits are grown with the help of irrigation.

East of the Sahara is the Arabian Peninsula. Most of the land on the Arabian Peninsula is desert. In some areas oases provide water for small farms and herds of animals. One desert, however, supports little life. This desert is

These Arabian camels, which have one hump, live in the deserts of North Africa and the Arabian Peninsula. Adults stand about 7 feet (2 m) tall at the shoulders.

called the Rub' al Khali (RUB al KAH•lee). Its name means "empty quarter." The Rub' al Khali covers most of the southern part of the Arabian Peninsula.

In the past, people could not have crossed this desert without using camels. Camels are often called the ships of the desert. A camel can travel several days on very little food and water. The hump on a camel's back stores fat that is used when food and water are scarce.

For many years people thought most of the deserts on the Arabian Peninsula were useless. It was almost impossible to grow anything there. Then, in the 1930s, oil and natural gas were discovered beneath the desert sands. Those oil fields soon became some of the world's most valuable land! Today they still supply oil and natural gas to much of the world.

✓ **What valuable fuels are found under the deserts of the Arabian Peninsula?**

ONE DESERT'S STORY

Northwest of the Arabian Peninsula is the small country of Israel (IZ•ree•uhl). Much of Israel is a desert, the Negev (NEH•gev). Less than 4 inches (10 cm) of rain falls on the Negev in most years. Yet the Israelis have turned this dry land into valuable farmland.

The Israelis got many of their ideas about farming in the desert from the Nabataeans (na•buh•TEE•uhnz). The Nabataeans were a group of people who lived in the Negev thousands of years ago. To raise crops, they learned to collect the little rain that fell in the desert. They built canals and tanks to store the water. They also put stones next to their plants.

THE NEGEV

LEBANON

SYRIA

GOLAN
HEIGHTS

Sea of
Galilee

Haifa

Nazareth

*Mediterranean
Sea*

Tel Aviv

WEST
BANK

Amman

Jerusalem

GAZA
STRIP

ISRAEL

*Dead
Sea*

Beersheba

EGYPT

JORDAN

```
0        25        50 Miles
0    25   50 Kilometers
Transverse Cylindrical Projection
```

Negev

National capital

Elat

Al 'Aqabah

*Gulf of
Aqaba*

LOCATION Irrigation has turned the Negev into fertile farmland.
■ In what part of Israel is the Negev?

Pipes carry water to irrigate the plants in this Israeli greenhouse.

farmers know when their plants need water. Underground pipes carry water to the plants' roots so that no water is wasted through evaporation.

✓ **Who did the Israelis get ideas about desert farming from?**

LESSON 4 REVIEW

Check Understanding

1. **Recall the Facts** Where is water often found in deserts?
2. **Focus on the Main Idea** How are deserts everywhere and the ways that people use them both alike and different?

Think Critically

3. **Think More About It** How might desert life in cold regions differ from desert life in hot regions?

Show What You Know

Art Activity Draw a cross-section diagram to show how the Nabataeans used dew to water their crops. Write labels to help explain your diagram.

At night, when temperatures dropped, dew formed on the stones and dripped down into the soil.

When Israel became a country, about 50 years ago, the Israelis remembered the Nabataeans' ways. The Israelis built water storage tanks and irrigation canals, just as the Nabataeans had. They even used some of the Nabataeans' old canals.

The Israelis also use new methods to farm the Negev. They have built large plastic greenhouses over fields to hold in moisture. Instruments measure the amount of moisture in the soil so that

REVIEW

CONNECT MAIN IDEAS

Use this organizer to show that you understand how the chapter's main ideas are connected. First copy the organizer onto a separate sheet of paper. Then complete it by writing three details about each main idea.

People affect deserts. → **A Land of Deserts** ← **Deserts affect people.**

Water Changes Deserts
Bringing more water to the deserts of the Southwest has changed them.

1. _____
2. _____
3. _____

Tucson: Desert City
The desert city of Tucson is both similar to and different from other cities in the United States.

1. _____
2. _____
3. _____

Deserts of the World
Deserts everywhere and the ways that people use them are both alike and different.

1. _____
2. _____
3. _____

WRITE MORE ABOUT IT

1. **Write a Speech** Suppose that you have been asked to speak to a group of citizens in Arizona about the need to conserve water. Write what you would say to the group.

2. **Write Clues** Create a riddle for each desert described in this chapter. Write several clues, and end with *Which desert is this?* Challenge classmates to name the deserts.

USE VOCABULARY

For each group of underlined words in the sentences, write the term that has the same meaning. Choose terms from the list.

arroyo   cloudburst
budget   nomads
city manager   oasis

1. At one time, the only people who lived in deserts were <u>people who have no permanent homes and move from place to place</u>.

2. Some places in a desert may get half of their yearly precipitation in one <u>sudden heavy rain</u>.

3. Water from a storm may follow the path of an ancient <u>water-carved gully</u>.

4. In Tucson, the city council and the mayor choose a <u>person who is hired to run a city</u>.

5. Like other cities, Tucson has a yearly <u>plan for spending and saving money</u>.

6. In the Sahara, water can be found near an <u>area that has water and is in the desert</u>.

CHECK UNDERSTANDING

1. How have people in the desert Southwest changed their environment to meet the growing demand for water?

2. What is an aqueduct?

3. What is the Central Arizona Project?

4. Who harvests many of the crops grown on farms in the desert Southwest?

5. What is a general election?

6. What feature do all deserts share?

7. Why is land so valuable in the deserts on the Arabian Peninsula?

THINK CRITICALLY

1. **Link to You**   Water conservation is important in every part of the country. What can you do to conserve water?

2. **Think More About It**   Suppose that people had never figured out ways to bring water to the desert. How would life in the Southwest be different today? How would the United States be different?

3. **Cause and Effect**   What caused the land in a large area between Phoenix and Tucson to sink more than 7 feet (2 m)?

APPLY SKILLS

How to Use a Time Zone Map
Use the time zone map on page 367 to answer these questions.

1. In what time zone is Chicago, Illinois?

2. In what time zone is eastern Kentucky? western Kentucky?

3. Is mountain time one hour earlier or one hour later than Pacific time?

4. If it is 7:00 P.M. in El Paso, Texas, what time is it in Detroit, Michigan?

READ MORE ABOUT IT

Sahara by Jan Reynolds. Harcourt Brace. This book tells about the people who live in the Sahara, the Earth's largest desert.

The Same Sun Was in the Sky by Denise Webb. Northland. A boy travels with his grandfather into Arizona's Hohokam country.

24 Hours in a Desert by Barrie Watts. Franklin Watts. Many changes can happen in just 24 hours in a desert.

BUILDING CLOSER TIES

The border between Mexico and the United States stretches 2,067 miles (3,326 km) from the Gulf of Mexico to the Pacific Ocean. There are close ties between communities on the two sides of this border. Each day thousands of people travel back and forth between the two nations. Many of them are Mexican citizens who come to the United States to shop, visit family, or go to work.

In many states in the Southwest, workers from Mexico are an important part of the local economies. "The Mexicans are taking jobs that no one here is taking," said a professor from the University of Texas. But some people think those jobs should be done by

Before people can legally cross the border, guards must check them and their cars.

workers from the United States. They want to stop Mexicans from coming to the United States to work.

Many people on both sides of the border have high hopes for NAFTA, the North American Free Trade Agreement, which went into effect in 1994. NAFTA makes it easier for the two countries to trade with each other. If NAFTA helps make the Mexican economy stronger, then Mexicans will be able to find jobs in their homeland instead of having to come to the United States. That way people on both sides of the border can work to build even closer ties. Other people, however, worry that the gain of jobs in Mexico will mean a loss of jobs in the United States.

THINK AND APPLY

Think about the ways in which people on the two sides of the border depend on one another. With a partner or in a small group, think of ways in which people might overcome their differences over jobs and workers. Present your ideas to the class.

BUILDING CITIZENSHIP

These workers (above) make and repair telephones in a factory in Mexico. The factory is owned by a business in the United States. These workers (right) are building a new shopping mall in Mexico.

This worker (above) has come to the United States from Mexico to help harvest oranges.

STORY CLOTH

Study the pictures shown in this story cloth to help you review what you read about in Unit 5.

Summarize the Main Ideas

1. The Southwest region has a variety of landforms, climates, and resources.

2. The Southwest's Spanish and Indian heritage lives on in the region today.

3. The Southwest is a changing region, and cities there have grown quickly.

4. Having to share the Rio Grande has caused the United States and Mexico both to disagree and to work together.

5. Bringing more water to the deserts of the Southwest has changed them.

6. Desert cities are similar to other cities in the United States in some ways but are different in other ways.

Write a Journal Imagine that you are visiting one of the places shown in this story cloth. Write a journal entry that describes that place.

Compare and Contrast Look closely at the scenes in this story cloth. Select two scenes, and think about how these scenes are alike and different. Then make a chart that compares and contrasts the two scenes.

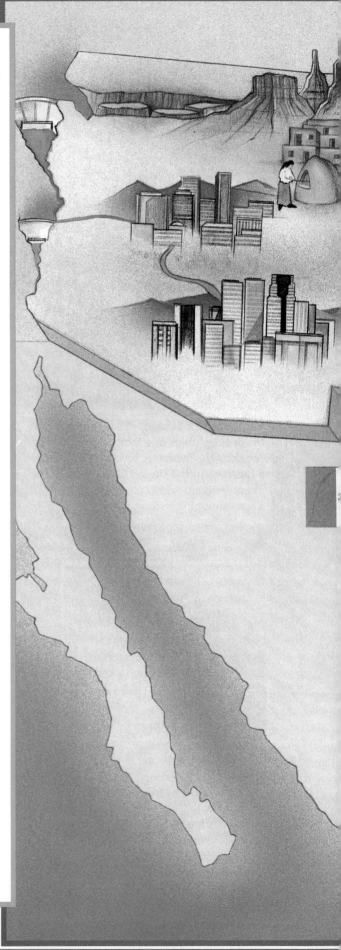

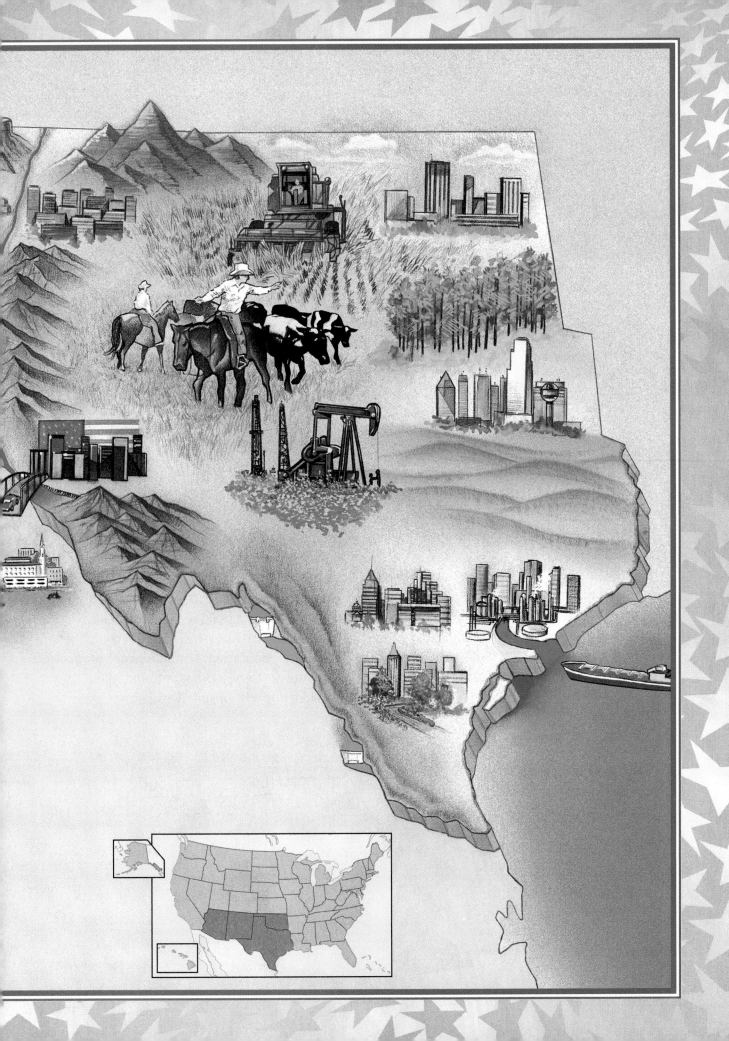

COOPERATIVE LEARNING WORKSHOP

Remember
- Share your ideas.
- Cooperate with others to plan your work.
- Take responsibility for your work.
- Show your group's work to the class.
- Discuss what you learned by working together.

Activity 1
Draw a Map
Work in a group to draw an outline map of the Southwest on a large sheet of paper. Maps in your textbook and in encyclopedias can help you. Add dots and labels to your map to show where the region's largest cities are located. Also label bodies of water and major landforms, such as the Coastal Plain and the Rocky Mountains. Draw symbols to show the region's most important resources. Then point out places on the map as your group takes the rest of the class on a "tour" of the Southwest.

Activity 2
Make a Time Line
Work in a group to make either a horizontal or a vertical time line. The time line should show some of the important events in the history of the Southwest. Find the events for the time line by using your textbook, encyclopedias, and library books. Be sure to show the date of each event on the time line.

Activity 3
Draw a Desert Scene
Work in a group to draw a scene showing some of the plants and animals that live in the desert Southwest. Use your textbook, encyclopedias, and library books to find information about the plants and animals. Then fasten a large sheet of paper to a wall in your classroom. Sketch the scene, and then color it. Present your desert scene to the class, and give facts about the plants and animals shown.

Activity 4
Celebrate a Mexican Holiday
Work together to plan a classroom celebration of a Mexican holiday, such as those celebrated by many people in the Southwest. First, research a holiday, such as Mexican Independence Day or Cinco de Mayo. Then, plan the celebration. You may want to make colorful costumes, prepare traditional Mexican foods, or sing Mexican songs.

USE VOCABULARY

Write the term that correctly matches each definition. Then use each term in a sentence.

aerospace   compromise
aqueduct   migrant worker
candidate   reservation

1. land set aside by the government for use by Indians

2. the technology used to build and test equipment for air and space travel

3. when each side in a conflict gives up some of what it wants in order to make an agreement

4. a large pipe or canal built to carry water

5. someone who moves from farm to farm with the seasons, harvesting crops

6. a person who is running for office in an election

CHECK UNDERSTANDING

1. What are the three largest plains regions in the Southwest?

2. What minerals and fuels that supply energy are found in the Southwest?

3. Why were missions started in the Southwest? How did they help the region grow?

4. How did Texas gain its independence from Mexico?

5. What is the largest city in the Southwest?

6. How does irrigation affect water levels in the Rio Grande?

7. What have people in Tucson done to adapt to their desert environment?

8. Which desert is the driest in the world? What caused that desert to form?

THINK CRITICALLY

1. **Explore Viewpoints**   Oklahoma settlers were supposed to wait at the starting line before racing to claim land. How do you think those who waited felt about the Sooners?

2. **Think More About It**   What are some good things that a fast-growing region like the Southwest can offer people? What are some problems caused by fast growth?

APPLY GEOGRAPHY SKILLS

How to Use a Time Zone Map
Use the time zone map below to answer these questions.

1. In which time zone is El Paso, Texas?

2. If it is 3:00 P.M. in Tulsa, Oklahoma, what time is it in Roswell, New Mexico?

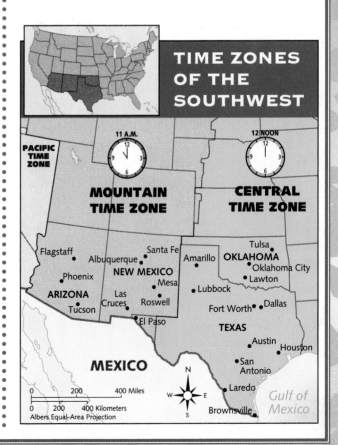

TIME ZONES OF THE SOUTHWEST

UNIT 6

*W*THE EST

Alaska　　**California**　　**Colorado**　　**Hawaii**　　**Idaho**

A team from the
Iditarod Trail
Sled Dog Race,
in Alaska

The Hollywood Sign,
in Hollywood, California,
a part of the city of
Los Angeles

The U.S.S. *Arizona* Memorial at Pearl
Harbor, in Hawaii

The West is the largest of the five regions of the United States. It is a land of contrast, with the wettest and the driest places and the warmest and the coldest places in the United States. The West also has the country's lowest place and its highest mountains. In fact, the West has more mountains than any other kind of landform. They cross every state in the region.

← The Golden Gate Bridge spans the entrance to San Francisco Bay, in northern California.

Montana   Nevada   Oregon   Utah   Washington   Wyoming

Glacier National Park, in Montana

Seattle, Washington

Grand Teton National Park, in Wyoming

ALMANAC
The West

Did You Know?

Eleven states make up the West. Those states are often divided into two smaller regions—the Mountain states and the Pacific states. All five of the Pacific states border the Pacific Ocean.

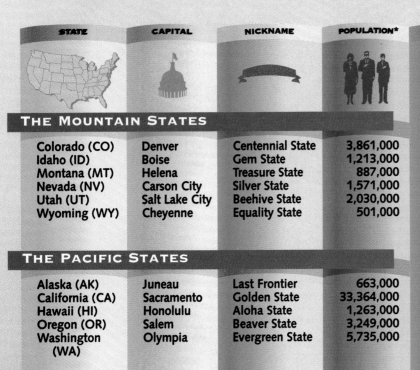

STATE	CAPITAL	NICKNAME	POPULATION*
THE MOUNTAIN STATES			
Colorado (CO)	Denver	Centennial State	3,861,000
Idaho (ID)	Boise	Gem State	1,213,000
Montana (MT)	Helena	Treasure State	887,000
Nevada (NV)	Carson City	Silver State	1,571,000
Utah (UT)	Salt Lake City	Beehive State	2,030,000
Wyoming (WY)	Cheyenne	Equality State	501,000
THE PACIFIC STATES			
Alaska (AK)	Juneau	Last Frontier	663,000
California (CA)	Sacramento	Golden State	33,364,000
Hawaii (HI)	Honolulu	Aloha State	1,263,000
Oregon (OR)	Salem	Beaver State	3,249,000
Washington (WA)	Olympia	Evergreen State	5,735,000

*The most recent figures available.

TEN LARGEST CITIES

1. Los Angeles, California
2. San Diego, California
3. San Jose, California
4. San Francisco, California
5. Seattle, Washington
6. Denver, Colorado
7. Portland, Oregon
8. Long Beach, California
9. Sacramento, California
10. Fresno, California

LEADING PRODUCTS AND RESOURCES

Farming:
Barley, beef cattle, coffee, cotton, dairy cows, fruits, hay, potatoes, rice, sheep, sugar beets, sugarcane, vegetables, wheat
Fishing:
Crabs, fish, oysters, scallops, shrimp
Manufacturing:
Chemicals, dairy products, electrical equipment, jet airplanes, lumber, metal products, paper products, processed foods, machinery
Mining:
Coal, copper, gold, lead, natural gas, oil, silver, uranium, zinc

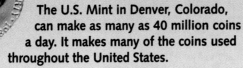

The U.S. Mint in Denver, Colorado, can make as many as 40 million coins a day. It makes many of the coins used throughout the United States.

Crater Lake, in Oregon, is the deepest lake in the United States. In one place it is 1,932 feet (589 m) deep.

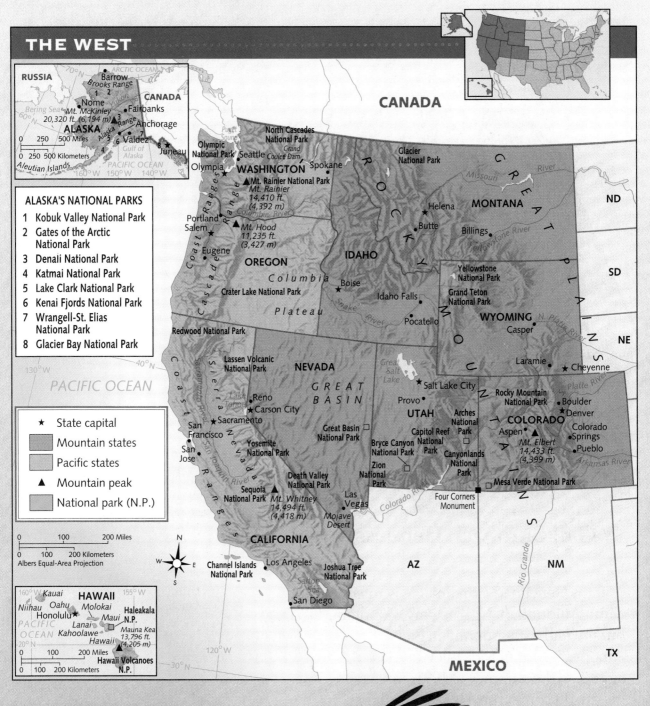

ALASKA'S NATIONAL PARKS

1 Kobuk Valley National Park
2 Gates of the Arctic National Park
3 Denali National Park
4 Katmai National Park
5 Lake Clark National Park
6 Kenai Fjords National Park
7 Wrangell-St. Elias National Park
8 Glacier Bay National Park

★ State capital

Mountain states

Pacific states

▲ Mountain peak

National park (N.P.)

0   100   200 Miles
0   100   200 Kilometers
Albers Equal-Area Projection

N

RUSSIA

ARCTIC OCEAN
Barrow
Brooks Range
1   2
Nome
Mt. McKinley
20,320 ft. (6,194 m)
Bering Sea
Fairbanks
Anchorage
ALASKA
Alaska Range
Valdez
Juneau
Gulf of Alaska
CANADA
Aleutian Islands
PACIFIC OCEAN
160°W 150°W 140°W
60°N

CANADA

North Cascades National Park
Olympic National Park
Seattle
Grand Coulee Dam
Glacier National Park
Olympia
WASHINGTON
Spokane
Mt. Rainier National Park
Mt. Rainier 14,410 ft. (4,392 m)
Missouri River
GREAT
Helena
MONTANA
Portland
Salem
Mt. Hood 11,235 ft. (3,427 m)
Butte
Billings
ND
Eugene
OREGON
IDAHO
Yellowstone River
Columbia
Boise
Idaho Falls
Yellowstone National Park
SD
Crater Lake National Park
Plateau
Snake River
Pocatello
Grand Teton National Park
WYOMING
NE
Redwood National Park
Casper
N. Platte River
ROCKY
Lassen Volcanic National Park
NEVADA
Great Salt Lake
Salt Lake City
Laramie
Cheyenne
Platte River
130°W
40°N
PACIFIC OCEAN
GREAT BASIN
Provo
Rocky Mountain National Park
Boulder
Reno
Carson City
UTAH
Arches National Park
COLORADO
Denver
San Francisco
Sacramento
Great Basin National Park
Capitol Reef National Park
Aspen
Colorado Springs
Mt. Elbert 14,433 ft. (4,399 m)
San Jose
Yosemite National Park
Bryce Canyon National Park
Zion National Park
Canyonlands National Park
Pueblo
Arkansas River
Death Valley National Park
Mesa Verde National Park
Sequoia National Park
Mt. Whitney 14,494 ft. (4,418 m)
Las Vegas
Colorado River
Four Corners Monument
Mojave Desert
CALIFORNIA
Channel Islands National Park
Los Angeles
Joshua Tree National Park
AZ
NM
Rio Grande
San Diego
120°W
30°N
TX
MEXICO

HAWAII
160°W 155°W
Kauai
Niihau Oahu Molokai
Honolulu Lanai Maui Haleakala N.P.
Kahoolawe
Mauna Kea 13,796 ft. (4,205 m)
Hawaii
Hawaii Volcanoes N.P.
PACIFIC OCEAN
20°N
0   100   200 Miles
0   100   200 Kilometers

Yosemite Falls, in California, is 13 times higher than Niagara Falls.

More bald eagles gather along the Chilkat River, in Alaska, than at any other place in the world. They fly there to catch salmon from the river.

CLIMB
Every Mountain

BY **Gail Skroback Hennessey**

Taras Genet had a dream. He wanted to climb a mountain. Not just any mountain, but the highest mountain in North America—Mount McKinley in Alaska! At age 12, in the summer of 1991, Taras made his dream come true. He became the youngest person ever to reach the summit of Mount McKinley's South Peak—a height of 20,320 feet.

"I've been wanting to do this all my life," says Taras, who lives near the base of Mount McKinley. In fact, both his parents were mountain climbers and guides. His father was the first person to climb Mount McKinley in the winter.

When Taras was just a baby, he "climbed" part way up the tallest mountain in the world, Mount Everest. Strapped to a Sherpa's back, he traveled with his mother to a camp on the side of Mount Everest in Nepal. (Sherpas are highly skilled mountain climbers who live at the base of the Himalayan mountains.) Taras's father, Ray, was finishing his climb to the top of the mountain. Taras and his mother were supposed to greet Ray on his way down. It was to be a joyous reunion.

But it never happened. Ray Genet was killed on a treacherous peak. When a friend told the family the tragic news, he looked over at baby Taras. The man promised that some day, when Taras was ready, he would take Taras to the mountain his father loved. Together they would climb Mount McKinley.

On June 5, 1991, Taras and six other members of his expedition flew to the base camp of Mount McKinley.

"From there, we traveled on skis to about 10,000 feet where we *cached* (labeled and left) our skis," Taras recalls. "Then we traveled with *crampons* through snow and ice." (Crampons are spikes made of steel that attach to the bottom of a boot to give traction.)

Taras lived through extreme heat during the day. At night, temperatures plummeted to 20 degrees below zero!

The climb wasn't just uncomfortable; it was also dangerous. Taras had to be alert at all times. A slip while crossing a crevasse (a deep hole in a glacier) would mean almost certain death. Once, an avalanche crashed down the slope, barely missing Taras's camp.

"It wasn't scary . . . most of the time," says Taras, "but I kept thinking, *I can't wait till I reach the summit.*"

It took days of hard work to reach the top. The expedition climbed five or more hours a day before setting up camp. But once the climbing was done for the day, the climbers still had plenty of work to do. Taras helped set up the tents. He helped make the outhouse. He gathered snow to be boiled into water for drinking and cooking.

"We had freeze-dried foods and lots of pasta to eat," Taras remembers. But life in camp wasn't all work and no play. About 16,000 feet up the side of the mountain, Taras and his fellow climbers had a great food fight!

Finally, after seventeen days of climbing, Taras reached 20,320 feet—the top of Mount McKinley.

"I could see lots of different mountain ranges and stuff," says Taras. He even spoke to his mother over a CB radio, waving to her as she flew overhead in an airplane.

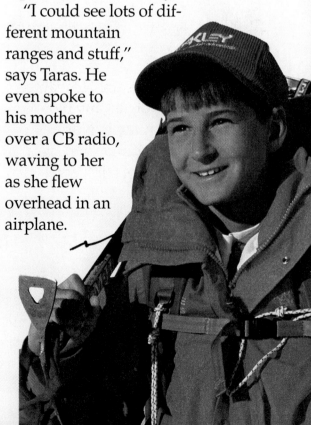

THE WESTERN MOUNTAINS

> 66 How glorious a greeting the sun gives the mountains! To behold this alone is worth the pains of any excursion a thousand times over. 99
>
> John Muir, on seeing the Sierra Nevada in California, 1894

A mountain climber in the Rocky Mountains of Colorado

MOUNTAINS
OLD AND NEW

Link to Our World

How are mountains similar, and in what ways are they different?

Focus on the Main Idea
As you read, compare and contrast the different mountain ranges in the United States.

Preview Vocabulary
lava
volcano
slope
Continental Divide
timberline

In a way, mountains have a lifetime. They form, they grow older, and they wear down. Some of those changes are so slow that they are hard to see. Others, however, can be quick and violent.

MOUNTAINS FORM

In 1943 a farmer in western Mexico heard a strange noise coming from his cornfield. "I heard a noise like thunder in a rainstorm," he said. "But I couldn't explain it, for the sky above was clear. I turned to speak to my wife when I saw the ground had swelled two meters (7 ft) and a kind of smoke—gray, like ashes—began to rise up with a loud hiss."

The next day, the farmer returned to find a mound 30 feet (9 m) high. The mound was growing larger by the minute as it spit out fire, ashes, and lava. **Lava** is hot, melted rock that comes from a volcano. A **volcano** is an opening in the Earth's surface from which hot gases, ashes, and lava may pour out. "Where only yesterday we had been waiting for the right time to plant our crop," the farmer said, "now we saw a flood of fire covering our footsteps' last traces."

As the lava that poured from the volcano's crater, or opening, cooled and became hard, the mound grew even higher. Over time it formed a tall, cone-shaped mountain. In eight months the volcano grew to be more than 1,500 feet (457 m) high. It was named Paricutín (pah•ree•koo•TEEN).

Paricutín formed in a cornfield in Mexico in 1943. Today the volcano rises more than 9,000 feet (2,743 m) above sea level.

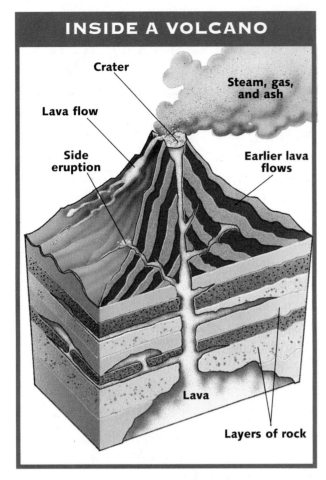

INSIDE A VOLCANO

Crater

Steam, gas, and ash

Lava flow

Side eruption

Earlier lava flows

Lava

Layers of rock

LEARNING FROM DIAGRAMS Many volcanoes form cone-shaped mountains.
■ From what parts of a volcano does lava spill out?

Some mountains, such as Paricutín, form quickly. Most mountains, however, form slowly as forces deep inside the Earth push up parts of the surface.

 How was the way Paricutín formed different from the way most mountains form?

MOUNTAINS CHANGE

When they are new, mountains often have high, pointed peaks. Over the years, however, mountains wear down. Rain, ice, blowing sand, and heat break up the rocks in a mountain. Then water and wind carry away tiny bits of the broken

rocks. This erosion causes mountain peaks to get lower and rounder.

Most mountains change their shapes slowly. A volcano, however, can change a mountain's shape quickly. When a volcano erupts, or begins to throw out lava, the blast can tear down the mountain.

On May 18, 1980, a small plane was flying near Mount St. Helens, a volcano in the state of Washington. At 8:32 A.M. the pilot and passengers saw the north **slope**, or side, of the mountain begin to move and slide. Suddenly, the mountain tore open, and a blast of steam, ash, and rock shot out.

The eruption of Mount St. Helens sent a cloud of steam, ash, and rock thousands of feet into the air. The energy released was equal to 10 million tons of dynamite.

The eruption of Mount St. Helens flattened entire forests (above). Ash from the eruption blanketed nearby cities (right).

DIFFERENT MOUNTAINS

The Appalachian Mountains, in the eastern part of the United States, are the oldest mountains in North America. Over the years, they have been worn down by erosion. Their peaks are mostly low and rounded. Even the Appalachians' tallest peak, Mount Mitchell in North Carolina, rises just 6,684 feet (2,037 m) above sea level. This is less than half as high as many peaks in the Rocky Mountains. Yet many scientists believe that the Appalachians were once taller and more rugged than the Rockies.

The newer and taller mountains in the United States are all found in the West. The largest are the Rocky Mountains. The Rockies are only about half as old as the Appalachians but are twice as high. In

A worker for the U.S. Forest Service remembers the blast. "There was no sound to it, not a sound—it was like a silent movie, and we were all in it. . . . I could see boulders—they must have been huge—being hurled out of the leading edge, and then being swept up again in the advancing cloud."

A cloud of smoke, steam, and ash made the sky dark for miles around. In Yakima (YA•kuh•maw), Washington, about 80 miles (129 km) away, the sky was so dark that streetlights went on at noon. On the mountain itself, rocks the size of cars tore down forests. Rock and ash up to 180 feet (55 m) deep covered other places. In all, more than 230 square miles (596 sq km) of the mountainside was destroyed. The mountaintop was lowered about 1,200 feet (366 m). Fifty-seven people died.

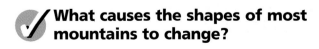 **What causes the shapes of most mountains to change?**

The Appalachian Mountains (top) are older than the Teton Range of the Rocky Mountains (bottom). How are their peaks different from each other?

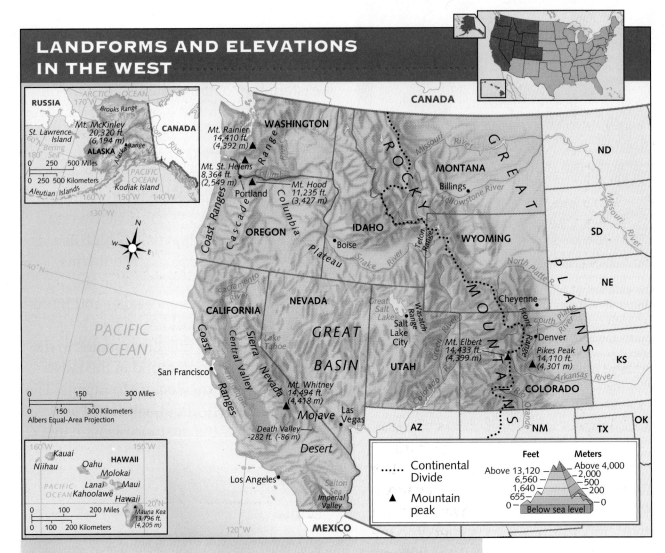

LANDFORMS AND ELEVATIONS IN THE WEST

RUSSIA

ARCTIC OCEAN
170°W

Brooks Range

St. Lawrence Island
Mt. McKinley 20,320 ft. (6,194 m)
ALASKA
Alaska Range

CANADA

Bering Sea

0 250 500 Miles
0 250 500 Kilometers

Aleutian Islands
Kodiak Island
PACIFIC OCEAN

CANADA

Mt. Rainier 14,410 ft. (4,392 m)
WASHINGTON

Mt. St. Helens 8,364 ft. (2,549 m)
Cascade Range
Columbia River
Mt. Hood 11,235 ft. (3,427 m)
Portland
Columbia
OREGON
Plateau
Coast Ranges

IDAHO
Boise
Snake River
Teton Range

MONTANA
Billings
Yellowstone River

ROCKY

WYOMING

Missouri River

GREAT

North Platte R.

CANADA

ND

SD

NE

Cheyenne

PACIFIC OCEAN

130°W
N
W E
S

40°N

Sacramento River

CALIFORNIA

Coast Ranges
Central Valley
Sierra Nevada
San Francisco

NEVADA

GREAT

BASIN

Lake Tahoe

Mt. Whitney 14,494 ft. (4,418 m)

Mojave
Death Valley -282 ft. (-86 m)

Desert

Los Angeles

Salton Sea
Imperial Valley

Great Salt Lake
Salt Lake City

Wasatch Range
UTAH

Colorado River

Las Vegas

0 150 300 Miles
0 150 300 Kilometers
Albers Equal-Area Projection

Mt. Elbert 14,433 ft. (4,399 m)
MOUNTAINS
Front Range
Denver
Pikes Peak 14,110 ft. (4,301 m)
COLORADO

South Platte River

PLAINS

Arkansas River

KS

Rio Grande

AZ

NM

TX

OK

160°W
Kauai
Niihau
Oahu
HAWAII
Molokai
Lanai
Maui
PACIFIC OCEAN
Kahoolawe
Hawaii
Mauna Kea 13,796 ft. (4,205 m)

155°W

20°N

0 100 200 Miles
0 100 200 Kilometers

120°W

MEXICO

	Feet	Meters
..... Continental Divide	Above 13,120	Above 4,000
	6,560	2,000
▲ Mountain peak	1,640	500
	655	200
	0	0
	Below sea level	

PLACE High mountain ranges stretch across many parts of the West. Several large rivers begin in these mountains.
■ What is the elevation of the land near the source of the Snake River?

Colorado alone, more than 50 peaks rise higher than 14,000 feet (4,267 m) above sea level. As in the Appalachians, some groups of mountains that are part of the Rocky Mountains have their own names. Among these are the Front Range in Colorado and Wyoming, the Teton Range in Wyoming, and the Brooks Range in Alaska.

An imaginary line runs north and south along the highest points of the Rocky Mountains. From this line, called the **Continental** (kahn•tuhn•EN•tuhl) **Divide**, rivers flow west or east. Most rivers that

begin west of the Continental Divide, such as the Yukon, the Columbia, and the Colorado, flow into or reach the Pacific Ocean. Rivers that begin east of the Continental Divide, such as the Missouri and the Rio Grande, flow into the Mississippi River or the Gulf of Mexico to reach the Atlantic Ocean.

As you know, other mountain ranges lie west of the Rockies—west of the Great Basin and the Columbia Plateau. Along the Pacific Ocean, from California to Alaska, are the Coast Ranges. Inland, along the California-Nevada border, are the Sierra Nevada. Farther north, in the states of Oregon and Washington, are the Cascades. Many of the Cascades' peaks are volcanoes. These include Washington's Mount St. Helens and Mount Rainier (ruh•NIR). Mount Rainier is the tallest peak in the Cascades.

 How are the Appalachian Mountains different from the Rocky Mountains?

CHANGING CLIMATES

In the western mountains a weather report may predict warm spring showers, sleet, and heavy snow—all for the same area. How is that possible? It can happen because temperatures change with elevation. Temperatures might be as much as 3°F lower for every 1,000 feet (305 m) higher in elevation. That is why weather reports in the West often give elevations. While a valley might have warm temperatures and showers, places higher in the mountains might have sleet or even snow.

....

Bighorn sheep can be found above the timberline in the Rocky Mountains.

Because the climate on a mountain changes at different elevations, plant and animal life changes, too. Trees, such as cottonwoods and pines, grow at lower elevations in the Rocky Mountains. Higher in the mountains, firs and spruces appear. Bears, deer, elk, and many other kinds of animals live among the trees.

Near the tops of the mountains, however, no trees grow. The Rockies, like all high mountains, have a distinct **timberline**. Above this elevation, temperatures are too low for trees to grow. Sure-footed mountain goats and bighorn sheep nibble on the grasses and other small plants that can grow above the timberline.

 What happens to temperatures as elevation becomes higher?

Check Understanding

1. **Recall the Facts** Into which large body of water do most rivers west of the Continental Divide flow?
2. **Focus on the Main Idea** How are mountain ranges in the United States alike, and how are they different?

Think Critically

3. **Cause and Effect** How do you suppose the volcano Paricutín affected the people living nearby?

Show What You Know

Art Activity Draw a diagram of a high mountain to show how climate and plant and animal life would change with elevation. Make sure your diagram shows and labels the timberline.

PEOPLE AND MOUNTAINS

LESSON 2

Link to Our World

How do mountains affect people's lives?

Focus on the Main Idea
Read to find out how mountains have affected transportation and communication in the United States.

Preview Vocabulary
**barrier
transcontinental railroad
labor
satellite**

Meriwether Lewis (right) and William Clark (left) led a small group of explorers on a journey to the Pacific coast.

The western mountains stand like giant walls across the American West. Those walls have shaped our country's history, and they still affect people's lives today. In some ways, however, people have learned to "tame" the mountains around them.

EXPLORING THE MOUNTAINS

In 1803 the United States bought the Louisiana Territory from France. This huge area of land stretched from the Mississippi River to the Rocky Mountains.

Americans knew very little about this land. They knew even less about the Rocky Mountains or the lands west of them. Was it possible to take a wagon through the Rockies? Was there a water route to the Pacific Ocean? The government sent Meriwether Lewis and William Clark to find out the answers to those questions.

Lewis and Clark, with a small group of explorers, left St. Louis, Missouri, in May 1804. They spent the summer going up the Missouri River. In the fall they camped at an Indian village near the Rockies. There they hired a trapper to help them find a way through the mountains. The trapper's wife, Sacagawea (sak•uh•juh•WEE•uh), was a Shoshone (shoh•SHOH•nee) Indian. She spoke English, so she helped them talk with the Indians they encountered.

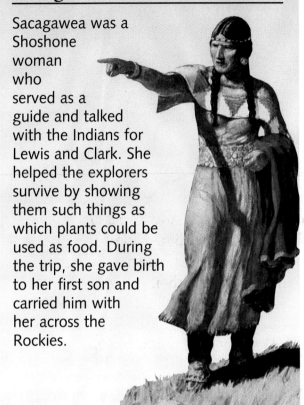

Sacagawea 1786?–1812?

Sacagawea was a Shoshone woman who served as a guide and talked with the Indians for Lewis and Clark. She helped the explorers survive by showing them such things as which plants could be used as food. During the trip, she gave birth to her first son and carried him with her across the Rockies.

In the spring the group reached Sacagawea's homeland. They asked the Shoshone people to trade them horses. At first the Indians did not want to trade their horses. When Sacagawea stepped forward, however, the chief saw that she was his sister! They had not seen each other for many years.

Sacagawea's brother agreed to trade the horses. The Indians also showed the group the way through the mountains. But the journey was hard. "Horrid bad going" was how one man described it. When the explorers finally reached the Pacific Ocean in November 1805, they were hungry and worn out.

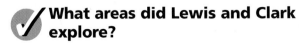 **What areas did Lewis and Clark explore?**

MOUNTAIN TRAVEL

In a few years pioneers began to cross the Rocky Mountains. Trappers had found other passes that made travel to California and Oregon easier. One group that joined the pioneers moving West was the Mormons. The Mormons came in search of religious freedom. They built Salt Lake City near the Great Salt Lake.

The mountains, however, still stood as barriers to travel. A **barrier** is something that blocks the way or makes it hard to move from place to place. Mountain travel remained slow and dangerous. The passes were often steep. Snowstorms and rock slides could happen at any time.

Most pioneers traveled by covered wagon. Their wagons carried all their belongings. One pioneer who made the trip west in the 1840s described people's feelings as they faced the mountains.

> ❝We had now arrived at a most critical period in our most adventurous journey; and we had many misgivings. . . . We could not anticipate at what moment we might be compelled to abandon our wagons in the mountains, pack our scant supplies upon our poor oxen, and make our way on foot through this terribly rough country, as best we could.❞

People wanted a faster and safer way to cross the country. In 1862 Congress agreed to plans to build a **transcontinental railroad**. It would cross the continent and link the East and West coasts. Two companies, the Union Pacific and the Central Pacific, would build the railroad. The Union Pacific would lay tracks west from Omaha, Nebraska, through the Rockies. The Central Pacific

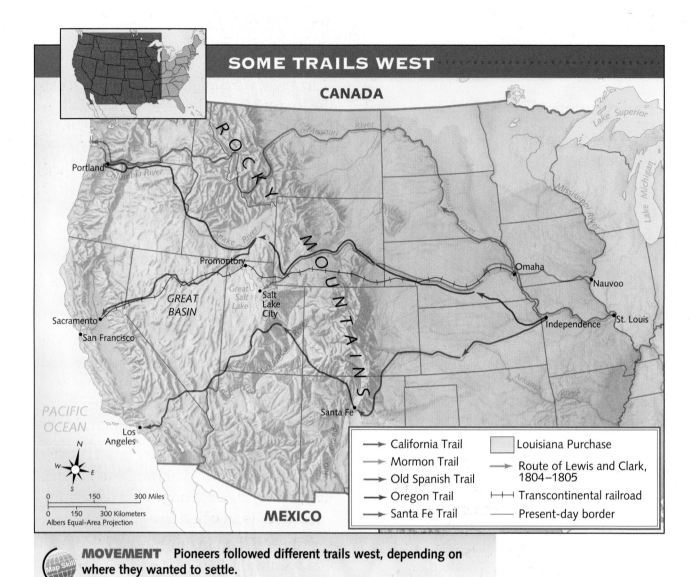

CANADA

R O C K Y

M O U N T A I N S

Portland
Columbia River
Snake River
Promontory
GREAT
BASIN
Great
Salt
Lake
Salt
Lake
City
Sacramento
San Francisco
PACIFIC
OCEAN
Los
Angeles
Santa Fe
Omaha
Nauvoo
Independence
St. Louis
Missouri River
Mississippi River
Lake Superior
Lake Michigan
Arkansas River
Rio Grande
Colorado River

MEXICO

N
W   E
S

0   150   300 Miles
0   150   300 Kilometers
Albers Equal-Area Projection

→ California Trail
→ Mormon Trail
→ Old Spanish Trail
→ Oregon Trail
→ Santa Fe Trail

☐ Louisiana Purchase
→ Route of Lewis and Clark,
   1804–1805
⊢⊣ Transcontinental railroad
── Present-day border

MOVEMENT Pioneers followed different trails west, depending on where they wanted to settle.
■ Which trail led to Portland, in present-day Oregon?

would lay tracks east from Sacramento, California, through the Sierra Nevada.

Building railroads through the mountains was hard work. Tracks sometimes had to be laid on narrow ledges around steep mountainsides. Bridges had to be built across deep canyons, and tunnels often had to be dug or blasted through some of the mountains.

Both companies hired thousands of workers to do this **labor**, or work. Most of the Union Pacific's workers were immigrants from Ireland or other European countries. Most of the Central Pacific's workers were immigrants from China.

All the immigrants worked long hours at low pay. The Chinese workers, however, risked great danger to complete the railroad, from hanging on ropes thousands of feet above the ground to using explosives to blast tunnels.

On May 10, 1869, the two railroads met at Promontory, Utah. The whole country celebrated as the last spike was driven to complete the railroad. Now it would be easier and less expensive for people and goods to cross the country.

✓ **Why were mountains barriers to travel?**

MOUNTAINS TODAY

Railroads and highways now cross mountains, and airplanes fly over them. Most mountain regions, however, have few people compared with other regions. Steep mountain slopes are not well suited for building large cities.

For example, the Mountain states—Montana, Idaho, Wyoming, Nevada, Utah, and Colorado—have few large cities. The large cities that are there, such as Salt Lake City, Utah, are built in valleys or on plateaus between mountains. Denver, Colorado, the region's largest city, is built on plains that lie just east of the Rocky Mountains.

Mountain land is also too steep and rocky for most farming. Most farms are found in lowlands between mountains. Some factories are found there, too, but there is less manufacturing in the western mountains than in other parts of the United States. Moving goods through the mountains to faraway markets is just too costly.

Mountains also make communication more difficult. Both radio and television

Workers test the antennas on the first North American satellite to broadcast television directly to homes.

reception can be poor because the mountains block signals. Communication satellites, however, have improved reception. A **satellite** is an object that orbits the Earth. Communication satellites travel high above the Earth, so they can send signals over the mountains.

 Why are there few large cities in mountain regions?

---

*L*ESSON 2 REVIEW

Check Understanding

1. **Recall the Facts** Why is mountain travel easier today than in the past?
2. **Focus on the Main Idea** How have mountains affected transportation and communication in the United States?

Think Critically

3. **Cause and Effect** How did the transcontinental railroad affect transportation?

Show What You Know

Simulation Activity Imagine that you are a pioneer traveling to California by covered wagon. List ten items that you are taking with you. When you reach the mountains, you discover that your wagon is much too heavy. Which five of the ten items would you leave behind? Why? Share your decisions with your classmates.

Use a Road Map and a Mileage Table

Why Is This Skill Important?

Imagine that this is the first day of your family's vacation trip to the Rocky Mountains of Colorado. The car is packed, you all jump in, and you are on your way. About an hour later your little sister asks, "How much farther do we have to go?"

To answer your sister's question, you can use a road map. As you know, a road map shows the routes between places. But a road map can also tell you the distances between places. Knowing distances helps people choose the best routes between places. It can also help you understand the geography of a region.

Understand the Process

Study the road map of Colorado on this page. It shows some of the state's major highways and cities.

1. Use the map index to find Denver and Glenwood Springs. Which interstate highway connects the two cities? From Denver, in which direction would you need to travel to reach Glenwood Springs?

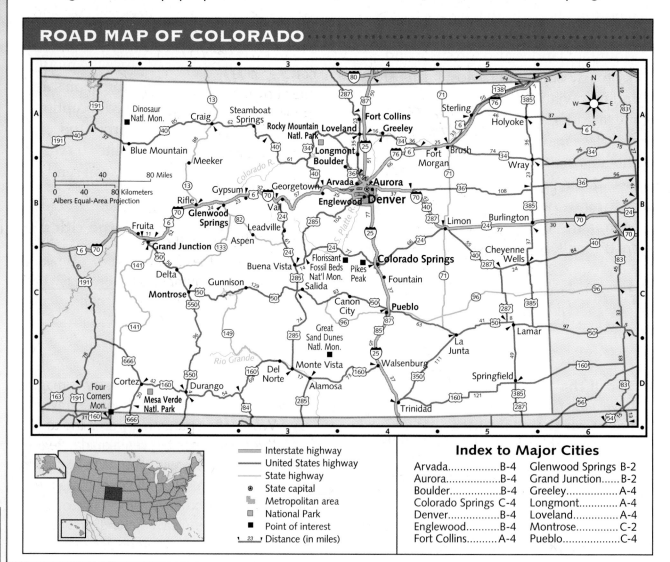

ROAD MAP OF COLORADO

Index to Major Cities

Arvada	B-4	Glenwood Springs	B-2
Aurora	B-4	Grand Junction	B-2
Boulder	B-4	Greeley	A-4
Colorado Springs	C-4	Longmont	A-4
Denver	B-4	Loveland	A-4
Englewood	B-4	Montrose	C-2
Fort Collins	A-4	Pueblo	C-4

Legend:
- Interstate highway
- United States highway
- State highway
- ⊛ State capital
- Metropolitan area
- ■ National Park
- ■ Point of interest
- 23 Distance (in miles)

COLORADO MILEAGE TABLE

	Boulder	Colorado Springs	Denver	Durango	Fort Collins	Glenwood Springs	Grand Junction	Greeley	Pueblo
Colorado Springs	96		70	311	137	208	299	121	42
Denver	26	70		339	62	159	246	54	109
Grand Junction	262	299	246	170	307	91		303	285
Greeley	50	121	54	403	29	212	303		166
Pueblo	138	42	109	272	174	236	285	166	

Suppose that you want to find the distance between Denver and Glenwood Springs. You can do this by using the map scale.

2. Use a ruler or a strip of paper and a pencil to find how far apart the cities are on the map. Then find the distance between the cities in miles. About how many miles is it from Denver to Glenwood Springs?

Using the map scale, you can estimate the distance along a straight line between the two cities. Mountain roads, however, are often winding, with steep hills and sharp curves. This can add to the driving distance, or mileage, between places.

You can find mileage by using special features of road maps. On most road maps main highways have small numbers next to them. These are the numbers of miles you would drive between places on the highways. The places are marked by wedges called distance markers. You can look at the map key to see what the distance markers look like.

3. Find the distance markers near Glenwood Springs and Gypsum, a town northeast of Glenwood Springs. Then find the number between those two markers. It tells you that Gypsum is 23 miles from Glenwood Springs.

Using distance markers is a good way to find the mileage between cities that are close to each other. However, using them to find the mileage between cities that are far apart—such as Denver and Glenwood Springs—would take a lot of time. You would have to find the mileage between lots of places and then add all the numbers together.

A much easier way to find the mileage between cities is to use a mileage table like the one above. A **mileage table** gives the number of miles between the listed cities. Most mileage tables, however, list only the largest cities in a state or country.

4. Suppose you want to know the mileage between Denver and Glenwood Springs. Find Denver on the mileage table. Move your finger along the row for Denver until you come to the column labeled Glenwood Springs. What number is in that box? That is the number of miles between the two cities.

5. What is the mileage between Denver and Pueblo? between Pueblo and Greeley?

Think and Apply

Work with a partner to plan a trip to three different cities in Colorado. Begin your trip in Denver. Use the road map to decide on the routes you will follow. Use the road map and the mileage table to find out the number of miles you will travel between these cities.

USING *W*ESTERN *L*ANDS

*L*ink to Our World

How can past events in a region affect the kinds of work that people do there?

Focus on the Main Idea
As you read, look for ways in which people still depend on the West's natural resources.

Preview Vocabulary
boomtown   public land
trade-off   geyser
opportunity cost

This early gold miner used a pick to break apart rocks. The large pan was filled with earth, and water was used to wash rock and dirt from the gold.

People were willing to face the dangers of crossing the western mountains because they believed life would be better on the other side. For many, their dreams came true. They found fertile land, thick forests, and rich deposits of minerals and fuels. Today many people in the West use those same resources to earn their living.

MINING IN THE WEST

It was gold that first brought many settlers to the West. When the Sierra Nevada pushed their way up into the California sky, they also pushed up rocks that held gold. A worker named James Marshall saw some of that gold shining in a ditch at Sutter's Mill in 1848. Sutter's Mill was a sawmill owned by a German immigrant named John Sutter.

The news spread like wildfire. Gold! There was gold in California! Thousands of people left their homes and jobs and rushed to California. Most came from states in the East. Many, however, came from other countries. They were all hoping to get a share of the riches.

Following the California gold rush, gold was discovered in other places—in the Colorado Rockies near Pikes Peak, along Montana's Yellowstone River, and in the mountains of Idaho and Alaska. Wherever gold was found, towns sprang up almost overnight. Because those towns grew so fast, they were called **boomtowns**. Boomtowns often had funny names, such as Rough and Ready, Bedbug, and Total Wreck.

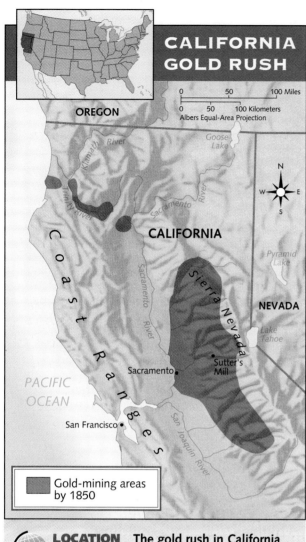

CALIFORNIA GOLD RUSH

OREGON

CALIFORNIA

NEVADA

PACIFIC OCEAN

San Francisco

Sacramento

Sutter's Mill

Coast Ranges

Sierra Nevada

Klamath River

Trinity River

Sacramento River

San Joaquin River

Goose Lake

Pyramid Lake

Lake Tahoe

0   50   100 Miles
0   50   100 Kilometers
Albers Equal-Area Projection

Gold-mining areas by 1850

LOCATION The gold rush in California began at Sutter's Mill.
■ About how far from Sutter's Mill was San Francisco?

Everything in boomtowns cost a lot of money. Goods were scarce, and store-keepers knew that miners would pay high prices for those items. For example, miners sometimes had to pay $1 for a slice of bread and $3 for an egg!

Most miners did not have enough money to buy everything they wanted or needed, so they had to make trade-offs. In a **trade-off**, a person gives up one thing he or she wants in order to get another.

A miner might have to make a choice between buying eggs or work gloves. Eggs would make a good breakfast, but without gloves, the miner might get blisters. To buy work gloves, the miner would have to miss the opportunity of a good breakfast. The value of what a person gives up to get something else is called the **opportunity cost**.

Most boomtowns did not last. When the gold was used up, people moved away. However, some boomtowns survived. When Montana's gold rush ended, the boomtown called Last Chance Gulch changed its name to Helena. Today Helena is the capital of Montana.

Mining is still an important industry in the West. Gold is mined in several states. Other metals mined in the West include silver, lead, zinc, and copper. The West also produces many kinds of minerals and important fuels, such as oil, natural gas, and coal.

✓ **How did gold mining affect the settling of the West?**

Helena, Montana, was one of the boomtowns that grew up in the West. This photograph shows Main Street in 1865.

MOUNTAIN FORESTS

The West also has many large forests. Forests cover the lower slopes of the Rocky Mountains. Even larger and thicker forests cover the Coast Ranges and the Cascades in Washington and Oregon. Together, these two states are sometimes called the Pacific Northwest.

The Pacific Northwest is an ideal place for thick forests to grow. The climate is mild, and coastal winds bring heavy rains. All along the Pacific Northwest coast, it rains and rains and rains. Some places get more than 130 inches (330 cm) of precipitation a year!

Some of the oldest, largest, and tallest trees in the world grow in the mountains of the Pacific Northwest and in the Sierra Nevada in northern California. These are the redwoods and the giant sequoias (sih•KWOY•uhz).

These people have just driven their car through a tunnel cut through a redwood. When this road was built, people thought little about conservation.

What?

The General Sherman

The world's largest tree, in amount of wood, is a giant sequoia called the General Sherman. It grows in Sequoia  National Park in California. The General Sherman is 275 feet (84 m) tall, and the base of its trunk is about 103 feet (31 m) around. Its bark is up to 24 inches (61 cm) thick.

Redwoods grow near the Pacific coast in California and Oregon. They often grow 300 feet (91 m) high. That is about as high as a 30-story building!

Giant sequoias are the Earth's largest living things. Many of the trees are more than 2,000 years old. While giant sequoias do not grow nearly as tall as redwoods, their trunks are much larger. In fact, some are as large as 40 feet (12 m) across. Once, after a giant sequoia was cut down, its leveled-off stump became a dance floor for 24 couples!

✔ Why is the Pacific Northwest an ideal place for large, thick forests to grow?

AVERAGE HEIGHT OF THREE KINDS OF TREES

White oak
60–80 feet
(18–24 m)

Giant sequoia
250 feet
(76 m)

Redwood
300 feet
(91m)

LEARNING FROM DIAGRAMS
■ About how much taller is the average redwood than the average giant sequoia?

THE LUMBER INDUSTRY

Laws now protect the giant sequoias from being cut. Many of the oldest and largest redwoods are protected, too. Many other kinds of trees also grow in the western forests. Among them are pines, spruces, cedars, and firs.

People in the West have used the region's many forests to build a huge lumber industry. Today Oregon leads the country in lumber production. California is second, and Washington ranks third.

Tens of thousands of people in the West work in the lumber industry. Some cut down trees. Others take them to sawmills and cut them into boards or grind them into wood chips for making pulp. Making paper and manufacturing wood products are huge industries in the West.

At one time the United States had so many forests that people did not worry about running out of lumber. They cut down huge forests, left the land bare, and went on to cut down more trees in other places. By 1900, however, only about one-fourth of the forests still stood that had been standing when the first European settlers arrived.

People began to worry that too many forests were being cut down. The United States set up national forests. The land and trees in national forests are taken care of by forest rangers. As trees are cut for lumber, new trees are planted. In fact, more new trees are now planted each year than are cut down. Some people still worry, however, because so many of the country's old-growth forests are being cut down. Old-growth forests are those in which trees have never been cut down.

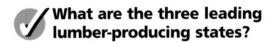
What are the three leading lumber-producing states?

Workers at this lumber mill located in Darrington, Washington, use heavy machinery to move logs cut from trees that have been cut down in nearby forests.

LAND USE AND RESOURCES IN THE WEST

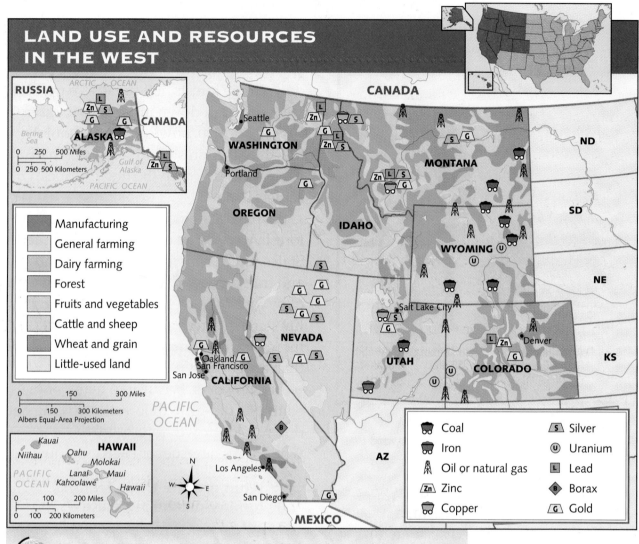

Map Skill **PLACE** The West provides the nation with many natural resources.
■ What are some leading resources in Colorado?

RANCHING AND FARMING

People in the United States depend on the West for metals, minerals, fuels, and wood. They also depend on the West for food. Both cattle and sheep are raised on the Great Plains in eastern Montana, Wyoming, and Colorado. Cattle and sheep are also raised in valleys and on plateaus between the western mountains.

In the hot summer months, the grasses at lower elevations dry up and turn brown. Ranchers move their herds up into the mountains, where the grasses are thick and green. Much of the land there is

public land, or land that is owned by the government. To use this land, ranchers must rent it from the government.

There are also many farms in the West. In the Pacific Northwest, where the climate is mild and rainy, farmers grow many kinds of vegetables, nuts, and fruits. Oregon is known for its winter pears. Washington is known for its cherries and apples.

Much of the rest of the land in the West is arid. The land east of the Cascades, for example, gets little rain. This high, dry land—the Columbia Plateau—gets only

10 to 20 inches (25 to 51 cm) of rain a year. Other places in the West get even less.

Irrigation has turned many of the West's driest places into good farmland. California's Central Valley, between the Sierra Nevada and the Coast Ranges, and Imperial Valley, in the Sonoran Desert, are now ideal for farming. In fact, irrigation has helped to make California the country's leading farming state.

The Snake River valley in Idaho is another arid place that has been made into good farmland through irrigation. The region is best known for its potatoes, but farmers there also grow beans and sugar beets.

 How are farmers able to grow crops in arid parts of the West?

Yellowstone's Old Faithful erupts faithfully every 35 to 120 minutes.

A LAND OF BEAUTY

Many places in the West remain wilderness. The United States government has set aside some of this land as national parks. The West has more national parks than any other region of the country.

Yellowstone National Park, which covers parts of Idaho, Wyoming, and Montana, is the oldest national park in the United States. Here visitors can see bubbling pools of mud and geysers. A **geyser** is a spring that shoots steam and hot water into the air. The most famous geyser in Yellowstone is Old Faithful.

What is the oldest national park in the United States?

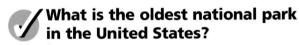

*L*SSON 3 REVIEW

Check Understanding

1. **Recall the Facts**   What were the towns called that grew up quickly near the mines?
2. **Focus on the Main Idea**   What are some ways in which people still depend on the West's natural resources?

Think Critically

3. **Personally Speaking**   Would you have been willing to leave your home and job to go to California in search of gold? Why or why not?

Show What You Know

Writing Activity   Describe an economic choice that you made recently. What trade-off did you have to make? What opportunity cost did you pay? Do you think you made the right choice? Tell why or why not.

How To

Form Conclusions and Predict Outcomes

Why Is This Skill Important?

A **conclusion** is a decision or idea reached by thoughtful study. To form a conclusion, you combine new facts with the facts you already know. Being able to form a conclusion will help you understand why things happen.

Once you have formed a conclusion about something, you may also make a **prediction**. This means that you will look at the way things are and say what you think will happen in the future or in another place. To predict an outcome, you use both the information that you know and your past experiences.

Remember What You Have Read

The western mountains once stood as mighty barriers to travel. Over time, however, people found ways to cross those mountains. You have read that gold first brought many settlers to the western mountains. Other settlers came to work in the region's forests. Still others came to start farms and ranches.

People today continue to use the land in the western mountains to earn their living. Mining is still an important industry there, and people have used the region's many forests to build a huge lumber industry. Ranching and farming are important industries, too, especially in the valleys and on plateaus between the mountains.

Understand the Process

Using the information you have read, what conclusions can you form about people and mountains? One conclusion you can form is that mountains affect the movement of people. Another conclusion is that mountains affect the way people earn their living. What other conclusions can you form?

There are many ways to form a conclusion. One way is to follow steps like these.

- Think about the information you have.
- Gather any new information that might help you.
- Make a statement that agrees with the information.

You can also use what you know about mountains in the United States to predict how mountains affect people in other places.

- Think about what you already know about mountains.
- Review the information about how the western mountains have affected people in the United States.
- Look for patterns in the ways people in the United States have used the western mountains to earn their living.
- Make a prediction about how mountains in other parts of the world affect the ways people earn their living.

Once you have made a prediction, you should continue to gather information. Ask yourself whether you still think your prediction is correct. You may need to go through the steps again to make a new prediction.

Think and Apply

Use the steps above to write several predictions about what you will learn about how mountains affect people in other parts of the world. Look at your predictions as you read the next lesson. Decide which of your predictions are true and which ones are false.

BUILDING CITIZENSHIP

MOUNTAINS AROUND THE WORLD

Link to Our World

How does living near mountains affect people in other parts of the world?

Focus on the Main Idea
Read to find out how people in mountain regions around the world have adapted to their environment.

Preview Vocabulary
terrace
bartering

To people in the United States, the Rockies are huge and grand. However, the Rockies are just one of the Earth's great mountain ranges. Wide bands of mountains cross all the continents. Those mountain ranges affect the Earth's climates and the directions in which its rivers flow. They also hold many of the Earth's valuable minerals and metals.

Snow and glaciers cover many of the Earth's highest mountain peaks, and powerful winds rush between them. Mountain land is steep and rocky, making travel difficult. Yet people have lived in mountain regions for thousands of years. They have learned to adapt to their mountain environment.

Long-haired oxen called yaks are used as pack animals by many people who live in the Himalayas.

THE HIMALAYAS

The Himalayas (hih•muh•LAY•uhz) are the world's highest mountain range. The Himalayas lie across southern Asia between the countries of China and India. They stand like a giant wall 5 miles (8 km) high. Mount Everest, the world's highest mountain, is in the Himalayas. It is 29,028 feet (8,848 m) high. The name *Himalaya* comes from an ancient word meaning "house of snow." This name tells something about these mountains. Because they are so high, many of their peaks are bitterly cold and covered with snow all year long.

Chapter 12 • **405**

There is not yet much modern transportation in the Himalayas, so travel there is still difficult. Because passes between the mountains are very high, snow often blocks them. A boy who traveled through one of the passes wrote, "The cold was cruel, and it was dangerous all the time."

People do live high in the Himalayas, however. Among these people are the Sherpas. The Sherpas live in the country of Nepal. They grow crops such as potatoes, rice, and soybeans on the mountain slopes. They also herd animals.

For many of their needs, the Sherpas depend on long-haired oxen called yaks. Tilen, a Sherpa, says, "Life would be impossible here without the yaks. They give yogurt and cheese, butter for tea, hide for shoes, wool for blankets. . . . They carry our loads. They take care of us."

Yaks have long, thick coats that help them live in the cold mountains.

✓ **What is the world's highest mountain range?**

THE ALPS

The Alps cross southern Europe. They are Europe's largest mountain range. Many people who live in the Alps farm and herd animals. They graze sheep, goats, and cattle on grassy mountain slopes. They use plows pulled by horses to till land that is too steep for tractors.

Dairy farmers in the Alps have adapted to their mountain environment in still another way. They have set up pipes to carry their cows' milk down to the villages in the valleys below. Some of the pipes are miles long!

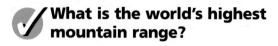

MOUNTAINS OF THE WORLD

LOCATION Mountain ranges cross all the continents. This map shows some of the world's largest mountain ranges.
■ On which continent are the Himalayas?

This house in Switzerland is typical of the houses built in the Alps.

A lot of snow falls in the Alps each winter. If it piled up on the roofs of the houses, the roofs would break. So people build their houses with steep roofs. That way the snow slides off.

For many years the Alps stood as barriers to travel in Europe. They separated people who lived on one side of a mountain from people who lived on the other side. Because of these barriers, people developed different customs, traditions, and languages. The small country of Switzerland has three national languages—German, French, and Italian.

Today dozens of highways and railroads cut through the Alps. This allows people to earn their living in many ways. People have used the Alps' forests to build a large lumber industry. Unlike the mountains in the United States, the Alps have few mineral resources.

✓ **How did the Alps affect people's languages in Switzerland?**

THE ATLAS MOUNTAINS

The Atlas Mountains lie across northwestern Africa. To the south of the mountains is the Sahara, the world's largest desert. Just as mountains in the western part of the United States keep moisture from reaching deserts there, the Atlas Mountains prevent moist winds from reaching the Sahara.

On the side of the Atlas Mountains nearest to the Atlantic and Mediterranean coasts, the climate is pleasant. There are

LEARNING FROM GRAPHS
■ Which mountain is taller, Kilimanjaro or Elbrus?

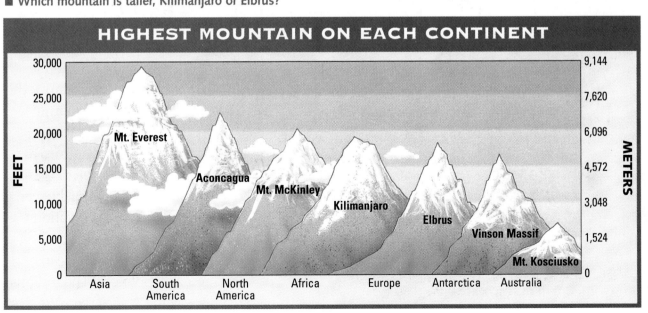

HIGHEST MOUNTAIN ON EACH CONTINENT

several small cities. At higher elevations there are even ski resorts.

The southern slopes of the Atlas Mountains, however, are mostly dry and rocky. Very little can grow there. The people who live in that arid region have small farms in the valleys, or they graze sheep and goats where plants can grow. Others mine phosphate and iron.

✓ **What desert formed because of the Atlas Mountains?**

THE ANDES MOUNTAINS

The Andes (AN•deez) Mountains lie along the whole length of South America near the Pacific coast. The Andes are the world's longest mountain range.

The Andes are also among the world's youngest mountains. Like the Rocky Mountains, they are high, rugged, and steep. Wind and water have not yet worn down their peaks. Some of the Andes

The Quechuas build rock walls up to 15 feet (5 m) high as part of terraces that prevent erosion on farmland. From far away, these terraces look like steps.

Mountains are more than 20,000 feet (6,096 m) high. Many are volcanoes.

Among the Andes are many high, dry plateaus. People have lived on these lands for thousands of years. One group that lives there is the Quechua (KEH•chuh•wuh) Indians.

Most Quechuas herd animals and farm. Farming, however, is difficult in the Andes. Water is scarce, and the soil is rocky. To grow crops on their steep mountain land, the Quechuas have built terraces. A **terrace** is a flat "shelf" dug into a mountainside.

The few crops that can grow at high elevations are a grain called quínoa (KEE•noh•wah), beans, and potatoes. The Indians of the Andes were the first

These Quechua women gather at an outdoor market in Cuzco, Peru. Notice the women's hats. In the Quechuan culture each village has its own style of hat.

people to grow potatoes, which are still their most important food.

The Quechuas have learned how to keep potatoes from spoiling. They leave the potatoes on the ground to freeze at night and dry in the sun the next day. After several days and nights, the dried potatoes are ground into a meal called *chuña* (CHOON•ya). *Chuña* keeps for many months.

An animal called the llama (LAH•muh) is important in Quechuan life. The llama looks a little like a camel without a hump. Its coat provides wool for clothing and blankets. The llama is also an excellent pack animal. It can carry heavy loads over long distances through the mountains.

The Quechuas often use llamas to carry goods to market. A Quechuan market can be an exciting place to visit. People wear brightly colored ponchos. A poncho is a blanket with a hole in the middle that the wearer's head slips through. The women wear different styles of hats, depending on the village they come from.

This Quechua girl leads her family's llama. The llama is the most important animal to the people of the Andes.

For many years the Quechuas traded for the goods they needed by bartering. **Bartering** is trading one kind of good for another without using money. Today, however, the Quechuas use money to buy goods. More Quechuas are now using trucks and railroads to take their goods to market.

Many Quechuas work in mines. The Andes are rich in natural resources. Silver, tin, and copper are some of the important metals mined in the Andes.

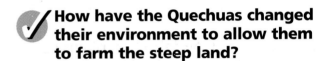

How have the Quechuas changed their environment to allow them to farm the steep land?

LESSON 4 REVIEW

Check Understanding

1. **Recall the Facts**   What is the world's longest mountain range?
2. **Focus on the Main Idea**   How have people in mountain regions around the world adapted to their environment?

Think Critically

3. **Think More About It**   How are modern communication and transportation changing life in the world's mountain regions?

Show What You Know

Table Activity   Make a table to compare the Andes, Alps, Atlas, Himalaya, Rocky, and Appalachian mountains. First, divide a sheet of paper into two columns. Then, write the names of the mountain ranges in the first column. Write facts about each one in the second column. Compare your table with those made by classmates.

CONNECT MAIN IDEAS

Use this organizer to show that you understand how the chapter's main ideas are connected. First copy the organizer onto a separate sheet of paper. Then complete it by writing two sentences about each main idea.

The Western Mountains

Mountain ranges in the United States are alike and different.

1. _____
2. _____

Mountains have affected transportation and communication in the United States.

1. _____
2. _____

People depend on the West's natural resources.

1. _____
2. _____

Mountains Around the World
People in mountain regions around the world have adapted to their environment.

1. _____
2. _____

WRITE MORE ABOUT IT

1. **Write a News Report** Imagine that you are a television news reporter. Your station has asked you to report on the volcanic eruption of Mount St. Helens, in Washington. Write what you will say in your news report. Tell how the mountain has changed as a result of the eruption.

2. **Write a Short Story** Write a short story about someone who travels to the West to mine gold. In your story, tell why that person decided to leave his or her home in the East to search for gold. Then describe what life is like for that person in a mining boomtown.

USE VOCABULARY

Write a term from this list to complete each of the sentences that follow.

bartering   timberline
Continental Divide trade-off
opportunity cost   volcano

1. A _____ is an opening in the Earth's surface from which hot gases, ashes, and lava may pour out.

2. Rivers that form in the Rocky Mountains flow east or west from an imaginary line called the _____.

3. Above the _____, temperatures are too low for trees to grow.

4. A _____ is giving something up in order to get something else.

5. The value of what a person gives up to get something else is the _____.

6. _____ is trading one kind of good for another without using money.

CHECK UNDERSTANDING

1. How is the shape of older mountains different from the shape of newer mountains?

2. Why was the transcontinental railroad built? How did it change travel?

3. Why do most mountain regions have few people, compared with other kinds of regions?

4. Why is there a large lumber industry in the Pacific Northwest?

5. How do ranchers depend on public land in the West?

6. Why have the Quechuas built terraces in the Andes Mountains?

THINK CRITICALLY

1. **Think More About It**   Why do you think people were willing to risk their lives to explore unknown lands?

2. **Link to You**   Satellites can send signals almost instantly to any place on the Earth. How does this technology help you understand current events?

APPLY SKILLS

How to Use a Road Map and a Mileage Table   Use the road map shown on page 396 and the mileage table shown on page 397 to answer these questions. For each question, explain whether you used the road map or the mileage table to find the answer.

1. How many miles is it from Colorado Springs to Boulder?

2. How many miles is it from Grand Junction to Montrose?

How to Form Conclusions and Predict Outcomes   Imagine that your best friend is standing in the hallway with your teacher, the principal, a newspaper reporter, and a photographer. You know that your friend recently entered a national contest for student poetry. What conclusion might you form? What predictions might you make?

READ MORE ABOUT IT

Jack Creek Cowboy by Neil Johnson. Dial. Ten-year-old Justin Whitlock helps his father on the Pitchfork Ranch in Wyoming.

Sierra by Diane Siebert. HarperCollins. The verses of this poem describe the beauty and glory of the Sierra Nevada.

THE PACIFIC COAST AND ISLANDS

> 66 Hawaiian rainbows, white clouds roll by,
> You show your colors against the sky.
> Hawaiian rainbows, it seems to me,
> Reach from the mountains down to the sea. 99
>
> from "Hawaiian Rainbows,"
> a Hawaiian folk song

A Hawaiian girl in traditional dress

ALONG THE PACIFIC COAST

*L*ink to Our World

Why are there such great differences along the same coast?

Focus on the Main Idea
As you read, look for ways in which places along the Pacific coast of the United States are alike and ways in which they are different.

Preview Vocabulary
fjord
earthquake
hunters and gatherers
aluminum
ecosystem

California sea lions, like this one, live along the rocky Pacific coast.

All coastal lands touch the sea, but the climates and landforms along a coast can be very different from place to place. Where people choose to live and how they use the land can be different, too.

A VARIED LANDSCAPE

The Pacific coast of the United States stretches north from Mexico to Canada. It borders the states of California, Oregon, and Washington. Farther north it borders Alaska. The island state of Hawaii lies about 2,400 miles (3,862 km) off the Pacific coast. Because these five states border the Pacific Ocean, they are sometimes called the Pacific states.

The Pacific coast covers a great distance, so the climate and landforms along it are very different. The southern coast of Alaska is cold and wet for much of the year. In Kodiak (KOH•dee•ak), a small town on an island off the coast, the average July temperature is just 50°F (10°C). This cold air is also very wet. Many places in Alaska receive as much as 100 inches (254 cm) of precipitation a year.

Alaska's southern coast has many bays and inlets. High cliffs jut out into the Pacific Ocean, forming fjords (fee•AWRDZ). A **fjord** is a narrow inlet of the ocean between cliffs. Steep mountains go right down to the shore. These mountains are part of the Alaska Range. Mount McKinley, North America's highest mountain, is part of this range.

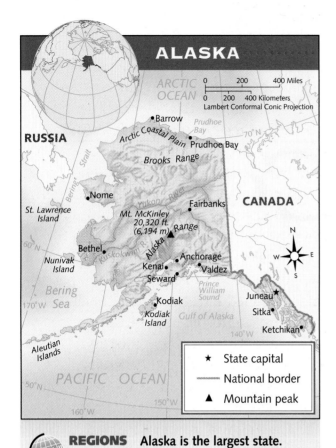

ALASKA

ARCTIC OCEAN

RUSSIA

0 200 400 Miles
0 200 400 Kilometers
Lambert Conformal Conic Projection

• Barrow

Arctic Coastal Plain
Prudhoe Bay
• Prudhoe Bay

70°N

Brooks Range

CANADA

• Nome

• Fairbanks

St. Lawrence Island

Yukon River

Mt. McKinley
20,320 ft.
(6,194 m) ▲ Range

Alaska Range

60°N

Bethel •

Kuskokwim

• Anchorage

Kenai •
• Valdez

Nunivak Island

Seward •

Prince William Sound

170°W

Bering Sea

• Kodiak

Juneau ★

Kodiak Island

Gulf of Alaska

Sitka •

Ketchikan •

140°W

Aleutian Islands

50°N

PACIFIC OCEAN

160°W

150°W

★ State capital
⬚ National border
▲ Mountain peak

REGIONS Alaska is the largest state.
■ What islands make up the most western part of the state?

The city of San Diego, California, lies more than 2,000 miles (3,219 km) south of Kodiak. San Diego is warm and dry. The

average July temperature is 70°F (21°C). Winter temperatures do not often fall below freezing. Rainfall averages about 10 inches (25 cm) a year.

San Diego is built on a large natural harbor. Most of southern California, however, has a smooth coastline. Los Angeles, the largest city and busiest port on the Pacific coast of the United States, lies about 120 miles (193 km) north of San Diego. Los Angeles has no natural harbor. Instead, workers made a harbor by piling up huge stone blocks to form an ocean wall 9 miles (14 km) long. Behind this wall, ships can dock in calm waters.

Near the coast of southern California are the Coast Ranges. Few trees grow on these mountains because the climate is too dry. Farther inland is the Mojave (moh•HAH•vay) Desert. In the Mojave is Death Valley, a place American Indians called "ground on fire." Death Valley is one of the hottest and driest places in the United States. In fact, the longest time without rain ever recorded in the United States—760 days—was in Death Valley!

Cities, such as Laguna (luh•GOO•nuh) Beach (above), line most of southern California's coast. The ocean's high waves make surfing a favorite pastime there.

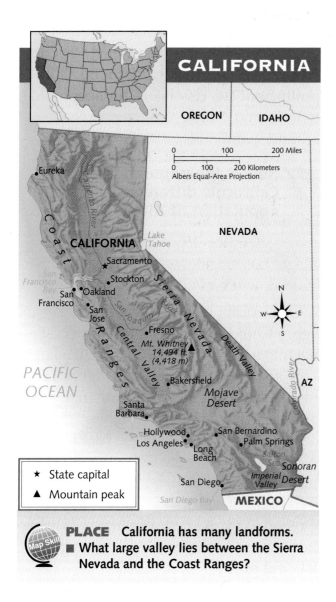

CALIFORNIA

OREGON

IDAHO

Eureka

0   100   200 Miles
0   100   200 Kilometers
Albers Equal-Area Projection

NEVADA

Lake Tahoe

CALIFORNIA

Sacramento

Stockton

San Francisco Bay

San Francisco

Oakland

San Jose

Fresno

Mt. Whitney 14,494 ft. (4,418 m)

PACIFIC OCEAN

Bakersfield

Mojave Desert

Santa Barbara

Hollywood
Los Angeles
Long Beach

San Bernardino
Palm Springs

Salton Sea

Sonoran Desert

San Diego

Imperial Valley

AZ

San Diego Bay

MEXICO

★ State capital
▲ Mountain peak

PLACE California has many landforms.
■ What large valley lies between the Sierra
Nevada and the Coast Ranges?

At 282 feet (86 m) below sea level, Death
Valley is also the lowest point in the
Western Hemisphere.

How do climates differ along the Pacific coast?

A SHAKY LAND

The land and climate along the southern coast of California are very different
from those farther north. Yet all places
along the Pacific coast share a danger—
earthquakes. An **earthquake** is a sudden
shaking of the ground. Earthquakes are
caused by the movement and cracking of
layers of rock deep inside the Earth.

Each year many small earthquakes
shake the Pacific coast. Often people do
not even feel them. Large earthquakes,
however, can cause major damage. The
shaking of the ground can cause buildings, bridges, and homes to fall down.

In recent years major earthquakes have
shaken several California cities, including
San Francisco and Los Angeles. Buildings
there are built to help protect against
earthquakes, but damage still happens. A
woman who lived in a second-floor apartment recalled the earthquake that shook
southern California in 1994. First, she
heard a loud crack. Then, the dining area
of her apartment moved downward. "I
felt a sensation of falling," she said. "But
until I actually saw what was on the outside, I really was not aware that it had
totally crushed the first floor."

What danger do places along the Pacific coast share?

This interstate highway in Northridge, California, was
destroyed by the earthquake that shook southern
California in 1994.

Instead of crowded cities, Alaska's coast has mostly small fishing villages, such as Sitka (above).

WHERE PEOPLE LIVE

People have lived along the Pacific coast for thousands of years. When Spanish explorers first sailed along the California coast in 1542, the land there was already densely populated by different groups of American Indians. Few people, however, lived in Alaska.

This pattern of settlement continues today. California has more people than any other state. Alaska, which is far bigger in area, has few people. In fact, only Wyoming and Vermont have fewer people.

As in most areas, population along the Pacific coast is not spread out evenly. Some places have many more people than other places. More than 15 million people live in the Los Angeles metropolitan area. The whole state of Alaska, on the other hand, has fewer than 700,000 people.

Many people like to live in Alaska because it is not crowded. One Alaskan gold miner was upset when just 40 people moved into his area to drill for oil. "I'll be pulling out any day now," he is reported to have said. "Too . . . many people around here."

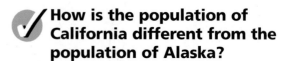 **How is the population of California different from the population of Alaska?**

FISH, TREES, AND FACTORIES

On a spring day more than 500 years ago, a Chinook (shuh•NUK) Indian cast a net into a mighty river and caught a large king salmon. He carried the fish back to his village, and the people gathered around to roast it.

The Chinooks lived in the Pacific Northwest, where the Columbia River meets the Pacific Ocean. That area is now part of the states of Washington and Oregon. As you know, ocean winds bring heavy rains to these states. Forests grow tall and thick.

The Chinooks did not farm the wet mountain land around them. Instead, they were hunters and gatherers. **Hunters and gatherers** are people who meet their food needs by hunting and gathering instead of by farming. In the

The chinook, also called the king salmon, is the largest kind of salmon. Chinooks are often 3 feet (1 m) long and weigh as much as 22 pounds (10 kg).

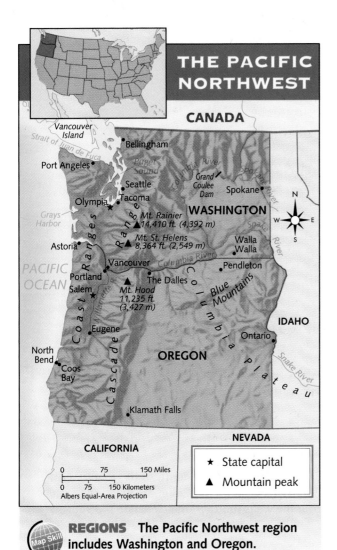

THE PACIFIC NORTHWEST

CANADA

Vancouver Island

Strait of Juan de Fuca

Bellingham

Port Angeles

Puget Sound

Seattle
Tacoma
Olympia ★

Grand Coulee Dam

Spokane

Spokane River

WASHINGTON

▲ Mt. Rainier 14,410 ft. (4,392 m)

Grays Harbor

Coast Ranges

Astoria

▲ Mt. St. Helens 8,364 ft. (2,549 m)

Walla Walla

Snake River

PACIFIC OCEAN

Vancouver

Columbia River

Pendleton

Portland
Salem ★

▲ Mt. Hood 11,235 ft. (3,427 m)

The Dalles

Blue Mountains

IDAHO

Eugene

Cascade Range

Willamette River

Columbia Plateau

Ontario

Snake River

North Bend

Coos Bay

OREGON

Klamath Falls

CALIFORNIA

NEVADA

| 0 | 75 | 150 Miles |
| 0 | 75 | 150 Kilometers |

Albers Equal-Area Projection

★ State capital
▲ Mountain peak

 REGIONS The Pacific Northwest region includes Washington and Oregon.
■ What river separates those two states?

forests, the rivers, and the ocean, the Chinooks found everything they needed.

Today many people who live along the Pacific coast still use the rivers, the forests, and the ocean to earn their living. Fishing is an important industry up and down the coast. Alaska leads all the other states in the amount of fish caught. In parts of Alaska, nearly everyone depends on the fishing industry in some way. In other places, lumbering is more important.

Fish also swim in Puget (PYOO•juht) Sound, a large inlet in northwestern Washington. Seattle, the state's largest city, lies on Puget Sound. Yet few workers there earn their living from fishing.

Instead, most workers have jobs in other industries.

Like many other cities near the Pacific Northwest coast, Seattle began as a port for shipping lumber. Today Seattle still ships large amounts of wood products. Workers at sawmills cut logs from nearby forests into lumber. Other workers use the wood to make furniture, paper, and other wood products.

Computer software, ships, and airplanes are also made in Seattle. In fact, many people around the world fly in airplanes made in and near Seattle. Aluminum (uh•LOO•muh•nuhm) is manufactured in Seattle, too. **Aluminum** is a metal used to make things that need to be strong and light, like airplane parts.

✓ **What are some leading products manufactured in and near Seattle?**

The state of Washington is the country's leading manufacturer of jet airplanes.

HYDROELECTRIC POWER

Factories in the Pacific Northwest use huge amounts of electricity. That electricity is produced by dams built across the Columbia River and its tributaries. The largest dam is the Grand Coulee Dam. It makes more electricity than any other dam in the United States.

Dams produce low-cost electricity, but every dam that is built also affects a river's ecosystem. An **ecosystem** is the relationship between living things and their nonliving environment. When a dam is built across a river, the reservoir behind it floods the land. The dam also affects the ecosystem downstream. The dam allows only so much water to flow through the river's channel. It can also threaten the fish that live in the river. Pacific salmon are a good example.

Pacific salmon live mostly in salt water, except at birth and death. Salmon hatch in a freshwater lake or river. Then, as young fish, they swim downstream to the sea.

When the salmon reach adulthood, they return to the place where they were born to spawn, or lay their eggs. Salmon sometimes swim hundreds of miles upstream just to reach that spot. Often they must jump shallow rapids or low waterfalls along the way.

Millions of Pacific salmon once followed the Columbia River upstream to spawn. One early settler wrote, "So thick were they that often, in riding a horse across at the ford, I have been compelled to get off and drive them away before my horse would go across."

Then came the dams. Not even the biggest salmon could leap them. The number of salmon in the river went down sharply.

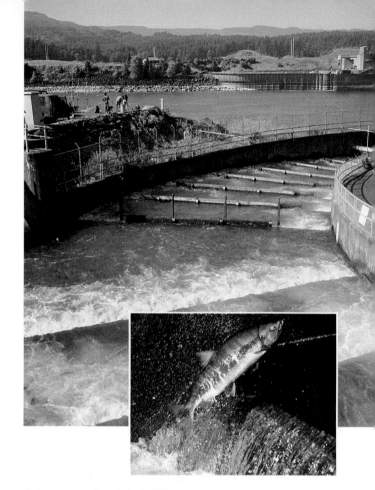

Salmon use this fish ladder (top) to swim past the Bonneville Dam on the Columbia River. They jump over the walls (bottom) that separate the pools.

To help the salmon get past the many dams on the river, people built fish ladders. A fish ladder is a group of pools of water like steps. Fish can either jump over the walls that separate the pools, or they can swim through openings in the walls. Using a fish ladder, the fish can go higher and higher until they reach the reservoir behind a dam.

Fish ladders help salmon get past many dams. But some dams, like the Grand Coulee, are much too tall for fish ladders. In those areas salmon that have been raised in tanks are put into the rivers.

 Where does the electricity used in the sawmills and factories in the Pacific Northwest come from?

THE LEADER IN MANUFACTURING

Hydroelectric power has helped turn many cities in the Pacific Northwest into manufacturing centers. The country's leading manufacturing state, however, is California. Its cities are crowded with factories that make many kinds of products, from computers to airplanes to movies. Hollywood, a part of Los Angeles, is the movie capital of the world.

Like the other Pacific states, California is rich in natural resources. Both petroleum and natural gas are found along the state's southern coast. Borax, a mineral used to make such products as laundry soap and glass, is mined in its desert areas.

Which state leads the country in manufacturing?

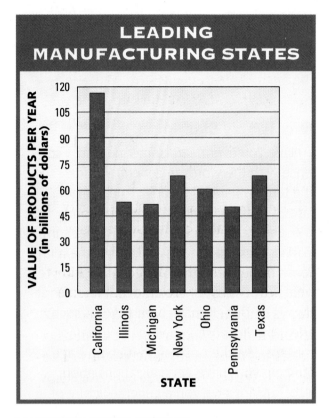

LEADING MANUFACTURING STATES

VALUE OF PRODUCTS PER YEAR (in billions of dollars)

STATE

California, Illinois, Michigan, New York, Ohio, Pennsylvania, Texas

LEARNING FROM GRAPHS
■ Which state produces about $60 billion of products each year?

Hollywood's Walk of Fame attracts thousands of tourists each year.

LESSON 1 REVIEW

Check Understanding

1. **Recall the Facts** Why are earthquakes dangerous?
2. **Focus on the Main Idea** How are places along the Pacific coast of the United States alike and how are they different?

Think Critically

3. **Think More About It** Why do you think more people choose to live in California than in Alaska?

Show What You Know

Art Activity Draw a picture that shows a place along the Pacific coast. Draw a second picture to show how another place along the coast is different.

Chapter 13 • **419**

Make a Generalization

Why Is This Skill Important?

Have you ever heard someone start a sentence with the words *In general, I think . . .?* The term *in general* means "true in most cases." It often begins a generalization.

A **generalization** is a statement that summarizes a group of facts and shows the relationships between them. A generalization tells what is true most of the time, but it may not always be true. It may contain words such as *often, many, most, generally,* or *usually*.

Maps, like the population map on page 421, can help you make generalizations about places. Maps give you a general picture of a place. They tell you such things as where most cities are located and where most people live.

Settlement Patterns Along the Pacific Coast

As you know, population along the Pacific coast is not spread out evenly. As in other regions of the United States, some places along the Pacific coast have many crowded cities and are densely populated. Other places,

however, are mostly rural areas with small towns or farms.

In southern California much of the state's population is in two large population centers—San Diego and Los Angeles. So many towns and cities surround Los Angeles that it is hard to tell where one town ends and another one begins.

Los Angeles is our country's second-largest metropolitan area. Why have so many people come to live in the Los Angeles area? Many have come for its pleasant, sunny climate and beautiful beaches. Others have come for jobs in its many businesses and factories.

In northern California most people live in one of the large cities built on the rolling hills around or near San Francisco Bay. These cities include San Francisco, Oakland, and San Jose. San Francisco is one of the country's busiest ports. Besides being an important business center, the San Francisco area draws thousands of tourists each year.

As in California the population in the Pacific Northwest is centered around large cities. In Oregon many people live in Portland or in one of the other cities along the Willamette (wuh•LA•muht) River. In the state of Washington, most people live in Seattle and other cities along Puget Sound.

The sprawling city of Los Angeles has little open land left.

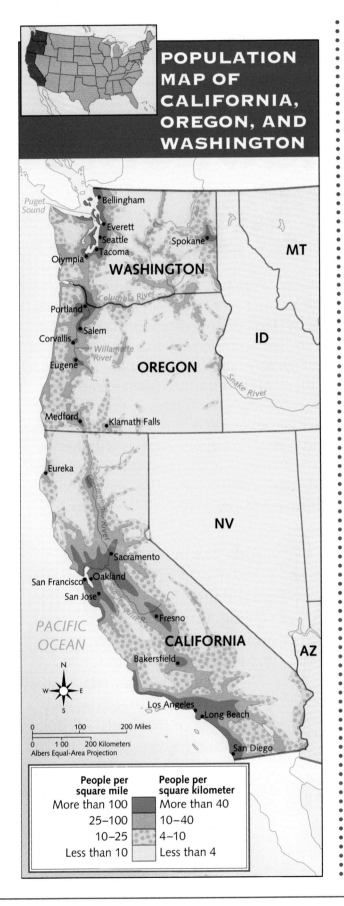

POPULATION MAP OF CALIFORNIA, OREGON, AND WASHINGTON

Bellingham
Puget Sound
Everett
Seattle
Spokane
Olympia
Tacoma
WASHINGTON
MT
Columbia River
Portland
Corvallis
Salem
ID
Willamette River
Eugene
OREGON
Snake River
Medford
Klamath Falls
Eureka
NV
Sacramento
San Francisco
Oakland
San Jose
Fresno
PACIFIC OCEAN
CALIFORNIA
Bakersfield
AZ
Los Angeles
Long Beach
San Diego

N
W E
S

0   100   200 Miles
0   1 00   200 Kilometers
Albers Equal-Area Projection

People per square mile	People per square kilometer
More than 100	More than 40
25–100	10–40
10–25	4–10
Less than 10	Less than 4

Understand the Process

Study the population map on this page. It shows settlement patterns in the states of California, Oregon, and Washington. By studying this map you can make some generalizations about where most of the people in California, Oregon, and Washington live.

1. Look at the map's key. What is the highest population density shown on the map? What is the lowest population density shown on the map?
2. Now look at the main part of the map. Where is the population density generally the greatest in all three states? From that observation you can state a generalization—*Most people in the states of California, Oregon, and Washington live in or near large cities.*
3. Look at the map again. Is the population density generally greatest in the eastern or the western part of each state?
4. Think about the geography of California and the Pacific Northwest. What large body of water borders all three states on the west? What generalization can you make about the population density near the coast as compared with the population density farther inland? Why do you think that is so?
5. By looking at the map, what other generalizations can you make about settlement patterns in the three states?

Think and Apply

Compare the population map on this page with the population density map of the United States on page A14. What generalizations can you make about settlement patterns in the United States? How do they compare with the settlement patterns in California, Oregon, and Washington?

BUILDING CITIZENSHIP

LESSON 2

LEARN with LITERATURE

Focus on Culture

Anna's Athabaskan Summer

BY Arnold Griese

ILLUSTRATED BY Charles Ragins

The Athabaskan (a·thuh·BAS·kuhn) Indians have lived along the Yukon River in Alaska for generations. In recent years, though, their life has changed a lot. Today they live in modern houses, and their children go to school, just as you do. Yet they keep many of their traditions alive. Each summer they fish for salmon in the river and gather berries along its banks. Read now about a girl named Anna, who travels with her family to their fish camp on the river. As you read, think about how life has stayed the same for Anna's family and how it has changed.

My world of winter is a world of snow, and of cold, and of darkness. It is a beautiful time, but for me it is a time of waiting. Waiting for the sun to warm the earth and to bring life again to our frozen land.

Then come warm days, pussy willows, melting snow, and the sound of birds. All this, and the breakup of the ice on the river, tell me spring has come again. The days go by quickly now, like the shadow of a soaring hawk. Soon school will be out.

One day Father takes Mother, Grandmother, Pup, and me in his boat to our summer fish camp. Mother says our people, the Athabaskan Indians, have always come to this place in the summer. Here fish swim close to the shore, big berries grow on the hillside, and soft winds off the water blow the mosquitoes away.

When the boat touches the beach, I jump out and climb the hill, then sit, resting. A fox runs past, carrying food to its family. Far away, the mountain we call "Denali" stands tall in the clear air. In front of me the river flows forever.

Mother's call stops my dreaming, and I hurry back to the beach. The open door, curling smoke from the stove pipe, and the rattle of pans are all signs. Work is waiting. But today I want to play. Then I remember Mother is going to have a baby. I smile and go inside.

In the busy days that follow, many things are done. Mother and I clean the house. We put food from town in the cache where animals cannot get it. Grandmother lays out a moose hide to be worked on.

cache (kash) a safe place to keep something

After going back to town to get the dogs, Father moves the fish wheel out into the fast current. Water gurgles as it pushes against the paddles that turn the wheel. The wheel groans and creaks as it moves.

Soon, the first swimming salmon will be scooped up on one of the baskets and dropped into the fish box. Then the hard work I do not like starts. The fish must be cleaned.

Now empty drying racks stand waiting. Father's dogs are tied close by to keep bears away. Everything is ready. It is time for father to leave. His hand rumples my hair as we walk to the boat. He and my older brother both have jobs in town.

Grandmother is scraping the moose hide as I walk toward the house. I see that now it is hard for her to do the work she loves.

Mother calls from the smokehouse and I go to her. "There is not much work to do today," she says. "Take Grandmother to the place she loves and sit with her."

smokehouse a building where smoke from a fire is used to preserve meat or fish

Grandmother and I go. While we sit looking down on our summer home, two ravens call to each other as they tumble through the air.

Grandmother looks up and says, "Old Grandfather, bring us luck."

"Why do you say that, Grandmother?"

She answers, "Our people say that Raven made the world. That, even though he plays tricks, he can bring luck."

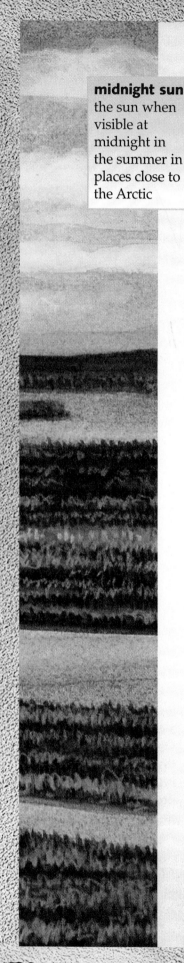

The sun warms me as I watch the ravens. "What luck will they bring?" I ask myself.

Late that same night, while the midnight sun is low in the sky, I watch as the fish wheel scoops up the first summer salmon. It flops down into the waiting box. There the salmon's strong tail pounds against the sides.

Long ago, our people would hold a feast for the first salmon. It meant more were coming. These salmon would supply food for the long winter to come.

Soon after, our fish box fills. Grandmother rests while she watches us clean fish during these long days of summer.

While I work, there is time to think. I hope the baby growing inside Mother is a girl. I could show a little sister the things I am learning from Mother.

One day I ask Mother, "Grandmother says we must show respect for all living things. Then why do we catch and kill the salmon?"

Mother brushes hair from her face and answers, "Our people believe living things die gladly for us. But we must show respect by killing only what we need and by returning to the river fish bones and other things we cannot eat."

After many days of hard work, the fish wheel brings us fewer salmon. Now Grandmother and I can walk to the hillside where big blueberries wait to be picked. The sun warms our backs as we kneel and pull the berries into our buckets. Grandmother watches as some of the berries find their way into my mouth. The quiet is broken as we laugh. It is good to hear Grandmother laugh the way she used to.

Once while we are picking blueberries, Grandmother puts her hand on my shoulder. I look up, and her eyes tell me not to move. She whispers, "A bear eats berries and does not see us."

Grandmother's hand stays on my shoulder as we crawl back slowly. Today the berries belong to the bear.

Early one morning, rain falling on the tin roof wakes me. Low gray clouds fill the sky. The air is chilly. I snuggle back under the covers.

After a while I go to walk in the rain. Ripe, red cranberries hang on the bushes along the bank. Their sweet smell fills the air.

Now, as Grandmother and I pick cranberries, the sky is deep blue, the air smells different, and the days grow shorter. The nights are dark again. Summer is ending.

Not many mornings later it comes—the cry of geese. I leave my warm bed and stand outside the door. In the sky, long lines of geese call to each other as they fly to warmer places.

The pebbles are cold under my bare feet as I walk to the beach. A spruce hen flies up. The leaves on the birch tree where it lands have turned golden.

That night, while Mother packs, I walk with Grandmother along the water in the soft light of a full moon. The warm glow from Mother's lamp shines through the window. It brings a special stillness. The soft sound of an owl's call floats through the air.

We go inside and I ask Grandmother, "Why does summer have to end?"

She answers, "Summer will come again as it always has since our people have lived by this river and fished on its banks." She stops, then adds, "Nothing ends. Someday I will leave you. But that is not the end. I will always be a part of your life."

I walk over and give her a hard hug. She holds me close for a long time.

The next morning, the sound of a motor from across the river reaches my ears. This time Father will take us home. Summer is over. It does not take long to load our things.

Bundled in my warm jacket, I take one last look at our summer home. But the sadness leaves me as I hold Grandmother tight.

When summer comes again we will come back and bring someone new. Someone I can teach about the ways of our people.

Literature Review

1. How has life stayed the same for Anna's family, and how has it changed?

2. In the story Grandmother teaches Anna about their family's beliefs and traditions. What kinds of things have you learned from members of your family?

3. Think about something that has changed in your life. Write a story about that change.

PROTECTING THE COASTAL ENVIRONMENT

Link to Our World

How can people work to protect the environment in coastal regions?

Focus on the Main Idea
Read to find out how people have both damaged the Pacific coast environment and worked to protect it.

Preview Vocabulary
tundra
oil slick
volunteer
wetlands
wildlife refuge

People who live near coasts depend on the resources around them in many ways. As people use those resources, they change the environment. Sometimes they damage it. However, people also work together to protect the coastal environment.

A COLD LAND

The northernmost part of Alaska is part of the Arctic Coastal Plain. This plain, much of which is tundra, stretches along the Arctic Ocean. **Tundra** is flat land without trees that stays frozen most of the year. In summer the top few inches of soil thaw and turn into a grassy marsh.

Most of the people who live along the Arctic coast call themselves Inupiat (ih•NOO•pee•aht) or Inuit (IH•nu•wuht). Both of these names mean "the people." The ancestors of the Inupiat and the Inuit were among the first people to live on the tundra of the Arctic Coastal Plain.

Beneath much of the tundra lies oil, Alaska's most valuable resource. In fact, Prudhoe (PROO•doh) Bay, which lies on the Arctic coast, is at the center of one of the world's major oil-producing areas. The huge Trans-Alaska Pipeline carries oil from Prudhoe Bay 800 miles (1,287 km) south to Valdez (val•DEEZ), a port on Prince William Sound.

An Inuit carving of a polar bear, an animal native to the Arctic Coastal Plain

✓ What kind of land is found on the Arctic Coastal Plain?

The Trans-Alaska Pipeline

The Trans-Alaska Pipeline carries about 1.5 million barrels of oil each day. The pipeline crosses three mountain ranges and hundreds of rivers.

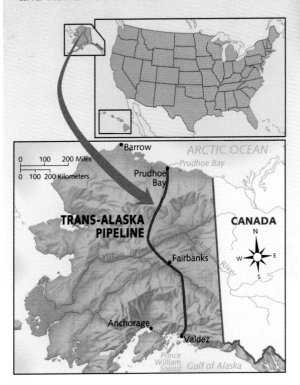

TRANS-ALASKA PIPELINE

Over the next few hours, almost 11 million gallons (42 million L) of oil poured into Prince William Sound. The oil polluted the water and killed fish and other animals. Much of the oil floated to the top of the water and formed an oil slick. An **oil slick** is the film of oil that coats the water after an oil spill. Strong winds and high waves swept the oil onto land. In time more than 1,200 miles (1,931 km) of beaches were covered with sticky oil.

✓ **How can oil from an oil spill harm a coastal environment?**

DANGEROUS WATERS

When oil tankers leave Valdez, they must pass by a sharp, rocky reef. This reef is called Bligh (BLY) Reef. It lies about 25 feet (8 m) under the waters of Prince William Sound. A reef can tear holes in the hulls, or bodies, of tankers and other ships. That is why a red light floats above Bligh Reef, warning ships away.

Just after midnight on March 24, 1989, the oil tanker *Exxon Valdez* came too close to Bligh Reef—much too close. The ship crashed into the reef and came to a stop. At that moment the most damaging oil spill in United States history began.

An oil-covered buoy with a red warning light on top

Workers used high-pressure sprayers to clean oil from the rocks along the shore of Hunter Island, in Prince William Sound.

A HELPING HAND

The ship's owners hired workers to clean up the oil. On beach after beach, the workers used shovels, hoses, and many other tools to try to clean up the mess. It took a long time, however, and the workers could not clean many spoiled beaches for months.

Some people got tired of waiting for the workers. They believed that as citizens they had a duty to help clean up the environment. So, working alone or in groups, hundreds of people began to help. One volunteer (vah•luhn•TIR) was Billy Day. A **volunteer** is a person who offers to do something without pay.

Soon after the spill Billy Day walked along Gore Point, a beach about 250 miles (402 km) southwest of Bligh Reef. He watched as hundreds of birds landed in the oil. He saw hundreds more washing up on shore, their bodies turned black by oil. "It was obvious to me," he said later, "that until we got this stuff picked up, we were going to have more and more dead birds. For me to just stand there and pick them up didn't seem like the right way to tackle the situation."

✓ **Why did volunteers offer to help clean up the Alaska beaches?**

Volunteers washed birds to remove the oil from their feathers. If the oil had not been removed, the birds would have died.

TAKING ACTION

Billy Day identified what the problem was—oil was polluting Gore Point and killing birds. What could he do to help solve the problem? Over the next few months, he found out.

Day noticed that in the sandy parts of Gore Point the oil could be scooped up with shovels and buckets. He spent day after day shoveling the oil-soaked sand into bags for ships to haul away. Soon other volunteers joined him.

It was harder to clean up the rocky parts of the beach. There the oil had to be washed off the rocks. That did not stop Billy Day, however. He spent $5,000 of his own money to design and build a machine that washed rocks.

Billy Day (right) built a machine (below) that he used to wash the oil from rocks.

The rock-washing machine worked! By early November, Day and the others had cleaned up about one-fourth mile (less than 1 km) of the beach. One-fourth mile does not seem like much, but it was an important start. "We realized," said Day, "that if we didn't take care of this beach, nobody was going to. I mean, it's not our mess, but it's our shoreline."

 **What did Billy Day do about the problems caused by the oil spill?**

OTHER PROBLEMS ALONG COASTS

Oil spills are not the only danger to the coastal environment. People sometimes pollute the ocean by dumping wastes into the water. Polluted water from the shore also gets into the ocean. In some places coastal waters become so polluted that people cannot use the beaches and fishing areas.

Polluted water is also a danger to animal life along beaches and in coastal wetlands. **Wetlands** are low-lying land where the water level is always near or above the surface of the land. Coastal wetlands are home to many birds and other animals.

Growth has changed the coastal environment, too. As the population has grown, more and more land has been used for buildings. Along many beaches high-rise buildings now block the ocean view. In some places people have dredged bays and filled in wetlands. In other places people have changed the natural coastline so much that some beaches have been washed away by the tides.

Over the years some people's actions have damaged the coastal environment.

At the same time, however, other people have worked for laws to help protect the coasts. The United States has made some of its coastal areas into wildlife refuges (REH•fyoo•juhz). A **wildlife refuge** is an area of land set aside to protect animals and other living things. People cannot build on land in a wildlife refuge.

Other laws help protect wetlands from development, stop the dumping of wastes into oceans, and control water pollution. One law says that most oil tankers must have thick, double hulls by the year 2015. People or businesses that break these laws can be punished.

The oil industry has taken action, too. Special ships built to clean up oil spills now follow tankers as they leave Prince William Sound. And above Bligh Reef, the warning light still shines.

✓ **What actions have people taken to help protect the coastal environment?**

LESSON 3 REVIEW

Check Understanding

1. **Recall the Facts** How can reefs damage tankers and other ships?
2. **Focus on the Main Idea** How have people both damaged the Pacific coast environment and worked to protect it?

Think Critically

3. **Personally Speaking** Do you think a citizen has a responsibility to clean up someone else's mess? Why or why not?

4. **Link to You** How have people in your community or state worked together to protect the environment?

Show What You Know

Brochure Activity Think about something that people working together could do to protect the coastal environment. Write and illustrate a brochure that asks volunteers to help with the project.

Act as a Responsible Citizen

Why Is This Skill Important?

Imagine that you are walking home from school with a few of your friends. Along the way, you pass the new park and notice some soda cans and candy wrappers on the ground. You pick them up and throw them into a garbage can. Your friends are surprised and say, "What are you doing? People get paid to do that. You shouldn't have to do it!"

By throwing the garbage away, you acted as a responsible citizen. Although government workers do many jobs, cities and states depend on their citizens to act responsibly. When a responsible citizen sees a problem, he or she takes action to help solve it. Acting responsibly is an important part of being an active citizen.

Remember What You Have Read

In the last lesson, you read about the most damaging oil spill in United States history. After the oil spill, hundreds of people acted as responsible citizens by volunteering to help clean up the mess. One of those responsible citizens was Billy Day. Think about what he did to help.

1. What problem did Billy Day notice at Gore Point after the oil spill?
2. What actions did he take to solve the problem?

Understand the Process

Acting as a responsible citizen is not always as difficult as helping to clean up after an oil spill. There are many other ways for citizens to act responsibly. They can learn about their community and state. They can take part in government and help choose wise leaders. They can do their jobs well, try to get along with other people, and work to solve community problems.

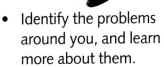

Sometimes, acting as a responsible citizen requires some special thought and action. Here are some steps that you can follow to help you act as a responsible citizen.

- Identify the problems around you, and learn more about them.
- Think about ways to solve these problems. Try to think of solutions that would be good for other people as well as for yourself.
- Decide what you can do to help, either acting alone or with other people. Then work to bring about change.
- Remember to be careful. Never try to solve a problem by risking your safety or the safety of someone else. If you cannot solve the problem yourself, get help from others, such as your family, a police officer, or a community official.

Think and Apply

Read your local newspaper to find out about a problem facing your community. Or identify a problem in your school or classroom. Use the steps above to decide how you and your classmates can act as responsible citizens.

BUILDING CITIZENSHIP

AMERICANS IN THE PACIFIC

LESSON 4

Link to Our World

How can location affect the ways of life of the people who live there?

Focus on the Main Idea
Read to find out how Hawaii's location has affected the state's history and people.

Preview Vocabulary
interest

Lava flows from Kilauea, one of the two active volcanoes in Hawaii Volcanoes National Park.

Thousands of miles off the Pacific coast, a chain of islands about 1,500 miles (2,414 km) long rises out of the water. Together these islands make up the state of Hawaii. Because Hawaii is so far away from the mainland, people who live there face special challenges. Hawaii's location has also given the state a mix of people from many backgrounds.

AN ISLAND WORLD

The state of Hawaii has eight main islands. People live on all of them except the dry and windy island of Kahoolawe (kah•hoh•uh•LAH•vay). Hawaii's 124 other islands are small and do not have fresh water.

The islands of Hawaii are really the tops of mountains that rise from the ocean floor. Volcanoes formed these mountains millions of years ago. Today only two volcanoes, Mauna Loa (MOW•nuh LOH•uh) and Kilauea (kee•low•AY•uh), are active. Both are part of Hawaii Volcanoes National Park, on the island of Hawaii, the state's largest island. *Hawaii* means "big island."

Hawaii is the state farthest south. Its temperatures are warm, but not hot. Ocean winds help cool the islands. Those same winds also bring heavy rains to parts of the islands. Mount Waialeale (wy•ah•lay•AH•lay), on the island of Kauai (KAU•eye), is the wettest place on Earth. It receives almost 40 feet (12 m) of rain a year! Other places on the islands are much drier.

 What formed the islands of Hawaii?

CROSSROADS OF THE PACIFIC

The first people to come to Hawaii were Polynesians (pah•luh•NEE•zhuhnz). They came from other islands in the Pacific more than 1,500 years ago. Guided only by the stars and the moon, they sailed to Hawaii in large canoes.

Captain James Cook was the first European to see Hawaii. This British explorer landed on Kauai in 1778. Ships from other countries soon began to visit the islands. Hawaii's location, in the middle of the Pacific between Asia and North America, made the islands a good place for trading ships to stop.

People from the United States started going to Hawaii during the 1800s. Some went to build schools and churches. Some went to start sugarcane and pineapple

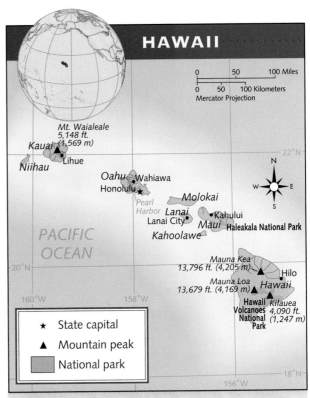

HAWAII

REGIONS This map shows the eight main islands that make up the state of Hawaii.
■ On which island is Hawaii's capital?

Beaches along the southeast coast of the island of Hawaii have black sand, formed from the lava of nearby volcanoes.

plantations. By 1900 Hawaii had become a territory of the United States. It became a state in 1959.

People from all over the world have moved to Hawaii. Many of them moved from countries in Asia, such as Japan, South Korea, and the Philippines. Because of Hawaii's location at the crossroads of the Pacific, it has a mix of cultures.

✓ **Where did many of the people who live in Hawaii come from?**

RESOURCES AND INCOME

Hawaii's warm climate allows farmers to grow sugarcane and pineapples. Other crops include coffee, macadamia nuts, and such tropical fruits as avocados and bananas. Many flowers are also grown in Hawaii for export to the mainland.

Diamond Head, an extinct volcano, towers over Honolulu's Waikiki Beach. Why do you think many tourists want to visit Hawaii?

Hula dancers, dressed in traditional grass skirts, often perform at festivals and other events in Hawaii. The hula is a Polynesian folk dance.

Hawaii has few minerals. It also has few factories, since transporting raw materials and finished products to and from the islands costs so much. One major industry on the islands is food processing.

Because of Hawaii's location, the United States government has built many military bases in Hawaii. Nearly one-fifth of the people in the state work on those bases.

Another important source of income is tourism, Hawaii's biggest industry. Millions of tourists from all over the world visit Hawaii every year.

Honolulu (hah•nuh•LOO•loo), Hawaii's largest city and capital, is the center of tourism in the state. Honolulu is on Oahu (oh•AH•hoo), Hawaii's most crowded island.

Honolulu is also a center of trade and banking. Its many banks do business in cities all over the Pacific region. Banks pay people interest when they put their money into them. **Interest** is the money a bank or a borrower pays for the use of money. In turn, the banks lend that money to other people.

Honolulu is like other port cities. It has many of the same problems that other large cities have. But Honolulu's island location makes life different from life in mainland cities. People in

Pineapple plants grow in Hawaii.

Honolulu and in other cities in Hawaii must pay more for most of the things they buy. That is because most goods have to be imported from other places, which adds to their costs.

 Why do most things cost more in Honolulu than in cities on the mainland?

GUAM

Hawaii is not the only place in the Pacific where Americans live. Some live on the island of Guam, a United States territory. Like people who live in Puerto Rico, people who live in Guam are citizens of the United States.

Guam is like Hawaii in many ways. Guam has warm weather all year. In the north the island is fairly flat, but there are mountains in the south. These mountains were formed by volcanoes.

Like Hawaii, Guam has a mix of cultures. Tourism and military bases are the two largest sources of income on the island. Many people on the island work at military bases. Many others work in hotels and restaurants, serving the

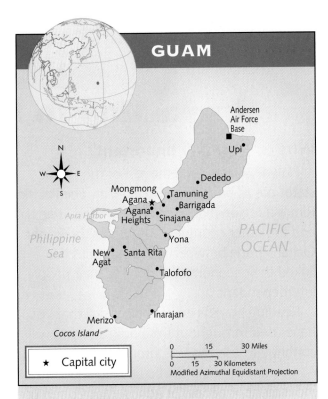

GUAM

 LOCATION Guam is an island in the Pacific Ocean. Guam became a United States territory in 1950.
■ What body of water lies to the west of Guam?

tourists who visit Guam each year. There is some farming on Guam, but it is not an important source of income.

 In what ways are Guam and Hawaii alike?

LESSON 4 REVIEW

Check Understanding

1. **Recall the Facts**   Who were the first people to settle Hawaii?
2. **Focus on the Main Idea**   How has Hawaii's location affected the state's history and people?

Think Critically

3. **Link to You**   How has the location of your state affected how you live?

Show What You Know

 **Map and Writing Activity** Draw a map showing the eight main islands of Hawaii. Label each one. Then plan a trip to some of the islands and show on the map the route you will follow. On another sheet of paper, tell what places you might visit and what you might see. Involve family members in your planning.

Use a Map to Show Movement

Why Is This Skill Important?

Hawaii, Alaska, and the rest of the Pacific states are all part of the Pacific Rim. The Pacific Rim is a region made up of the United States and the other countries that border the Pacific Ocean. Trade between these countries has linked their economies and made their people interdependent.

Reading maps is an important skill that you have used throughout this book, and you will continue to use this skill throughout your life. As you know, maps can be used to show the movement of people or goods. Maps often use arrows to show such movement. Sometimes the arrows show routes between places. On some maps, however, the arrows show general movement between regions. Figuring out the arrow symbols will help you understand the maps.

Understand the Process

The map on page 437 shows the value of imports and exports between the United States and three Pacific Rim countries in recent years. The arrows on this map point from one country to another. That tells you that the map shows imports and exports for the whole country rather than for single cities or ports.

1. Look at the map. The green arrows show exports from the United States to each of two countries in Asia and to Australia. The other colors show imports from those countries to the United States. Read the map key to identify which country each color stands for. What country does the color purple stand for?

2. Trace each arrow from beginning to end with your finger. Then use the compass rose to find out the directions in which the

arrows are pointing. In what general direction do goods move from countries in Asia to the United States? from the United States to Australia?

Notice that some arrows on the map are wider than other arrows. The thickness of each arrow depends on the total value of the goods being imported or exported. The thicker the arrow, the greater is the value of the imports or exports.

Find China on the map. The pink arrow from China to the United States is thicker than the green arrow from the United States to China. That tells you that the value of imports coming from China into the United States is greater than the value of exports going from the United States to China. Unlike tables and graphs, this map does not give you the exact value of the imports or exports. But it does allow you to quickly see which values are greater or less than others. It also allows you to see the locations of different places involved in trade.

3. Now find Australia on the map. Is the value of imports coming from Australia to the United States greater or less than the value of exports going from the United States to Australia?

4. From which country does the United States import the greatest value of goods?

5. Does the United States export more to Japan or to China?

Think and Apply

Write a paragraph comparing the map on page 437 with a table or graph that gives the same kind of information. How is the map better than a table or graph? How would a table or graph be better?

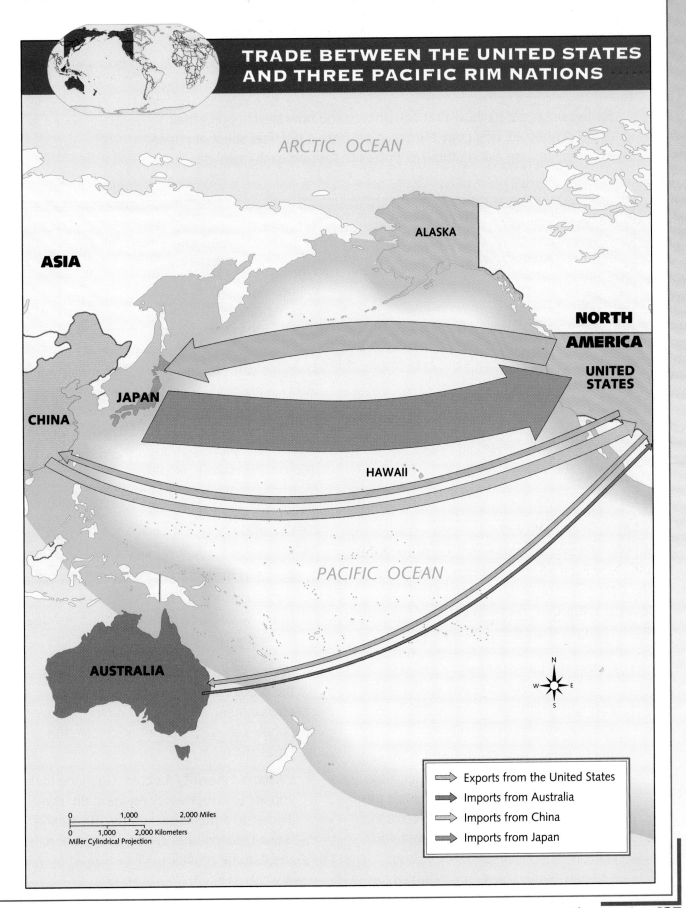

TRADE BETWEEN THE UNITED STATES
AND THREE PACIFIC RIM NATIONS

ARCTIC OCEAN

ALASKA

ASIA

NORTH
AMERICA

UNITED
STATES

JAPAN

CHINA

HAWAII

PACIFIC OCEAN

AUSTRALIA

N
W · E
S

0   1,000   2,000 Miles
0   1,000   2,000 Kilometers
Miller Cylindrical Projection

⇒ Exports from the United States
⇒ Imports from Australia
⇒ Imports from China
⇒ Imports from Japan

CONNECT MAIN IDEAS

Use this organizer to show that you understand how the chapter's main ideas are connected. First copy the organizer onto a separate sheet of paper. Then complete it by writing three examples to support each main idea.

Places along the Pacific coast of the United States are alike and different.

1. _____
2. _____
3. _____

People have both damaged the coastal environment and worked to protect it.

1. _____
2. _____
3. _____

The Pacific Coast and Islands

Life for Alaska's Athabaskan Indians has both changed and stayed the same.

1. _____
2. _____
3. _____

Hawaii's location has affected the state's history and the state's people.

1. _____
2. _____
3. _____

WRITE MORE ABOUT IT

1. **Compare Landscapes**   Compare the landscapes of southern Alaska and southern California. Describe the land and the climate in both places.

2. **Write Interview Questions**   Imagine that you are a newspaper reporter. You have been asked to interview people after the earthquake that shook California in 1994. Write a list of questions that you would like to ask the people.

3. **Write Your Opinion**   Choose one of the problems that threaten the coastal environment. Write your opinion of how people can cooperate to help solve this problem.

4. **Write a Friendly Letter**   Imagine that you are visiting Hawaii on vacation. Write a letter to a friend back home, describing Hawaii's landscape, climate, vegetation, and cultural activities.

Write the term that correctly matches each definition. Then use the term in a sentence.

ecosystem   tundra
fjord   volunteer
interest   wetlands

1. a narrow inlet of the ocean between cliffs

2. the relationship between living things and their nonliving environment

3. flat land without trees that stays frozen most of the year

4. a person who offers to do something without pay

5. low-lying land where the water level is always near or above the surface of the land

6. the money a bank or a borrower pays for the use of money

CHECK UNDERSTANDING

1. Which state has the most people?

2. Why is aluminum an important metal for manufacturing airplanes?

3. What carries oil from Prudhoe Bay to Valdez?

4. What is a wildlife refuge?

5. What city is the center of tourism, trade, and banking in Hawaii?

THINK CRITICALLY

1. Personally Speaking Would the threat of natural disasters, such as earthquakes or yearly flooding, stop you from living in a place that you like? Explain your response.

2. Cause and Effect What effect can oil spills have on the environment?

3. Explore Viewpoints Many of the people who lived along Prince William Sound believed that they should help clean up after the oil spill. Do you agree with their point of view? Explain.

PPLY SKILLS

How to Make a Generalization Study a population map of your state or another state. What generalizations can you make about the settlement patterns of the state you have chosen?

How to Act as a Responsible Citizen Watch the people around you. Identify a person that you think is acting as a responsible citizen in some way. Write a paragraph telling why you think that person is acting responsibly.

 How to Use a Map to Show Movement Use the map on page 437 to answer these questions.

1. To which country does the United States export the most, as measured in dollars?

2. Is the value of imports coming into the United States from China greater or less than the value of exports going to China?

READ MORE ABOUT IT

Arctic Hunter by Diane Hoyt-Goldsmith. Holiday House. An Inupiat travels with his family to their summer camp to fish and hunt for food.

Sanctuary by Mary Ann Fraser. Henry Holt. In the early 1900s two men try to persuade lawmakers to set aside the nation's first protected area for wildlife.

MAKING SOCIAL STUDIES
RELEVANT

Preserving the
NATIONAL PARKS

The West has more national parks than any other region of the United States. These parks are places of beauty and recreation for the millions of people who visit them each year. The parks are also a source of income for nearby towns. Park visitors spend lots of money in the towns' restaurants, gift shops, and hotels.

Among the best-known national parks in the West are Yosemite (yoh•SEH•muh•tee), in California, and Yellowstone, which covers parts of Idaho, Wyoming, and Montana. Both of these parks have serious problems that may affect the future of all the national parks.

More people visit Yosemite than any other national park in the West. Often the park must be closed because of overcrowding. Some people even joke that roads in Yosemite have the longest traffic jams in the United States! At Yellowstone there is not always enough money to keep up the park's

buildings, trails, and roads. Many of the national parks get so much use that they need repair badly. Many people think that we are loving our parks to death!

The beauty of Yosemite National Park, including Upper and Lower Yosemite Falls (above), attracts thousands of visitors each year.

THINK AND APPLY

Find out more about the problems faced by our national parks or the state or city parks near you. Then work with other students to plan ways to let people know about the problems and to ask them to take better care of the parks. You may want to invite speakers to your school, design bumper stickers, write advertisements, or draw posters.

Meadow Damage

Signs like the one above remind visitors to Yellowstone National Park of the damage they can cause. Other visitors (above right) enjoy an eruption by Yellowstone's most famous geyser—Old Faithful.

Arch Rock
Entrance Station
Elevation 2855

All Park Campgrounds FULL

Entrance Fees
Per vehicle   5.00
Bicycle/Bus Passenger/Walk-in

STORY CLOTH

Study the pictures shown in this story cloth to help you review what you read about in Unit 6.

Summarize the Main Ideas

1. The newer and taller mountains in the United States are all found in the West.

2. Mountains were barriers to early westward travel. People have changed their mountain environments to allow for better transportation and communication.

3. The West's rich supply of natural resources first attracted people to the region. People today continue to use the region's resources to earn their living.

4. The Pacific coast of the United States is long, so it has many differences from place to place.

5. People have both damaged the Pacific coast environment and worked to protect it.

6. Hawaii's location has affected its history and people.

Make a Class Scrapbook   Look at the story cloth, and think about something that interests you about the West. Then find out more about that topic. Your local library can be a source for more information. Write a one-page report that describes your findings. Include pictures or maps. Put your report in a class scrapbook. Display the scrapbook in the school library.

Make a Generalization   Study the story cloth. Then write three generalizations about the region known as the West.

COOPERATIVE LEARNING WORKSHOP

Remember

- Share your ideas.
- Cooperate with others to plan your work.
- Take responsibility for your work.
- Show your group's work to the class.
- Discuss what you learned by working together.

Activity 1
Draw a Map

Work in a group to draw an outline map of the West on a large piece of paper. Maps in your textbook and in encyclopedias and atlases can help you. Use two different colors to show the Mountain states and the Pacific states. Add dots and labels to show the region's largest cities. Also label large bodies of water and major landforms, such as the Rocky Mountains, the Great Basin, and the Sierra Nevada. Draw symbols to show the region's most important resources. Then point out places on the map as your group takes the rest of the class on a "tour" of the West.

Activity 2
Make a Relief Map

Work in a group to make a relief map of the United States. First, draw an outline map of the United States on a piece of posterboard, and color the major bodies of water. Then, use construction paper, clay, or papier mâché to show the Appalachian Mountains, the Rocky Mountains, the Sierra Nevada, and the Coast Ranges. Color your map to show elevations from level plains to mountain peaks. Create a map key to identify the elevation each color stands for. Display your group's map in the classroom.

Activity 3
Publish a Classroom Travel Magazine

Work with your classmates to put together a magazine about places to visit in the West. First, plan your magazine by preparing a table of contents. Books and magazines from the library can help you decide which places to include. Decide what articles, illustrations, and special features your magazine will have. Then, form several small groups, with each group working on a different part of the magazine. Once the parts have been put together, ask permission to display the magazine in the principal's office or the school library.

USE VOCABULARY

For each group of terms, write a sentence or two that explains how the terms are related.

1. lava, volcano

2. slope, timberline

3. barrier, transcontinental railroad, labor

4. trade-off, opportunity cost

5. hunters and gatherers, ecosystem

CHECK UNDERSTANDING

1. How do mountains change over time?

2. What happens to the temperature as the elevation increases?

3. Why is there less manufacturing in the western mountains than in some other parts of the United States?

4. What is the world's longest mountain range?

5. How are rivers and dams important to manufacturing in the Pacific Northwest?

6. How has growth changed the coastal environment?

7. Why does Hawaii have few factories?

THINK CRITICALLY

1. **Cause and Effect** How have mountains affected transportation and settlement in the West?

2. **Personally Speaking** Billy Day volunteered to help clean up the environment of Prince William Sound. What can you do to help clean up the environment where you live?

APPLY GEOGRAPHY SKILLS

How to Use a Road Map and a Mileage Table Use the map and the table below to answer these questions.

1. How many miles is it from Corvallis to Portland? Did you use the map or the mileage table to find this answer? Explain.

2. How many miles is it from Cannon Beach to Tillamook? Did you use the map or the mileage table to find this answer? Explain.

MILEAGE TABLE

	Corvallis	Portland	Salem
Corvallis		81	34
Portland	81		47
Salem	34	47	

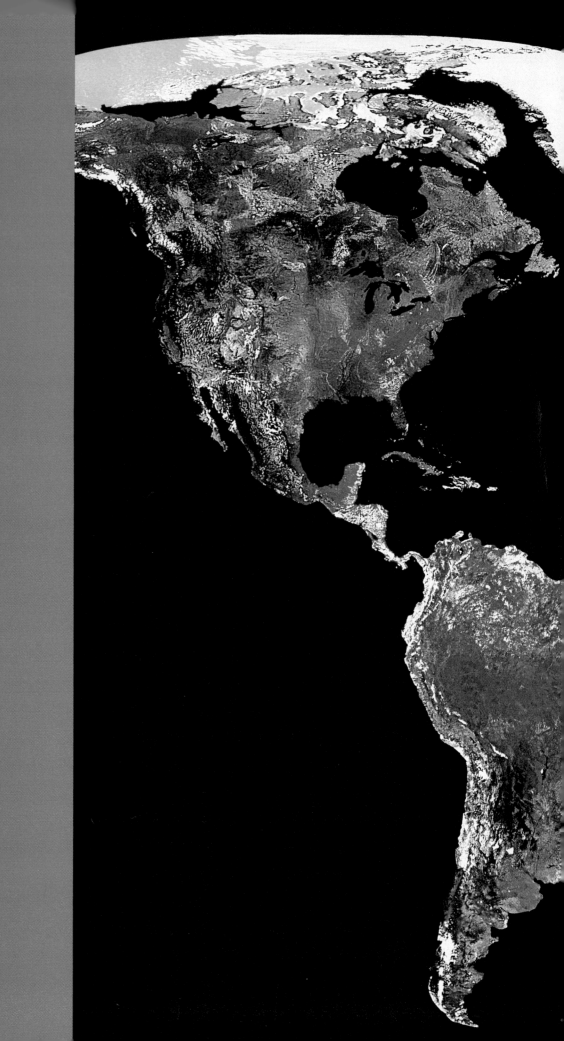

FOR YOUR REFERENCE

CONTENTS

HOW TO GATHER AND REPORT INFORMATION

To write a report, make a poster, or do many other projects in your social studies class, you may need information that is not in your textbook. You can gather this information from reference books, electronic references, or community resources. The following guide can help you gather information from many sources and report what you find.

HOW TO USE REFERENCE TOOLS

Reference works are collections of facts. They include books and electronic resources, such as almanacs, atlases, dictionaries, and encyclopedias. Books in libraries are organized through a system of numbers. Every book in a library has its own number, called a call number. The call number on the book tells where in the library the book can be found. In a library a reference book has an *R* or *REF* for *reference* on its spine along with the call number. Most reference books are for use only in the library. Many libraries also have electronic references on CD-ROM and the Internet.

WHEN TO USE AN ENCYCLOPEDIA

An encyclopedia is a good place to begin to look for information. An encyclopedia has articles on nearly every subject. The articles are arranged in alphabetical order by subject. Each article gives basic facts about people, places, and events. Some electronic encyclopedias allow you to hear music and speeches and to see short movies about the subject.

WHEN TO USE A DICTIONARY

A dictionary gives information about words. Dictionaries explain the meanings of words and show how the words are pronounced. A dictionary is a good place to check the spelling of a word. Some dictionaries also include the origins of words and lists of foreign words, abbreviations, well-known people, and place names.

WHEN TO USE AN ATLAS

You can find information about places in an atlas. An atlas is a book of maps. Some atlases have road maps. Others have maps of countries around the world. Some atlas maps show where certain crops are grown and where certain products are made. Others show the populations of different places. Ask a librarian to help you find the kind of atlas you need.

WHEN TO USE AN ALMANAC

An almanac is a book or an electronic resource containing facts and figures. It shows information in tables and charts. The population of a city and the largest industries of a country are the kinds of facts given in an almanac.

The subjects in an almanac are grouped in broad categories, not in alphabetical order. To find a certain subject, such as health and sports, you need to use the index, which lists the subjects in alphabetical order. Most almanacs are brought up to date every year. So an almanac can give you the latest information on a subject.

HOW TO FIND NONFICTION BOOKS

Unlike fiction books, which tell stories that are made up, nonfiction books give facts about real people, places, and events. In a library all nonfiction books are placed in order on the shelves according to their call numbers.

You can find a book's call number by using a card file or a computer catalog. To find this number, however, you need to know the book's title, author, or subject. Here are some sample entries for a book about the Rocky Mountain states.

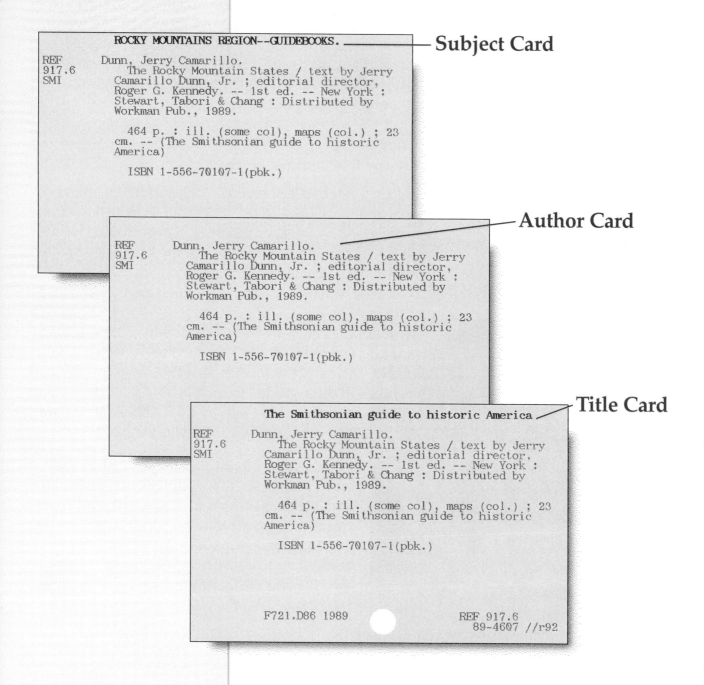

Subject Card

ROCKY MOUNTAINS REGION--GUIDEBOOKS.

REF
917.6
SMI

Dunn, Jerry Camarillo.
    The Rocky Mountain States / text by Jerry
Camarillo Dunn, Jr. ; editorial director,
Roger G. Kennedy. -- 1st ed. -- New York :
Stewart, Tabori & Chang : Distributed by
Workman Pub., 1989.

    464 p. : ill. (some col), maps (col.) ; 23
cm. -- (The Smithsonian guide to historic
America)

    ISBN 1-556-70107-1(pbk.)

Author Card

REF
917.6
SMI

Dunn, Jerry Camarillo.
    The Rocky Mountain States / text by Jerry
Camarillo Dunn, Jr. ; editorial director,
Roger G. Kennedy. -- 1st ed. -- New York :
Stewart, Tabori & Chang : Distributed by
Workman Pub., 1989.

    464 p. : ill. (some col), maps (col.) ; 23
cm. -- (The Smithsonian guide to historic
America)

    ISBN 1-556-70107-1(pbk.)

Title Card

The Smithsonian guide to historic America

REF
917.6
SMI

Dunn, Jerry Camarillo.
    The Rocky Mountain States / text by Jerry
Camarillo Dunn, Jr. ; editorial director,
Roger G. Kennedy. -- 1st ed. -- New York :
Stewart, Tabori & Chang : Distributed by
Workman Pub., 1989.

    464 p. : ill. (some col), maps (col.) ; 23
cm. -- (The Smithsonian guide to historic
America)

    ISBN 1-556-70107-1(pbk.)

F721.D86 1989   REF 917.6
                                 89-4607 //r92

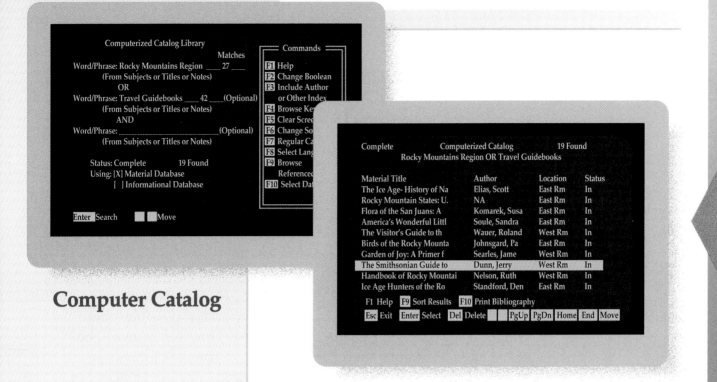

Computer Catalog

How to Find Periodicals

Libraries have special sections for periodicals—newspapers and magazines. A periodical, which is usually published every day, week, or month, is a good source for the most up-to-date information and for topics not yet covered in books. The latest issues of periodicals are usually displayed on a rack. Older issues are stored away, sometimes on film.

Most libraries have an index that lists magazine articles by subject. The most widely used are the *Children's Magazine Guide* and the *Readers' Guide to Periodical Literature*. The entries in these guides are in alphabetical order by subject and author, and sometimes by title. Abbreviations are used for many parts of an entry, such as the name of the magazine and the date of the issue. Here is a sample entry for an article about autumn in the state of Arizona.

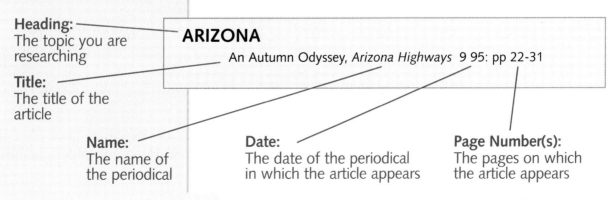

Heading:
The topic you are researching

Title:
The title of the article

ARIZONA

An Autumn Odyssey, *Arizona Highways* 9 95: pp 22-31

Name:
The name of the periodical

Date:
The date of the periodical in which the article appears

Page Number(s):
The pages on which the article appears

How to Conduct an Interview

Conducting interviews, or asking people questions, is a good way to get facts and points of view on a topic.

Planning an Interview

1. Make a list of people to interview. Think about who the experts are on the subject you are researching.
2. Call or write to each person to ask for an interview. Identify yourself, and let the person know what you want to talk about.
3. Ask the person you will interview to set a time and place to meet.

Before the Interview

1. Read more about your topic and, if possible, about the person you are interviewing. That way you will be better able to talk with the person.
2. Make a list of questions to ask.

During the Interview

1. Listen carefully. Do not interrupt or argue with the person.
2. Take notes as you talk with the person, and write down the person's exact words.
3. If you want to use a tape recorder, first ask the person if you may do so.

After the Interview

1. Before you leave, thank the person you interviewed.
2. Follow up by writing a thank-you note.

How to Conduct a Survey

A good way to get information about the views of people in your community is to conduct a survey.

1. Identify your topic, and make a list of questions. Write the questions so that they can be answered with "yes" or "no" or with "for" or "against." You may also want to give a "no opinion" or "not sure" choice.
2. Make a tally sheet to use for recording your responses.
3. Decide how many people you will ask and where you will conduct your survey.
4. During the survey, carefully record each person's responses on the tally sheet.
5. When you have finished your survey, count your responses and write a summary statement or conclusion that your survey supports.

HOW TO WRITE FOR INFORMATION

You can write a letter to ask for information about a certain topic. When you write, be sure to do these things:

- Write neatly or use a word processor.
- Say who you are and why you are writing.
- Make your request specific and reasonable.
- Provide a self-addressed, stamped envelope for the answer.

You may or may not get a reply, but if you do, you may find it was worth your time to write.

HOW TO WRITE A REPORT

You may be asked to write a report on the information you have gathered. Knowing how to write a report will help you make good use of the information you have collected. You should take the following steps when writing a report.

GATHER AND ORGANIZE YOUR INFORMATION

- Gather information about your topic from reference books, electronic references, or community resources.
- Take notes as you find information that you need for your report.
- Review your notes to make sure you have all the information you want to include.
- Organize your information in an outline.
- Make sure the information is in the order in which you want to present it.

DRAFT YOUR REPORT

- Review your information. Decide if you need more.
- Remember that the purpose of your report is to share information about your topic.
- Write a draft of your report. Put all your ideas on paper. Present your ideas in a clear and interesting way.

REVISE

- Check to make sure that you have followed the order of your outline. Move sentences that seem out of place.
- Add any information you feel is needed.
- Add quotations to show people's exact words.
- Reword sentences if too many follow the same pattern.

PROOFREAD AND PUBLISH

- Check for errors.
- Make sure nothing has been left out.
- Make a clean copy of your report.

Alabama

Alaska

Arizona

Arkansas

California

Colorado

Connecticut

Delaware

Florida

Georgia

HOW TO STUDY YOUR STATE

ACTIVITY BANK

In social studies you read about different regions of the United States and of the world. You study the geography and history of those regions and the way people in each place live. The following activities will help you learn more about a special region—the state in which you live. For each activity, you may choose to work alone, with a partner, or in a group.

GEOGRAPHY

Atlases, encyclopedias, almanacs, and library books can help you learn more about the geography of your state.

- Find out how your state compares in size with other states. Figure out the greatest distance in miles across your state.
- Make a bar graph that compares the populations of the five largest cities in your state.
- Draw scenes that show what the climate of your state is like in the winter and in the summer. Then make a table that shows the average high and low monthly temperatures and the average monthly precipitation for some of the cities in your state.

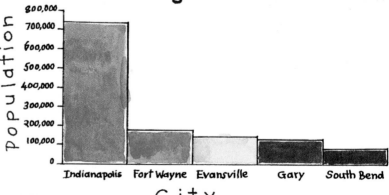

Five Largest Cities in Indiana

Hawaii

Idaho

Illinois

Indiana

Iowa

Kansas

Kentucky

Louisiana

Maine

MAPS AND GLOBES

- Draw a large outline map of your state. Then add and label your state's major landforms, bodies of water, and natural regions. Identify the state's highest and lowest places.

- Make a political map of your state. Label large cities, including the state capital, and other important human features. Also label the states that border your state.

- Make a latitude and longitude card game. On separate index cards, write the names of towns and cities in your state. On other cards, write the latitude and longitude for each place. Challenge classmates to use a map to match each place with its latitude and longitude clues.

- Draw a land use map for your state. Add a key to explain what each color or symbol on the map stands for.

- Make a map that shows where natural resources are located in your state. Then write a paragraph explaining how people in your state and in other places depend on those resources.

PLACES TO VISIT

Every state has interesting places to visit. You can write to your state's department of tourism or its department of natural resources for information about some of them. Most road maps also show places of interest.

- Use a road map to plan a tour of your state. Tell what places you would visit and why. List the highways you would use to reach those places.

- Make a postcard. Draw or cut out a picture of a famous landmark in your state, and glue it to an index card. On the other side, write a sentence or two about the object or place you have shown.

- Create a brochure that tells about a state park, a national park, or a historical site in your state. Tell what people could see if they visited that place.

- Design a magazine advertisement inviting tourists to visit your state. Your advertisement should tell about some of the outdoor activities people can enjoy there. Add pictures to illustrate your advertisement.

Maryland

Massachusetts

Michigan

Minnesota

Mississippi

Missouri

Montana

Nebraska

Nevada

New Hampshire

HISTORY

Resources such as encyclopedias and library books can give you information about the history of your state. You can get more information by writing to historical societies, museums, or historical sites.

- Create a mural that shows the way of life of an early American Indian group in your state. Tell your class where that group lived, and explain how its people depended on natural resources.
- Research the first European explorers to visit your state. Share your findings with classmates.
- Write a report that describes the first settlement in your state. Tell who settled there, and explain why they chose to settle where they did.
- Write a scene for a play that explains how your state became part of the United States.
- Prepare an oral report about an important event in your state's history. Tell where and when the event took place.
- Make a time line of your state's history. Include at least five important events.

Some Important Dates in Illinois History

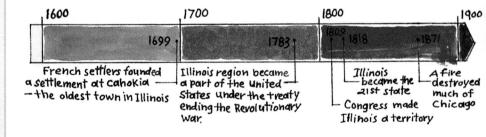

1600   1699   1700   1783   1800   1809   1818   1871   1900

French settlers founded a settlement at Cahokia —the oldest town in Illinois

Illinois region became a part of the United States under the treaty ending the Revolutionary War.

Illinois became the 21st state

Congress made Illinois a territory

A fire destroyed much of Chicago

New Jersey

New Mexico

New York

North Carolina

North Dakota

Ohio

Oklahoma

Oregon

Pennsylvania

CIVICS AND GOVERNMENT

Newspapers and almanacs are good sources of information about your state's government. You can get more information by writing letters to state leaders. Their addresses are often given in the telephone book.

- Draw a chart showing the three branches of your state's government. Then explain the main job of each branch.
- Make a table that lists the names of your state's elected officials and the titles of their jobs. Include the names of the people who represent your community in the state legislature.
- Keep a current-events notebook. Cut out newspaper articles about your state's government. Paste the articles in your notebook, and write a summary of each one.
- Make a flow chart that shows how a bill becomes a law in your state.
- Draw a picture of the state flag. Then find out what each symbol on the flag stands for.
- Make a poster showing state symbols, such as the state bird, the state flower, and the state tree. Find out why each was chosen as a state symbol.
- Learn the words to the state song, and sing it with classmates.

ECONOMICS

Almanacs and encyclopedias are good sources of information about your state's economy. You can learn more by writing to the state chamber of commerce or to the secretary of state.

- List your state's most important manufacturing and farm products. Then use the names of those products to make a word-search puzzle.
- Do research to find out how people in other states and in other parts of the world depend on raw materials and products from your state. Report your findings to the class.
- Write a descriptive paragraph about a service job or a manufacturing job that people in your state do. Tell whether you would like to do that job, and explain your feelings about it.

Rhode Island

South Carolina

South Dakota

Tennessee

Texas

Utah

Vermont

Virginia

Washington

West Virginia

Wisconsin

Wyoming

CULTURE

Both now and in the past, many groups of people have lived in your state. Each of those groups has added to the way of life of people in your state. Encyclopedias, magazines, museums, and historical sites can help you learn about those groups and how they have affected your state.

TRADITIONS

- Make a calendar that shows the dates of festivals, fairs, and holiday celebrations that take place in your state. Circle the names of events that celebrate the culture of one of your state's ethnic groups.
- Videotape a television advertisement for one of your state's festivals. In your advertisement, explain how the festival began and who started it.

PEOPLE WHO HAVE MADE A DIFFERENCE

- Collect some interesting facts about a well-known person from your state. Give an oral report to your class, telling why that person is well known.
- Make Who's Who cards about well-known people from your state. Write each person's name on an index card, and then list several facts about that person's life. Read the facts, one at a time, to other students, and challenge them to name the person you are describing.
- Write a short biography about a person from your state whom you admire. Tell why you admire that person.

AMERICAN DOCUMENTS

THE PLEDGE OF ALLEGIANCE

I pledge allegiance to the Flag
of the United States of America,
and to the Republic
for which it stands,
one Nation under God, indivisible,
with liberty and justice for all.

THE NATIONAL ANTHEM

"The Star-Spangled Banner"

Oh, say can you see by the dawn's early light

What so proudly we hail'd at the twilight's last
  gleaming,

Whose broad stripes and bright stars through the
  perilous fight

O'er the ramparts we watch'd were so gallantly
  streaming?

And the rockets' red glare, the bombs bursting in air,

Gave proof through the night that our flag was
  still there.

Oh, say does that star-spangled banner yet wave

O'er the land of the free and the home of the brave?

The flag is a symbol of the United States of America. The Pledge of Allegiance says that the people of the United States promise to honor the flag and their country.

"The Star-Spangled Banner" was written by Francis Scott Key during the War of 1812, but it did not become the national anthem until 1931. "The Star-Spangled Banner" has four verses, but the first verse, shown here, is the one that is most commonly sung.

BIOGRAPHICAL DICTIONARY

The Biographical Dictionary lists many of the important people introduced in this book. The page number tells where the main discussion of each person starts. See the Index for other page references.

A

Antin, Mary *1881–1949* A writer who was born in Russia and came to the United States in 1894. p. 74

B

Boone, Daniel *1734–1820* One of the first American pioneers to cross the Appalachian Mountains. p. 220

C

Carnegie, Andrew *1835–1919* A leader in the early U.S. steel industry who was well known for his gifts of money to schools and libraries. p. 170

Carver, George Washington *1864?–1943* An African American scientist who became well known for his work with peanuts and with ways to improve farming. p. 195

Cather, Willa *1873–1947* An American novelist. p. 258

Clark, William *1770–1838* An American explorer who, with Meriwether Lewis, explored the Louisiana Territory and lands west of the Rocky Mountains. p. 392

Clemens, Samuel *1835–1910* An American writer who wrote many stories and books under the pen name Mark Twain. p. 293

Clinton, De Witt *1769–1828* An American lawyer who led the group of people that wanted to build the Erie Canal. He later served as governor of New York. p. 174

Clinton, William *1946–* 42nd U.S. President and a former governor of Arkansas. p. 92

Columbus, Christopher *1451–1506* An Italian-born Spanish explorer who, in 1492, sailed west from Spain. He thought he reached Asia but actually reached islands near the Americas, lands that were unknown to Europeans. p. 73

Cook, James *1728–1779* An English sea captain and explorer who was the first European to see Hawaii. p. 433

Coronado, Francisco Vásquez de (kawr•oh•NAH•doh) *1510?–1554* A Spanish explorer who led a group from Mexico City into what is now the southwestern United States in search of gold. p. 323

D

Deere, John *1804–1886* An American inventor who, in 1837, made a steel plow. p. 267

E

Estevan *See* Estevanico.

Estevanico (ehs•tay•vahn•EE•koh) *1500–1539* An African who was brought to America as a slave and who later explored the Southwest United States; also called Estéban. p. 318

F

Flagler, Henry *1830–1913* An American millionaire who built a railroad across the Florida Keys, linking Miami and Key West. p. 212

Ford, Henry *1863–1947* An American automobile manufacturer who mass-produced cars at low cost by using assembly lines. p. 289

Fulton, Robert *1765–1815* An American engineer and inventor who, in 1807, built the *Clermont*, the country's first moneymaking steamboat. p. 293

G

Gingrich, Newt *1943–* A member of the House of Representatives from Georgia since 1979. He became Speaker of the House in 1995. p. 91

Gore, Al *1948–* A former member of the House of Representatives and a former U.S. senator from Tennessee. He became Vice President of the United States in 1993. p. 49

Gregory, Fred *1941–* An African American astronaut who traveled on the space shuttle three times, twice as commander. p. 96

Guthrie, Woody *1912–1967* An American singer and songwriter. Many of his songs describe the people and land of the United States. p. 36

H

Houston, Sam *1793–1863* A leader in the fight for Texas independence and president of the Republic of Texas. He later served as governor of the state of Texas. p. 333

Hughes, Langston *1902–1967* One of the best-known African American writers. p. 284

J

Jefferson, Thomas *1743–1826* 3rd U.S. President and the main writer of the Declaration of Independence. p. 90

K

King, Martin Luther, Jr. *1929–1968* An African American civil rights leader who worked for integration in nonviolent ways. He won the Nobel Peace Prize in 1964. p. 83

L

Lazarus, Emma (LAZ•uh•ruhs) *1849–1887* An American poet whose poem "The New Colossus" is displayed at the base of the Statue of Liberty. p. 139

Lewis, Meriwether *1774–1809* An American explorer who, with William Clark, explored the Louisiana Territory and lands west of the Rocky Mountains. p. 392

Lincoln, Abraham *1809–1865* 16th U.S. President, who served during the Civil War. p. 73

Love, Nat *1854–1921* An African American cowhand who worked in the great cattle drives from Texas. p. 273

M

Marshall, James *1810–1885* A worker who discovered gold in a ditch at Sutter's Mill in 1848, an event that sparked the California gold rush. p. 398

McCormick, Cyrus *1809–1884* An American inventor who built a reaping machine for harvesting wheat. p. 267

McCoy, Joseph *1837–1915* A cattle trader who built stockyards near the railroad at Abilene, Kansas, which led to the growth of a major cattle ranching industry in the Great Plains states. p. 272

Melville, Herman *1819–1891* A well-known American writer. p. 72

Muir, John *1838–1914* A naturalist who persuaded the U.S. government to set aside more than 150 million acres of land for national parks, forests, and wilderness areas. p. 386

N

Newman, Pauline *1891?–1986* A Jewish immigrant who lived on the Lower East Side in New York City and later became a leader of the International Ladies' Garment Workers' Union. p. 140

O

Oliver, James *1823–1908* An inventor from Indiana who built a plow that was especially good for cutting through the sod of the Great Plains. p. 268

P

Percy, Charles One of the founders of Jamestown, in what is now Virginia. p. 194

Pitts, Hiram *1800–1860* An American inventor who, with his brother, built a threshing machine in 1834. p. 267

Pitts, John *1800–1840* An American inventor who, with his brother, built a threshing machine in 1834. p. 267

Powell, John Wesley *1834–1902* An American geologist who was one of the first people to explore the Grand Canyon. p. 46

R

Rockwell, Norman *1894–1978* An American painter and illustrator who is best known for his paintings of the everyday activities of American people. His illustrations often appeared on the covers of the *Saturday Evening Post.* p. 84

Rogers, Will *1879–1935* An American actor, lecturer, and humorist. p. 337

Roosevelt, Theodore *1858–1919* 26th U.S. President, who worked to protect the nation's natural resources and wilderness areas. p. 66

S

Sacagawea (sak•uh•juh•WEE•uh) *1786?–1812?* A Shoshone woman who acted as an interpreter for the Lewis and Clark expedition. p. 392

Smith, John *1580–1631* An English explorer who explored the northeast coast of what is now the United States and named the area New England. He also helped found the colony of Jamestown, in what is now Virginia. p. 131

Squanto *See* Tisquantum.

Stevenson, Robert Louis *1850–1894* A Scottish writer who, in 1879, traveled across the United States and wrote a book about his journey. p. 39

Sutter, John *1803–1880* A German immigrant who owned the California sawmill where gold was discovered in 1848, leading to the California gold rush. p. 398

T

Teach, Edward *?–1718* An English pirate, also known as Blackbeard, who robbed ships off the coast of the Carolinas and Virginia. p. 210

Tisquantum (tih•SQUAN•tuhm) *1585?–1622* An American Indian who spoke English and helped the colonists at the Plymouth colony. p. 132

W

Washington, George *1732–1799* 1st U.S. President and leader of the Continental army during the American Revolution. p. 83

White, Peregrine *1620–1704* The first child of English heritage born in New England. She was born on the *Mayflower.* p. 132

Winslow, Edward *1595–1655* One of the founders of the Plymouth colony in Massachusetts. p. 131

GAZETTEER

The Gazetteer is a geographical dictionary that will help you locate places discussed in this book. The page number tells where each place appears on a map.

A

Acadia National Park A national park on the coast of Maine. p. 125

Adirondack Mountains (a·duh·RAHN·dak) A mountain range in northeastern New York. p. 125

Alabama River A river in the southeastern United States. p. 48

Alaska Range A mountain range in southern Alaska. p. 40

Albany (AWL·buh·nee) The capital of New York. (43°N, 74°W) p. 145

Albuquerque (AL·buh·ker·kee) The largest city in New Mexico. (35°N, 107°W) p. 317

Aleutian Islands (uh·LOO·shuhn) A chain of islands extending west from the Alaska Peninsula. p. 414

Allegheny Mountains (a·luh·GAY·nee) A mountain range that is part of the Appalachian Mountains. p. 125

Allegheny River A river in the northeastern United States. p. 45

Alps A mountain range in south-central Europe. p. 406

Amazon Rain Forest A tropical forest in South America, located mainly in Brazil. p. 299

Amazon River A river in South America; the second-longest river on Earth. p. 297

Anchorage (ANG·kuh·rihj) The largest city in Alaska. (61°N, 150°W) p. 414

Andes Mountains (AN·deez) A mountain range in South America; the longest chain of mountains on Earth. p. 280

Annapolis (uh·NAH·puh·luhs) The capital of Maryland. (39°N, 76°W) p. 125

Antarctic Circle (ant·AHRK·tihk) The line of latitude that is located at 66½°S. p. 102

Appalachian Mountains (a·puh·LAY·chee·uhn) A mountain range in the eastern United States. p. 240

Appalachian Trail A trail extending from Mt. Katahdin, in Maine, to Springer Mountain, in Georgia. p. 240

Arctic Circle (AHRK·tihk) The line of latitude located at 66½°N. p. 102

Argentina A country in South America. p. 280

Arkansas River A tributary of the Mississippi River. p. 28

Atacama Desert (a·tah·KAH·mah) A desert region in South America; the driest desert in the world. p. 369

Atlanta The capital of Georgia. (34°N, 84°W) p. 249

Atlas Mountains A mountain range in northern Africa. p. 406

Augusta The capital of Maine. (44°N, 70°W) p. 125

Austin The capital of Texas. (30°N, 98°W) p. 317

B

Baltimore A city in north-central Maryland. (39°N, 77°W) p. 125

Baton Rouge (BA·tuhn ROOZH) The capital of Louisiana. (30°N, 91°W) p. 189

Bering Sea A sea separating Alaska and Russia. p. 414

Big Bend National Park A national park on the big bend of the Rio Grande, in western Texas. p. 342

Birmingham A city in Alabama. (34°N, 87°W) p. 189

Biscayne National Park (bis·KAYN) A national park in southern Florida. p. 189

Bismarck The capital of North Dakota. (47°N, 101°W) p. 253

Black Hills A mountain range in South Dakota. p. 40

Boise (BOY·zee) The capital of Idaho. (44°N, 116°W) p. 383

Boston The capital of Massachusetts. (42°N, 71°W) p. 133

Brazil The largest and most populous country in South America; the fifth-largest nation in the world. p. 299

Brooks Range A mountain range in northern Alaska. p. 40

Buffalo A city in western New York. (43°N, 79°W) p. 125

C

Cape Canaveral (kuh·NAV·ruhl) A cape on the Atlantic coast of Florida. (28°N, 81°W) p. 189

Cape Cod A cape on the southeastern coast of Massachusetts, located between Cape Cod Bay and the Atlantic Ocean. p. 125

Cape Hatteras (HA·tuh·ruhs) A cape on Hatteras Island, in North Carolina. (36°N, 76°W) p. 189

Caribbean Sea (kair·uh·BEE·uhn) A part of the Atlantic Ocean bounded by the West Indies and Central and South Americas. p. 214

Carlsbad Caverns National Park A national park near Carlsbad, New Mexico. p. 317

Carson City The capital of Nevada. (39°N, 120°W) p. 383

Cascade Range A mountain range in the northwestern United States. p. 40

Catskill Mountains A mountain range in southeastern New York. p. 125

Central Arizona Project An engineering project that uses canals, tunnels, and pipelines to carry water from the Colorado River to desertlands in Arizona. p. 352

Central Valley A large valley in central California. p. 40

Chang Jiang (CHAHNG jee·AHNG) The longest river in Asia. p. 297

Charles River A river in eastern Massachusetts. p. 133

Charleston A port city in South Carolina. (33°N, 80°W) p. 199

Charleston The capital of West Virginia. (38°N, 82°W) p. 189

Charlotte The largest city in North Carolina. (35°N, 81°W) p. 189

Chattahoochee River (cha·tuh·HOO·chee) A river in the southeastern United States. p. 224

Chattanooga (cha·tuh·NOO·guh) A city in southeastern Tennessee. (35°N, 85°W) p. 222

Chesapeake Bay (CHEH·suh·peek) A bay on the Atlantic coast of the United States, which has its lower section in Virginia and its upper section in Maryland. p. 125

Cheyenne (shy•AN) The capital of Wyoming. (41°N, 105°W) p. 383

Chicago A city in Illinois; the third-largest city in the United States. (42°N, 88°W) p. 253

Chihuahuan Desert (chee•WAH•wahn) A desert region that covers part of Mexico, New Mexico, and Texas; part of the North American Desert. p. 324

China A country in East Asia. p. 437

Cincinnati (sin•suh•NA•tee) A city in southern Ohio. (39°N, 84°W) p. 121

Ciudad Juárez (SEE•u•dahd HWAR•ays) A city in northern Mexico, near El Paso, Texas. (32°N, 106°W) p. 342

Cleveland A city in northern Ohio. (41°N, 82°W) p. 260

Coast Ranges The mountain ranges that stretch along the Pacific coast of North America. p. 40

Coastal Plain One of two major plains in the United States; located along the coasts of the Atlantic Ocean and the Gulf of Mexico. p. 40

Colorado Plateau A plateau in the southwestern United States; covers most of northern New Mexico and Arizona. p. 40

Colorado River A river in the southwestern United States. p. 48

Columbia The capital of South Carolina. (34°N, 81°W) p. 230

Columbia Plateau A plateau located to the east of the Cascade Range. p. 40

Columbia River A river in the northwestern United States and southwestern Canada. p. 48

Columbus The capital of Ohio. (40°N, 83°W) p. 121

Concord The capital of New Hampshire. (43°N, 72°W) p. 125

Connecticut River The longest river in New England. p. 48

Continental Divide A ridge that divides eastern and western North America and extends from northwest Canada to South America. p. 390

Corpus Christi (KOHR•puhs KRIS•tee) A city in southern Texas. (28°N, 97°W) p. 317

Cuba An island country in the Caribbean Sea; the largest and westernmost island of the West Indies. p. 35

Cumberland Gap A pass through the Appalachian Mountains in Tennessee. p. 189

D

Dallas A city in northeastern Texas. (33°N, 97°W) p. 260

Dead Sea A salt lake on the boundary between Israel and Jordan; the lowest point on the Earth's surface. p. 371

Death Valley The lowest point in the Western Hemisphere; located in the Mojave Desert in California. (36°N, 117°W) p. 35

Delaware Bay A bay on the coast of the Atlantic Ocean, located between New Jersey and Delaware. p. 125

Delaware River A river in the northeastern United States. p. 125

Denver The capital of Colorado. (40°N, 105°W) p. 396

Des Moines (DUH MOYN) The capital of Iowa. (42°N, 94°W) p. 253

Deserts of the Arabian Peninsula A desert region in southwestern Asia on the Arabian Peninsula. p. 369

Detroit The largest city in Michigan. (42°N, 83°W) p. 288

Detroit River A river in southeastern Michigan, which forms part of the United States–Canada border. p. 288

Dismal Swamp A swamp that covers part of Virginia and North Carolina. p. 189

Dodge City A city in southern Kansas, which was a major railroad center on the Santa Fe Trail. (38°N, 100°W) p. 272

Dover The capital of Delaware. (39°N, 76°W) p. 125

Duluth (duh•LOOTH) The third-largest city in Minnesota. (47°N, 92°W) p. 286

E

Egypt (EE•juhpt) A country in northeastern Africa. p. 371

El Paso A city in western Texas. (32°N, 106°W) p. 342

Equator An imaginary line that circles the Earth halfway between the North Pole and South Pole. The line divides the Earth into the Northern Hemisphere and the Southern Hemisphere. p. 102

Erie A city in northwestern Pennsylvania. (42°N, 80°W) p. 125

European Plain A plains region that extends across most of Europe. p. 279

Everglades A large area of wetlands in southern Florida. p. 211

Everglades National Park A national park in southern Florida. p. 189

F

Falcon Reservoir A reservoir in southern Texas on the Rio Grande. p. 342

Florida Bay The body of water located between the southern tip of Florida and the Florida Keys. p. 211

Florida Keys A chain of islands off the southern tip of the Florida peninsula. p. 211

Fort Worth A city in north-central Texas. (33°N, 97°W) p. 329

Four Corners The point where four states—New Mexico, Colorado, Utah, and Arizona—meet. (37°N, 109°W) p. 317

Frankfort The capital of Kentucky. (38°N, 85°W) p. 189

Fresno A city in southern California. (37°N, 120°W) p. 415

G

Galveston A city on Galveston Island, in Texas. (29°N, 95°W) p. 317

Galveston Bay A bay on the Gulf of Mexico near Houston, Texas. p. 337

Ganges River (GAN•jeez) A river in India that flows into the Bay of Bengal. p. 297

Gary A city in northwestern Indiana. (42°N, 87°W) p. 286

Gila River (HEE•lah) A river in the southwestern United States. p. 48

Gobi (GOH•bee) A desert region in central Asia. p. 369

Grand Canyon A canyon in northwestern Arizona, formed by the Colorado River. p. 352

Grand Canyon National Park A national park in northwestern Arizona. p. 317

Grand Rapids A city in western Michigan. (43°N, 86°W) p. 253

Great Basin An area of low, dry land in the western United States, including parts of Nevada, Utah, California, Idaho, Wyoming, and Oregon. p. 383

Great Plains The western part of the Interior Plains of the United States. p. 260

Great Salt Lake The largest lake in the Great Basin, located in Utah. p. 46

Great Smoky Mountains National Park A national park on the Tennessee–North Carolina state line. p. 189

Green Mountains A mountain range in the northeastern United States that extends from Canada through Vermont and into Massachusetts. p. 125

Greenland The largest island on Earth, located in the northern Atlantic Ocean, northeast of Canada. p. 73

Greensboro A city in north-central North Carolina. (36°N, 80°W) p. 189

Guadalupe Mountains National Park (gwah·dah·LOO·pay) A national park near El Paso, Texas. p. 317

Guam (GWAHM) An island territory of the United States in the western Pacific Ocean. p. 435

Gulf of California A part of the Pacific Ocean, located off northwestern Mexico. p. 317

Gulf of Mexico A body of water off the southeastern coast of North America that is bounded by the United States, Cuba, and Mexico. p. 26

H

Harrisburg The capital of Pennsylvania. (40°N, 77°W) p. 125

Hartford The capital of Connecticut. (42°N, 73°W) p. 146

Helena (HEH·luh·nuh) The capital of Montana. (46°N, 112°W) p. 383

Hilton Head Island An island off the coast of South Carolina. (32°N, 81°W) p. 189

Himalayas (hih·muh·LAY·uhz) A mountain range in southern Asia. p. 406

Honolulu (hah·nuh·LOO·loo) The capital of Hawaii. (21°N, 158°W) p. 433

Hoover Dam A dam on the Colorado River on the Nevada–Arizona state line. (36°N, 114°W) p. 351

Hot Springs National Park A national park in the Ouachita Mountains in Arkansas. p. 189

Houston The largest city in Texas. (30°N, 95°W) p. 337

Houston Ship Channel A waterway that connects Houston, Texas, with the Gulf of Mexico. p. 337

Huang He River (HWAHNG HUH) The second-largest river in China. p. 297

Hudson River A river in the northeastern United States. p. 48

Huntsville A city in northern Alabama. (35°N, 86°W) p. 189

I

Illinois River A river in Illinois. p. 48

Illinois Waterway A waterway that connects Lake Michigan with the Illinois River. p. 253

Indianapolis (ihn·dee·uh·NA·puh·luhs) The capital of Indiana. (40°N, 86°W) p. 313

Interior Plains One of two major plains in the United States; located between the Appalachian Mountains and the Rocky Mountains; includes the Central Plains and the Great Plains. p. 40

Isle Royale National Park A national park near the northwestern shores of Lake Superior. p. 253

Israel (IZ·ree·uhl) A country on the eastern coast of the Mediterranean Sea. p. 371

J

Jackson The capital of Mississippi. (32°N, 90°W) p. 189

Jacksonville A city in northern Florida. (30°N, 82°W) p. 189

James River A river in central Virginia. p. 48

Jamestown The first permanent English settlement in America, located on the James River. p. 194

Japan A country in East Asia; consists of Honshu, Hokkaido, Kyushu, Shikoku, and other islands in the western Pacific Ocean. p. 437

Jefferson City The capital of Missouri. (39°N, 92°W) p. 253

Jersey City A port city in northeastern New Jersey. (41°N, 74°W) p. 185

Juneau (JOO·noh) The capital of Alaska. (58°N, 134°W) p. 414

K

Kahoolawe (kah·hoh·uh·LAH·vay) A Hawaiian island, located west of Maui. p. 433

Kalahari (ka·luh·HAHR·ee) A desert region in southern Africa. p. 369

Kansas City The largest city in Missouri, located on the Missouri River on the Kansas-Missouri state line. (39°N, 95°W) p. 277

Kauai (KAU·eye) The fourth largest of the eight major Hawaiian islands. p. 433

Key West A city in southwestern Florida, on the island of Key West. (25°N, 82°W) p. 211

Klamath River (KLA·muhth) A river that flows through southern Oregon and northwestern California. p. 399

Kodiak Island (KOH·dee·ak) An island in the Gulf of Alaska. p. 414

L

Lake Champlain (sham·PLAYN) A large lake on the New York–Vermont state line. p. 125

Lake Erie The fourth largest of the Great Lakes, bordering New York, Pennsylvania, Ohio, Michigan, and Canada. p. 286

Lake Havasu (HAV·uh·SOO) A human-made lake on the Arizona–California state line. p. 352

Lake Huron The second largest of the Great Lakes, bordering Michigan and Canada. p. 286

Lake Itasca (eye·TAS·kuh) A lake in northern Minnesota; the source of the Mississippi River. p. 291

Lake Mead A reservoir on the Colorado River, formed by Hoover Dam. p. 324

Lake Michigan The third largest of the Great Lakes, bordering Michigan, Indiana, Illinois, and Wisconsin. p. 286

Lake Okeechobee (oh·kuh·CHOH·bee) The largest lake in the southern United States, located in southern Florida along the northern edge of the Everglades. p. 189

Lake Ontario The smallest of the Great Lakes. p. 286

Lake Powell A human-made lake in Glen Canyon National Recreation Area in southern Utah. p. 317

Lake Sidney Lanier A lake in northern Georgia. p. 224

Lake Superior The largest of the Great Lakes, bordering Michigan, Wisconsin, Minnesota, and Canada. p. 286

Lanai (luh·NY) A Hawaiian island, located west of Maui. p. 433

Lansing The capital of Michigan. (43°N, 85°W) p. 253

Las Vegas A city in Nevada. (36°N, 115°W) p. 260

Lexington A city in north-central Kentucky. (38°N, 84°W) p. 189

Lincoln The capital of Nebraska. (41°N, 97°W) p. 253

Little Rock The capital of Arkansas. (35°N, 92°W) p. 28

Long Beach A port city in southwestern California. (34°N, 118°W) p. 415

Long Island An island located east of New York City and south of Connecticut. p. 125

Long Island Sound The body of water separating Connecticut and Long Island, New York. p. 98

Los Angeles The largest city in California; the second-largest city in the United States. (34°N, 118°W) p. 56

Louisville The largest city in Kentucky. (38°N, 86°W) p. 189

M

Madison The capital of Wisconsin. (43°N, 89°W) p. 253

Mammoth Cave National Park A national park in south-central Kentucky. p. 189

Marquette (mahr·KET) A city in northern Michigan. (47°N, 87°W) p. 286

Massachusetts Bay An inlet on the coast of Massachusetts, surrounded by Cape Ann and Cape Cod. p. 133

Maui (MOW·ee) The second largest of the eight major Hawaiian islands. p. 433

Mediterranean Sea (meh·duh·tuh·RAY·nee·uhn) The sea south of Europe, north of Africa, and west of Asia. p. 297

Memphis A city in southwestern Tennessee. (35°N, 90°W) p. 189

Mesabi Range (muh·SAH·bee) An area of low hills in northeastern Minnesota. p. 253

Miami A city in south Florida. (26°N, 80°W) p. 189

Middle West Region One of the five regions of the United States. p. 253

Milwaukee (mil·WAH·kee) The largest city in Wisconsin. (43°N, 88°W) p. 260

Mississippi Delta The landform at the mouth of the Mississippi River, created by silt deposited by the river. p. 199

Mississippi River A river that flows from Minnesota to the Gulf of Mexico; the longest river in the United States. p. 291

Missouri River A tributary of the Mississippi River. p. 297

Molokai (mah·luh·KY) A Hawaiian island. p. 433

Monongahela River (muh·nahn·guh·HEE·luh) A river that flows through Pennsylvania and West Virginia. p. 45

Montgomery The capital of Alabama. (32°N, 86°W) p. 189

Montpelier (mawnt·PEEL·yer) The capital of Vermont. (44°N, 73°W) p. 125

Mount McKinley The highest mountain in North America, located in central Alaska. (64°N, 150°W) p. 414

Mount Rainier (ruh·NIR) The highest mountain in the Cascade Range. (47°N, 121°W) p. 35

Mount Rushmore A mountain in the Black Hills of South Dakota. (44°N, 103°W) p. 253

Mount St. Helens A volcano in the Cascade Range that erupted in 1980. (47°N, 122°W) p. 390

Mount Washington A mountain in the White Mountains of New Hampshire. (44°N, 71°W) p. 158

N

Nashua River (NA·shuh·wuh) A river in the northeastern United States. p. 125

Nashville The capital of Tennessee. (36°N, 87°W) p. 222

Negev (NEH·gev) A desert region in southern Israel. p. 371

New Orleans (AWR·lee·uhns) The largest city in Louisiana. (30°N, 90°W) p. 199

New York City The largest city in the United States. (41°N, 74°W) p. 145

New York State Barge Canal System A system of canals that links the Great Lakes with the Hudson River and the Atlantic Ocean. p. 125

Newark A city in northeastern New Jersey. (41°N, 74°W) p. 185

Niagara Falls (ny·AG·ruh) The large waterfalls on the Niagara River. (43°N, 79°W) p. 125

Niagara River A river in western New York that forms part of the United States–Canada border. p. 174

Niihau (NEE·how) A Hawaiian island, located southwest of Kauai. p. 433

Nile River A river in northeastern Africa; the longest river in the world. p. 297

Norfolk (NAWR·fawk) A port city in Virginia. (37°N, 76°W) p. 189

North American Desert A desert region in western North America. p. 369

North Pole The northernmost point on the Earth. (90°N) p. 103

North Sea A part of the Atlantic Ocean, located east of Great Britain and west of Denmark. p. 297

Northeast Region One of the five regions of the United States. p. 125

O

Oahu (oh·AH·hoo) The third-largest of the eight major Hawaiian islands. p. 433

Ogallala (oh·guh·LAHL·uh) A city in western Nebraska. (41°N, 102°W) p. 272

Ohio River A tributary of the Mississippi River. p. 45

Okefenokee Swamp (oh·kee·fuh·NOH·kee) A swamp that covers part of southeastern Georgia and northern Florida. p. 189

Oklahoma City The capital of Oklahoma. (35°N, 98°W) p. 317

Olympia (oh·LIM·pee·uh) The capital of Washington. (47°N, 123°W) p. 35

Omaha The largest city in Nebraska. (41°N, 96°W) p. 253

Orlando A city in central Florida. (28°N, 81°W) p. 189

Ouachita Mountains (WAH·shuh·tah) A mountain range in western Arkansas and southeastern Oklahoma. p. 317

Outer Banks A chain of sand islands and peninsulas along the coast of North Carolina. p. 189

Ozark Plateau (OH·zahrk) A plateau extending from southeastern Missouri across Arkansas and into eastern Oklahoma. p. 40

P

Painted Desert A desert region in Arizona. p. 324

Pampa (PAHM·puh) A plains region in central South America. p. 279

Pecos River (PAY·kohs) A river that flows through eastern New Mexico and western Texas. p. 331

Pee Dee River A river that flows through North Carolina and South Carolina. p. 230

Peru A country in western South America. p. 299

Petrified Forest National Park A national park in eastern Arizona. p. 317

Philadelphia A city in southeastern Pennsylvania. (40°N, 75°W) p. 151

Phoenix (FEE·niks) The capital of Arizona. (33°N, 112°W) p. 352

Piedmont (PEED·mahnt) A region of high land that lies east of the Appalachian Mountains. p. 228

Pierre (PIR) The capital of South Dakota. (44°N, 100°W) p. 253

Pittsburgh A city in southwestern Pennsylvania. (40°N, 80°W) p. 45

Platte River A river that flows through central Nebraska and is a tributary of the Missouri River. p. 48

Plymouth (PLIH·muhth) A town on Plymouth Bay in Massachusetts; the site of the first settlement built by Pilgrims who sailed on the *Mayflower*. (42°N, 71°W) p. 125

Plymouth Bay An inlet on the eastern coast of Massachusetts. p. 132

Pocono Mountains (POH·kuh·noh) A mountain range in eastern Pennsylvania. p. 125

Portland A city in southern Maine. (44°N, 70°W) p. 158

Portland The largest city in Oregon. (46°N, 123°W) p. 417

Potomac River (puh·TOH·muhk) A river in the eastern United States. p. 125

Prime meridian An imaginary line that divides the Earth into the Eastern Hemisphere and the Western Hemisphere. p. 103

Providence (PRAW·vuh·duhns) The capital of Rhode Island. (42°N, 71°W) p. 125

Puerto Rico (PWAIR·tuh REE·koh) A commonwealth of the United States, located southeast of Florida, in the Caribbean Sea. p. 214

R

Raleigh (RAH·lee) The capital of North Carolina. (36°N, 79°W) p. 189

Red River A tributary of the Mississippi River. p. 48

Reno (REE·noh) The second-largest city in Nevada. (40°N, 120°W) p. 104

Rhine River A river in western Europe. p. 297

Richmond The capital of Virginia. (38°N, 77°W) p. 189

Rio Grande (REE·oh GRAND) The river that forms the Texas–Mexico border. p. 35

Rochester A city in western New York. (43°N, 78°W) p. 145

Rocky Mountains A mountain range that extends through the western United States into Canada. p. 40

Russia A country in northeastern Europe and northern Asia; a historic empire and the largest republic of the former Soviet Union. p. 26

S

Sacramento (sa·kruh·MEN·toh) The capital of California. (39°N, 121°W) p. 415

Sacramento River A river in northwestern California. p. 48

Sahara (suh·HAIR·uh) A desert region in northern Africa. p. 369

Salem (SAY·luhm) The capital of Oregon. (45°N, 123°W) p. 417

Salt Lake City The capital of Utah. (41°N, 112°W) p. 46

San Antonio A city in central Texas. (29°N, 98°W) p. 272

San Diego A city in southern California. (33°N, 117°W) p. 415

San Francisco A city in northern California. (38°N, 122°W) p. 107

San Francisco Bay A bay on the northern coast of California. p. 107

San Joaquin River (wah·KEEN) A river in central California. p. 399

San Jose (hoh·ZAY) A city in western California. (37°N, 122°W) p. 421

San Juan (WAHN) The capital of Puerto Rico. (18°N, 66°W) p. 214

Santa Fe (SAN·tah FAY) The capital of New Mexico. (36°N, 106°W) p. 331

Santee River (san•TEE) A river in central South Carolina. p. 220

Savannah (suh•VA•nuh) The oldest city in Georgia. (32°N, 81°W) p. 199

Savannah River A river that forms the border between Georgia and South Carolina. p. 48

Scranton (SKRAN•tuhn) A city in northeastern Pennsylvania. (41°N, 76°W) p. 125

Seattle (see•AT•uhl) The largest city in Washington. (48°N, 122°W) p. 260

Shenandoah National Park (shehn•uhn•DOH•uh) A national park in the Blue Ridge Mountains, in northern Virginia. p. 189

Sierra Nevada (see•AIR•ah neh•VAH•dah) A mountain range in eastern California. p. 40

Silicon Valley An area in California, near San Jose, where many computer chips are produced. p. 107

Snake River A river in the western United States. p. 48

Sonoran Desert (soh•NOHR•ahn) A part of the North American Desert, located in southwestern Arizona. p. 324

South Pole The southernmost point on the Earth. (90°S) p. 103

Southeast Region One of the five regions of the United States. p. 189

Southwest Region One of the five regions of the United States. p. 317

Springfield The capital of Illinois. (40°N, 90°W) p. 253

St. Augustine (AW•guhs-teen) A city on the Atlantic coast of Florida; the oldest city founded by Europeans in the United States. (30°N, 81°W) p. 189

St. Croix (KROY) An island in the Caribbean Sea; the largest of the Virgin Islands. p. 214

St. Lawrence River A river that forms part of the border between Canada and the United States. p. 48

St. Louis The largest city in Missouri. (39°N, 90°W) p. 253

St. Paul The capital of Minnesota. (45°N, 93°W) p. 253

St. Thomas An island in the Caribbean Sea; one of the Virgin Islands. p. 214

Straits of Florida A narrow waterway separating the Florida Keys and Cuba. p. 211

Susquehanna River (suhs•kwuh•HA•nuh) A river in Pennsylvania. p. 48

T

Tallahassee (ta•luh•HA•see) The capital of Florida. (30°N, 84°W) p. 189

Tampa A city on the west coast of Florida. (28°N, 82°W) p. 189

Tampa Bay An inlet of the Gulf coast of Florida. p. 199

Tennessee River A tributary of the Ohio River. p. 222

Topeka (tuh•PEE•kuh) The capital of Kansas. (39°N, 96°W) p. 253

Trenton The capital of New Jersey. (40°N, 75°W) p. 185

Tropic of Cancer The line of latitude at 23½°N. p. 102

Tropic of Capricorn The line of latitude at 23½°S. p. 102

Tucson (TOO•sahn) A city in Arizona. (32°N, 111°W) p. 364

Tulsa (TUHL•suh) A city in Oklahoma. (36°N, 96°W) p. 329

U

Ural Mountains (YOOR•uhl) A mountain range in Russia that extends south from the Kara Sea. p. 406

Utica (YOO•tih•kuh) A city in New York. (43°N, 75°W) p. 169

V

Virgin Islands A group of islands between the Caribbean Sea and the Atlantic Ocean that are United States territories. p. 214

Virginia Beach A city and ocean resort in Virginia. (37°N, 76°W) p. 189

Volga River (VAHL•guh) A river in Russia; the longest river in Europe. p. 297

Voyageurs National Park A national park in northern Minnesota. p. 253

W

Wabash River (WAW•bash) A river in Indiana and Illinois that empties into the Ohio River. p. 48

Washington, D.C. The capital of the United States. (39°N, 77°W) p. 125

Welland Ship Canal (WEH•luhnd) A ship waterway that connects Lake Erie and Lake Ontario; part of the St. Lawrence Seaway. p. 177

West Region One of the five regions of the United States. p. 383

Wheeler Peak A mountain in New Mexico. (36°N, 105°W) p. 317

White Mountains A mountain range in northern New Hampshire. p. 158

Wichita Falls (WIH•chuh•taw) A city in northern Texas. (34°N, 98°W) p. 317

Wilmington A city in Delaware. (40°N, 76°W) p. 125

Wilmington A city in North Carolina. (34°N, 78°W) p. 189

Wind Cave National Park A national park in southwestern South Dakota. p. 253

Winston-Salem (win•stuhn•SAY•luhm) A city in north-central North Carolina. (36°N, 80°W) p. 227

Wisconsin River A river in central Wisconsin. p. 253

Y

Youngstown A city in northern Ohio. (41°N, 81°W) p. 121

Yukon River (YOO•kahn) A river that flows through Alaska and the southwestern Yukon Territory in Canada. p. 35

Yuma (YOO•muh) A city in southwestern Arizona. (33°N, 115°W) p. 317

GLOSSARY

The Glossary contains important social studies words and their definitions. Each word is respelled as it would be in a dictionary. When you see this mark ´ after a syllable, pronounce that syllable with more force than the other syllables. The page number at the end of the definition tells where to find the word in your book.

add, āce, câre, pälm; end, ēqual; it, īce; odd, ōpen, ôrder; tŏŏk, pōōl; up, bûrn; yŏŏ as u in fuse; oil; pout; ə as a in above, e in sicken, i in possible, o in melon, u in circus; check; ring; thin; this; zh as in vision

A

absolute location (ab´sə•lŏŏt lō•kā´shən) An exact position on the Earth's surface. p. 102

adapt (ə•dapt´) To change in order to make more useful. p. 64

adobe (ah•dō´bā) Clay brick. p. 331

aerospace (âr´ō•spās) The technology used to build and test equipment for air and space travel. p. 338

agricultural economy (ag•rə•kul´chər•əl i•kon´ə•mē) An economy in which people meet most of their needs by farming. p. 168

agriculture (a´gri•kəl•chər) Farming. p. 107

aluminum (ə•lŏŏ´mə•nəm) A strong and light metal. p. 417

analyzing (an´ə•līz•ing) A way of thinking in which something is broken down into its parts to more closely see how the parts are connected. p. 29

ancestor (an´ses•tər) An early family member. p. 72

Antarctic Circle (ant•ärk´tik sûr´kəl) The line of latitude at 66½°S. p. 102

aqueduct (a´kwə•dəkt) A large pipe or canal built to carry water. p. 351

Arctic Circle (ärk´tik sûr´kəl) The line of latitude at 66½°N. p. 102

arid (ar´əd) Dry. p. 341

arroyo (ə•roh´yō) A deep, water-carved gully or ditch. p. 350

assembly line (ə•sem´blē līn) A line of workers along which a product moves as it is put together one step at a time. p. 288

axis (ak´səs) An imaginary line that runs through the Earth from the North Pole to the South Pole. p. 53

B

ballot (ba´lət) A sheet of paper or some other method used to mark a secret vote. p. 365

barge (bärj) A large, flat-bottomed boat used on rivers and other inland waterways. p. 294

barrier (bar´ē•ər) Something that blocks the way or makes it hard to move from place to place. p. 393

barrier island (bar´ē•ər ī´lənd) A low, narrow island that is near a coast. p. 210

bartering (bär´tər•ing) The trading of one kind of good for another without using money. p. 409

basin (bā´sən) Low, bowl-shaped land with higher ground all around it. p. 42

bayou (bī´ŏŏ or bī´ō) A slow-moving body of water. p. 203

blizzard (bliz´ərd) A snowstorm driven by strong, freezing winds. p. 263

boomtown (bŏŏm´toun) A town that grew up quickly, almost overnight. p. 398

boundary (boun´də•rē) The border or edge of a place. p. 27

broadleaf tree (brôd´lēf trē) A tree with wide, flat leaves. In autumn, the leaves turn colors and fall to the ground. p. 106

budget (bu´jət) A plan for spending and saving money. p. 364

C

campaign (kam•pān´) What a candidate running for an elected office does to get votes, such as running advertisements on television, displaying signs, making speeches, and talking with voters. p. 365

canal (kə•nal´) A waterway dug across land. p. 174

candidate (kan´də•dāt or ka´nə•dət) A person who is running for office in an election. p. 365

canyon (kan´yən) A deep, narrow valley with steep sides. p. 42

cape (kāp) A point of land that reaches out into the ocean. p. 131

capital resource (kap´ə•təl rē´sôrs) The money, a building, a machine, or a tool needed to run a business. p. 287

cardinal directions (kär´də•nəl də•rek´shənz) The four main directions: north, south, east, and west. p. 27

cause (kôz) Something that makes something else happen. p. 202

central business district (sen´trəl biz´nəs dis´trikt) The downtown area in the center of a city; often the oldest part of a city. p. 141

century (sen´chə•rē) A period of 100 years. p. 335

channel (chan´nəl) The deepest part of a river or other body of water. p. 44

citizen (sit´ə•zən) A member of a town or city, a state, or a country. p. 19

city manager (sit´ē ma´ni•jər) A person who is hired to run a city. A city manager hires city workers and oversees all the day-to-day operations of a city. p. 364

classify (klas´ə•fī) To put into groups. p. 300

climate (klī´mət) The kind of weather a place has over a long time. p. 23

cloudburst (kloud´bərst) A sudden, heavy rain. p. 350

coastal plain (kōs´təl plān) Low land that lies along an ocean. p. 39

colony (kä´lə•nē) A settlement started by people who leave their own country to live in another land. p. 132

commonwealth (käm´ən•welth) A territory that governs itself. p. 214

communication (kə•myoo•nə•kā´shən) The way people send and receive information. p. 112

compass rose (kum´pəs rōz) The direction marker on a map. p. 27

competition (käm•pə•ti´shən) In business, the contest among companies to sell the most products. p. 171

compromise (kom´prə•mīz) Each side in a conflict giving up some of what it wants in order to make an agreement. p. 343

conclusion (kən•kloo´zhən) A decision or idea reached by thoughtful study. p. 404

conflict (kon´flikt) A disagreement between two or more people or groups. p. 342

Congress (kon´grəs) The legislative branch of the federal government. p. 91

consequence (kon´sə•kwens) What happens because of an action. p. 76

conservation (kon•sər•vā´shən) The protecting of natural resources and the using of them wisely. p. 65

Constitution (kon•stə•too´shən) The plan for the federal government. It describes the rights that people in the United States have, and it is the supreme law of the land. p. 90

continent (kon´tə•nənt) One of the seven main areas of land on the Earth. p. 25

Continental Divide (kän•tən•en´təl də•vīd´) An imaginary line running north and south along the highest points of the Rocky Mountains. p. 390

coral (kôr´əl) A stony material formed by the skeletons of tiny sea animals. p. 211

county (koun´tē) A part of a state, usually larger than a city, that has its own government. p. 99

county seat (koun´tē sēt) A town or city that is the center of government for a county. p. 99

cross section (krôs sek´shən) A slice or piece cut straight across something. p. 208

cross-section diagram (krôs sek´shən dī´ə•gram) A drawing or picture that shows what you would see if you could slice through something and then look at the cut surface. p. 208

crude oil (krood oil) The name given to petroleum pumped from the ground. p. 204

culture (kul´chər) A way of life. p. 75

custom (kus´təm) A usual way of doing things. p. 71

cutaway diagram (ku´tə•wā dī´ə•gram) A diagram that shows the outside and inside of an object at the same time. p. 136

D

dam (dam) A wall built across a river to hold back water. p. 49

decade (dek´ād) A period of 10 years. p. 335

Declaration of Independence (dek•lə•rā´shən uv in•də•pen´dəns) A statement, written by Thomas Jefferson in 1776, explaining why the United States wanted to be free from England. p. 90

delta (del´tə) The triangle-shaped land at a river's mouth. p. 48

demand (di•mand´) A desire for a good or service by people who are willing to pay for it. p. 273

democracy (di•mä´krə•sē) A form of government in which the people rule and are free to make choices about their lives and their government. p. 84

downstream (doun´strēm) Toward a river's mouth. p. 51

drainage basin (drā´nij bā´sən) The land drained by a river system. p. 45

dredge (drej) To dig out the bottom and sides of a waterway to make it deeper and wider. p. 336

drought (drout) A time of little or no rain. p. 261

E

earthquake (ûrth´kwāk) A sudden shaking of the ground caused by the movement and cracking of rock deep inside the Earth. p. 415

economics (ek•ə•nom´iks *or* ē•kə•nom´iks) The study of how people provide and use goods and services. p. 30

economy (i•kä´nə•mē) A system for providing and using goods and services. p. 61

ecosystem (ē´kō•sis•təm) The relationship between living things and their nonliving environment. p. 418

effect (i•fekt´) What happens because of an earlier action. p. 202

elevation (e•lə•vā´shən) The height of the land. p. 50

entrepreneur (än•trə•prə•nûr´) A person who sets up a new business. p. 273

environment (in•vī´rən•mənt) Surroundings. p. 20

equator (i•kwā´tər) An imaginary line that circles the Earth halfway between the North Pole and the South Pole. The line divides the Earth into the Northern Hemisphere and the Southern Hemisphere. p. 24

erosion (i•rō´zhən) The wearing away of the Earth's surface. p. 47

estancia (is•stän´sē•a) A large ranch. p. 281

ethnic group (eth´nik grōōp) A group made up of people from the same country, people of the same race, or people with a common way of life. p. 74

executive branch (ig•ze´kyə•tiv branch) A branch of the federal government. Its main job is to see that the laws passed by Congress are carried out. p. 91

export (eks´pôrt) A good shipped from one country to another, most often to be sold. p. 135

F

fact (fakt) A statement that can be checked and proved to be true. p. 161

factors of production (fak´tərz uv prə•duk´shən) The natural, human, and capital resources that a business needs to produce goods or services. p. 287

fall line (fôl līn) The place where rivers drop from higher to lower land. p. 219

federal (fed´ər•əl) National. p. 88

fertile (fûr´təl) Good for growing crops, as rich land is. p. 42

fertilizer (fûr´təl•ī•zər) Matter added to the soil to help crops grow. p. 268

finished product (fin´isht prod´əkt) A manufactured good made from raw materials. p. 169

fjord (fē•ôrd´) A narrow inlet of the ocean between cliffs. p. 413

flatboat (flat´bōt) A large raft made of boards that are tied together. p. 291

floodplain (flud´plān) The low land along a river. p. 47

food processing (fōōd pros´es•ing) The cooking, canning, or freezing of food and the preparing of it for market. p. 198

free enterprise (frē en´tər•prīz) A kind of economy in which people own and run their own businesses with only some control by the government. p. 273

fuel (fyōō´əl) A natural resource, such as coal, oil, or natural gas, used to make heat or energy. p. 58

G

gaucho (gou´chō) A skilled rider who lived on the open land of the Pampa of South America and who hunted cattle for food and hides. Today a gaucho is a ranch hand on an estancia. p. 280

general election (jen´ər•əl i•lek´shən) An election in which the voters choose the people who will represent them in government. p. 365

generalization (jen•ər•əl•ə•zā´shən) A statement that summarizes a group of facts and shows the relationships between them. p. 420

generation (je•nə•rā´shən) The average time between the birth of parents and the birth of their children. p. 193

geography (jē•og´rə•fē) The study of the Earth's surface and the ways people use it. p. 22

geyser (gī´zər) A spring that shoots steam and hot water into the air. p. 403

glacier (glā´shər) A huge, slow-moving mass of ice. p. 157

government (guv´ərn•mənt) A group of people who lead a community, state, or nation. The main job of government is to make and carry out laws. p. 84

governor (guv´ər•nər) The head of the executive branch of state government. p. 229

grid (grid) On a map the lines that cross each other to form a pattern of squares used to locate places. p. 28

groundwater (ground´wô•tər) Water beneath the Earth's surface. p. 44

growing season (grō´ing sē´zən) A time when the weather is warm enough for plants to grow. p. 195

H

hailstorm (hāl´stôrm) A storm that drops hail, or lumps of ice. p. 263

harbor (här´bər) A place where ships can dock safely. p. 131

hemisphere (hem´ə•sfir) Half of a sphere, such as a ball or a globe; a half of the Earth. p. 24

heritage (her´ə•tij) A way of life, a custom, or a belief that has come from the past and continues today. p. 86

history (his´tə•rē) The study of the past. p. 29

human feature (hyōō´mən fē´chər) A feature, such as a building or a highway, that has been made by people. p. 23

human resources (hyōō´mən rē´sôr•səz) Workers and the ideas and skills that they bring to their jobs. p. 59

humidity (hyōō•mi´də•tē) The amount of moisture in the air. p. 55

hunters and gatherers (hun´tərz and ga´thər•ərz) People who meet their needs by hunting and gathering instead of by farming. p. 416

hurricane (hûr´ə•kān) A huge storm with heavy rains and high winds. Near its center, winds blow at 74 miles (119 km) per hour or more. p. 206

hydroelectric power (hī•drō•i•lek´trik pou´ər) Electricity made by waterpower. p. 221

I

immigrant (i´mi•grənt) A person who comes to live in a country from another place. p. 71

import (im´pôrt) A good brought into one country from another country, most often to be sold. p. 135

independence (in·də·pen´dəns) Freedom from control by others. p. 83

industrial economy (in·dus´trē·əl i·kä´nə·mē) An economy in which factories and machines manufacture most goods. p. 169

industry (in´dus·trē) All the businesses that make one kind of product or provide one kind of service. p. 107

inlet (in´let *or* in´lət) A narrow strip of water leading into the land from a larger body of water. p. 203

inset map (in´set map) A small map within a larger map. p. 27

interdependence (in·tər·də·pen´dəns) Depending on one another for resources and products. p. 112

interest (in´tə·rəst) The money a bank or a borrower pays for the use of money. p. 434

intermediate directions (in·tər·mē´dē·it də·rek´shənz) The directions between the cardinal directions: northeast, southeast, southwest, and northwest. p. 27

international trade (in·tər·nash´ən·əl trād) Trade among nations. p. 135

interstate highway (in·tər·stāt´ hī´wā) A divided highway that goes through more than one state and connects large cities. p. 276

irrigation (ir·ə·gā´shən) The use of canals, ditches, or pipes to move water to dry areas. p. 296

isthmus (is´məs) A narrow piece of land that connects two larger land areas. p. 72

J

judicial branch (jōō·di´shəl branch) A branch of the federal government. Its main job is to see that laws are carried out fairly. p. 92

L

labor (lā´bər) Work. p. 394

land use (land yōōs) How most of the land in a place is used. p. 62

landform (land´fôrm) One of the shapes that make up the Earth's surface, such as mountains, hills, or plains. p. 19

lava (lä´və) Hot, melted rock that comes from a volcano. p. 387

legend (lej´ənd) A story that has come down from the past; parts of it may or may not be true. p. 210

legislative branch (le´jəs·lā·tiv branch) The lawmaking branch of the federal government. It is also called Congress. p. 91

levee (le´vē) A high wall that is made of earth and is built along the banks of a river to control flooding. p. 49

line graph (līn graf) A graph that uses a line to show changes over time. p. 172

lines of latitude (līnz uv la´tə·tōōd) The set of imaginary lines on a globe or a map that run east and west. They are used to tell how far north or south of the equator a place is. p. 102

lines of longitude (līnz uv lon´jə·tōōd) The set of imaginary lines on a globe or a map that run north and south. They are used to tell how far east or west of the prime meridian a place is. p. 103

location (lō·kā´shən) Where something can be found. p. 22

locator (lō´kāt·ər) A small map or globe that shows where the place on a main map is located in a state, in a country, or in the world. p. 27

lock (läk) A part of a canal in which the water level can be raised or lowered to bring a ship to the level of the next part of the canal. p. 175

M

mainland (mān´land) The continent, or part of a continent, nearest to an island. p. 210

majority rule (mə·jôr´ə·tē rōōl) A way of deciding something. Whoever or whatever gets the most votes wins. p. 84

manufacturing (man·yə·fak´chə·ring) The making of goods. p. 59

map key (map kē) The part of a map that explains what the symbols on the map stand for. p. 27

map scale (map skāl) The part of a map that compares a distance on the map to a distance in the real world. p. 27

marsh (märsh) Low, wet land where cattails, tall grasses, and other similar plants grow. p. 193

mass production (mas prə·duk´shən) A way of manufacturing in which many goods that are alike can be made quickly and cheaply. p. 288

meat packing (mēt pak´ing) The preparing of meat for market. p. 275

megalopolis (me·gə·lä´pə·ləs) A huge urban region formed when two or more metropolitan areas grow together. p. 143

meridians (mə·ri´dē·ənz) Lines of longitude. p. 103

mesa (mā´sa) A hill or small plateau with a flat top and steep sides. p. 326

metropolitan area (me·trə·pä´lə·tən âr´ē·ə) A large city together with its suburbs. p. 142

migrant worker (mī´grənt wur´kər) Someone who moves from farm to farm with the seasons, harvesting crops. p. 353

migration (mī·grā´shən) The movement of many people who leave one country or region to settle in another. p. 291

mileage table (mī´lij tā´bəl) A table that gives the number of miles between the listed cities. p. 397

mineral (min´rəl) A natural substance found in rocks. p. 58

mission (mish´ən) A settlement started by Catholic priests where they taught Native Americans about Christianity. p. 331

monument (mon´yə•mənt) Something that is built to remind people of the past. p. 87

mountain range (moun´tən rānj) A group of connected mountains. p. 42

mouth (mouth) The place where a river empties into some larger body of water. p. 45

municipal court (myōō•ni´sə•pəl kôrt) A court that decides the cases of people accused of breaking city laws. p. 365

N

natural resource (nach´ə•rəl rē´sôrs) Something found in nature that people can use. p. 22

natural vegetation (nach´ə•rəl ve•gə•tā´shən) The plant life that grows naturally in an area. p. 105

navigable river (na´vi•gə•bəl riv´ər) A river that is deep and wide enough for ships to use. p. 173

needleleaf tree (nē´dəl•lēf trē) A tree with long, sharp leaves that look like needles. It stays green all year. p. 106

nomad (nō´mad) A person who has no permanent home but keeps moving from place to place. p. 349

nonrenewable resource (non•ri•nōō´ə•bəl rē´sôrs) A resource that cannot be made again by nature or by people. p. 204

O

oasis (ō•ā´səs) An area that is in a desert but has water. p. 370

oil slick (oil slik) The film of oil that coats the water after an oil spill. p. 427

opinion (ə•pin´yən) A statement that tells what a person thinks or believes. It cannot be proved. p. 161

opportunity cost (ä•pər•tōō´nə•tē kôst) The value of the thing a person gives up in order to get something else. p. 399

ore (ôr) Rock that contains one or more kinds of minerals. p. 239

P

paddy (pad´ē) A rice field. p. 298

parallels (par´ə•lelz) Lines that are always the same distance apart, such as lines of latitude. p. 102

pass (pas) A low place between mountains. p. 219

peninsula (pə•nin´sə•lə) Land almost entirely surrounded by water. p. 39

petrochemical (pe•trō•ke´mi•kəl) A chemical made from oil. p. 205

petroleum (pə•trō´lē•əm) Oil. p. 204

physical feature (fiz´i•kəl fē´chər) A feature, such as a landform, body of water, or resource, that has been formed by nature. p. 22

pictograph (pik´tə•graf) A graph that uses symbols to stand for numbers. p. 264

plantation (plan•tā´shən) A type of farm where tobacco, cotton, and rice were the main crops. p. 195

plateau (pla•tō´) An area of high, mostly flat land. p. 41

pollution (pə•lōō´shən) Anything that makes a natural resource, such as air, soil, or water, dirty or unsafe to use. p. 66

population (pop•yə•lā´shən) The number of people who live in a place. p. 138

population density (pop•yə•lā´shən den´sə•tē) The number of people living in an area of a certain size, usually one square mile or one square kilometer. p. 144

port (pôrt) A trading center where ships are loaded and unloaded. p. 134

poverty (pä´vər•tē) Being very poor. p. 74

prairie (prâr´ē) An area of flat or rolling land covered mostly by grasses and wildflowers. p. 259

precipitation (pri•si•pə•tā´shən) Water, as in rain, sleet, or snow, that falls to the Earth's surface. p. 52

prediction (pri•dik´shən) Looking at the way things are and saying what you think will happen in the future or in another place. p. 404

prejudice (pre´jə•dəs) An unfair feeling of hatred or dislike for a group because of their background, race, or religion. p. 140

primary source (prī´mâr•ē sôrs) Firsthand information from someone who saw an event or took part in it. p. 340

prime meridian (prīm mə•rid´ē•ən) An imaginary line that divides the Earth into the Eastern Hemisphere and the Western Hemisphere. p. 103

produce (prō´dōōs) Fresh fruits and vegetables. p. 167

product (prod´əkt) Something that people make or grow, usually to sell. p. 58

public land (pub´lik land) Land that is owned by the government. p. 402

pulp (pulp) A soft mixture of ground-up wood chips and chemicals that is used to make paper. p. 198

Q

quarry (kwôr´ē) A large open pit cut into the ground in which stone is mined. p. 159

R

rain forest (rān fôr´əst) A warm, wet area where tall trees, vines, and other plants grow close together. p. 299

rain shadow (rān sha´dō) On a mountain, the drier side that receives little or no precipitation. p. 327

rapid (ra´pəd) A rocky place in a river where a sudden drop in elevation causes fast-moving, dangerous water. p. 174

raw material (rô mə•tir´ē•əl) A resource in its natural state, such as a mineral, that can be used to manufacture a product. p. 134

reclaim (ri•klām´) To return something, such as land, to its natural condition. p. 237

recreation (rek•rē•ā´shən) What people do to have fun. p. 106

recycle (rē•sī´kəl) To use again. p. 66

reef (rēf) A ridge of rocks, sand, or coral near the surface of the sea. p. 212

refinery (ri•fī´nər•ē) A factory that turns crude oil into useful products such as gasoline and other fuels. p. 205

region (rē´jən) An area with at least one feature that makes it different from other areas. p. 23

relative location (re´lə•tiv lō•kā´shən) The position of a place in relation to other places on the Earth. p. 97

relief (ri•lēf´) Differences in elevation. p. 50

religion (ri•li´jən) Beliefs about God or gods. p. 73

renewable resource (ri•nōō´ə•bəl rē´sôrs) A resource that can be used again or made again by people or nature. p. 199

representative democracy (rep•ri•zen´tə•tiv di•mok´rə•sē) A system of government in which citizens elect representatives, or leaders, to make decisions about the laws for all the people. p. 84

reservation (rez•ər•vā´shən) Land set aside by the government for use by American Indians. On reservations, Indians govern themselves. p. 334

reservoir (re´zə•vwär) A lake that stores water held back by a dam. p. 221

responsibility (ri•spän•sə•bi´lə•tē) Something that a person should do. p. 85

revolution (rev•ə•lōō´shən) A complete trip of the Earth around the sun. It takes the Earth one year to make one revolution. p. 53

revolution (rev•ə•lōō´shən) A large, sudden change in government or in people's lives. p. 90

right (rīt) A freedom that belongs to a person. p. 85

river system (ri´vər sis´təm) A river and its tributaries. p. 45

rotation (rō•tā´shən) A complete turn of the Earth on its axis from west to east. It takes the Earth one day to make one rotation. p. 53

route (rōōt) A path from one place to another. p. 276

runoff (run´ôf) Surface water that does not soak into the ground. p. 344

rural (rŏŏr´əl) Of or like a country region. p. 108

S

sand dune (sand dōōn) A hill-like mound formed by blowing sand. p. 370

satellite (sa´təl•īt) An object that orbits the Earth. p. 395

scarce (skers *or* skars) Limited. p. 66

sea level (sē lev´əl) Land that is level with the surface of the ocean. p. 50

secondary source (sek´ən•dâr•ē sôrs) A description of an event by someone who did not directly observe or take part in the event. p. 340

self-sufficient (self sə•fish´ənt) The state in which people can do almost everything for themselves, with no help from other people. p. 267

sequence (sē´kwəns) The order in which one thing comes after another. p. 270

service (sûr´vəs) An activity that someone does for others for pay. p. 61

shaman (shä´mən) A spiritual leader. p. 290

slavery (slā´vər•ē) Making one person the property of another person. p. 73

slope (slōp) The side of a mountain. p. 388

society (sə•sī´ə•tē) A group of people who have many things in common. p. 332

sod (sod) A layer of soil held together by the roots of grasses. p. 266

source (sôrs) The place where a river begins. p. 44

specialize (spe´shə•līz) To work at only one kind of job. p. 111

sphere (sfir) An object having a ball-like shape, such as a globe of the Earth. p. 24

state legislature (stāt le´jəs•lā•chər) The legislative branch of state government. p. 229

strait (strāt) A narrow channel that connects two larger bodies of water. p. 211

suburb (sub´ərb) A town or small city built near a larger city. p. 108

suburban (sə•bər´bən) Made up of all the suburbs around a large city, as a suburban region is. p. 108

Sun Belt (sun belt) A wide area of the southern United States that has a mild climate all year. p. 201

supply (sə•plī´) A good or service that a business offers for sale. p. 274

Supreme Court (sə•prēm´ kôrt) The highest court in the country. p. 92

swamp (swämp) A low, wet area, usually covered by shallow water at least part of the year. p. 197

symbol (sim´bəl) Something that stands for something else. Colors, patterns, lines, and other special marks are sometimes used as symbols on maps. p. 27

T

technology (tek·nä´lə·jē) The way people use new ideas to make tools and machines. p. 110

terrace (ter´əs) A flat "shelf" dug into a mountainside to make farming there possible. p. 408

territory (ter´ə·tôr·ē) A place owned and governed by a country. p. 214

textile (teks´tīl) Cloth. p. 198

timberline (tim´bər·līn) On a mountain, the elevation above which the temperatures are too low for trees to grow. p. 391

time zone (tīm zōn) A region in which people use the same clock time. p. 366

toll road (tōl rōd) A road that drivers must pay to use. p. 276

tornado (tôr·nā´dō) A funnel-shaped, spinning windstorm, sometimes called a cyclone or twister. p. 263

tourism (toor´iz·əm) The selling of goods and services to tourists. p. 201

tourist (toor´·ist) Someone who travels to a place for pleasure. p. 201

trade (trād) The buying and selling of goods. p. 111

trade-off (trād´of) The giving up of one thing in order to get another. p. 399

tradition (trə·dish´ən) A way or an idea that has been handed down from the past. p. 160

transcontinental railroad (trans·kon·tə·nen´təl rāl´rōd) A railroad built to link the East and West coasts of North America. p. 393

transportation (trans·pər·tā´shən) The way people and goods are moved from place to place. p. 111

tributary (trib´yə·ter·ē) A stream or river that flows into a larger stream or river. p. 45

Tropic of Cancer (trop´ik uv kan´sər) The line of latitude at 23½°N. p. 102

Tropic of Capricorn (trop´ik uv ka´pri·kôrn) The line of latitude at 23½°S. p. 102

tropics (trop´iks) A band of warm climate that circles the Earth near the equator. p. 213

truck farm (truk färm) A farm that grows produce and is located close to a city so that the produce can be taken quickly by trucks to nearby markets. p. 167

tundra (tun´drə) Flat land without trees that stays frozen most of the year. p. 426

U

unemployment (un·im·ploi´mənt) Being without a job. p. 150

upstream (up´strēm) Toward a river's source. p. 51

urban (ûr´bən) Of or like a city region. p. 108

urban growth (ûr´bən grōth) The growth of cities. p. 139

urban sprawl (ûr´bən sprôl) The spreading of urban areas and the growth of new centers of business and shopping. p. 142

urbanization (ûr·bə·nə·zā´shən) The spread of city life. p. 269

V

volcano (vol·kā´nō) An opening in the Earth's surface from which hot gases, ashes, and lava may pour out. p. 387

volunteer (vä·lən·tir´) A person who offers to do something without pay. p. 428

W

waterpower (wô´tər·pou·ər) The power produced by rushing water. p. 220

waterway (wô´tər·wā) A body of water that boats can use. p. 170

wealth (welth) Riches. p. 73

wetlands (wet´landz) Low-lying land where the water level is always near or above the surface of the land. p. 429

wildlife refuge (wīld·līf re´fyooj) An area of land set aside to protect animals and other living things. p. 430

INDEX

Page references for illustrations are set in italic type. An italic m indicates a map. Page references set in boldface type indicate the pages on which vocabulary terms are defined.

Abilene, Kansas   *Charleston, South Carolina*

For permission to reprint copyrighted material, grateful acknowledgment is made to the following sources:

Boyds Mills Press: *Anna's Athabaskan Summer* by Arnold Griese, illustrated by Charles Ragins. Text copyright © 1995 by Arnold Griese; illustrations copyright © 1995 by Charles Ragins.

Curtis Brown Ltd.: "Stone Wall" by Ann Turner from *A New England Scrapbook: A Journey Through Poetry, Prose, and Pictures* by Loretta Krupinski. Text copyright © 1994 by Ann Turner. Published by HarperCollins Publishers.

Cherry Lane Music Publishing Company, Inc. (ASCAP): From "Take Me Home, Country Roads" by John Denver, Bill Danoff, and Taffy Danoff. Text copyright © 1971 by Cherry Lane Music Publishing Company, Inc.

Children's Better Health Institute, Indianapolis, IN: From "Climb Every Mountain" by Gail Skroback Hennessey in *U. S. Kids, A Weekly Reader* Magazine, November/December 1992. Text copyright © 1992 by Children's Better Health Institute, Benjamin Franklin Literary & Medical Society, Inc.

Chronicle Books, San Francisco, CA: From *Alejandro's Gift* by Richard E. Albert, illustrated by Sylvia Long. Text copyright © 1994 by Richard E. Albert; illustrations copyright © 1994 by Sylvia Long.

Harcourt Brace & Company: From *A River Ran Wild* by Lynne Cherry. Copyright © 1992 by Lynne Cherry. From *Appalachia: The Voices of Sleeping Birds* by Cynthia Rylant, illustrated by Barry Moser. Text copyright © 1991 by Cynthia Rylant; illustrations copyright © 1991 by Pennyroyal Press, Inc. "The Sea" from *Everything Glistens and Everything Sings* by Charlotte Zolotow. Text copyright © 1987 by Charlotte Zolotow.

HarperCollins Publishers: From *Heartland* by Diane Siebert, illustrated by Wendell Minor. Text copyright © 1989 by Diane Siebert; illustrations copyright © 1989 by Wendell Minor.

Henry Holt and Company, Inc.: From *Lobster Boat* by Brenda Z. Guiberson, illustrated by Megan Lloyd. Text copyright © 1993 by Brenda Z. Guiberson; illustrations copyright © 1993 by Megan Lloyd. From "Waves" in *Is Somewhere Always Far Away?* by Leland B. Jacobs. Text copyright © 1993 by Allan D. Jacobs. "Ten miles to the nearest water..." from *It Happened in America: True Stories from the Fifty States* by Lila Perl.

Alfred A. Knopf, Inc.: From "The Negro Speaks of Rivers" in *Selected Poems* by Langston Hughes. Text copyright 1926 by Alfred A. Knopf, Inc., renewed 1954 by Langston Hughes.

Ludlow Music, Inc., New York: "This Land Is Your Land" by Woody Guthrie. TRO – © lyrics copyright 1956 (renewed), 1958 (renewed), 1970 by Ludlow Music, Inc.

Open Hand Publishing Inc.: From *Black Heroes of the Wild West* by Ruth Pelz. Copyright © 1990 by Open Hand Publishing Inc.

Random House, Inc.: From "City, Oh City!" by Jack Prelutsky in *The Random House Book of Poetry for Children,* selected by Jack Prelutsky. Text copyright © 1983 by Jack Prelutsky.

Simon & Schuster Books for Young Readers, Simon & Schuster Children's Publishing Division: Amazon Boy by Ted Lewin. Copyright © 1993 by Ted Lewin.

Tilbury House, Publishers, Gardiner, Maine: From *Who Belongs Here? An American Story* (Retitled: "Nary's Story") by Margy Burns Knight, illustrated by Anne Sibley O'Brien. Text copyright © 1993 by Margy Burns Knight; illustrations copyright © 1993 by Anne Sibley O'Brien.

University of Missouri—Kansas City, University Libraries: "Maps" by Dorothy Brown Thompson.

Every effort has been made to locate the copyright holders for the selections in this work. The publisher would be pleased to receive information that would allow the correction of any omissions in future printings.

ILLUSTRATION CREDITS:

PHOTO CREDITS:

Stock, Boston; 175 (c) Marshall Prescott/Unicorn Stock Photos; 175 (bl) Erie Canal Museum, Syracuse NY; 175 (br) Buffalo & Erie County Historical Society; 176 Imagery; 180 (l), 180 (r), 181 (t), 181 (b) Philadelphia Anti Graffiti Network.

Unit 3
Harcourt Brace & Company
Page 197 (b) Harcourt Brace & Company; 200 Len Kaufman/Black Star; 221 (r) Weronica Ankarorn; 227 Maria Paraskevas; 233-235 (bg) Victoria Bowen; 248 Terry D. Sinclair.

Other
Page 186 (bl) Matt Bradley; 186 (bc) Jim Stamates/Tony Stone Images; 186 (br) David Madison/Tony Stone Images; 186-187 NASA; 187 (bl) David Muench; 187 (bc) David Barnes/The Stock Market; 187 (br) Henley & Savage/Tony Stone Images; 188 (l) Jonathan Nourok/PhotoEdit; 188 (inset) David Young-Wolff/PhotoEdit; 188 (r) John Elk III/Stock, Boston; 189 (l) Chuck O'Rear/Westlight; 189 (c) Doris De Witt/Tony Stone Images; 189 (r) Douglas A. Faulkner/Photo Researchers; 190, 191 Richard T. Nowitz/National Geographic Society; 192 Robert E. Daemmrich/Tony Stone Images; 193 Bruce Hands/Stock, Boston; 194 (l) William Johnson/Stock, Boston; 194 (c), 194 (r) Courtesy of the Jamestown-Yorktown Educational Trust, Jamestown Settlement Museum; 195 Culver Pictures; 196 (t) Kenneth W. Fink/Photo Researchers; 196 (b), 197 (t) David Frazier Photolibrary; 198 Frank Fortune/Stock South; 199 David R. Frazier Photolibrary; 201 (inset) Myrleen Ferguson/PhotoEdit; 201 James Blank/The Stock Market; 203 Kunio Owaki/The Stock Market; 204 Jean Anderson/The Stock Market; 205 Bob Daemmrich/Stock, Boston; 206 Kristin Finnegan/Tony Stone Images; 207 (l) Reuters/Bettmann; 207 (r) NOAA/SPL/Photo Researchers; 208 (t) Ken M. Highfill/Photo Researchers; 208 (b) A.W. Ambler/Photo Researchers; 210 The Granger Collection, New York; 211 (t) Tom Till/Tony Stone Images; 211 (b) Larry Lipsky/Bruce Coleman, Inc.; 212 (l) Florida State Archives; 212 (r) Dallas & John Heaton/Westlight; 214 Harvey Lloyd/The Stock Market; 215 (l) Mark E. Gibson; 215 (r) Cosmo Condina/Tony Stone Images; 218 Michael Newman/PhotoEdit; 219 B. Thomas/H. Armstrong Roberts; 221 (l) D. & I. MacDonald/Photri; 223 Champion International Corp.; 225 Terri Froelich/Southern Stock Photo Agency; 226 Kunio Owaki/The Stock Market; 228 John Elk/Tony Stone Images; 229 Michael Moore Photography; 236 UPI/Bettmann; 237 Larry Smith/H. Armstrong Roberts; 239 Shorty Wilcox/The Stock Market; 240 (t), 240 (b) Martin Fox/Picturesque Stock Photo; 241 (l), 241 (c) Chuck Wyrostok/AppaLight; 241 (r) Kent & Donna Dannen; 244 (t) Wendell Metzen/Bruce Coleman, Inc.; 244 (b) R. Tully; 244-245 (bg) J. Carmichael/Bruce Coleman, Inc.; 245 (t), 245 (b) R. Tully.

Unit 4
Harcourt Brace & Company
Page 254-257 (bg) Corel; 290 Wellington Photography/Courtesy Chickasaw National Headquarters; 296 (r) Harcourt Brace & Company; 296 (c) Rich Franco; 312 P&F Communications.

Other
Page 250 (bl) Michael Dunn/The Stock Market; 250 (bc) Philip & Karen Smith/Tony Stone Images; 250 (br) Tom Algire/Tom Stack & Associates; 250-251 Jim Blakeway/Panoramic Images; 251 (bl) David Muench; 251 (bc) Bachmann/Stock, Boston; 251 (br) Charles Thatcher/Tony Stone Images; 252 (l) Culver Pictures; 252 (inset) Lawrence Migdale/Stock, Boston; 252 (c), 252 (r) Missouri Historical Society; 253 (l) Kansas State Historical Society; 253 (r) The Granger Collection, New York; 258 Charlie Westerman/Liaison International; 259 Jeff Greenberg/Unicorn Stock Photos; 261

Thomas Hovland/Grant Heilman Photography; 262 (t) Grant Heilman Photography; 262 (inset) David Young-Wolff/PhotoEdit; 263 Merrilee Thomas/Tom Stack & Associates; 265 The Farmers' Museum, Inc., Cooperstown, N.Y.; 266 Nebraska State Historical Society; 267 Kevin Horan/Tony Stone Images; 268 (t) Deere & Company; 268 (c) Joe Bator/The Stock Market; 268 (b) Michael Rosenfeld/Tony Stone Images; 270 The Bettmann Archive; 271 The Granger Collection, New York; 272 Bob Daemmrich/Stock, Boston; 273 (l) The Bettmann Archive; 273 (r) Kansas State Historical Society; 275 Mark E. Gibson; 275 (inset) General Mills; 276 (t) Aneal Vohra/Unicorn Stock Photos; 276 (b) Sohm/The Stock Market; 278 Kenneth W. Fink/Bruce Coleman, Inc.; 280 H. Armstrong Roberts; 281 Robert Frerck/Woodfin Camp & Associates; 284 David R. Frazier Photolibrary; 285 Joseph Nettis/Stock, Boston; 287, 287 (inset) Calumet Regional Archives/Indiana University Northwest; 288 (t) Culver Pictures; 288 (b) Andy Sacks/Tony Stone Images; 289 (l), 289 (r) The Bettmann Archive; 292 The Granger Collection, New York; 293 (t) Detail of: *Clemens, Samuel Langhorne ("Mark Twain"), 1835-1910* by Frank Edwin Larson/National Portrait Gallery/Smithsonian Institute; 293 (b) John Elk III/Stock, Boston; 294 Ryan-Beyer/Tony Stone Images; 295 The Granger Collection, New York; 296 (l) Charlie Waite/Tony Stone Images; 297 Tony Stone Images; 298 (l) Keren Su/Stock, Boston; 298 (r) Michele Burgess/The Stock Market; 299 Claudia Parks/The Stock Market; 308 (bg) Grant Faint/The Image Bank; 308 Reuters/Bettmann; 309 (bg) Michel Euler/Wide World Photos; 309 Reuters/Bettmann.

Unit 5
Harcourt Brace & Company
Page 378 P & F Communications.

Other
Page 314-315 Lukasseck/Tony Stone Images; 314 (bl) Bill Ross/Westlight; 314 (bl inset) Mark E. Gibson; 314 (bc) David Hiser/Tony Stone Images; 314 (br) Larry Ulrich/Tony Stone Images; 315 (bl) Wayne Eastep/Tony Stone Images; 315 (bc) Wes Thompson/The Stock Market; 315 (br) John M. Roberts/The Stock Market; 316 (l) E.R. Degginger/Color-Pic; 316 (inset) Willard Clay/Tony Stone Images; 316 (r) Richard Pasley/Stock, Boston; 317 (l) Mark Burnett/Photo Researchers; 317 (r) Jim Pickerell/WestLight; 322 John Running; 323 Detail of portrait of Coronado by Peter Hurd, permanent collection Roswell Museum and Art Center, Gift of the artist, 1955.23; 325 (l) David Stoecklein/The Stock Market; 325 (r) David R. Frazier Photolibrary; 326 E.R. Degginger/Color-Pic; 328 (t) E.R. Degginger/Color-Pic; 328 (bl) Robert A. Ross/Color-Pic; 328 (br) Stan Osolinski/Tony Stone Images; 330, 331 Craig Aurness/WestLight; 332 The Granger Collection, New York; 333 E.R. Degginger/Color-Pic; 334 (t), 334 (b) E. Burciaga/The Picture Cube; 336, 337 David R. Frazier Photolibrary; 338 Courtesy: Arizona Historical Society/Tucson, #22978; 339 Brian Stablyk/Tony Stone Images; 341 Bob Daemmrich/Stock, Boston; 343 David R. Frazier Photolibrary; 344 Ron/Blakeley/The Stockhouse; 348 Benn Mitchell/The Image Bank; 349 Arizona State Museum, The University of Arizona; 350 Peter Bianchi © National Geographic Society; 351 Andrew Pernick/Bureau of Reclamation; 352 J. Madrigal, Jr./Central Arizona Project; 355 Bureau of Reclamation; 361 Charles Krebs/The Stock Market; 362 Randy Prentice; 363 (t) Christine Keith; 363 (c) Tom Bean; 363 (b) A. Ramey/Woodfin Camp & Associates; 365 (t) Arizona Historical Society; 365 (b) Mark E. Gibson/The Stock Market; 366 John Livzey/AllStock; 368 Michael Fogden/Animals Animals; 369 Guido Alberto Rossi/The Image

Bank; 370 Noboru Komine/Photo Researchers; 371 A. Ramey/Leo de Wys, Inc.; 374-375 Alyx Kellington/Gamma Liaison; 374 Ron Dorsey/Stock, Boston; 375 (t) David R. Frazier/Tony Stone Images; 375 (b) Bob Daemmrich/Stock, Boston.

Unit 6
Harcourt Brace & Company
Page 382 (l) Carroll Morgan; 384 (t) Corel; 431 P&F Communications; 444 P&F Communications.

Other
Page 380-381 Harold Sund/The Image Bank; 380 (bl) Gamma Liaison; 380 (bc) Rob Lewine/The Stock Market; 380 (br) Bob Abraham/The Stock Market; 381 (bl) Mark E. Gibson; 381 (bc) Raymond Barnes/Tony Stone Images; 381 (br) Paola Koch/Photo Researchers; 382 (r) Greg Vaughan/Tom Stack & Associates; 383 (l) William S. Helsel/Tony Stone Images; 383 (c) Thomas H. Brakefield/The Stock Market; 383 (r) Vince Streano/The Stock Market; 384 (b), 385 Stephanie Hollyman/Sygma; 386 Litz/Monkmeyer; 387 Robert Frerck/Woodfin Camp & Associates; 388 Roger Werth/Woodfin Camp & Associates; 389 (t) Owen Franken/Stock, Boston; 389 (inset) Bill Thompson/Woodfin Camp & Associates; 389 (c) William Johnson/Stock, Boston; 389 (b) Bill Ross/Tony Stone Images; 391 Thomas Kitchin/Tom Stack & Associates; 392, 393 The Granger Collection, New York; 395 Hughes Space and Communications Company; 398, 399 The Bettmann Archive; 400 (t) Ken Biggs/Tony Stone Images; 400 (b) The Bettmann Archive; 401 Bruce Hands/Stock, Boston; 403 Peter Southwick/Stock, Boston; 405 Keren Su/Stock, Boston; 407 Lescourret/Explorer/Photo Researchers; 408 (t) Martin Rogers/Stock, Boston; 408 (bl) Elene Perlman/Stock Boston; 408 (br) Owen Franklen/Stock, Boston; 409 Ken Biggs/Tony Stone Images; 412 Phil Kramer/The Stock Market; 413 Jeff Foott/Bruce Coleman, Inc.; 414 James Blank/The Stock Market; 414 (inset) Elan Sun Star/Tony Stone Images; 415 Jonathan Nourok/Tony Stone Images; 416 (t) Larry Ulrich/Tony Stone Images; 416 (b) Tom McHugh/Photo Researchers; 417 David R. Frazier Photolibrary; 418 Eric Carle/Bruce Coleman, Inc.; 418 (inset) Lee Rentz/Bruce Coleman, Inc.; 419 Mark E. Gibson; 419 (inset) Lee Foster/FPG International; 420 Dave Lawrence/The Stock Market; 426, 427 (t) McCutcheon/Monkmeyer; 427 (b) Charles Mason/Black Star; 428 (t) Ken Graham/Bruce Coleman, Inc.; 428 (b) Al Grillo/Alaska Stock Images; 429, 429 (inset) Hal Spence Photography; 430 Tom Bean/The Stock Market; 432 Don King/The Image Bank; 433 Peter French/Bruce Coleman, Inc.; 434 (tl) Harald Sund/The Image Bank; 434 (tr) John Penisten/The Gamma Liaison Network; 434 (b) Obremski/The Image Bank; 440-441 (bg) Archive Photos/American Stock; 440 James D. Wilson/The Gamma Liaison Network; 441 (tl) P.F. Bentley/Black Star; 441 (tr) Claude Poulet/Gamma Liaison; 441 (b) P.F. Bentley/Black Star.

Reference
Harcourt Brace & Company
Page R1(t) Victoria Bowen; R2, R3, R6, R7 P&F Communications.

Other
Facing R1 Earth Satellite Corporation/SPL/Photo Researchers; R1(b) NASA; R13 Jeffry W. Myers/FPG International.

COVER CREDIT:
Keith Gold & Associates

All maps by GeoSystems